An Activity-Based

Approach to Early Intervention

An Activity-Based Approach to Early Intervention

Fourth Edition

by

JoAnn (JJ) Johnson, Ph.D.
St. Cloud State University
Minnesota

Naomi L. Rahn, Ph.D.
West Virginia University
Morgantown

and

Diane Bricker, Ph.D.
University of Oregon
Eugene

·P A U L·H·
BROOKES
PUBLISHING C?®

Baltimore • London • Sydney

Paul H. Brookes Publishing Co.
Post Office Box 10624
Baltimore, Maryland 21285-0624

www.brookespublishing.com

Typeset by Scribe Inc., Philadelphia, Pennsylvania.
Manufactured in the United States of America by
Sheridan Books, Chelsea, Michigan.

Cover image ©istockphoto/quavondo

Section opener art ©istockphoto/quavando/MarkGoddard/BananaStock

Figures 4.1 and 4.2 courtesy of Jennifer Craun.

Photograph on p. xii by David Loveall (http://loveallphoto.com/).

Library of Congress Cataloging-in-Publication Data

The Library of Congress has cataloged the print edition as follows:
Johnson, JoAnn.
 An activity-based approach to early intervention / by JoAnn (JJ) Johnson, Naomi L. Rahn and Diane
Bricker. — Fourth edition.
  pages   cm
 Revised edition of: An activity-based approach to early intervention / by Kristie Pretti-Frontczak and
Diane Bricker. 3rd ed. c2004.
 Summary: "This textbook and professional guide presents thorough, research based coverage of child
directed intervention in which multiple learning opportunities are embedded into authentic activities.
Expanded with 4 new chapters, this comprehensive update includes a chapter on observation skills,
2 new chapters on application, and a chapter on using the approach with children with significant
impairments"—Provided by publisher.
 ISBN 978-1-59857-801-0 (paperback) — ISBN 1-59857-801-4 (paperback) —
ISBN 978-1-59857-940-6 (epub)
1. Children with disabilities—Education (Preschool)—United States. 2. Education, Preschool—Activity
programs—United States. 3. Child development—United States. I. Rahn, Naomi L. II. Bricker,
Diane D. III. Pretti-Frontczak, Kristie. Activity-based approach to early intervention. IV. Title.
 LC4019.2.B74 2015
 371.9'0472—dc23   2014044924

British Library Cataloguing in Publication data are available from the British Library.

2019   2018   2017   2016   2015

10   9   8   7   6   5   4   3   2   1

Contents

About the Ancillary Materials

Purchasers of this book may download, print, and/or photocopy the forms for clinical or educational use. These forms are included with the book and are also available at **www.brookespublishing.com/johnson/materials**.

Online course companion materials are available for instructors using *An Activity-Based Approach to Early Intervention, Fourth Edition,* in a course. Please visit **www.brookespublishing.com/johnson** to access chapter activities, study questions, PowerPoints, links, and more.

About the Authors

JoAnn (JJ) Johnson, Ph.D., Associate Professor, Child and Family Studies Department, School of Education, B109 Education Building, St. Cloud State University, 720 4th Avenue South, St. Cloud, Minnesota 56301

Dr. Johnson is an associate professor in Child and Family Studies at St. Cloud State University in Minnesota, where she provides professional development education in early childhood education, early intervention, and early childhood special education. She completed her undergraduate degree in special education and elementary education at the University of Idaho and her master's and doctoral degrees in early intervention at the University of Oregon under the advisement of Dr. Diane Bricker. In her professional life she has worked at University Centers for Excellence in Developmental Disabilities in Louisiana, Oregon, and Nevada, as program coordinator, teacher, service coordinator, grant and contract administrator, director, principal investigator, and instructor. Dr. Johnson served as Director of the Research and Educational Planning Center and the Nevada University Center for Excellence in Developmental Disabilities from 2001 to 2008, where she developed and administered lifespan programs, services, and supports for individuals with disabilities and their families. Her professional experiences encompass all service settings for young children, including neonatal intensive care units, pediatric intensive care units, well-baby clinics, home- and center-based programs for infants and young children (including Head Start and Early Head Start), nursing homes, supported employment, transition programs, special education schools, and university lab school programs. Much of her professional career has been focused on development and refinement of assessment and curriculum systems to support interventions for young children, birth to age 6, with disabilities and their families. Dr. Johnson is an author, developer, and trainer of the *Assessment, Evaluation, and Programming System (AEPS®) for Infants and Children, Second Edition* (Paul H. Brookes Publishing Co., 2002) and has been involved with the system since her days as a graduate student at the University of Oregon.

Naomi L. Rahn, Ph.D., Assistant Professor, Department of Special Education, College of Education and Human Services, Allen Hall, West Virginia University, 355 Oakland Street, P.O. Box 6122, Morgantown, West Virginia 26506

Dr. Rahn is an assistant professor of special education at West Virginia University. She completed her undergraduate degree in communicative disorders at the University of Wisconsin–Madison, her master's degree in early intervention at the University of Oregon, and her doctoral degree in special education at the University of Minnesota under the advisement of Dr. Scott McConnell. She has worked as a preschool special education teacher with children having a range of needs, including children with significant disabilities, and as an early interventionist providing services to infants and toddlers with special needs and their families. While at the University of Oregon, she provided outreach training on the AEPS and earlier editions of *An Activity-Based Approach to Early Intervention* to programs around the country as part of an outreach training grant. Her areas of interest include naturalistic intervention strategies, early language and literacy interventions, response to intervention, and personnel preparation. Dr. Rahn's research is focused on vocabulary and language interventions for young children with disabilities and at risk for disabilities.

Diane Bricker, Ph.D., Professor Emerita, Early Intervention Program, Center on Human Development, College of Education, 5253 University of Oregon, Eugene, Oregon, 97403

Dr. Bricker completed her undergraduate work at The Ohio State University, her master's degree in special education at the University of Oregon, and her doctoral degree in special education at Vanderbilt University, Peabody College. Her initial work focused on improving language skills of children with severe disabilities in institutions. That work led to the development of one of the first community-based integrated early intervention programs in the early 1970s. Since then, her work has continued in the area of early intervention/early childhood special education. She has focused on the preparation of early intervention/early childhood special education personnel at the graduate level. Many previous students now serve in leadership positions in academic and governmental entities in the United States and abroad. She has also been concerned with the development of policy to guide both training programs and service delivery models. In particular she has advocated for the adoption of a systems approach to assessment, intervention, and evaluation that links important components efficiently and effectively.

Her work in curricula-based assessment/evaluation has focused on the development of the AEPS. This comprehensive measure and curricula provides intervention personnel with a system for the comprehensive assessment of young children with results that link directly to curricular content and subsequent evaluation of child progress. The AEPS has an accompanying online system for data input, tracking progress, and report writing.

Dr. Bricker's work in developmental-behavioral screening that began in 1980 has culminated in the creation (with Jane Squires) of the *Ages & Stages Questionnaires® (ASQ-3): A Parent-Completed Child Monitoring System, Third Edition* (Paul H. Brookes Publishing Co., 2009), and (with Jane Squires and Elizabeth Twombly) *Ages & Stages Questionnaires®: Social-Emotional (ASQ:SE): A Parent-Completed Child Monitoring System for Social-Emotional Behaviors* (Paul H. Brookes Publishing Co., 2002). She and her colleagues have collected psychometric and utility information on these screening measures for more than 30 years. These data have been most recently summarized in the *ASQ-3® User's Guide* (with Jane Squires, Elizabeth Twombly, and LaWanda Potter; Paul H. Brookes Publishing Co., 2009). The ASQ has been translated into over 25 languages and is used throughout the world.

Acknowledgments

During the 1970s a predominate educational approach to typical young children was to offer them a variety of enriching activities associated with little formal instruction. Conversely, during this same decade, a predominate approach to young children with disabilities was to offer them carefully structured learning routines largely directed by adults—if anything at all was offered. When examining these offerings, one approach appears too laissez faire for children who need help in learning while the other approach does not seem to appreciate the importance of human motivation as a basis for learning. Thus, in the 1980s, many of us struggling to create effective intervention approaches for young children with disabilities began to explore other options.

It was during the ensuing decade of the 1980s that a group of researchers and interventionists at the University of Oregon began to formalize an approach that has come to be called activity-based intervention or ABI. During the 1980s we struggled to create a framework for the approach and the associated "how to" content. By the end of this decade we felt sufficiently emboldened to develop the first text to describe the approach. The first edition was published in 1992; the second in 1998; and the third in 2004.

This fourth edition, some 20-plus years since publication of the first, still retains the underlying conceptual framework, the basic elements that compose the approach, and some of the organizational structure designed to assist the user in the application of ABI. However, this volume also reflects significant expansions and changes in the approach. In particular, our collective years of experience have suggested the need for more clarity in the daily/weekly application of the approach. Thus, the most significant change between this volume and earlier editions is the expansion of information on how to use the approach with a range of children and families.

As we noted, the information in this fourth edition is expanded from previous volumes; however, we would be remiss not to acknowledge the many contributions made by previous volume authors: Julianne Woods, Kristie Pretti-Frontczak, and Natalya McComas.

We also wish to acknowledge the feedback we have received since the publication of the third edition in 2004 from users of the approach. Comments by teachers, interventionists, specialists, and administrators have been extremely valuable in helping us understand what parts and pieces of the approach need further refinement and clarification.

As noted in previous editions, the assistance of the Paul H. Brookes Publishing Co. staff has been consistently helpful. In addition, we greatly appreciate their commitment to quality and their tolerance for getting content accurate even if it means several rewrites. As most writers know, good editors are an essential element to quality products.

JJ would like to acknowledge her colleagues and co-authors for numerous in-depth conversations about ABI and her friends and family, who understood her hibernation. She would also like to acknowledge the great influence of the many children and families she has been privileged to work with over the years.

Naomi would like to acknowledge her husband, Jason, who listened patiently and gave feedback during the writing process; her son, Calvin, who brightened her day when she needed a writing break; her son, Jack, who shaped her understanding of early intervention; and her co-authors for their kind suggestion to dedicate this book to Jack.

Finally, Diane would like to acknowledge the work and contributions of the many graduate students and staff who have participated in the University of Oregon Early Intervention Program since 1978. Their contributions have been and continue to be the sustenance that propels this approach forward.

To Jack, who taught us so much

I

A Comprehensive Systems Approach and the Field of Early Intervention/Early Childhood Special Education

1

Purpose and Overview

The primary purpose of intervention for young children with disabilities or children who are at risk for disabilities is to assist them in the acquisition and generalization of critical developmental skills so that they can, to the extent possible, achieve independent functioning across environments. This purpose requires intervention efforts focused on helping children reach their individual learning and developmental goals. This book provides a description of activity-based intervention (ABI), an approach developed in the United States at the University of Oregon that is specifically designed to help children reach their individual goals within the context of daily activities and familiar routines. The authors have been closely associated with the development of ABI and represent different generations of professionals who have contributed to the approach's evolution.

The driving force behind ABI is the attainment of functional skills that children with disabilities or those at risk for disability can use adaptively across environments and situations. To maximize opportunities for children to acquire their individual goals, ABI maps intervention efforts onto or integrates them into daily interactions that children initiate and experience. The approach makes explicit the use of children's daily environmental transactions for this purpose and provides a structure for doing so.

The heart of ABI is the use of children's daily activities and initiations to embed or target their individualized developmental and therapeutic goals. ABI can be defined as

An approach that uses behavioral principles to encourage child interactions and participation in meaningful (i.e., authentic) daily activities with the explicit purpose of assisting the child in acquiring, generalizing, and strengthening functional skills.

Kerry, a toddler with developmental delays, has two important developmental goals: 1) to improve her pincer grasp in order to pick up and manipulate small objects and 2) to expand her vocabulary of common objects in order to better communicate her wants and needs. Sitting in her high chair, she points at a box of crackers and vocalizes. Her mother, who is washing dishes, turns and says, "What do you want?" Kerry again points and her mother says, "Oh cracker, you want a cracker. Can you say 'cracker'?" Kerry says, "Ka ka." Her mother immediately smiles, nods, and places a small bit of cracker on Kerry's tray. Kerry tries to pick up the cracker by using a raking grasp, but her mother physically prompts Kerry to use her finger and thumb (i.e., pincer grasp) to pick up the cracker. Kerry's mother returns to washing dishes while waiting for Kerry to ask for another cracker.

The mother's use of this routine activity allows her to address Kerry's goals in meaningful ways with just a little extra time and effort. This scenario is a prime example of ABI in practice.

The Fresh Start Early Childhood Program is a center-based program for children ages 3–6 years both with and without disabilities. One of the classes is preparing to take a walk in a nearby park. One important general curriculum goal for the children in this class is to follow directions. The interventionist, aide, and parent volunteers tell the children they will play a game while walking to the park. The game entails following specific directions: stop, walk, bend, and hold hands. As the children walk in pairs, the interventionist calls out a direction. The children are prompted to follow the direction if necessary. The children enjoy the game and are eager to follow the directions when given. As the walk progresses, the interventionist selects individual children to also give a direction. One child adds a new direction, "Jump up and down." The interventionist follows the new direction and encourages all the other children to do so as well.

This activity is fun for the children but also addresses an important curricular goal and demonstrates ABI in action for a group of children.

    As illustrated in the two examples, the foundation of ABI is the use of daily transactions that occur between infants and young children and their physical and social environments. These daily transactions account for the primary means by which children learn. Within an ABI approach, learning opportunities that address children's educational and therapeutic goals and objectives are specifically embedded into authentic child-directed, routine, and planned activities. These authentic (i.e., meaningful for individual children) activities provide a range of practice opportunities for young children. Furthermore, an ABI approach has a comprehensive framework that enables the user to capitalize on child–environment transactions and maximize development and learning.

As noted previously, the purpose of this book is to describe in detail the ABI approach. This includes making clear its conceptual framework and discussing its application across children, families, and settings. Perhaps the greatest strength of this approach is its adaptability for use across a wide variety of settings (e.g., home, child care, center-based classes, community) and children (i.e., from typically developing to those with significant impairments) and by a range of individuals (e.g., parents, caregivers, professionals).

As useful and flexible as ABI is, no intervention approach can function well in isolation from other components critical to comprehensive quality service delivery programs. Our years of experience have permitted the creation of a comprehensive system that complements intervention efforts and ensures all essential service delivery components are present and linked.

LINKED SYSTEM APPROACH: THE LARGER CONTEXT FOR INTERVENTION

As noted, intervention is an essential component of early intervention/early childhood special education (EI/ECSE) service delivery programs; however, it must be supported by other essential service delivery components to ensure quality and breadth. The ABI approach is situated in the larger context of a linked system framework that is composed of five essential components: screening, assessment, goal development, intervention, and progress monitoring. Embedding ABI as the intervention component into a linked system approach is important for two reasons. First, a comprehensive system provides a broad context for formulating and delivering necessary services to children, and second, it helps ensure that a solid and cyclical relationship exists between the components that compose comprehensive service delivery systems.

ABI is directly relevant to the intervention component of the linked system; however, the information provided by the other components is essential to its successful application. That is, without objective, detailed, relevant, and appropriate assessment data, quality goals cannot be written, and quality goals are essential to the efficient and effective application of ABI. Chapter 3 describes each component of the linked system and how they inform and support each other.

BOOK OVERVIEW

Since the publication of the first three editions of this book, the study, refinement, and expansion of the ABI approach has moved forward at a steady pace. At the time of this edition, the ABI approach is seen as 1) a viable option for blending practices from multiple perspectives, 2) reflective of recommended intervention practice, and 3) a means of providing individualized intervention within the context of naturalistic or daily activities. Since 1998, our continued work with interventionists, teachers, and specialists across the country have provided better insight into the critical elements of the approach and better strategies to ensure successful implementation. The impetus for this fourth edition has been the acquisition of new knowledge and improved practice for employing ABI. The conceptual and practical knowledge gained since the inception of the approach has been examined, synthesized, and incorporated into this book.

Although the organization and some of the content contained in this fourth edition have changed from earlier editions, the major features and elements of this approach remain the same. This book contains three major sections:

I.   A Comprehensive Systems Approach and the Field of Early Intervention/Early Childhood Special Education

II. Conceptual Framework for Activity-Based Intervention

III. Application of Activity-Based Intervention

Section I contains three chapters that describe the book's purpose and overview, address the field of EI/ECSE, and discuss the larger linked system framework that supports the application of ABI. Section II contains five chapters that offer a more detailed description of ABI; address its conceptual framework, its organizational structure, and issues associated with its application; and discuss challenges of intervention research and the empirical base of ABI. Section III contains six chapters that discuss how to use ABI with an emphasis on topics important to ABI, such as observational skills; address application of ABI in centers, in the home, and with children having significant impairments; and describe the implementation of ABI by a team and training strategies for use with paraprofessionals and parents/caregivers.

The changes in this edition are based on our considerable experience in assisting teachers, therapists, interventionists, paraprofessionals, and caregivers in learning and using ABI. These professionals and caregivers have shown us clearly what parts of the approach were understandable and which were problematic for them to implement. We have attempted to remedy the latter through improving procedures, adding examples, and describing more clearly the structural framework. We believe that the changes introduced in this book will enable users of ABI to grasp the underlying conceptual framework of the approach and to use the approach effectively in a variety of settings with a range of children and families.

AUDIENCE

As noted earlier, the purpose of this book is to describe ABI and provide the necessary structure to enable interventionists and caregivers to use the approach. Although words alone may not be entirely satisfactory when attempting to learn and employ new information, strategies, and skills, the hope is that the detailed descriptions provided in this book will permit most readers to 1) understand the major assumptions that underlie the approach and the necessary assessment processes, goal setting, and environmental arrangements that provide the guiding structure; and 2) incorporate into their teaching repertoires the essential elements that define ABI.

For several reasons, we believe that the individuals for whom this book is intended will vary in their ability to understand and incorporate the approach. Some readers will be experienced in using child-directed techniques and find adoption of the approach relatively straightforward. Others may have been educated in adult-directed approaches and will find it challenging to learn to become observers of, and responders to, children. Often, ingrained habits are difficult to relinquish even with the intent to do so. For example, adults who direct children through individual activities as well as through the entire school/home day may find it difficult to permit children to engage frequently in self-directed activities or may find it challenging to use routines and daily activities as teaching vehicles.

We have also found that many are eager to learn the concrete elements of an approach and are less interested in the conceptual base and underlying structure of the approach. These individuals may be tempted to focus on the chapters contained in Section III. We believe the material presented particularly in Section II is essential to the effective and generalized application of ABI. When we observe a teacher, therapist, interventionist, or caregiver having significant problems in applying the approach, we find that these individuals often have a limited appreciation of the conceptual base of the approach or have little or no knowledge about the framework and structure that underlie the approach. As with so much of life, understanding the underlying fundamentals is essential to effective application and absolutely vital to diagnosing and remedying problems.

DEFINITION OF TERMS AND CONCEPTS

To help ensure clarity of the material presented in this book, it is useful to define several terms that appear throughout the chapters. For populations with disabilities we use early intervention (EI) to refer to the age range from birth through 2 years, we use early childhood special education (ECSE) to refer to children ages 3–5 years, and we use early intervention/early childhood special education (EI/ECSE) to refer to the entire age range of children with disabilities from birth through 5 years. These terms refer to a field of study and a method of intervention focused on children who have or who are at risk for disabilities from birth through preschool and their families. Although the principles and strategies contained in an ABI approach may be appropriate for other groups, the examples and research base described in this book address systems and programs that target children in this specific age range, including children served in community-based and inclusive programs. We generally use early childhood to refer to the broad population of children birth through age 5 years, including both children with and without disabilities.

The term *interventionist* is used to represent the array of professionals and paraprofessionals who deliver services to young children who participate in EI/ECSE and early childhood education programs. We find the term *teacher* to be overly limiting when the team of professionals who work in EI/ECSE programs includes speech-language pathologists, occupational therapists, physical therapists, psychologists, and medical personnel, as well as early childhood teachers, aides, and parents.

We agree with the federal mandate that children with disabilities and their families require a team of professionals to offer the array of needed services specified in their individualized education program (IEP)/individualized family service plan (IFSP). We therefore use the term *team* to refer to the group of professionals, paraprofessionals, and parents/caregivers who work together to deliver the needed services. In addition, we use the terms *interventionists* and *teams* interchangeably throughout the book. Finally, the term *caregiver* is used throughout this book to describe individuals who provide primary care to young children (e.g., parents, foster parents, grandparents, other extended family members, child care providers, neighbors).

SUMMARY

ABI is an intervention approach that relies primarily on the use of children's daily activities to address therapeutic and educational goals. This book's content is designed for students in training, EI/ECSE and early childhood professionals, and child care workers who are delivering community services to infants, toddlers, and preschool-age children and their families. This introductory chapter has set a context for understanding ABI by stating its purpose, and by providing an overview of the book. It further addresses the importance of embedding intervention approaches into larger service delivery systems that are designed to offer comprehensive and quality services to young children and their families.

2

History and Contemporary Status of Early Intervention/ Early Childhood Special Education Programs

This chapter addresses the history of intervention efforts with young children and also describes contemporary programs that operate in the United States. Although the primary focus of this chapter—and the book—is on young children with disabilities, we also offer a brief examination of programs for young children living in poverty and programs for typically developing children. We do this because of the significant overlap between these populations and the type of programs offered (e.g., Head Start serves both children from low-income families and those with disabilities; many child care programs serve typically developing children and their peers with disabilities).

This chapter begins by providing a rationale for EI as a background for the development of intervention efforts with young children. It then provides a brief history of early childhood programs and programs specifically created for children living in poverty, along with a more detailed picture of program evolution for children with disabilities. The final part of the chapter provides a description of contemporary programs designed for children with disabilities.

Specific eligibility categories for children can range from *typical* to *disabled,* and these categories have been employed for a variety of purposes (e.g., population descriptions). The potential overlap between categories, however, and the increasing number of children at risk and with disabilities who

Portions of this chapter were taken from Bricker, 1989; Bricker, Pretti-Frontczak, & McComas, 1998; and Bricker, Macy, Squires, & Marks, 2013.

are being "included" in programs designed for typically developing children requires a reexamination of the certainty with which children are placed into these categories.

We find it useful to visualize populations of children on a continuum that covers five categories—from severe impairment to none—as shown in Figure 2.1. As the figure shows, approximately .01% of children have severe impairments, 2% have moderate impairments, 12% have mild impairments, 25% are at risk for impairments, and 60% have no impairments (U.S. Department of Education, 2013). These approximate percentages suggest that the majority of children are classified as typical on most scales, whereas a much smaller percentage of children are classified as having disabilities.

An important feature of Figure 2.1 is the crosshatch marks that appear between each category. These marks are used to suggest that the categorical borders may change for some children. How a child's disability is characterized may vary for many different reasons, including, for example, the type of measurement used, the child's familiarity with the setting and people, the time of day, and the child's condition (e.g., hungry, tired). For example, on a measure of literacy a child may score in the moderately impaired category, whereas on a measure of motor skills the child may score in the typical category. It is important to note that some children likely will not change categories (e.g., those with significant impairments) regardless of changing conditions or factors. However, other children (e.g., those at risk) may change categories depending on a number of factors, resulting in the lines between categories overlapping or blurring for at least some children. In addition, over time the guidelines for program participation have expanded to accommodate broader ranges of children. For example many community-based child care programs accept a range of children from typically developing to those with disabilities. As noted, Head Start is required to accommodate a percentage of children with diagnosed disabilities. Many school programs are inclusive in that they enroll children with a range of needs. It is this overlap of populations and expanded program accommodation that underlies the historical importance of early childhood programs, programs for children from low-income families, and programs specially designed for children with disabilities. Before discussing the evolution of intervention programs, however, it is important to explore the rationale underlying EI for young children.

THE RATIONALE FOR EARLY INTERVENTION

Over the years, researchers have argued over the contributions rendered by nature versus nurture. Perhaps since the release of Joseph McVicker Hunt's book, *Intelligence and Experience* (1961), most psychologists and educators in the United States acknowledge the importance that environmental influences have on developing children. Indeed, for years, many investigators placed such an emphasis on environmental variables that the genetic and physiological contributions were overlooked or, at least, undervalued. The

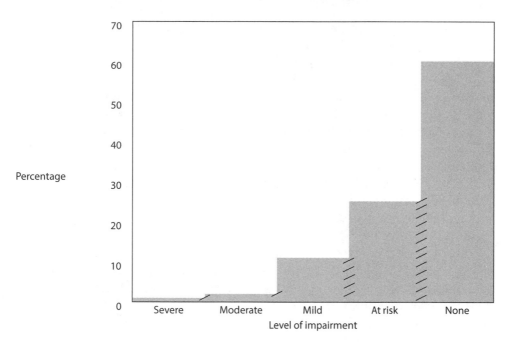

Figure 2.1. The percentage of children associated with level of impairment. Crosshatch marks indicate possible overlap between categories.

work of theorists such as Sameroff and Chandler (1975), however, empha-sized the interaction between reproductive risk (e.g., child's physical status) and caregiving variables (e.g., quality of parenting), leading to the adoption of conceptual frameworks that take into account genetic, physiological, and experiential variables. The rationale for EI offered in this chapter comprises arguments that address both experiential and genetic/physiological factors, including 1) maximizing developmental outcomes, 2) preventing the develop-ment of secondary disabilities or problems, 3) providing support for families, and 4) cost-effectiveness.

Maximizing Developmental Outcomes

The first argument that informs the rationale for EI derives from the prem-ise that environmental–child interactions form the bases for the acquisition of knowledge and skills. This premise further suggests that early learning lays the experiential and neural foundations for subsequent development. That is, early environmental feedback creates the soil from which grows sub-sequent development. The better the soil, the better the development. Conse-quently, without solid early learning children do not have the experiential or neural building blocks from which to evolve more complex understanding or knowledge of their physical and social world.

A child's early experiences are critically important for evolving brain architecture. Brain development research suggests, for example, that quality early experiences with caregivers can enhance neural structures, whereas negative experiences can adversely affect brain development (National Scientific Council on the Developing Child, 2007).

The investigative work on the impact of early experiences on brain development is clear, and other lines of research suggest that the quality of EI services is also important. Data have been accumulating since the 1960s that suggest that the quality of services delivered to children and families make a difference in child outcomes (Guralnick, 1997). That is, the more the content (i.e., curriculum) is considered, the more effective the staff, and the longer and more intense the offered services, the greater the impact and longevity of impact on participating children. Table 2.1 presents a series of studies that provide information on the positive effects of quality EI services on varying populations of young children.

Data from the studies of brain development and intervention efforts strongly suggest that quality early experiences are essential for promoting sound developmental growth; consequently, the first piece in our rationale for EI is the necessity of providing early and quality experiences for infants and young children if they are to thrive and grow into productive citizens.

Preventing the Development of Secondary Disabilities or Problems

A second argument for EI is the prevention of secondary or associated problems through appropriate handling of and responding to children. Many infants and young children who are at risk or who have a disability are inclined to develop a variety of undesirable behaviors if not managed properly. The onset of such behavior is not an inevitable accompaniment to impairment but instead is often learned. For example, the reciprocal nature of child–caregiver interactions assumes a time-sequence framework in which one individual responds and the other reacts. The synchrony of responding between the pair may do much to color the nature of the interaction and refers generally to the caregiver's ability to monitor the state, mood, or needs of the child and to respond in a facilitating manner. Such synchrony of responding appears to come naturally to many parents; however, when faced with an infant or child who is nonresponsive or responds in ways that are asynchronous (e.g., infants who arch their backs when lifted), caregivers may be hard pressed to respond in ways that shape more positive and developmentally advanced responses.

A second facet of the prevention argument is the apparent irreversible nature of some conditions if steps are not taken for correction during the formative years. For example, without proper exercising and positioning, a child with severe spasticity may develop contractures that become permanent. Children with hearing impairments may not learn to use their residual hearing unless trained to do so early in life. Children with major disabilities may never function completely within the normal range across a number of behavioral domains, but there are data to suggest that children

Table 2.1. Studies addressing the effects of early intervention on young children

Project	Place	Year(s)	Purpose and strategy	Outcomes	References
Early Training Project–Gray	Murfreesboro, Tennessee	Early 1960s	Enhance development in children with intellectual disabilities. Random assignment to an experimental or control group and weekly home visits.	Initial IQ differences in favor of the experimental group. By fourth grade the differences in IQ/achievement were no longer significant.	Consortium for Longitudinal Studies, 1983
Project Head Start (HS)	Nearly 2,500 communities	1965	Improve social, academic, and health competence of economically disadvantaged preschool children through comprehensive academic and health services.	A national evaluation of the first 3 years reported no favorable cognitive effects from participation in the summer program, but found that in the first and second grade the full-year participants performed better on a school readiness test than non–Head Start participants.	Kean, 1970; Mills, 1999; Washington & Bailey, 1995; Zigler & Styfco, 2000
Chicago Child-Parent Center (CPC) and Expansion Program	11 public schools in Chicago, Illinois	Started in 1967	Serve economically disadvantaged children ages 3–5 years by providing a structured half-day program during the 9-month school year and comprehensive services (i.e., health & social and parent involvement).	At age 9, children who participated in CPC had significantly higher reading and math scores, lower rates of grade retention, and higher ratings of parental involvement.	Reynolds & Ou, 2011; Reynolds, Temple, White, Ou, & Robertson, 2011
Syracuse Family Development Research Program (FDRP)	Syracuse, New York	1969–1975	Provide primarily African American sample of first-time mothers from impoverished communities an array of health and human service resources. The program began prior to the birth of the baby and lasted through the preschool years.	A 10-year follow-up evaluation reported reduced juvenile delinquency and improved school functioning for participants in the experimental group.	Honig, 2004; Honig, Lally, & Mathieson, 1982

(continued)

Table 2.1. *(continued)*

Project	Place	Year(s)	Purpose and strategy	Outcomes	References
Houston Parent–Child Development Center (PCDC)	Houston, Texas	1975–1982	Promote social and intellectual competence among low-income, Mexican American families with 1-year-olds.	Significantly higher IQ scores for treatment at age 2, but differences were marginal by age 3. Significantly higher achievement test scores for the treatment group, but no differences in grade retention, special education referral, or school grades.	Johnson & Walker, 1987, 1991
Infant, Toddler, and Preschool Research and Intervention Project	Tennessee	1970 1974	Enhance the developmental achievements of children with disabilities by offering individually tailored intervention services using a developmentally integrated center-based approach.	All participating children consistently showed developmental gains across areas.	Bricker & Bricker, 1971, 1972
Carolina Abecedarian Project	North Carolina	1972	Provide quality child care services to infants from low-income families using center-based approach. Children were randomly assigned to a treatment and nontreatment group.	Children in the treatment group were significantly more likely to be in school at age 21, and employment rates were higher (65%) for the treatment group than for the control group (50%), although the trend was not statistically significant.	Campbell & Ramey, 1995; Campbell, Ramey, Pungello, Miller-Johnson, & Burchinal, 2001
Milwaukee Project	Milwaukee, Wisconsin	1977–1983	Examine the effectiveness of early intervention in preventing intellectual delay/disability in young children at risk.	Children who received intervention had higher IQ scores and language skills that were 2 years more advanced than the children in the control group.	Garber, 1988
Project CARE	North Carolina	1978	A follow-up study to the Abecedarian Project. Children were randomly assigned to intervention services that lasted 5 years and compared intensity of intervention with no treatment.	The strongest cognitive outcomes were for the children who received both the home-based and center-based programs.	Burchinal, Campbell, Bryant, Wasik, & Ramey,1997

Project	Place	Year(s)	Purpose and strategy	Outcomes	References
Elmira Prenatal/Early Infancy Project (PEIP)	University of Rochester, Elmira, New York	1978–1982	Examine the effects of home visiting on children from low-income families. The first intervention group received home visiting only during pregnancy, and the second intervention group received home visits until the children were 2 years old.	Treatment group reported 33% fewer emergency room visits through age 4 than children in the control group, and their mothers were less welfare dependent. Mothers in the intervention group reported less cigarette use, better nutrition, improved childbirth class attendance, and more social supports.	Sameroff, 1994; Sameroff, Seifer, Baldwin, & Baldwin, 1993
Infant Health and Development Program (IHDP)	AK, CT, FL, MA, NY, PA, TX, and WA	1985–1988	Provide intervention to infants who were born prematurely (less than 37 weeks gestation) and with low birth weight (less than 2,500 grams).	Babies who received the intervention had higher IQs than the control group by nearly 10 points at the end of the intervention (36 months).	Brooks-Gunn, 2003; Brooks-Gunn et al., 1994; IHDP, 1990
National Institute of Child Health & Human Development (NICHD) Study of Early Child Care	AR, CA, KS, MA, NC, PA, VA, WA, and WI	1991–1994	Examine the relationship between child care experiences and developmental outcomes.	Children in poverty received lower quality care than children not living in poverty. Cognitive and social-emotional outcomes were more consistently predicted by family factors rather than child care factors.	NICHD, 2001

From Bricker, D., Macy, M., Squires, J., & Marks, K. (2013). *Developmental screening in your community: An integrated approach for connecting children with services* (pp. 19–21). Baltimore, MD: Paul H. Brookes Publishing Co.; reprinted by permission.

with disabilities can be assisted in becoming more adaptive and independent if exposed to early and continuous quality intervention (Guralnick & Bricker, 1987; Spiker, Hebbler, & Mallik, 2005). Thus, EI may do much to assist infants and young children in moving toward the most positive developmental and behavioral trajectory possible and to offset or attenuate other associated debilitating conditions that may occur.

Providing Support for Families

The third argument for EI is the need to assist parents and other caregivers of children with special needs who may display a broad range of complex and challenging behaviors. There seems to be little doubt that the birth of a child with a disability may produce trauma, fear, and stress for many caregivers (Orsmond, 2005). EI services can be a valuable resource for caregivers to help offset the effects of coping with a child with disabilities in at least two areas.

The first area is helping caregivers to adjust to and cope with having a child with disabilities by listening and responding appropriately to requests and needs. EI personnel can listen to caregiver concerns and offer resources to assist the family in learning to manage the child's challenges. Another important service that staff can extend is putting caregivers in touch with other parents who have had similar experiences and may be able to provide reassurance or other information that parents may find valuable. Finally, personnel can impart important knowledge about community resources that caregivers may need to access to assist in learning to cope with having a child with disabilities, such as counseling or respite services.

A second area is helping caregivers to acquire the knowledge and skills necessary to manage their child's behavior and to help the child acquire important cognitive, adaptive, language, and motor skills. To maximize development, learning opportunities need to be generalized across people and settings, including the home. Although the number of infants and preschool-age children remaining full time in their home is diminishing and group child care is on the rise, primary caregivers still spend time with their children. Consequently, it is essential that caregivers be an integral part of the intervention team. They should be critical players in selecting intervention goals, and they need to understand how to address these goals throughout the child's day wherever the setting (i.e., staff in child care facilities, parents in the home). EI personnel need to assist caregivers in learning the skills necessary to be effective intervention agents with their children. Caregiver participation in intervention efforts is essential if children are to grow and thrive, and many caregivers need assistance in learning how to effectively manage and teach children with disabilities.

Cost-Effectiveness

The fourth rationale for EI is focused on cost-effectiveness. The cost-effectiveness for EI can be viewed from two perspectives: 1) the cost of avoiding more intensive and expensive services, and 2) the savings incurred by better preparing children for the future. Although costs vary across states, schools, and communities, it is well known that special education services are more expensive than general education, and that institutional care is the most costly and likely the least effective of all services provided to children in the United States. Consequently, if EI services for a young child keep that child in a program designed for typically developing children (e.g., child care, kindergarten), the cost savings can be substantial even if additional support services are necessary to ensure that children thrive in blended settings.

The cost-effectiveness of EI is supported by economic analyses of the effects of EI on long-term child outcomes. Most of these analyses have been conducted on risk groups, but we think the conclusions are also relevant for children with disabilities. Heckman (2012) investigated the economic benefits of EI services and estimated between a $4 and $17 return for every dollar invested in EI. This investment return is generated through greater earning power, improved mental health outcomes, and job productivity (Reynolds, Temple, Robertson, & Mann, 2002; Temple & Reynolds, 2007). Lynch (2003) reported that if every child living in poverty received 2 years of quality early childhood education, this investment would yield a 16% annual return rate in cost savings by improving children's academic skills, lowering grade retention and placement in special education, decreasing substance abuse, reducing teenage pregnancy rates, lowering crime rates, reducing welfare dependent adults, and increasing the number of educated workers.

The growing evidence that intervening early in a child's life saves resources by 1) ensuring a solid developmental base for subsequent learning, 2) attenuating disability and behavior problems, 3) assisting caregivers in providing more facilitative environments, and 4) yielding significant cost benefits all build what we believe is a powerful argument for EI.

Finally, although apart from the rationale for EI, we need to point out that effective EI is highly dependent upon early detection. The earlier a child's problem is identified, the earlier remedial action can be undertaken. The data are clear that the delivery of quality services as early as possible is almost always more effective in producing desired outcomes than delaying services until the child becomes older (Bricker, Macy, Squires, & Marks, 2013).

HISTORY OF PROGRAM DEVELOPMENT FOR YOUNG CHILDREN

Given the importance of EI, this section addresses the historical evolution of intervention programs for young children. It traces separately the development of 1) early childhood programs, 2) programs for children living in poverty, and 3) programs for children with disabilities.

Early Childhood Programs

According to Lazerson (1972), the historical roots of early childhood education in this country are intertwined with three major themes. The first is
that early schooling can be instrumental in social change. Thus, much of the
historical and more recent emphasis in education has been focused on social
reform for children from low-income families. The second theme is that the
early developmental period is unique and important. And the third is that
early childhood programs have been viewed by some as a means to reform
rigid and narrow educational approaches often found in the public schools.

Educators before the 1900s recognized the importance of the early childhood period; however, the actual catalyst for the development of early education programs appears to have been the concern for children growing up in
the squalid conditions of poverty, thus representing a blurring between populations of children from this early time. According to Maxim (1980), important educational reforms for young children were stimulated by a number of
concerned individuals living in different countries. For example, programs
for young children living in poverty were initiated in the late-1800s and early
1900s by Robert Owen of Scotland, Friedrich Frobel in Germany, Margaret
McMillan in England, and Marie Montessori in Italy. These programs bore
some interesting similarities. Owen, McMillan, and Montessori, in particular, began programs because of their concern for the health of young children
living in poverty, many of whom were physically abused. Their programs
were developed to offer these children the opportunity to thrive physically
and intellectually.

Inspired in particular by the work of Frobel, kindergarten programs
were introduced in the United States in the mid-1880s, and by 1900, public school kindergartens were well established (Maxim, 1980). In Lazerson's
(1972) view, the growth of kindergarten programs in the country was inti-
mately tied to social reform. That is, workers such as Jane Addams, Robert Woods, and Kate Wiggin saw the need to assist children living in cities
who were growing up in conditions of extreme poverty. An underlying goal
appeared to be identifying and educating children living in poverty early so
that they could develop a sense of middle-class values. Another goal of these
initial kindergarten programs was to influence the family life of families
living in poverty through education of the parents (Lazerson, 1972), a theme
that gained support again in the 1960s.

The nursery school movement in the United States also had European
roots, and its development was subject to many of the same forces. Nursery school programs, however, developed separately from the kindergarten
movement (Maxim, 1980). As with kindergarten programs, nursery schools
were originally developed to serve children living in poverty. During the
1920s, few nursery school programs were available, but following the Great
Depression, a significant growth in programs occurred largely because of
support from the federal government to create jobs. The operation of nursery

schools provided jobs for unemployed teachers and also provided facilities where working mothers could leave their children.

Child care also began in this same time period, initially so women could join the work force and later to permit welfare recipients to return to work (Belsky, Steinberg & Walker, 1982). Then, during World War II, there was a need for child care facilities so that women could join the war effort. However, these child care programs were custodial in the sense that little attention was given to the children's educational needs (Maxim, 1980). After the war, federal support for child care was discontinued, whereas support for programs from private agencies began to grow. This shift meant that many of the programs for young children began serving privileged rather than underprivileged children. During the postwar era, little was done in the way of program development for young children from low-income families or for those with disabilities.

In the 1960s, two important movements began: A new view of young children's learning abilities emerged, and a renewed attack on the impact of poverty on young children was launched. A burgeoning era of research on infants and young children began to suggest that infants were more capable learners than generally believed. For example, researchers began to report that infants could perform sophisticated discriminations and memory feats (Schaffer, 1977; Trehub, Bull, & Schneider, 1981). Such data provided strong support for the view that learning could begin early in a child's life. Furthermore, in 1956, Bloom's taxonomy of learning domains indicated much of a child's cognitive growth occurred during the first 4 years of life.

Paralleling these findings, a number of investigators were beginning to present information that supported the plasticity of children's intellectual growth and the enormous impact of the environment on child outcomes (Hunt, 1961). Other researchers and theorists, such as Bowlby (1973) and Spitz (1946), pointed to the catastrophic effects of placing young children in nonstimulating environments (e.g., orphanages). This work among others (Thompson, 2001) added fuel to the arguments of the importance of early experiences, the sustained impact of early environments, and the importance of critical periods (Bruer, 2001). These positions, along with political motivation, provided the foundation for the development of a massive social program in the United States called "The War on Poverty," which was designed to provide support for children being raised in poverty (Beller, 1979).

During the 1970s and 1980s, early childhood programs, kindergarten programs, and child care programs adopted a variety of approaches, ranging from structured, adult-directed activities to nonstructured, children-led activities. The debate over the merits of the various approaches continues today (Kirp, 2007).

In 1926, the National Association for the Education of Young Children (NAEYC) was created. NAEYC provided the first nationwide vehicle to create and disseminate policy for the education of young children. In 1987,

NAEYC published its first guidelines on developmentally appropriate practice (Bredekamp, 1987). Such guidelines as well as other published documents have brought consistency and improved standards to the field of early childhood and the services being delivered to young children in communities all over the nation.

Of recent historical importance for early childhood programs was the advent of concrete steps taken to develop cooperation between organizations and professionals who serve all populations of children, from typically developing children to those with disabilities. In 1997, the NAEYC guidelines (Bredekamp & Copple, 1997) for developmentally appropriate practices were revised with an eye toward "addressing the needs of all young children, including those with disabilities, in a more comprehensive way" (Grisham-Brown, Hemmeter, & Pretti-Frontczak, 2005, p. 7). This was indicative of a move by professional organizations (e.g., NAEYC, Division for Early Childhood, Council for Exceptional Children) to create quality services appropriate for all children. This goal was surely a laudable aim and a high note for the evolution of early childhood programs.

Programs for Children Living in Poverty

As noted previously, many of the earliest nursery school and kindergarten programs were created to offset the impact poverty was having on young children; however, without doubt, the major EI effort in this country for families of children living in poverty is Head Start. In 1964, the Johnson administration created the Office of Economic Opportunity, from which Operation Head Start was created. Head Start funds were contracted to local community action groups throughout the nation to develop preschool programs for children living in poverty. The goals were to improve children's physical health and abilities, improve children's social-emotional development, improve children's conceptual and verbal skills, and establish a pattern of expectations to help ensure future success (Maxim, 1980).

The evolution of Head Start has been fraught with challenges. According to Zigler and Cascione (1977), the goals of Head Start were poorly understood from the beginning, which may have contributed to some of the controversy that has surrounded the program over the years. In addition, the impact this program has had on children has been debated over the years (Clarke & Clarke, 1977; Farran, 2005; Peters & Deiner, 1987). In the early years, a source of this controversy was likely the variety of programs subsumed by the Head Start umbrella. Approaches used in local programs varied over the years in terms of curriculum focus, staffing patterns and qualifications, structure, and service delivery models. Recent federally issued Head Start requirements and regulations are producing more consistency across programs. In 1972, the Head Start legislation was amended to ensure that enrollment included at least 10% children with disabilities (Ackerman & Moore, 1976). This legislative change created an opportunity for many children with disabilities to be served in programs that followed many tenets of early childhood programs, although compensatory interventions were often offered.

Studies investigating the impact of early education programs on populations considered at risk have produced mixed results. One early study by Blatt and Garfunkel (1969) randomly assigned 59 preschool-age children from low-income homes to experimental and nonexperimental groups. The experimental group attended a structured intervention program, whereas the nonexperimental group did not. Evaluation of the results suggested that the children appeared to be more influenced by the home setting than by the school environment. This conclusion suggested that other factors present in children's environments could outweigh the effect of even sound school-based intervention.

Other early studies have reported more positive outcomes. For example, the work of Gray and Klaus (1976) with children from low-income families offered potent evidence on the effects of EI. The findings were based on data from a 7-year follow-up study of 88 African American children from low-income families living in rural Tennessee. The children were assigned to one of four conditions: two experimental conditions that differed in length of intervention or two control groups. A comparison of performances found that measured intelligence of children in the experimental conditions significantly exceeded that of the controls, and this difference was retained for several years.

In 1997, Bryant and Maxwell summarized 3 decades of research on early education programs for children living in poverty. These writers noted that

> The Consortium for Longitudinal Studies provided powerful evidence of the effectiveness of such programs by conducting long-term follow-up of 11 experimentally designed programs serving children between 1962 and 1973, finding that the children in intervention groups were placed in special education less often and retained in grade less often, even though their initial IQ advantage over controls had largely disappeared after three years in public schools. (p. 23)

Echoing this conclusion, Kirp (2007) noted 10 years later that the studies conducted by the Perry Preschool Project, the Abecedarian Project, and the Child Parent Centers in Chicago have made clear the value of providing quality preschool education to children living in poverty.

Additional research has addressed some of the complexity associated with determining the effects of compensatory education on young children living in poverty. Although findings of effects are often positive, they require careful qualification in terms of conditions, such as quality of services, length of intervention, curricular focus, and intensity (Bricker et al., 2013; Bryant & Maxwell, 1997; Farran, 2005).

Although controversy continues to swirl around program offerings for children living in poverty, they are clearly here to stay as a political reality; however, as noted by Kirp (2007),

> Today the prekindergarten movement has arrived at a crossroads. Even as more states are offering preschool, more children are enrolling, and more public dollars are being spent, the quality of instruction remains mixed and the amount of money being spent on each child has declined. (p. 266)

Thus, enormous challenges remain, and the subsequent growth and quality of preschool education for children living in poverty remains an unanswered question.

Programs for Children with Disabilities

Concerns for children living in poverty have been paralleled by concerns for children with disabilities or impairments. As noted previously, impairments exist on a continuum, from typically developing children to children with severe challenges. As shown in Figure 2.1, often the boundaries between contiguous classifications (e.g., at risk and mildly impaired) can be blurred as children's level and quality of performance varies either over time or over conditions. Nonetheless, data provided by the federal government have suggested that 15%–17% of children born in the United States are diagnosed with a disability (U.S. Department of Education, 2013). That is, these children have developmental delays or behavior problems that are sufficiently discrepant from the norm to warrant the label of disability consistently overtime. By definition these children receive publicly supported services to assist them and their families; however, the availability and quality of services for this population of children has changed significantly over time, as have federal and state policies.

One of the first formal efforts to educate a child with a disability occurred in the 1800s by French physician Jean Marc Gaspard Itard. The child, Victor, was found wandering in a wooded area near Paris and was assumed to be approximately 11 years old. His behavior was primitive and unsocialized, and some labeled him as a hopeless case. Itard disagreed with this label and took on the task of educating Victor (Ball, 1971). Itard developed a carefully designed educational program designed to address Victor's many impairments. Although Itard's success with Victor was relatively modest, his work established the idea that individuals with severe disabilities could acquire skills. Itard's initial work was continued by Edouard Seguin, a student of Itard's who refined Itard's approach and again demonstrated that people with severe disabilities could learn.

Despite some success associated with educational intervention efforts undertaken in the community, a movement was initiated in the U.S. in the mid-1800s to place individuals with disabilities into institutional settings. Initially, these institutional facilities were created with the purpose of helping those with impairments gain skills so that they would be better accepted by individuals in the larger community; however, over time, these large institutions became human warehouses. They ceased to provide treatment and educational programs and instead substituted custodial care (MacMillan,

1977). Not until the 1950s did institutions once again begin to offer compensatory services to those who were institutionalized; however, these remedial services were slow to begin, slower to expand, and often available only to a small number of residents.

In the 1970s, perspectives about individuals with disabilities began to shift dramatically to more optimistic and hopeful views. The impetus for these changing views was spurred by three factors. First, parent groups as well as some professionals began to argue for the rights of individuals with impairments and to create groups (e.g., the National Association for Retarded Children, now ARC) to advocate for these rights. Second, judicial action such as *Mills v. Board of Education of the District of Columbia* (1972), and *Pennsylvania Association for Retarded Children (PARC) v. Pennsylvania* (1971) provided the legal basis for subsequent court rulings and for change in federal and state policies (Bricker, 1989). These legal decisions and policy changes laid the foundation for equal rights and treatment of individuals with disabilities. Third, the perspective about the constancy of a person's IQ began evolving in concert with the growing appreciation of the impact of environments on young children (Gallagher & Ramey, 1987). Increasingly, professionals as well as the general public were coming to understand the importance and impact of early developmental periods on children's outcomes.

In the late 1950s to early 1960s, students and interpreters of B.F. Skinner began to apply the principles of the experimental analysis of behavior to people with intellectual disabilities and mental illness (Ayllon & Michael, 1959). The early work was conducted with institutionalized adults thought to be unteachable and uncontrollable. Using the principles of arranging antecedents, defining responses, and providing immediate feedback, investigators were able to demonstrate their ability to teach individuals with severe disabilities to perform a variety of functional behaviors (Staats, 1964).

Although the application of behavioral principles and interventions began with institutionalized adult populations, the principles were subsequently transferred for use with younger and younger populations. The first children to be involved in behavioral analytical interventions were institutionalized; however, this approach was applied with children living at home beginning in the 1960s (Baer, 1962; Risley & Wolf, 1967). Using behavior analytical principles, investigators began to demonstrate that a range of children with disabilities could be helped.

Sam Kirk, often called the Father of Special Education, began another line of work in the late 1940s to early 1950s. In 1948 Kirk received support to begin an experiment that was the first formal attempt to provide an EI program to a group of preschool-age children with intellectual disability. Kirk's investigation included 81 preschool children between 3 and 6 years of age. Children were assigned to one of four groups: a group of community-based children who attended a preschool program, a group of community-based children who did not attend a preschool program, a group of institutionalized children who attended a preschool program, and a group of institutionalized children who did not attend a preschool program. Upon completion of the project, the children who attended a preschool program, either community-based or institutional, outperformed those children who had received no schooling (Kirk, 1977). Although the initial differences tended to be lost over time, Kirk concluded that the intervention did have a positive impact on the participating children.

During the 1950s to 1970s, other investigators began exploring the potential of EI with children with impairments. Some of this early work is described in a 1976 volume edited by Theodore Tjossem. In general, investigators reported that quality intervention undertaken early in the lives of children with diagnosed and often substantial impairments consistently produced positive outcomes (e.g., Bricker & Bricker, 1976). And then community-based programs for young children with disabilities began to appear. Though initially many employed strict behavioral principles, over time personnel found that young children responded better to these principles being embedded in familiar routines and play activities, which prompted the onset of more naturalistic approaches such as ABI (Bricker & Cripe, 1992) and milieu training (Warren & Kaiser, 1988).

Parallel to programmatic developments were changes in federal law and policy. In 1968, the United States Congress enacted the Handicapped Children's Early Education Program (HCEEP). The purpose of this federal program for preschool-age children with disabilities was "to demonstrate the feasibility of early education to the American public" (Ackerman & Moore, 1976, p. 669). The outcomes of the HCEEP-funded programs were reviewed by Swan (1980), who concluded they were successful in demonstrating the positive impact on children's performance and on stimulating the growth of community-based programs for young children with disabilities.

Perhaps the single most important piece of federal legislation for children with disabilities was the Education for All Handicapped Children Act of 1975 (PL 94-142). This law and its subsequent amendments put in place the federal commitment to ensure that all children are entitled to a free appropriate public education, nondiscriminatory evaluation, an individualized education program (IEP), due process, and parent participation. The Education of the Handicapped Act Amendments of 1986 (PL 99-457) expanded these services to preschool-age children. In addition, this law created a discretionary program designed to provide EI services to children birth through age 2 and their families.

The law was later renamed the Individuals with Disabilities Education Act (IDEA; PL 101-476). IDEA and its subsequent amendments (the Individuals with Disabilities Education Improvement Act of 2004; PL 108-446) continue to clarify federal policy that addresses the educational treatment of and services for individuals with disabilities.

During the 1980s and 1990s programs for young children with disabilities emerged as a synthesis of philosophies, curricular approaches, and instructional methodologies (Odom, 1988; Warren & Kaiser, 1988); however, this synthesis has not occurred without debate and controversy (e.g., Atwater, Carta, Schwartz, & McConnell, 1994 Novick, 1993). The trend appears to be moving toward the inclusion of children with disabilities into programs designed for typically developing children or creating blended programs (Grisham-Brown et al., 2005). (More detail on contemporary programs is offered in the next section.)

Since their inception, intervention approaches have evolved from being adult directed with little attention given to children's interests and motivation to becoming child directed with the use of authentic assessment and curricular approaches. Other substantial changes associated with educational and therapeutic interventions with young children with disabilities will likely be reflected in the years to come.

CONTEMPORY PROGRAMS FOR CHILDREN WITH DISABILITIES

The previous sections have offered a rationale for EI and an historical review of early childhood programs, programs for children living in poverty, and programs for children with disabilities. This historical foundation provides a basis for understanding the range and variety of contemporary services for young children, birth to age 6 years, with disabilities. Federal law and regulations have helped shape the national landscape for many of these programs and have provided some consistency across programs. Courts have also weighed in, and generally rulings uphold the need for equality and fairness in the provision of educational and therapeutic services for children, no matter their disability. Nevertheless, significant variation exists in service delivery systems depending on many factors such as state legislation and regulation, community expertise and leadership, population density, economic resources, and theoretical influences.

Today, EI/ECSE services are generally provided in either home- or group/center-based settings. Home-based services were and often still are considered the most appropriate setting for infants and toddlers birth through age 2 with disabilities. The home is considered by many to be the natural or most appropriate place for infants and toddlers to spend their time because home is safe and familiar, and because parents are available. However, historical and contemporary change (e.g., mothers working outside of the home) and economic necessity (e.g., the need for two working adults in the family) have rendered this traditional picture of home often unrealistic for a large number of infants and toddlers. Many programs for infants and toddlers still deliver services in the home, but increasingly services for this young population are being delivered in other settings (e.g., Early Head Start centers, community child care centers). Many very young children spend many hours a day in center-based or child care programs while their parent(s) work (Lombardi, 2003).

Service delivery settings for children ages 3–6 years with disabilities are most frequently provided outside of the home in a community-based program designed to accommodate groups of children; however, variations exist in that some preschool children are seen at home and some children receive individual therapy sessions in medical settings. Huge variation exists in the types of center/group-based settings that are available across states and communities, but generally these services can be classified as 1) typical child care settings that operate all day and sometimes into the evening, 2) settings specifically designed for children with disabilities that may operate all day or for specific time periods (e.g., mornings, afternoons, alternate days), or 3) settings for children with ranges of abilities (e.g., inclusive programs). Settings also vary in terms of what they offer children, ranging from programs with a strong academic focus to programs that provide little or no educational opportunities.

The following sections examine the significant changes or shifts that have taken place in more recent years in services for children birth through age 2 years and those 3–6 years with disabilities. For infants and toddlers, the program descriptions are divided into home-based services and child care–based services. For preschool-age children, the program descriptions are divided into center-based services and child care–based services.

Home-Based Services for Infants and Toddlers

Since their inception in the early 1970s, home visit programs have undergone significant modifications by embracing more contemporary beliefs about child development and motivation, family systems, and authentic assessment and intervention strategies. Much of this change has been motivated by federal legislation.

As noted earlier, the Handicapped Children's Early Education Act of 1968 (PL 90-538) offered states an impetus for serving young children with disabilities by providing funding for model demonstration programs through the Bureau for the Education of the Handicapped. In addition, this agency along with other government agencies such as the Division of Maternal and Child Health began offering grants to universities for the preparation of professionals to work with children with disabilities. Although these programs did not mandate services to nonschool-age populations, they were instrumental in creating a nationwide movement to develop EI/ECSE programs and prepare quality personnel to operate these programs.

Beginning in 1974, the federal government offered competitive funding to states for the planning and development of services for preschoolers with disabilities; however, no legislation addressed services for infants and toddlers until 12 years later. The Education of the Handicapped Act Amendments of 1983 (PL 98-199) permitted states to use Preschool Incentive Grant funds to serve children with disabilities younger than age three. Then in 1986, PL 99-457 was enacted; this new grant program was designed to assist states to provide services to infants and toddlers with disabilities. This legislation required states to create plans and develop and implement appropriate services for children birth through age 2 and their families.

In the mid-1980s, home-based services for infants and toddlers with disabilities and their caregivers consisted of regularly scheduled 60–90 minute visits (e.g., weekly, monthly) in the home by trained personnel, such as an early interventionist/early childhood special educator, therapist, or social worker. A home visit often followed routines during which the professional demonstrated a number of important tasks to be conducted with the child during the ensuing days or weeks (e.g., activities to encourage walking or babbling). During the first visits to the home, the professional would gather assessment information through observation and from the caregiver about the child's skills and participation in family activities. This information was used to create or to update the individualized family service plan (IFSP) and intervention activities.

As the child's assessment and the resulting IFSP were completed or updated, the focus of the home visits became intervention-oriented. In large measure, home visits were planned and controlled by the professional who brought toys and materials selected to address the child's intervention targets. The home visitor would introduce the toys and materials, engage the child in intervention and play activities, and provide multiple opportunities for the child to practice targeted skills with the hope of providing a positive model for the caregiver. The home visitor and caregiver would observe the child as he or she played, encouraging the child to practice targeted skills, and conclude with a discussion of strategies to be used by the caregiver between visits. The caregiver and home visitor also discussed a range of other topics, such as the child's progress since the previous visit, new issues or concerns, and plans for future visits. At the end of the visit, the home visitor would provide the caregiver with instructions to follow until the next scheduled visit.

With the passage of amended federal legislation designed to enhance services to young children with disabilities (e.g., IDEA), and with the collection of data on program effectiveness (Bailey, 1987; Crais, 1991; Dunst, Trivette, & Deal, 1988; Turnbull & Turnbull, 1990), three important changes in the delivery of home-based services occurred: 1) the adjustment of IFSP goals and objectives from those chosen by professionals to those deemed valuable and important by families, 2) the shift to include parents/caregivers as partners in assessment and intervention efforts, and 3) the use of authentic activities and meaningful materials.

The first shift from professionally chosen goals to addressing family determined goals required the adoption of different assessment/evaluation measures than had previously been used. Measures were needed that asked caregivers about their interests and needs and desires for their children. Numerous new measures were developed and used throughout the 1990s

(Bricker & Cripe, 1992; Dunst & Leet, 1986). Family-completed measures were specifically designed to obtain information from caregivers about their own values and hopes for their children (Dinnebeil & Rule, 1994).

The *Assessment, Evaluation, and Programming System (AEPS®) for Infants and Children* Family Report (Bricker, 2002) is an example of a family friendly measure that was created to gather information from caregivers that can be used in developing IFSPs and in planning and conducting intervention. The AEPS Family Report consists of two sections that families can complete. Section I asks caregivers to indicate 1) the family's typical daily routines and activities, 2) the child's participation in each routine or activity, and 3) what makes the activity pleasant and/or difficult in terms of the child's participation. The content addressed in Section I includes eating, sleeping, dressing, bathing/showering, toileting, playing and interacting, communicating with others, and family and community activities. Section II contains a set of questions that ask about children's developmental skills. Caregivers are asked to mark each item with a *y* (yes), *s* (sometimes), or *n* (not yet). At the end of each developmental area caregivers are asked to list the skills they want their child to learn next or what they would like to target on the IFSP.

Other new measures reflected alternative foci. For example, the Family Support Scale (Dunst, Jenkins, & Trivette, 2007) addresses parents' satisfaction with their support systems. Caregivers are asked to respond using a 5-point Likert scale to identify their informal kinship, social organizations, formal kinship, nuclear family, specialized professional services, and generic professional services. Providers then identify areas that need assistance to better meet families' needs.

A second significant modification that occurred in home visits was the exchange of roles between the home visitor and caregiver during interactions with the child. This shift entailed the caregiver taking on the role of primary intervener with the child and the professional observing and providing constructive feedback. A range of terms and descriptions has been used to describe this modification in roles; however, the term *coaching* perhaps best captures the role exchange (Friedman, Woods, & Salisbury, 2012). Other terms include *dyadic and triadic interactions* (Marvin & Yates, 2007) and *caregiver teaching* (Sawyer & Campbell, 2012).

In a coaching model, the caregiver and child are the primary participants, interacting with each other, as they would while engaged in daily routines or activities. The home visitor joins the dyad, as a guide or coach who can offer information on child development and intervention strategies and techniques. As interactions occur between the caregiver and child, the home visitor coach can suggest information and feedback on intervention strategies such as positioning, supporting growing independence, de-escalating tense interactions, and creating supportive environmental arrangements. This role reversal produces a significant benefit to the child by trading

60–90 minutes of massed practice trials led by the home visitor to a range of logical and meaningful practice opportunities occurring throughout the day with the caregiver. This shift enhances the generalization of targeted skills across time, materials, people, and settings.

A third significant shift adopted by many home visit programs involves using authentic activities and materials. Rather than introducing specific or specialized training activities, the home visitor helps the caregiver learn how to use or adapt children's daily routines and play to practice targeted goals and objectives. Thus, the caregiver uses routines such as meal times, bath times, and play times to introduce and practice IFSP goals.

In addition to using authentic activities, home visitors shifted to using toys and materials found in the child's home (McWilliam, 2010). This modification supplants the home visitor practice of bringing new and unfamiliar toys for each visit and then packing them back up and removing them when they leave. Ending the toy bag practice requires using materials that are available in the child's home and encouraging families to support the child's developmental progress with familiar materials. An alternative practice is the use of lending toy libraries. Toys and other materials can be checked out and can remain in the home for extended periods of time.

These three important shifts have resulted in contemporary home visit services that are more cognizant of the importance of family input and more responsive to their needs as well as the role that caregivers can fill. Quality home visit services now entail selecting intervention goals and objectives that reflect family values and needs; assisting caregivers in becoming their child's teacher throughout daily routines; and using activities, toys, and materials that are meaningful, familiar, and consistently available to the child.

Child Care–Based Services for Infants and Toddlers

As noted previously, many children younger than 3 with disabilities attend child care programs outside of the home while their parents work. Out-of-home child care services can be classified as family care and group care. Family care, as the title suggests, takes place in a family residence and provides a home-like environment for participating children. These settings generally accommodate only a few children and generally lack a schedule of organized activities. Group care services are usually located in a community facility such as a church or home that has been converted to accommodate groups of children. These programs can range from small (i.e., fewer than 10 children) to large (i.e., more than 30 children). Recommended practices for adult-to-child staffing is 1:3 for infants and 1:4 for toddlers younger than 3 years. The physical facilities may vary enormously depending largely on program resources. However, most programs have separate rooms for play, napping, and eating. State licensing often dictates the size of the various areas; however, the quality of these separate areas and the materials they contain can vary from relatively modest to expensive.

In child care settings for infants and toddlers, the daily schedule is generally less fixed than in programs designed for older children. In many of these programs, the majority of the day is spent in routine child care activities (e.g., eating, changing diapers, cleanup, getting ready for and being put down for naps) than in planned events.

Perhaps the most significant change for infants and toddlers in child care–based programs has been the expansion of professional services to these programs. Until the mid-1990s, infants and toddlers with disabilities attending child care did not receive EI/ECSE services in those settings. Instead, EI/ECSE professionals met with the parents in the home. This practice overlooked the many hours a week the child spent in the care of others. Beginning in the late 1990s, home visitors began extending their EI/ECSE visits and services to child care settings where they could work with child development workers as well as with parents. With collaboration and planning between EI/ECSE and child care staff, intervention services were extended to settings in which children spent much of their time. Although a significant step forward, the quality of the services offered in child care settings is highly dependent upon the expertise and tact of the EI/ECSE professional, the training and experience of the child care worker, and the willingness and ability of child care staff to work with EI/ECSE professionals and to engage in intervention activities. When EI/ECSE services are provided to infants and toddlers with disabilities in child care settings, the EI/ECSE professional usually makes regular visits to both the home and child care facility to observe the child, exchange information with the family and child care staff, and support the child's participation in daily and routine activities. Some visits are also arranged to occur with both parent and child care staff so that team members can plan intervention strategies that can be used in both settings. The EI/ECSE professional usually meets separately with the child's parent(s) periodically (e.g., monthly) to provide additional service coordination and support.

The expansion of intervention services to child care settings for infants and toddlers has provided greater continuity of effort to the child and family by working with all the primary adults who care for the child. As a result of growing flexibility of federal and state regulations and the recognition of the need for the continuity of intervention across a child's environment, an expansion of EI services to all settings in which children spend significant amounts of time has occurred. This change has the potential of enhancing intervention efforts and consequently maximizing child progress and family satisfaction.

Center-Based Services for Preschool-Age Children

To review, the Handicapped Children's Early Education Act of 1968 (PL 90-538) authorized funding for the development, evaluation, refinement, and dissemination of model demonstration programs for the education of infants and preschoolers with disabilities and their parents. Under this law, grants for demonstration programs and specialized university teacher-training programs in early childhood special education were funded. In 1975, the Education for All Handicapped Children Act (PL 94-142) was passed. This law established the right to a free appropriate public education for all children ages 6–21, and also established preschool incentive grant programs specifically to provide services to children with disabilities ages 3–5 years. In 1986, PL 99-457 was enacted, which strengthened incentives for states to serve all eligible children ages 3–5 years old by tying federal preschool funds to it, thus mandating rights and protections to eligible children. PL 101-476 was enacted in 1990 and renamed the Individuals with Disabilities Education Act. This Act was amended in 1997 and again in 2007, and once again renamed the Individuals with Disabilities Education Improvement Act.

Most children in this country ages 3–5 who are identified with a disability or are at risk for disability now participate in some type of center-based program (U.S. Department of Education, 2014). An exception to center-based programs for children in this age range are medically fragile children with compromised immune systems who are homeschooled and/or participate with a preschool class through technology.

As noted in the history discussion earlier in this chapter, community-based programs for children with disabilities began in the late 1970s to early 1980s, and over the decades they have moved from more adult-directed, highly structured, decontextualized training activities to more child-focused and child-directed, authentic assessment and intervention efforts provided by inclusive teams. By the mid-1980s, many communities offered center-based services for children ages 3–5 years. Most of these programs enrolled children with diagnosed disabilities who were eligible for free public services. With some notable exceptions (Bricker & Bricker, 1976), it was not until the mid-to-late 1980s that inclusive, or blended, programs (i.e., children with and without disabilities placed and educated in the same setting) became available. Early federal legislation addressing individuals with disabilities did not mandate inclusion, but rather required school districts to "place students in the least restrictive environments, that to the maximum extent appropriate means in the regular classroom" (PL 94-142) with their peers without disabilities. Consequently, states' interpretation of the federal mandate has resulted in preschool-age services for children with disabilities varying widely in terms of the mix between children with and without disabilities.

Historically, preschool-age center-based services for children with disabilities tended to be half-day programs that were provided 2 to 5 days per week—although many exceptions existed. The children in the classroom were usually similarly aged, and all had disabilities. The classroom setting was equipped with child-sized furniture and facilities. Furniture usually consisted of small tables and chairs, pillows, large rugs for children to sit on at circle time, sand and water tables, book cases, room dividers, child mail boxes, and child-sized cubbies to hang coats or extra clothing.

As center-based services for children with disabilities became more educationally oriented, they began to follow a daily schedule, similar to that of preschools for typically developing children. Although schedules varied, they generally consisted of large group, small group, and individualized activities. During individualized activities each child worked on his or her targeted IEP goals and objectives.

A typical schedule might include

1. Independent or free play upon arrival

2. Large-group instruction often taking place in a circle and following a theme

3. Individual activities for each child

4. Outside or gymnasium play

5. Cleanup and bathroom time

6. Snack time

7. Individual activities

8. Circle time and good-bye

As with programs for infants and toddlers, there have been significant changes in center-based services for children ages 3–5 with disabilities. Most of the change that has occurred was inspired by university-based demonstration programs and research outcomes that suggested approaches more likely to produce improved outcomes for children and families.

The first change in preschool programs has been the gradual shift away from adult-directed and -controlled activities. Intervention efforts such as ABI take into account children's likes and motivations—a practice that usually produces better outcomes (see Chapter 8). Using child-initiated or directed activities removes the problem of motivation and offers a context that apparently makes sense to the child (see Chapter 4). Mesmerizing a child with 10 trials of nonmeaningful actions is no longer seen as appropriate. Rather, caregivers observe and use children's natural interests and actions for addressing intervention goals and objectives.

A second significant change focuses on what the field has come to label authentic assessment and intervention activities. The dimension of *authentic* emphasizes the real-life nature of a task and the natural context in which it occurs (Bagnato, 2007). As a contrast to more conventional assessment and intervention practice, authentic approaches make use of everyday, familiar settings (i.e., typically home, community-based, or classroom settings) and use activities and routines that occur throughout the day (Bagnato, Neisworth, & Pretti-Frontczak, 2010).

Bagnato and Yeh-Ho defined authentic assessment as the "systematic recording of developmental observations over time about the naturally occurring behaviors of young children in daily routines by familiar and knowledgeable caregivers in the child's life" (2006, p. 29). Authentic intervention unites learning opportunities to practice targeted skills with regularly occurring activities and routines in which those skills are functionally used. Authentic intervention is provided in settings where children are more likely to need and use the skills, and will learn to generalize their use.

Thus, center-based services for preschool-age children are increasingly shifting their focus to the use of authentic assessment and intervention activities. This shift is yielding better information about children's developmental repertoire that in turn provides better information to target important goals and objectives. Subsequent authentic intervention activities should also accrue better outcomes.

A third significant change in center-based group services for preschool-age children has been the development of team approaches that organize, coordinate, and unify assessment and intervention activities. The primary professions/disciplines associated with EI/ECSE are EI providers/ECSE teachers; however, these interventionists/teachers are supported by a wide range of related service personnel including speech-language pathologists, occupational therapists, physical therapists, social workers, psychologists, nutritionists, audiologists, and medical specialists. Each of these professionals experience separate and unique preservice programs of study; require special licenses, certificates, or degrees to practice; and differ in their philosophies of service delivery (Bruder, 2005).

Historically, related service professionals have operated according to their disciplinary training when providing services to young children and their families. The preservice training for related service professionals has differed from the preparation of EI/ECSE specialists in four important ways. First, related services professionals' training programs often offer only limited course work focused on young children, so these professionals frequently enter the world of EI/ECSE with little prior experience or knowledge of this age group or home/center/school settings. Second, related services training programs often do not provide course work about working with families—meaning that these professionals typically have little experience interacting with families and collaborating with caregivers as team members. Third, related services training programs often advocate approaches that emphasize individualized, pull-out training sessions rather than the use of daily, authentic activities, routines, and play as primary times to embed opportunities for children to practice target skills. Fourth, related service training programs often do not foster the concept of "role release" or the transfer of expertise and information to those who work with children consistently throughout the day and over time (e.g., parents, teachers).

Changes in university training programs and disciplinary practice are gradually occurring; consequently, related service personnel are becoming better prepared to work with young children and families. Related service personnel are coming to understand the inherent usefulness of using authentic activities to both garner information about children and to use as intervention vehicles. In addition, rather than pull-out therapy that removes a child from his or her usual environment, push-in therapy is being conducted within the home, classroom, or child care setting.

An array of different types of center-based services exist for preschool children: general education, blended general education co-taught, blended general education with dual certificated teacher, reverse mainstream special education, inclusive special education, and special education. Each type of preschool program serving children with disabilities requires the services of a teacher certified in EI/ECSE; however, the teacher's role may be as an itinerant teacher, as a co-teacher, or as the only teacher, depending on the program type. School districts often provide several types of EI/ECSE programs to accommodate the district size and range of disabilities. Table 2.2 lists the program type with the associated role of the EI/ECSE teacher.

Many preschoolers with disabilities now spend some part of their day with typically developing same-age peers. The benefits obtained from inclusive play and learning experiences are widely accepted as best practice in preschool education by offering appropriate models for learning new skills, increasing social and communication skills, and producing greater independence.

In the short time since services to young children, birth to age 6, with disabilities became law, intervention services and practices have expanded significantly, and services have shifted from professionally directed to family driven. Intervention services better reflect modern family lifestyles, and the caregiver role has evolved from service recipient to active team member.

CHILD CARE SERVICES FOR PRESCHOOL-AGE CHILDREN

As noted, increasing numbers of infants and toddlers are in out-of-home child care placements. This trend is equally true for preschool-age children. Many 3–6-year-olds spend all day 5 days a week in a child care setting making it necessary and important to include the staff in intervention efforts with children who have disabilities or who are at risk for disability. Much of the discussion in this section mirrors the information contained in the Infant and Toddler Child-Care–Based Services section of the chapter presented earlier.

As with infants and toddlers, preschool child care services can be classified as family care and group care. Family care generally occurs in someone's home and provides a home-like environment for participating children. Family care may have only one or two child care workers and thus generally accommodates only a few children. Family care may offer children a variety of activities but often does not follow a schedule of organized activities. Alternatively, group child care services are operated in a facility such as a

Table 2.2. Type of preschool center-based programs and associated early intervention/early childhood special education (EI/ECSE) teacher roles

Preschool center-based program type	EI/ECSE professional staff
General education	Early childhood (EC) teacher with special education services provided by itinerant EI/ECSE teacher
Blended general education co-taught	EC teacher and ECSE teacher co-teach
Blended general education with dual certificate	EC/ECSE teacher with dual certification
Reverse mainstream special education	ECSE teacher
Integrated special education	ECSE teacher
Special education	ECSE teacher

Source: Kansas State Department of Education (2014).

recreation center, church, or home that has been remodeled to accommodate groups of children. These programs can range from small (i.e., fewer than 10 children) to large (i.e., more than 30 children), and the type of facilities, furnishings, and play materials may vary substantially. Staff varies considerably in terms of training and experience. Many workers have no formal child development training, and many have only high school diplomas. A few workers may have associate degrees, and even fewer have a bachelor's degree.

As with infants and toddlers, the most significant change in preschool child care services is the expansion of professional services to these programs. Until the late 1990s, few children received ECSE services in child care settings. As with infants and toddlers, initially ECSE professionals' interactions with the parents were in the home; however, beginning in the mid-1990s, home visitors began extending their EI/ECSE visits and services to group child care settings where they could work with child care workers as well as with parents. With collaboration and planning between EI/ECSE and child care workers, intervention services were extended to settings in which children spend much of their time. Although significant progress has occurred in the delivery of services to children, the quality of these services is tied to the EI/ECSE professional's expertise and ability to communicate, as well as the personal and program resources available to child care workers.

When ECSE services are provided to preschoolers with disabilities in group child care settings, recommended practice dictates that the ECSE professional makes regular visits to both the home and child care facility to observe the child, exchange information with the family and child care staff, and support the child's participation in daily and routine activities. Visits should also be arranged with both parents and child care staff, so that team members can plan intervention strategies that can be used in both settings.

The expansion of intervention services to child care settings for preschool-age children has provided greater continuity of effort to the child and family by working with all the primary adults who care for the child. As a result of growing flexibility of federal and state regulations and recognition of the need for the continuity of intervention across a child's environment, an expansion of early childhood special education services to all settings in which children spend significant amounts of time has occurred. This change has the potential of enhancing intervention efforts and consequently maximizing child progress and family satisfaction.

SUMMARY

This chapter presented an overview of EI/ECSE programs in the United States. It began by discussing the rationale for EI as a basis for appreciating the development of intervention efforts for young children in this country. It also traced the historical development of early childhood programs, programs for children living in poverty, and programs for children with disabilities. The chapter discussed federal legislation that has undergirded programs for young children and the evolution of services for these originally distinct populations of children. The chapter concluded with descriptions of contemporary programs for infants, toddlers, and preschool-age children with disabilities. It also highlighted the significant changes that have shaped and reshaped practices in programs for infants and toddlers and preschool-age children with disabilities.

REFERENCES

Ackerman, P., & Moore, M. (1976). Delivery of educational services to preschool handicapped children. In T. Tjossem (Ed.), *Intervention strategies for high risk infants and young children*. Baltimore, MD: University Park Press.

Atwater, J., Carta, J., Schwartz, I., & McConnell, S. (1994). Blending developmentally appropriate practice and early childhood special education: Redefining best practice to meet the needs of all children. In B. Mallory & R. New (Eds.), *Diversity and developmentally appropriate practice*. New York, NY: Teachers College Press.

Ayllon, T., & Michael, J. (1959). The psychiatric nurse as a behavioral engineer. *Journal of the Experimental Analysis of Behavior, 2*, 323–334.

Baer, D. (1962). Laboratory control of thumbsucking by withdrawal and representation of reinforcement. *Journal of the Experimental Analysis of Behavior, 5*, 525–528.

Bagnato, S. (2007). *Authentic assessment for early childhood intervention: Best practices.* New York, NY: Guilford Press.

Bagnato, S.J., Neisworth, J.T., & Pretti-Frontczak, K. (2010). *LINKing authentic assessment and early childhood intervention: Best measures for best practices* (2nd ed.). Baltimore, MD: Paul H. Brookes Publishing Co.

Bagnato, S.J., & Yeh-Ho, H. (2006). High-stakes testing of preschool children: Viola standards for professional and evidence-based practice. *International Journal of Korean Educational Policy, 3*, 23–43.

Bailey, D. (1987). Collaborative goal-setting with families: Resolving differences in values and priorities for services. *Topics in Early Childhood Special Education, 7*(2), 59–71.

Ball, T. (1971). *Itard, Seguin, and Kephart: Sensory education: A learning interpretation.* Columbus, OH: Merrill.

Beller, E. (1979). Early intervention programs. In J. Osofsky (Ed.), *Handbook of infant development*. New York, NY: John Wiley and Sons.

Belsky, J., Steinberg, L., & Walker, A. (1982). The ecology of day care. In M. Lamb (Ed.), *Nontraditional families*. Mahwah, NJ: Lawrence Erlbaum Associates.

Blatt, B., & Garfunkel, F. (1969). *The educability of intelligence*. Washington, DC: The Council for Exceptional Children.

Bloom, B.S. (Ed.) (1956). *Taxonomy of Educational Objectives, the classification of educational goals—Handbook I: Cognitive Domain* New York, NY: McKay.

Bowlby, J. (1973). *Attachment and loss: Separation, anxiety, and anger.* New York, NY: Basic Books.

Bredekamp, S. (Ed.). (1987). *Developmentally appropriate practice in early childhood programs serving children from birth through age 8.* Washington, DC: National Association for the Education of Young Children.

Bredekamp, S., & Copple, C. (Eds.). (1997). *Developmentally appropriate practice in early childhood programs* (Rev. ed). Washington, DC: National Association for the Education of Young Children.

Bricker, D. (1989). *Early intervention for at-risk, and handicapped infants, toddlers, and preschool children.* Palo Alto, CA: VORT.

Bricker, D. (Series Ed.). (2002). *Assessment, Evaluation and Programming System (AEPS®) for Infants and Children* (2nd ed.). Baltimore, MD: Paul H. Brookes Publishing Co.

Bricker, D., & Bricker, W. (1971). *Toddler research and intervention project report: Year I.* IMRID Behavioral Science Monograph No. 21. Nashville: George Peabody College Institute on Mental Retardation and Intellectual Development.

Bricker, D., & Bricker, W. (1972). *Toddler research and intervention project report: Year II.* IMRID Behavioral Science Monograph No. 22. Nashville: George Peabody College Institute on Mental Retardation and Intellectual Development.

Bricker, W., & Bricker, D. (1976). The infant, toddler, and preschool research and intervention project. In T. Tjossem (Ed.), *Intervention strategies with at-risk infants and young children.* Baltimore, MD: University Park Press.

Bricker, D., & Cripe, J. (1992). *An activity-based approach to early intervention.* Baltimore, MD: Paul H. Brookes Publishing Co.

Bricker, D., Macy, M., Squires, J., & Marks, K. (2013). *Developmental screening in your community.* Baltimore: MD. Paul H. Brookes Publishing Co.

Bricker, D., Pretti-Frontzcak, K., & McComas, N. (1998). *An activity-based approach to early intervention.* Baltimore, MD: Paul H. Brookes Publishing Co.

Brooks-Gunn, J. (2003). Do you believe in magic? What we can expect from early childhood programs. *Social policy report: Giving child and youth development knowledge away, 17,* 3–14.

Brooks-Gunn, J., McCarton, C.M., Casey, P.H., McCormick, M.C., Bauer, C.R., & Bernbaum, J.C., et al. (1994). Early intervention in low birth weight premature infants results through age 5 years from the Infant Health and Development Program. *JAMA, 272*(16), 1257–1262.

Bruder, M. (2005). Service coordination and integration in a developmental systems approach to early intervention. In M.J. Guralnick (Ed.), *A developmental systems approach to early intervention* (pp. 29–58). Baltimore, MD: Paul H. Brookes Publishing Co.

Bruer, J.T. (2001). A critical and sensitive period primer. In D.B. Bailey, J.T. Bruer, F.J. Symons, & J.W. Litchtman (Eds.), *Critical thinking about critical periods.* Baltimore, MD: Paul H. Brookes Publishing Co.

Bryant, D., & Maxwell, K. (1997). The effectiveness of early intervention for disadvantaged children. In M. Guralnick (Ed.), *The effectiveness of early intervention.* Baltimore, MD: Paul H. Brookes Publishing Co.

Burchinal, M.R., Campbell, F.A., Bryant, D.M., Wasik, B.H., & Ramey, C.T. (1997). Early intervention and mediating processes in cognitive performance of children of low-income African American families. *Child Development, 68,* 935–954.

Campbell, F.A., & Ramey, C.T. (1995). Cognitive and school outcomes for high-risk African-American students at middle adolescence: Positive effects of early intervention. *American Educational Research Journal, 32*(4), 743–772.

Campbell, F.A., Ramey, C.T., Pungello, E.P., Miller-Johnson, S., & Burchinal, M. (2001). The development of cognitive and academic abilities: Growth curves from an early childhood educational experiment. *Developmental Psychology, 37*(2), 231–242.

Campbell, P., & Sawyer, B. (2009). Changing early intervention providers' home visiting skills through participation in professional development. *Topics in Early Childhood Special Education, 28*(4), 219–223.

Clarke, A., & Clarke, A. (1977). Prospects for prevention and amelioration of mental retardation: A guest editorial. *American Journal of Mental Deficiency, 81,* 523–533.

Consortium for Longitudinal Studies. (1983). *As the twig is bent: Lasting effects of preschool programs.* Mahwah, NJ: Lawrence Erlbaum Associates.

Crais, E.R. (1991). Moving from parent involvement to family-centered services. *American Journal of Speech-Language Pathology, 1*(1), 5–8.

Cripe, J., & Bricker, D. (1998). *Family interest survey for Assessment, Evaluation, and Programming System (AEPS®) for infants and children.* Baltimore, MD: Paul H. Brookes Publishing Co.

Dinnebeil, L., & Rule, S. (1994). Variables that influence collaboration between parents and service coordinators. *Journal of Early Intervention, 18*(4), 349–361.

Dunst, C., Jenkins, V., & Trivette, C. (2007). *Family Support Scale.* Asheville, NC: Winterberry Press.

Dunst, C., & Leet, H. (1986). *Family Resource Scale.* Asheville, NC: Winterberry Press.

Dunst, C., Trivette, C., & Deal, A. (1988). *Enabling and empowering families: Principles and guidelines for practice.* Cambridge, MA: Brookline Books.

Education for All Handicapped Children Act of 1975, PL 94-142, 20 U.S.C. §§ 1400 *et seq.*

Education of the Handicapped Act Amendments of 1983, PL 98-199, 20 U.S.C. §§ 1400 *et seq.,* 97 Stat. 1357.

Education of the Handicapped Act Amendments of 1986, PL 99-457, 20 U.S.C. §§ 1400 *et seq.*

Farran, D. (2005). Developing and implementing preventive intervention programs for children at risk: Poverty as a case in point. In M.J. Guralnick (Ed.), *The developmental systems approach to early intervention* (pp. 267–304). Baltimore, MD: Paul H. Brookes Publishing Co.

Friedman, M., Woods, J., & Salisbury, C. (2012). Caregiver coaching strategies for early intervention providers: Moving toward operational definitions. *Infants & Young Children, 25*(1), 62–82.

Gallagher, J., & Ramey, C. (1987). *The malleability of children.* Baltimore, MD: Paul H. Brookes Publishing Co.

Garber, H.L. (1988). *The Milwaukee Project: Preventing mental retardation in children at risk.* Washington, DC: American Association on Mental Retardation.

Gray, S., & Klaus, R. (1976). The early training project: A seventh year report. In A. Clarke & A. Clarke (Eds.), *Early experience: Myth and evidence.* New York, NY: The Free Press.

Grisham-Brown, J., Hemmeter, M.L., & Pretti-Frontczak, K. (2005). *Blended practices for teaching young children in inclusive settings.* Baltimore, MD: Paul H. Brookes Publishing Co.

Gurlnick, M. (1997). *The effectiveness of early intervention.* Baltimore, MD: Paul H. Brookes Publishing Co.

Gurlnick, M., & Bricker, D. (1987). The effectiveness of early intervention for children with cognitive and general developmental delays. In M. Guralnick & F. Bennet (Eds.), *The effectiveness of early intervention for at-risk and handicapped children.* New York, NY: Academic Press.

Handicapped Children's Early Education Act of 1968, PL 90-538, 20 U.S.C §§ 621 *et seq.*

Heckman, J. (2012). Invest in early childhood development: Reduce deficits, strengthen the economy. Retrieved from http://heckmanequation.org/content/resource/invest-early-childhood-development-reduce-deficits-strengthen-economy

Honig, A.S. (2004). Longitudinal outcomes from the family development research program. *Early Child Development and Care, 174*(2), 125–130.

Honig, A.S., Lally, J.R., & Mathieson, D.H. (1982). Personal and social adjustment of school children after five years in the Family Development Research Program. *Child Care Quarterly, 11,* 136–146.

Hunt, J.M. (1961). *Intelligence and experience*. New York, NY: Ronald Press.

Individuals with Disabilities Education Act (IDEA) of 2004, PL 108-446, 20 U.S.C §§ 1400 *et seq.*

Individuals with Disabilities Education Improvement Act (IDEA) of 1990, PL 101-476, 20 U.S.C §§ 1400 *et seq.*

Infant Health and Development Program. (1990). Enhancing the outcomes of low-birth-weight premature infants: A multisite, randomized trial. *JAMA, 263*(22), 3035–3042.

Johnson, D.L., & Walker, T. (1987). Primary prevention of behavior problems in Mexican-American children. *American Journal of Community Psychology, 15*(4), 375–386.

Johnson, D.L., & Walker, T. (1991). A follow-up evaluation of the Houston Parent-Child Development Center: School performance. *Journal of Early Intervention, 15*(3), 226–236.

Kean, J.M. (1970). The impact of Head Start: An evaluation on the effects of Head Start on children's cognitive and affective development. *Childhood Education, 46*(8), 449–452.

Kirk, S. (1977). General and historical rationale for early education of the handicapped. In N. Ellis & L. Cross (Eds.), *Planning programs for early education of the handicapped*. New York, NY: Walker & Co.

Kirp, D. (2007). *The sandbox investment*. Cambridge, MA: Harvard University Press.

Lazerson, M. (1972). The historical antecedents of early childhood education. *Education Digest, 38,* 20–23.

Lombardi, J. (2003). Time to care: Redesigning child care. *Zero to Three, 25,* 4.

Lynch, R.G. (2003). *Early childhood investment yields big payoff.* Retrieved from http://www.wested.org/online_pubs/pp-05-02.pdf

MacMillan, D. (1977). *Mental retardation in school and society*. Boston, MA: Little Brown.

Marvin, C., & Yates, T. (2007, October 27). *Promoting parent-child interactions during home visits*. Presentation at Council for Exceptional Children, Division for Early Childhood (DEC) 23rd Annual International Conference on Young Children with Special Needs and their Families. Niagara Falls, Ontario, Canada.

Maxim, G. (1980). *The very young: Guiding children from infancy through the early years*. Belmont, CA: Wadsworth.

McWilliam, R.A. (2010). *Routines-based early intervention: Supporting young children and their families*. Baltimore, MD: Paul H. Brookes Publishing Co.

Mills, K. (1999). *Something better for my children: How Head Start has changed the lives of millions of children*. New York, NY: Penguin Books.

Mills v. Board of Education of the District of Columbia, 348 F. Supp. 866 (D. D.C. 1972).

National Institute of Child Health & Human Development Early Child Care Research Network. (2001). Nonmaternal care and family factors in early development. *Journal of Applied Developmental Psychology, 22,* 457–492.

National Scientific Council on the Developing Child. (2007). *A science-based framework for early childhood policy: Using evidence to improve outcomes in learning, behavior, and health for vulnerable children*. Cambridge, MA: Harvard University Press.

Novick, R. (1993). Activity-based intervention and developmentally appropriate practice: Points of convergence. *Topics in Early Childhood Special Education, 13*(4), 403–417.

Odom, S. (1988). Research in early childhood special education: Methodologies and paradigms. In S. Odom & M. Karnes (Eds.), *Early intervention for infants and children with handicaps: An empirical base*. Baltimore, MD: Paul H. Brookes Publishing Co.

Orsmond, G. (2005). Assessing interpersonal and family distress and threats to confident parenting in the context of early intervention. In M. Guralnick (Ed.), *The developmental systems approach to early intervention*. Baltimore, MD: Paul H. Brookes Publishing Co.

Pennsylvania Association for Retarded Children (PARC) v. Pennsylvania, 334 F. Supp. 1247 (E.D. PA 1971).

Peters, D., & Deiner, P. (1987). The reality of early childhood: Head Start and the child development associate. *Topics in Early Childhood Special Education, 7*(3), 48–58.

Reynolds, A.J., & Ou, S. (2011). Paths of effects from preschool to adult well-being: A confirmatory analysis of the Child-Parent Center Program. *Child Development, 82*(2), 555–582.

Reynolds, A., Temple, J., Robertson, D., & Mann, E. (2002). Age 26 cost-benefit analysis of the Child-Parent Center early education program. *Child Development, 82*(1), 379–404.

Reynolds, A.J. Temple, J.A., White, B., Ou, S., & Robertson, D.L. (2011). Age-26 cost-benefit analysis of the Child-Parent Center early education program. *Child Development, 82*(1), 379–404.

Risley, T., & Wolf, M. (1967). Establishing functional speech in echolalic children. *Behavior Research and Therapy, 5,* 73–88.

Sameroff, A. (1994). Ecological perspectives on longitudinal follow-up studies. In S. Friedman & H. Haywood (Eds.), *Concepts, domains and method* (pp. 45–64). New York, NY: Academic Press.

Sameroff, A., & Chandler, M. (1975). Reproductive risk and continuum of caretaking causality. In F. Horowitz, M. Hetherington, S. Scarr-Salapatek, & G. Siegel (Eds.), *Review of child development research* (vol.4). Chicago, IL: University of Chicago Press.

Sameroff , A.J., Seifer, R., Baldwin, A., & Baldwin, C. (1993). Stability of intelligence from preschool to adolescence: The influence of social and family risk factors. *Child Development, 64,* 80–97.

Sawyer, B., & Campbell, P. (2012). Early interventionists' perspectives on teaching caregivers. *Journal of Early Intervention, 34*(2), 104–124.

Schaffer, H. (1977). *Studies in mother-infant interaction.* New York, NY: Academic Press.

Spiker, D., Hebbler, K., & Mallik, S. (2005). Developing and implementing early intervention programs for children with established disabilities. In M.J. Guralnick (Ed.), *The developmental systems approach to early intervention* (pp. 271–306). Baltimore, MD: Paul H. Brookes Publishing Co.

Spitz, R. (1946). Hospitalism: A follow up report. *Psychoanalytical Study of the Child, 2,* 313–332.

Staats, A. (1964). *Human learning.* New York, NY: Holt, Rinehart & Winston.

Swan, W. (1980). The handicapped children's early education program. *Exceptional Children, 47,* 12–16.

Temple, J., & Reynolds, A. (2007). Benefits and costs of investment in preschool education: Evidence from the child-parent centers and related programs. *Economics of Education Review, 26*(1), 126–144.

Thompson, R. (2001). Sensitive periods in attachment? In D.B. Bailey, J.T. Bruer, F.J. Symons, & J.W. Litchtman (Eds.), *Critical thinking about critical periods.* Baltimore, MD: Paul H. Brookes Publishing Co.

Tjossem, T. (1976). (Ed.). *Intervention strategies for high risk infants and young children.* Baltimore, MD: University Park Press.

Trehub, S., Bull, D., & Schneider, B. (1981). Infant speech and nonspeech perception. In R. Schielfelbusch & D. Bricker (Eds.), *Early language acquisition and intervention.* Baltimore, MD: University Park Press.

Turnbull, A., & Turnbull, H. (1990). *Families, professionals, and exceptionality: A special partnership.* Upper Saddle River, NJ: Merrill Publishing.

U.S. Department of Education. (2013). *Digest of Education Statistics 2012* (NCES 2014-015). Retrieved from http://nces.ed.gov/pubs2014/2014015.pdf

U.S. Department of Education. (2014). *Thirty-third annual report to Congress on the implementation of the Individuals with Disabilities Education Act, Parts B and C.* U.S. Department of Education, 2013. National Center for Education Statistics.

Warren, S., & Kaiser, A. (1988). Research in early language intervention. In S. Odom & M. Karnes (Eds.), *Early intervention for infants and children with handicaps: An empirical base* (pp. 89–108). Baltimore, MD: Paul H. Brookes Publishing Co.

Washington, V., & Bailey, U.J. (1995). *Project Head Start: Models and strategies for the twenty-first century.* New York, NY: Garland Publishing.

Weikart, D.P. (1989). *Quality preschool programs: A long-term social investment.* New York, NY: Ford Foundation.

Zigler, E., & Cascione, R. (1977). Head Start has little to do with mental retardation: A reply to Clarke and Clarke. *American Journal of Mental Deficiency, 82,* 246–249.

Zigler, E., & Styfco, S.J. (2000). Pioneering steps (and fumbles) in developing a federal preschool intervention. *Topics in Early Childhood Special Education, 20*(2), 67–70.

3

Comprehensive Linked System Framework for Service Delivery with Young Children

As noted in Chapter 1, ABI is a comprehensive approach to intervention that focuses on what young children do throughout their day. The approach is largely child-directed and embeds teaching/training into daily or routine activities, play, and child initiations. For example, for a child with a gross motor delay who frequently chooses to play with blocks, the child care worker can consistently move the blocks beyond the child's reach so he must move to obtain them.

Recognizing and using each child's interests serves as the basic platform from which intervention efforts are orchestrated. An intervention strategy that uses children's motivation produces significant progress in critical areas of development; however, neither ABI nor any other intervention approach can operate effectively in isolation. The effectiveness and impact of any intervention approach is enhanced by its placement in a more comprehensive framework that takes into account other factors or variables that produce systematic change in children. A review of many service delivery programs that operate in the United States provides strong evidence that many intervention efforts are not situated within a comprehensive framework. Rather, as the example that follows demonstrates, services and activities are often disconnected, producing inefficiency and oversight resulting in compromised outcomes for children and families.

The Oakdale Early Intervention Program provides services to 25 children with disabilities and their families. The children range in age from 12 to 48 months and have identified developmental delays (e.g., Down syndrome, autism, sensory impairments). The stated overall goals of the program are to 1) enhance parent–child interactions, 2) build peer interaction skills, and 3) assist children in gaining preacademic skills.

To be eligible for participation in the Oakdale Program, children must have a significant developmental delay (at least two standard deviations below mean age performance in two or more developmental areas), and therefore before entering the program, children must be assessed and their disability or delay documented. The local community does not have a screening program. Children in the community with suspected or known problems are referred to an evaluation agency for a multidisciplinary assessment. Because a community screening program does not exist, timely referral of children often does not occur.

When children are referred to the evaluation agency—usually after their development or behavior is noted to be significantly atypical—they are seen by an interdisciplinary team, including a pediatrician, psychologist, physical therapist, and speech-language pathologist, and are given at least one individualized standardized test (e.g., Bayley Scales of Infant Development; Bayley, 2005). Based on the child's performance, the team writes intervention goals and plans for those children who meet eligibility requirements.

The goals and intervention suggestions are then forwarded to the staff of community-based services such as the Oakdale Program. However, because the members of the interdisciplinary team are not familiar with the goals or operation of the Oakdale Program, the staff usually finds the children's goals to be inconsistent with their overall program goals and curriculum. This inconsistency requires that the Oakdale Program staff develop additional goals for each child. The development of more appropriate goals requires that staff conduct systematic observations and/or administer additional measures, both of which require time and effort as well as delay the initiation of intervention efforts.

Once children's goals are developed, intervention efforts focus on providing events and activities that address the children's individual goals, as well as those goals targeted by the program's general curriculum. At the end of the school year, each child's progress is evaluated by the re-administration of the standardized measure that was used to determine eligibility. Unfortunately there is little relationship between the goals the staff targets for intervention efforts and the content of the standardized measure. Consequently, caregivers and program staff have no objective way to determine the effectiveness of their intervention efforts.

The practices outlined in this example highlight a model of service delivery that is fragmented and disconnected. A screening program does not exist, and the assessment component is not connected to the service program. The initial assessment does not provide adequate information to develop sound intervention goals, and the goals that come from the initial assessment do not reflect the overall goals of the Oakdale Program. Relevant intervention content has to be derived from other sources that are not linked to the initial assessment conducted by the interdisciplinary team. Subsequent follow-up progress monitoring is not related to the children's goals, intervention efforts, or the program's overall goals. Such models of service delivery do not have a coordinated system and consequently often waste resources and compromise quality.

Alternatives to service delivery programs that do not attempt to create systems are those that focus on building coordination and linkages with and between all of the necessary activities to ensure the delivery of quality services to young children and their families. The purposes of this chapter are to

1. Describe one such comprehensive system

2. Discuss how this comprehensive framework can be used with ABI

3. Present an example that demonstrates the application of a linked system framework

THE LINKED SYSTEM FRAMEWORK

We believe that the application of ABI is most successful when conceptualized and implemented within a linked system framework. That is, intervention activities cannot stand alone; rather, to be maximally effective they need to be supported by and linked to other critical components of service delivery. The linked system framework that we are proposing is composed of five interrelated components: screening, assessment, goal development, intervention, and monitoring progress (Bagnato, Neisworth, & Pretti-Frontczak, 2010; Bricker, 1989, 1996a, 1996b, 2002).

These five components address all critical service delivery activities from the first step of screening for potential developmental–behavioral problems to the final activity of monitoring progress toward targeted goals. As shown in Figure 3.1, each component is directly linked to the next component, or in the case of monitoring progress, linked back to assessment, goal development, and intervention efforts.

To reiterate, it is important to recognize that although ABI focuses directly on the intervention component of a linked system, the approach cannot be fully implemented without attention to all of the components necessary for quality service delivery. The following sections explain the linked system by describing each of its components. Each component then includes the following sections: Definition, Goal, Application, and Outcomes.

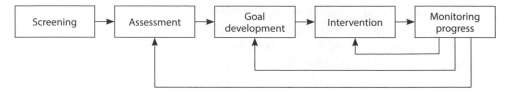

Figure 3.1. Five components of the linked system approach.

Screening

As indicated in Figure 3.1, we advocate for screening as the first component of the linked system framework. Communitywide screening programs are essential if children with potential developmental or behavior problems are to be detected in a timely manner. Early detection is fundamental to ensuring the best outcomes for children and their families (Bricker, Macy, Squires, & Marks, 2013).

Definition Screening is a quick, simple, and economical procedure to determine if more comprehensive assessment is in order (Bricker et al., 2013). Screening is often conceptualized as the administration of a brief test (e.g., Ages & Stages Questionnaires® [ASQ; Squires & Bricker, 2009]; Denver Developmental Screening Test II [Frankenburg et al., 1992]) or brief procedure (e.g., newborn hearing screening); however, effective screening needs to be communitywide and connected to a referral system, the administrative/operational context for conducting the actual screening, and strategies for providing feedback and taking subsequent appropriate action. Efficient and effective screening programs can be thought of as a subsystem embedded in the more comprehensive linked system framework.

Goal In the linked system framework, the primary goal for the screening component is the early detection of children with potential problems. More specifically, screening determines if children require a more thorough, detailed assessment of their developmental–behavioral repertoire. That is, does the child's performance on the screening measure or procedure fall significantly below established age expectations? If so, the family should be provided feedback and referred for follow-up assessment: the next component in the linked system framework.

Application A variety of relatively new measures exist for conducting developmental screening of large groups of children (Squires & Bricker, 2007; Macy, 2012). These measures can be sorted into two groups: measures administered by professionals, and those administered by parents or other caregivers. For the linked system framework we recommend the use of parent-completed measures even for comprehensive screening programs for several important reasons. First, in most cases, primary caregivers have the most detailed information about their children's development. When provided with an easy-to-complete, straightforward measure focused on observable behavior, caregivers can reliably assess their child's developmental repertoire (Squires, 1996). Second, having parents complete simple screening measures such as the ASQ (Squires & Bricker, 2009) is far more economical than using professional or paraprofessional staff. Third, the inclusion of parents or other primary caregivers in the child's assessment from the beginning sends an important message—that parental input and involvement is fundamentally important.

Outcomes   For children who are screened (i.e., children who have been identified as needing more comprehensive developmental assessment), this component yields three important outcomes that are directly relevant to the subsequent component of assessment. The first and perhaps most important piece of information to be passed on is that the child's performance on the screening measure was below established cutoffs for developmental age expectations. That is, the child's performance on the screening measure was well below the expected performance for his or her chronological age. Second, an analysis of the child's performance on a particular measure can offer hints about the nature of the delay or problem. That is, the child's performance in the critical areas of gross motor, fine motor, social-communication, adaptive, social, and cognitive can be examined. Finally, the initial information provided by the caregiver (e.g., address, date of birth) can be passed on to personnel in the assessment team.

Passing on family demographics and specific information about the child's performance on the screening measure is important because it will assist the personnel operating the assessment component to decide what type of follow-up eligibility assessment should be used. Further, passing on family information should increase efficiency for the assessment personnel as well as the family by not having to ask the same questions and collect the same information again. Passing on child data and family information requires a connected or linked system and trust in screening data (i.e., accuracy and reliability).

Assessment

The second component of the linked system is assessment. Assessment refers to "an ongoing collaborative process of systematic observations and analysis" (Greenspan & Meisels, 1996 p. 23). In our framework, assessment can be conceived as two parts or two steps. First, the child's eligibility for services must be established. Second, the content for developing relevant and essential intervention goals and objectives must be delineated. Many programs are developing strategies to combine these two steps into a more efficient procedure that simultaneously permits establishing eligibility and also generating appropriate intervention content.

Definition   For children who have been screened, the next step is to determine if they meet the stipulated criteria for receiving services and, if so, to determine appropriate goals and intervention content for eligible children. Most government-sponsored programs require that children meet established eligibility guidelines in order to receive services. In the United States, most jurisdictions require that children demonstrate significant developmental problems (e.g., Down syndrome) or developmental delays (e.g., a performance at least two standard deviations below their age norm in two or more developmental areas). Therefore assessment can be defined as collecting information to determine a child's eligibility for services and for development of appropriate goals and intervention content.

Goal   As noted, the assessment component has two important goals. The first is to reliably determine those children who meet stipulated state and federal criteria for eligibility to receive services. The second goal is to collect a range of developmental information that will permit the intervention team to develop appropriate, functional, and individualized developmental goals.

Application   Until the late 1990s–2000s, it was necessary to administer two different types of measures to obtain the necessary information to determine eligibility and to develop high-quality individual intervention goals. Standardized, norm-referenced tests such as the Battell Developmental Inventory (Newborg, 2004) yield information that is appropriate for determining if children meet established eligibility guidelines; however, information provided by these tests is not particularly useful for the development of intervention goals and content. Rarely can information generated by standardized, norm-referenced tests be used directly to formulate functional, high-quality goals for young children.

Curriculum-based measures (CBMs) such as the AEPS (Bricker, 2002) have, since their inception, been the choice to develop goals and intervention content because these measures have been created precisely for these purposes. CBMs have been defined as "a form of criterion-referenced measurement wherein curricular objectives act as the criteria for the identification of instructional targets and for the assessment of status and progress" (Bagnato & Neisworth, 1991, p. 87). CBMs have advantages over standardized norm-referenced assessments when linking assessment outcomes to goal development and intervention. CBMs such as the AEPS are composed of items directly relevant to the development of high-quality and individually appropriate goals. CBMs are comprehensive in that their content addresses all major developmental domains. In addition, items from curriculum-based assessments can be modified to meet children's individual needs and can be observed across settings, time, materials, and people to ensure generalizability.

As noted, developmental information generated by a CBM permits the development of appropriate goals. In addition, research suggests that CBMs such as the AEPS can also be reliably used to determine children's eligibility for services. Children's performance outcomes on the AEPS can be compared with empirically derived cutoffs (Bricker, Yovanoff, Capt, & Allen, 2003). If children's scores fall below the established cutoffs, they are eligible for services. Therefore, the linked system framework can use curriculum-based assessment outcomes for dual purposes: to establish eligibility for services and to generate information directly relevant to goal development.

Besides gathering developmental information on children, it is usually equally important to assess or gather information about the family's strengths and challenges. As noted in Chapter 2, the AEPS has an associated tool called the AEPS Family Report. This family friendly measure is designed to assist family members in describing their living context and identifying areas in need of attention.

Outcomes   In the linked system framework, the assessment component produces two important outcomes. First, it determines if a child is eligible for services. Second, it produces information that can be used to develop individualized intervention goals and objectives. CBMs are composed of items directly relevant to the development of high-quality and individually appropriate goals; therefore, the assessment outcomes are directly relevant to the creation of appropriate, functional, and measurable goals. In addition, most curriculum-based assessments address all major areas of development and offer concrete guidelines for developing individualized goals. Thus, in the linked system framework, the information produced by the assessment component is directly relevant to the next component of goal development.

Goal Development

The third component of the linked system is goal development. The purpose of goal development is to individualize and prioritize a set of goals and objectives that are developmentally appropriate, functional, and important behaviors that will advance children's behavioral repertoires. The development of high-quality, developmentally appropriate, and functional goals is dependent on comprehensive information gathering during the assessment process.

Definition   Goals (or objectives) are written statements that serve to describe an end point or developmental target for a child. Goals can be formulated as general statements (e.g., the child will learn to walk), or they can be formulated as precise and specific statements (e.g., the child will take at least six steps consecutively by alternately lifting feet off the ground and propelling the entire body forward while remaining in an upright position). The linked system framework requires that goals meet five important criteria to ensure quality. Goals should be 1) functional, 2) teachable, 3) generative, 4) measurable, and 5) able to be addressed within daily activities.

To develop goals to meet these quality criteria, it is essential that assessment outcomes provide the necessary developmental information. Assessment outcomes that are vague, irrelevant, or nonfunctional do not provide sufficient information to formulate quality goals.

Goal   The goal of this component is to develop written statements for individual children that meet the five criteria for quality noted previously. In addition, assessment information generated by the AEPS Family Report or similar assessments may suggest family outcomes. As noted, the quality of these goals is highly dependent on the type and quality of assessment information gathered during the assessment component. The development of quality goals is essential because it is these goals that drive and guide intervention efforts.

Application   CBMs such as the AEPS offer the user a range of developmental items that address essential behaviors. Frequently items have associated examples of a high-quality goal, as shown in Table 3.1. The first item and associated goal is from the Social Area, and the second goal is from the Gross Motor Area of the AEPS.

The associated goal examples are offered only as guidelines, and most will require some modification and adjustment in order to meet the needs of individual children.

Outcomes   The outcome from the goal development component for each child is the development of two to four individualized goals, such as those shown in Table 3.1. High-quality goals (i.e., those that meet the criteria of being functional, measurable, and addressable across the day) will ensure that important, functional behaviors have been targeted and that these behaviors can be integrated into a broad range of intervention activities.

The selected goals are of critical importance in the linked system framework because it is these goals that direct subsequent intervention efforts. Children's individual goals dictate the curricular content and how to plan opportunities for practice throughout the day. Rather than offering random activities, training efforts are carefully orchestrated to address children's goals.

Intervention

The fourth component of the linked system framework is intervention. The purpose of intervention is to assist children in acquiring and using prioritized individualized goals and objectives. Specifically, ABI is designed to assist caregivers and interventionists in using daily activities as the context for delivering specially designed instruction that will produce desired change in children.

Definition   Intervention refers to the planning and executing of actions and events by caregivers and teachers/interventionists/therapists that are designed to assist children in the acquisition of their individual

Table 3.1. Sample items from the *Assessment, Evaluation, and Programming System* (AEPS®) with their associated goals

AEPS test item	Associated goal
Initiates cooperative activity	The child will use verbal or nonverbal strategies to initiate cooperative activities and encourage peer(s) to participate (e.g., the child says, "Come on, let's build a house," to a group of peers).
Rides and steers two-wheel bicycle	While sitting on a two-wheel bicycle, the child will pedal forward and steer the bicycle at least 20 feet.

AEPS items adapted by permission from Bricker, D. (2002). *Assessment, evaluation, and programming system for infants and children* (2nd ed., Vols. 1–4). Baltimore, MD: Paul H. Brookes Publishing Co.

developmental goals and the program's general curriculum goals. Intervention is composed of planned and incidental actions and responses by adults and peers, as well as the arrangement of the physical environment, which provides guidance and practice opportunities for children to address their individual goals.

Intervention content can be conceptualized as two parts: 1) children's individual developmental goals and 2) general curriculum goals. Individual child goals are those that were specifically derived from the child's performance on a CBM and address the child's specific impairments identified during the assessment component. The general curriculum goals refer to the universal content and behavior that most children must acquire to be successful in home and school environments. An example of a universal goal for children is that they should be able to focus their attention and follow directions. Such important general curriculum goals should be addressed throughout the day. Effective intervention requires that children be given multiple opportunities to address their individual goals as well as general curriculum goals.

Goal   The goal of the intervention component is to develop and execute an intervention plan that will assist children in meeting their individualized goals as well as the general curriculum goals. Reaching this outcome requires that intervention staff in conjunction with caregivers undertake two actions. First, they need to develop an individualized intervention plan for each child (an example plan is contained in Chapter 6). This plan should be designed to address the child's individualized goals. Second, a strategy to address the targeted general curriculum goals should be created in order to ensure that children are presented with numerous opportunities to acquire these important goals.

Application   It is important that intervention plans—both the individualized plans and the general curriculum activities—focus on authentic activities and events that can be used to embed training on targeted goals. Authentic refers to events and activities that have meaning and relevance for children. For example, learning to use the pincer grasp by picking up bits of food when you are hungry is likely a meaningful activity for most children, whereas picking up pegs to insert in a board may be of questionable relevance or importance for many young children. Learning to use a word to obtain a desired object will likely be more meaningful (i.e., authentic) than naming picture cards.

Outcomes   There are two major outcomes for the intervention component. First, each child should have an individualized intervention plan that specifies his or her goals, intervention strategies for reaching the goals, and methods for collecting data to ensure adequate progress is being made toward goals. The second outcome should be the systematic and coordinated presentation of events and activities that target children's individual goals as well as those goals deemed essential by the general curriculum used by a program.

Monitoring Progress Monitoring progress is the final component of the linked system framework and refers to documenting key behaviors in which children's previous performance in an area is compared with later performances. That is, this component is designed to permit comparisons of children's behavior over time to determine whether or not the offered intervention is being effective.

Definition   Monitoring progress in the linked system framework refers to monitoring the child's progress toward targeted goals and objectives. Monitoring progress can be defined as a cyclical process that involves the systematic comparison of the child's current behavior (i.e., performance) with previous performance(s). Useful progress monitoring requires the collection of objective information or data that accurately and reliably describes the child's performance of target goals and objectives so that these performances can be compared with subsequent performances. It is only through appropriate comparisons that the effectiveness of intervention can be assessed.

Goal   The goal of the monitoring progress component is the systematic collection of objective data to document and compare children's performances of targeted goals and objectives over time. Systematic refers to the collection of data on a preset schedule, such as once per week following an intervention activity. Objective data refers to targeting behaviors or responses that are observable and measurable. For example, an observable and measurable response would be "the child uses descriptor words such as color and size," in contrast to a vague response such as, "the child's language improves."

Application   In most cases, weekly collection of data is necessary to ensure that children are making adequate progress toward targeted goals. If goals are of high quality (i.e., meet the quality criteria), it should be possible to collect systematic information on children's progress. The collection of weekly data is generally necessary to make timely and informed decisions about the effectiveness of intervention for individual children. If a child's goal is to "initiate peer interactions at least three or more times during an activity," staff should keep track of the number of initiations that occur at least once a week during, for example, free play, to measure whether the frequency of child initiations is growing over time.

Weekly data collection should focus on the acquisition and use of targeted goals. Often these data may not address child progress on general curriculum goals and, therefore, it is also necessary to collect more global data three to four times per year by re-administering a CBM such as the AEPS.

Outcomes Including the monitoring progress component in a linked system framework is essential. There are two outcomes from this component that inform staff about the success of the assessment, goal development, and intervention components. First, as noted earlier, a child's progress can only be determined through the adequate collection of objective information that allows staff and caregivers to determine whether or not children are acquiring targeted goals in a timely manner.

Although the collection of objective data is necessary, it is not sufficient. To be useful (i.e., assist in making sound decisions) data must be translated into visual (e.g., graphs) or written descriptions that permit an examination of children's progress. Generally this requires graphing or plotting findings so that legitimate comparisons can be made. Such comparisons need to be made for weekly as well as quarterly and annual data. Thus, a graph or written presentation of comparative data is the second outcome of the progress monitoring component. These comparative data provide the mechanism to determine if children are making acceptable progress toward individual as well as general curriculum goals.

ABI AND THE LINKED SYSTEM FRAMEWORK

Employing a linked system framework permits 1) efficient use of personnel and other resources, 2) accountability in terms of documenting intervention program impact over time, and 3) individualization through the design of intervention content specific to the needs of children and their families. A comprehensive system provides the necessary context for the implementation of ABI. The successful application of ABI is dependent on the use of an assessment measure (i.e., CBM) that yields information that can be translated into appropriate goals and objectives for children. The ABI approach is also dependent on targeting goals and objectives that are functional and developmentally appropriate and that can be addressed within daily activities, play, and child initiations. Finally, the approach requires careful and continuous progress monitoring and that information be transmitted or passed on (linked) to each subsequent component of the system. That is, as the system accumulates data, it passes this information forward, and this information is, in turn, used as the basis for the next component.

Figure 3.2 illustrates how data and information collected over time are transmitted across components. That is, screening findings offer information

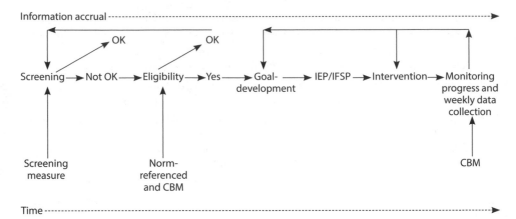

Figure 3.2. Schematic of recommended sequence of child data and information moving forward to subsequent components to create quality individualized education program/individualized family service plan goals and subsequent intervention content. (*Key:* IEP/IFSP, individualized education program/individualized family service plan; CBM, curriculum-based measure.)

that permits targeting the approximate developmental level of children when determining eligibility and developing IEP/IFSP goals and objectives. In turn, these goals and objectives guide the development of intervention content and finally, as shown in Figure 3.2, monitoring progress links directly to the assessment, goal development, and intervention components of the system. This cyclical feedback assists in evaluating the effectiveness of intervention efforts and when and if modification is in order.

ABI and Screening

Screening measures are designed to sort children into one of two categories: those whose development appears okay, and those whose development is suspect. Screening measures, in most cases, are used with large groups of children, thus requiring the measures be administered quickly and economically. Given these conditions, screening measures make relatively gross discriminations about children (i.e., further testing is or is not needed).

Although the screening component is part of the linked system framework, screening activities should occur as the first step in service delivery and prior to conducting intervention activities. Communities that have widespread screening efforts are able to identify children with potential problems in a timely manner. Timely identification of problems increases the likelihood that appropriate services will be offered to young children and their families, which, in turn, generally results in better outcomes (Bricker et al., 2013).

ABI and Assessment

When using an ABI approach, it is critical to obtain information regarding children's strengths, interests, and emerging skills. Meaningful intervention efforts can be designed and monitored only through ongoing observations and conversations with people who interact frequently with the child. It is therefore essential that assessment information provide a continuous, accurate, and comprehensive profile of children's behavioral repertoires in order to accurately determine eligibility and to identify appropriate goals and intervention content.

Many formal and informal procedures have been developed to guide teams in observing and documenting children's behaviors across a wide variety of settings. Formal procedures may include completing norm-referenced and/or standardized tests (e.g., Bayley Scales of Infant Development [Bayley, 2005], Battelle Developmental Inventory [Newborg, 2004]), criterion-referenced or CBMs (e.g., AEPS [Bricker, 2002], Hawaii Early Learning Profile [HELP; VORT Corporation, 1995]), or structured interviews with caregivers (e.g., Vineland Adaptive Behavior Scales [Sparrow, Cicchetti, & Balla, 2005]). Informal procedures may include observations of young children during daily activities, completion of program-created checklists, the collection of anecdotal notes, or conversations with caregivers and other team members.

Traditionally eligibility measures are standardized and norm-referenced and are used by teams to determine a child's performance in relation to a normative sample. These measures are typically administered by trained professionals (e.g., psychologists, speech-language pathologists) under controlled conditions using standardized materials and procedures. Results from such measures often provide a summary of children's development in one or more areas, and document the child's level of delay and areas of need; however, most of these measures do not yield outcomes that are directly relevant to the development of quality goals and objectives needed by the child.

Fortunately, state agencies are increasingly permitting the use of CBMs to establish eligibility for services. The ABI approach is predicated on the use of a CBM to establish eligibility and to generate content for goal development. CBMs are criterion-referenced measures in which curricular objectives act as the criteria for the identification of goals and objectives. CBMs have several advantages in comparison with standardized norm-referenced assessments when linking assessment and goal development to intervention. In general, CBMs are composed of items directly relevant to the development of high-quality and individually appropriate goals. Some CBMs are also comprehensive in that their content addresses all major developmental domains (e.g., motor, communication, social development). In addition, CBM items can be modified to meet children's individual needs and can be observed across settings, time, materials, and people.

As noted, CBMs can be used to determine eligibility and also to generate the necessary content for the development of quality goals. These measures often encourage family involvement and are specifically designed to assist teams in describing a child's level of functioning; selecting, prioritizing, and writing appropriate goals; designing appropriate intervention content; and monitoring child progress.

ABI and Goal Development

ABI addresses children's individual needs by embedding multiple and varied learning opportunities into their daily activities and by providing timely feedback/consequences designed to promote children's acquisition and use of functional and generative skills. Fundamental to the successful application of this approach is the development of children's goals that provide direction and guidance for the design and implementation of intervention.

When developing IFSPs/IEPs, teams should follow federal and state mandates. For example, the Individuals with Disabilities Education Act (IDEA) of 1990 (PL 101-476) and the Individuals with Disabilities Education Act Amendments (IDEA) of 1997 (PL 105-17) specify that teams develop IEP intervention targets as measurable annual goals and short-term objectives or benchmarks and develop IFSP intervention targets as outcomes. How the terms *goals, objectives,* and *benchmarks* are used across states and written sources varies. Throughout this book, *goals* are defined as measurable skills targeted for a child to acquire or master within approximately 6 months to 1 year. Goals often address general or broad classes of behaviors, are needed by children across settings, and are written to reflect their independence in performing the target skill(s). Goals are composed of a set of more specific skills often referred to as objectives or benchmarks.

Objectives or *benchmarks,* as defined in this book, represent intermediate or measurable steps toward the goal, as well as earlier milestones or building blocks of a goal. Target objectives or benchmarks should be related to the annual goal and serve as an indicator of a child's progress toward attaining the annual goal (e.g., Michnowicz, McConnell, Peterson, & Odom, 1995; Notari & Bricker, 1990; Notari & Drinkwater, 1991; Tymitz, 1980). For some children objectives or benchmarks may need to be further delineated into simpler or smaller components referred to as *program steps.* Last, throughout this book, the term *target skill* is used generically to refer to behaviors (i.e., goals, objectives/benchmarks, or program steps) selected for children to learn, strengthen, and/or use as part of their functional behavioral repertoire.

The primary method of ensuring a wise choice of specific intervention activities is through the development of high-quality individual goals for children. If skills targeted for intervention are well chosen and operationally defined, intervention efforts become clear, and the selection of teaching strategies or capitalization on learning opportunities, as well as the reinforcement of child-directed and child-initiated activities, becomes straightforward. Developmentally appropriate and functional goals help ensure that interventionists and caregivers can select with confidence intervention activities that ensure the learning of target skills.

ABI and Intervention

As noted previously, intervention refers to the planning and executing of actions by caregivers and professionals designed to assist children in the acquisition and use of target skills. In ABI, intervention is conceptualized as the intentional and incidental actions and responses by adults and peers as well as the arrangement of the physical environment that provides guidance and practice opportunities for children to learn target skills.

Intervention efforts during the early childhood years are intended to occur during daily activities, routines, and play. Selection of daily activities and events should be guided by children's individual interests and needs and should ensure that all children 1) have access to the general curriculum, 2) make progress within the general curriculum, and 3) accomplish or achieve their individualized skills.

To ensure appropriate intervention efforts within routines, play, and daily activities or events, teams employing ABI should 1) derive content for intervention from children's performance on CBMs, 2) target functional and generative skills, 3) incorporate a variety of evidence-based instructional procedures designed to meet children's individual needs, and 4) systematically monitor children's progress to ensure that effective intervention is consistently provided (i.e., employ components of the linked system framework). Furthermore, to ensure that children make desired progress toward target skills, an organizational structure should be present that directs teams to develop activities that provide frequent opportunities for practicing and learning target skills. Creating and maintaining such a structure requires ongoing, consistent, and thoughtful planning among team members. The literature on quality practices cites the importance of planning to ensure successful intervention and, in particular, individualized instruction for young children with disabilities (e.g., Bennett, DeLuca, & Bruns, 1997; Hoyson, Jamieson, Strain, & Smith, 1998; McDonnell, Brownell, & Wolery, 2001; Salisbury et al., 1994). Adequate planning time is necessary for teams to successfully use ABI (e.g., Grisham-Brown & Pretti-Frontczak, 2003).

ABI and Monitoring Progress

Monitoring progress is a cyclical process that involves making decisions regarding what to observe, when to observe, who to observe, where to observe, and how to document observations. When considering the type of evaluative data desired, it is important to determine how the data will be used (e.g., as a description of the child's performance or an evaluation of their progress over time). Evaluation data are comparative in that children's individual or group performances are compared with either their previous performance or to some other criterion such as norms for a specific chronological age. Typically, teams document a child's progress on targeted IFSP/IEP skills, monitor a child's progress in the general curriculum, and determine whether broad program goals are being met.

To successfully use ABI, teams will need to collect weekly, quarterly, and annual progress monitoring data to ensure effective intervention over time. Weekly data collection permits monitoring children's performance during play, daily activities, and routine events. Data should be collected weekly regarding children's progress toward target skills (i.e., typically those targeted on the IFSP/IEP for individualized intervention). The weekly data that are collected regarding both a child's performance and progress should be systematically summarized and reviewed by team members to make sound decisions regarding intervention efforts.

Weekly data collection should focus on the acquisition and use of target skills that are designed to move children toward individual target goals; therefore, these data often do not address children's progress on more global outcomes or their progress toward skills associated with the general curriculum. In addition, weekly data are often difficult to combine across children, making them inappropriate for examining group effects or program efficacy. The collection of more global evaluation data three to four times per year can provide useful feedback on children's progress toward goals selected from a programmatic measure (e.g., AEPS [Bricker, 2002]) and/or from the program's general curriculum. In addition, quarterly data may permit examining group effects and/or program outcomes. Finally, web-based programs now exist such as AEPSi that permit daily or weekly data entry to track children's progress.

Teams should also be prepared to collect annual data regarding children's progress and program outcomes. The collection of annual data can be an extension of the quarterly data collection procedures if teams decide to use the same measure. For example, if a programmatic measure is administered to children quarterly, these data can also be used for annual evaluations. Teams should develop strategies to keep their data collection activities focused and efficient.

USING THE LINKED SYSTEM FRAMEWORK: AN EXAMPLE

The purpose of this example is to illustrate how teams can use and pass on information gathered within each component of the linked system. The example begins with the first component, screening, in which a potential problem with the child's development is identified and the family is referred for more comprehensive assessment. The assessment process includes administration of a CBM and assessing family resources, priorities, and concerns. Assessment information is summarized to determine the child's eligibility for services as well as her strengths and emerging skills. Priority needs serve as the basis for developing individualized goals that then become the focus of intentional intervention efforts and require systematic progress monitoring.

In this example, the team chooses to use the AEPS to meet the goals for the assessment component of establishing eligibility and developing IEP/ IFSP goals. In terms of eligibility, the AEPS has objectively derived cutoff points that can be used to determine eligibility for services. For goal development, the AEPS offers several important features. First, most items are written to reflect conceptual or generative response classes rather than specific responses (e.g., target stacking a variety of objects such as books, clothes, carpet squares, and cups vs. stacking three 1-inch cubes). Second, many items are composed of skills essential for young children to function independently and to cope with environmental demands (e.g., moving around their environment, expressing their wants and needs). Third, the AEPS contains prototype goals that can serve as guides or models for writing children's individualized goals and objectives.

Screening

Katie is 3 years old and has been slow to acquire typical developmental milestones. Both parents work, so Katie attends an all-day child care program. Before her last well child visit, Dr. Andrews, Katie's pediatrician, asked her parents to complete the 36-month interval of the ASQ online. During Katie's appointment, Dr. Andrews informed her mother that Katie's performance on the screening measure was below expectations for her age. Given this finding, Dr. Andrews referred Katie to the EI/ECSE community-based team to gather more in-depth information. Accompanying the referral was a copy of the completed ASQ, a medical summary, and demographic information on the family.

Prior to Katie's eligibility determination assessment, the team reviewed the information forwarded from the physician's office. In particular they examined her performance on the ASQ. They noted that Katie's performance in fine motor and social-communication areas were of particular concern, and this provided them with useful information for beginning the more comprehensive assessment necessary to establish eligibility for EI/ECSE services.

Gathering Assessment Information

Katie's team was composed of her parents, the ECSE teacher, and therapists. The professionals completed the AEPS by observing Katie at her child care program as well as talking to others familiar with Katie's behavior (e.g., grandparents). Her parents completed the AEPS Family Report, which provides information about the family's daily routines. The Family Report allows caregivers the opportunity to record a child's strengths, interests, and emerging skills across areas of development. This comprehensive approach to gathering assessment information was designed to meet two purposes: 1) to determine if Katie was eligible for services and, if so, 2) to assist the team in developing meaningful goals that, in turn, would guide intervention efforts.

Summarizing Findings

Following administration of the AEPS, completion of the AEPS Family Report, and review of existing and relevant documents, the team summarized the assessment information. In general, teams are encouraged to summarize assessment results in several ways (e.g., numerically, visually, anecdotal). When summarizing assessment information, teams are encouraged to focus on a child's strengths, interests, and emerging skills. Teams should identify patterns in the demonstration of skills (e.g., with or without assistance, consistently or inconsistently, in certain locations) and identify the relationship between the child's performances across areas of development (e.g., teams may look for a common feature that impedes the child from performing related tasks).

Katie's team reviewed the information they gathered and summarized their findings in three ways. First, they calculated an area percent score for each of the six developmental areas of the AEPS. Area percent scores represent the percentage of items the child can perform independently/consistently and those items they are beginning to demonstrate or can demonstrate with assistance across the six areas assessed (e.g., gross motor, adaptive, social). Second, they summarized the information visually by completing the AEPS Child Progress Record. The Child Progress Record was developed to monitor individual children's progress over time and provides teams with a visual record of the child's accomplishments, current targets, and future targets (Bricker, 2002). Third, the team summarized information anecdotally by noting Katie's strengths, interests, and needs.

Goals Development

Skills (i.e., goals) selected for intervention should meet at least five quality criteria. They should be 1) functional, 2) teachable, 3) generative, 4) measurable, and 5) able to be addressed within daily activities (Pretti-Frontczak & Bricker, 2000). Katie's team used the Revised Goals and Objectives Rating Instrument (adapted from Notari-Syverson & Schuster, 1995) to ensure that potential goals selected from assessment results meet the quality criteria. For example, the team identified cutting paper in half and cutting out shapes with straight lines as a need. Using the Revised Goals and Objectives Rating Instrument, the team noted that this skill did not meet all of the quality criteria to be selected as an IEP goal. The team then decided that manipulating objects with both hands (a broader skill that includes cutting out shapes with straight lines) met the five quality criteria listed on the Revised Goals and Objectives Rating Instrument, and, therefore, considered the broader skill as a potential target for intervention. In all, the team identified the following seven skills that met the quality criteria and served as potential intervention targets:

1. Manipulates toys and materials with both hands

2. Draws simple shapes and letters

3. Eats and prepares (e.g., taking the wrapper off of foods, removing the peel from fruits) more types of foods

4. Follows directions

5. Talks more and increases intelligibility

6. Plays with other children

7. Plays with toys and materials

Prioritizing Individualized Education Program Goals

After the team selected potential intervention targets (i.e., goals and objectives) and ensured the target skills met quality criteria, they determined which skills were of highest priority and required specialized services. The team prioritized goals by reviewing Katie's strengths and needs and by answering a series of questions:

- Do all team members understand the nature of the target skills?

- Are the skills deemed to be a priority by all team members?

- Will intentional and individualized instruction be provided for the child to acquire and use the skills?

- Are the target skills developmentally and individually appropriate?

- Are the skills necessary for the child's participation in the general curriculum (i.c., daily activities) or necessary for the completion of most daily routines?

- Are the skills related to or aligned with the general curriculum and state standards for all children, and/or do they represent the critical function of the standard versus a restatement of the standard?

Table 3.2 contains a list of potential goals and their rationale for inclusion on Katie's IEP. The prioritization process resulted in the following skills selected to serve as IEP goals:

- Manipulates toys and materials using both hands (e.g., cutting, drawing, zipping, pouring)

- Plays with toys and materials (i.e., functional use and representational use)

- Talks more and is intelligible to others (i.e., uses words to greet, inform, and request)

Table 3.2. Summary of potential individualized education program (IEP) goals and rationale for inclusion or exclusion

Potential IEP goals	Rationale for inclusion or exclusion on IEP
Manipulates toys and materials with both hands	This goal remains a priority for Katie's IEP because she needs the skill during most daily activities, and individualized intervention is needed for her to acquire the skill.
Draws simple shapes and letters	It is not necessary to target this goal on Katie's IEP because the team can address drawing simple shapes and letters as a part of targeting the manipulation of toys and materials.
Eats and prepares more types of foods	It is not necessary to target this goal on Katie's IEP because the team feels that learning to eat more types of food will come with time and does not require individualized intervention. Furthermore, by addressing the skill of manipulating materials, the team is addressing Katie's need to be more independent with preparing foods.
Follows directions	It is not necessary to target this goal on Katie's IEP because the skill is required by all children in the preschool and is addressed within the context of the general curriculum, not through individualized intervention efforts.
Talks more and increases intelligibility	This goal is a high priority that requires individualized intervention and will therefore be included on Katie's IEP.
Plays with other children	This goal is not necessary to target on Katie's IEP because the team feels the skill will emerge as Katie improves her ability to play with toys/ materials and to be understood by others. Katie also receives exposure to play with others at the preschool.
Plays with toys and materials	This goal remains a priority for Katie's IEP because she needs skills to increase her participation in activities with other children, and individualized intervention is needed for her to acquire the skill.

Writing Individualized Education Program Goals and Objectives/Benchmarks

Katie's team listed the priority skills and wrote them as IEP goals and associated objectives or benchmarks that met their state's and agency's guidelines. The team used the AEPS goal/objective examples for writing Katie's IEP. The AEPS goal/objective examples are designed to assist teams in writing meaningful goals/objectives and subsequent intervention. Katie's team used the examples from the AEPS as a starting point. They modified and individualized the examples using a straightforward ABC formula, in which A represents an antecedent, B represents the child's target behavior, and C represents the criterion or level of acceptable performance. Table 3.2 provides a comparison of AEPS goals/objectives examples and how the team individualized them for Katie. Katie's team then used the individualized goals and objectives/benchmarks to guide intervention efforts.

Linking assessment information and goal development is a critical aspect of ABI. This example illustrates how a team used screening findings to target where to begin their comprehensive assessment. The team then used that information to determine eligibility and to develop functional and generative goals.

SUMMARY

This chapter described a linked system framework that provides the broader context for situating ABI as an intervention approach. The linked system framework encompasses five essential components: screening, assessment, goal development, intervention, and monitoring progress. These five components are critical to the delivery of effective services for young children and for the use of ABI in particular. The chapter also explained the relationship between ABI and the linked system framework, concluding with an example of the application of the linked system framework with a young child.

REFERENCES

Bagnato, S., & Neisworth, J. (1991). *Assessment for early intervention: Best practices for professionals*. New York, NY: The Guilford Press.

Bagnato, S., Neisworth, J., & Pretti-Frontczak, K. (2010). *Linking authentic assessment and early childhood intervention, 2nd edition*. Baltimore, MD: Brookes Publishing.

Bayley, N. (2005). *Bayley Scales of Infant Development–III*. San Antonio, TX: Pearson.

Bennett, T., DeLuca, D., & Bruns, D. (1997). Putting inclusion into practice: Perspectives of teachers and parents. *Exceptional Children, 64*(1), 115–131.

Bricker, D. (1989). *Early intervention for at-risk and handicapped infants, toddlers, and preschool children*. Palo Alto, CA: VORT Corp.

Bricker, D. (1996a). Assessment for IFSP development and intervention planning. In S. Meisels & E. Fenichel (Eds.), *New visions for the developmental assessment of infants and toddlers* (pp. 169–192). Washington, DC: ZERO TO THREE: National Center for Infants, Toddlers, and Families.

Bricker, D. (1996b). Using assessment outcomes for intervention planning: A necessary relationship. In M. Brambring, H. Rauh, & A. Beelmann (Eds.), *Early childhood intervention theory, evaluation, and practice* (pp. 305–328). Berlin/New York, NY: Aldine de Gruyter.

Bricker, D. (Series Ed.). (2002). *Assessment, Evaluation, and Programming System (AEPS®) for Infants and Children* (2nd ed., Vols. 1–4). Baltimore, MD: Paul H. Brookes Publishing Co.

Bricker, D., Macy, M., Squires, J., & Marks, K. (2013). *Developmental screening in your community: An integrated approach for connecting children with services*. Baltimore, MD: Paul H. Brookes Publishing Co.

Bricker, D., Yovanoff, P., Capt, B., & Allen, D. (2003). Use of a curriculum-based measure to corroborate eligibility decisions. *Journal of Early Intervention, 26*(1), 20–30.

Frankenburg, W.K., Dodds, J.B., Archer, P., Bresnick, B., Maschka, P., Edelman, N., & Shapiro, H. (1992). *Denver II* (2nd ed.). Denver, CO: Denver Developmental Materials.

Greenspan, S.J., & Meisels, S. (1996). Toward a new vision for the developmental assessment of infants and young children. In S.J. Meisels & E. Fenichel (Eds.), *New visions for the developmental assessment of infants and young children* (pp. 11–26). Washington DC: Zero to Three, National Center for Infants, Toddlers, and Families.

Grisham-Brown, J., & Pretti-Frontczak, K. (2003). Using planning time to individualize instruction for preschoolers with special needs. *Journal of Early Intervention, 26*(1), 31–46.

Hoyson, M., Jamieson, B., Strain, P., & Smith, B. (1998). Duck, duck—colors and words: Early childhood inclusion. *Teaching Exceptional Children, 30*(4), 66–71.

Individuals with Disabilities Education Act Amendments (IDEA) of 1997, PL 105-17, 20

U.S.C. §§ 1400 *et seq.*

Individuals with Disabilities Education Act (IDEA) of 1990, PL 101-476, 20 U.S.C. §§ 1400 *et seq.*

Macy, M. (2012). The evidence behind developmental screening instruments. *Infants and Young Children: An Interdisciplinary Journal of Special Care Practices, 25*(1), 19–61.

McDonnell, A., Brownell, K., & Wolery, M. (2001). Teachers' views concerning individualized intervention and support roles within developmentally appropriate preschools. *Journal of Early Intervention, 24*(1), 67–83.

Michnowicz, L., McConnell, S., Peterson, C., & Odom, S. (1995). Social goals and objectives of preschool IEPs: A content analysis. *Journal of Early Intervention, 19*(4), 273–282.

Newborg, J. (2004). *Battelle Developmental Inventory, 2nd Edition (BDI-2)*. Chicago, IL: Riverside Publishing.

Notari, A., & Bricker, D. (1990). The utility of a curriculum-based assessment instrument in the development of individualized education plans for infants and young children. *Journal of Early Intervention, 14*(2), 117–132.

Notari, A., & Drinkwater, S. (1991). Best practices for writing child outcomes: An evaluation of two methods. *Topics in Early Childhood Special Education, 11*(3), 92–106.

Notari-Styverson, A., & Schuster, S.L. (1995). Putting real life skills into IEP/IFSPs for infants and young children. *Teaching Exceptional Children, 27*(2), 29–32.

Pretti-Frontczak, K., & Bricker, D. (2000). Enhancing the quality of IEP goals and objectives. *Journal of Early Intervention, 23*(2), 92–105.

Salisbury, C., Mangino, M., Petrigala, M., Rainforth, B., & Syryca, S. (1994). Innovative practices: Promoting the instructional inclusion of young children with disabilities in the primary grades. *Journal of Early Intervention, 18*(3), 311–322.

Sparrow, S., Cicchetti, D., & Balla, D. (2005). *Vineland Adaptive Behavior Scales* (2nd ed.). Circle Pines, MN: American Guidance Service.

Squires, J. (1996). Parent-completed developmental questionnaires: A low cost strategy for child-find and screening. *Infants and Young Children, 9*(1), 16–28.

Squires, J., & Bricker, D. (2007). An activity-based approach to developing young children's social emotional competence. Baltimore, MD: Paul H. Brookes Publishing Co.

Squires, J., & Bricker, D. (with Twombly, E., Nickel, R., Clifford, J., Murphy, K., Hoselton, R., Potter, L., Mounts, L., & Farrel, M.S.). (2009). *Ages & Stages Questionnaires® (ASQ): A parent-completed child monitoring system* (3rd ed.). Baltimore, MD: Paul H. Brookes Publishing Co.

Tymitz, B. (1980). Instructional aspects of the IEP: An analysis of teachers' skills and needs. *Educational Technology, 9*(20), 13–20.

VORT Corporation. (1995). *Hawaii Early Learning Profile (HELP)*. Palo Alto, CA: Author.

II

Conceptual Framework for Activity-Based Intervention

4

Description of Activity-Based Intervention

A main purpose of intervention for young children with disabilities or children who are at risk for disabilities is to assist them in the acquisition and generalization of critical developmental skills so that they can, to the extent possible, achieve independent functioning across environments. This purpose requires intervention efforts that are focused on helping children reach their individual learning and developmental goals and objectives. This chapter provides a description of ABI—an approach that is specifically designed to help children reach their individual goals within the context of play, routines, and daily activities. In effect, the driving force behind ABI is the attainment of functional skills that can be used across environments and situations.

To maximize opportunities for children to acquire their individual goals, ABI maps intervention efforts onto or integrates them into daily interactions that children experience. The strength of this approach is that it makes explicit the use of children's daily environmental transactions, and it provides a structure for doing so. Figure 4.1 illustrates how daily interactions between children and their social and physical environments appear to provide much of the information and feedback necessary for children to learn.

In the first frame of the figure, Tobia, a 3-year-old with a language delay, looks at a book and says, "Horsie!" Her mother, who is nearby, asks her to repeat what she said, and Tobia again says "Horsie." In the second frame,

---

The target goals listed in this chapter are taken from Bricker, D. (Series ed.). (2002). *Assessment, Evaluation, and Programming System (AEPS®) for Infants and Children* (2nd ed.). Baltimore, MD: Paul H. Brookes Publishing Co. The reader is referred to this source for more information.

Figure 4.1.   Illustration of how daily interactions between children and their social and physical environments provide the information and feedback necessary for learning.

Tobia's mother looks to see what her daughter is referring to and states, "Oh. Where do you see a horsie?" Tobia responds, "Here . . . lookie," while pointing to a picture of a horse in the book. Tobia's mother affirms her understanding by saying, "Oh, I see the horse." She then expands on Tobia's comment by saying, "It's brown." Tobia looks again at the picture and asks, "Brown?" In the third frame, Tobia's mother joins her on the carpet and points to the picture of the horse. She says, "Yes, the horse is brown. The horse also has a brown mane." Again, the mother's introduction of new words and ideas not only maintains Tobia's original interest in the horse but also expands her observation to other attributes of the horse. In response to her mother's comment, Tobia asks, "Mane?" and her mother responds, "Yes, the hair on the horse's neck is called a mane." Tobia repeats a portion of her mother's comment by saying, "Mane." In the fourth frame, her mother expands on her attention to the horse's mane by asking, "Do you have a mane?" Tobia responds, "No, I have hair." The mother affirms her daughter's response by saying, "You're right. Horses have manes, and people have hair." Tobia again repeats part of her mother's comment by saying, "I have brown hair."

A review of the interaction between Tobia and her mother suggests several interesting features. First, the interactions were at least equally initiated and directed by the child. Tobia's mother followed Tobia's lead and provided information and feedback that appeared to address her child's interest. Second, the transactions between mother and daughter were a meaningful sequence of reciprocal exchanges that were appropriate to Tobia's level of development. Third, the interactions had some novel characteristics—that is, they were not static but evolved and changed in meaningful ways. Fourth, when both partners are responsive, then the interaction is somewhat obligatory yet positive.

ABI is designed to capitalize on daily interactions such as those between Tobia and her mother. The following vignettes provide further examples of ABI used in daily interactions.

RASHID

Rashid is 17 months old and has Down syndrome. He is side-stepping down the length of the couch when he notices a favorite ball that is just beyond his reach. He points to the ball and asks, "Ba?" His father passes by, and Rashid looks at him and then back to the ball, again pointing and asking, "Ba?"

His father stops, leans over him, and says, "Ball. You want the ball?"

The toddler says, "Ba," and his father responds, "Do you want to play with the ball?"

Rashid first looks at his father, then at the ball, then back to his father and says, "Ba." His father picks up the ball and places it on the couch beside Rashid, and Rashid reaches to pick up the ball.

His father holds out his hands and says, "Throw the ball to me." Rashid releases the ball, laughs, and waves his arms. His father laughs and picks up the ball and holds it out to Rashid. "Do you want the ball? Come and get it."

The toddler says, "Ba," and takes several steps along the couch toward his father.

His father, still holding out the ball, says, "Here's the ball."

MAYA

Maya is 10 months old and has mild cerebral palsy. She is sitting in an infant seat in the kitchen while her older brother puts away groceries. She waves her arms and babbles. Her brother leans toward her and imitates her arm waving. He then picks up a paper bag to discard it, and the crackling paper attracts Maya's attention. She looks intently at the paper and waves her arms again. Her brother shakes the paper bag, and she immediately quiets and stares at the paper bag. Her brother then places the paper bag within easy reach. Maya reaches for the paper bag but misses it. Her brother moves the bag closer and helps her grasp it. He then guides her arm to shake the paper bag. As the bag moves, the crackling sound occurs, and Maya stops her activity. After a few seconds, her brother gently shakes her arm again, causing the paper to make the crackling noise. Maya pauses but soon independently shakes her arm to produce the crackling noise.

CARSON

Carson, a 5-year-old with behavioral challenges, walks into his house in tears. His grandmother asks him what happened. He sniffles and says that his playmate took his toy truck. His grandmother comforts him and then asks, "What should we do about it?" Carson shrugs his shoulders. His grandmother says, "Could you ask your friend to share the truck? Or could we find another truck for you?"

Carson runs to his bedroom but soon yells to his grandmother, "I can't find a truck!"

His grandmother replies, "Where did you look?"

"I looked in my toy box," says Carson.

"Where else can you look?" asks his grandmother.

In a few minutes, Carson stands before his grandmother with a red fire truck in his hands and explains, "It was under my bed."

In all of these scenarios, Tobia, Rashid, Maya, and Carson were permitted to initiate and lead the activities. The sequence of events for these four children was logical and continuous, and the interaction was meaningful to both partners in each situation. ABI promotes the use of daily child interactions and activities; however, the approach is selective about the nature and type of interactions and activities it uses because not all daily interactions that occur are meaningful or relevant to children.

Now consider the following vignettes for Sonja and Alberto.

SONJA

Sonja, a 16-month-old with a developmental delay, is crawling toward a toy on the floor. Her mother intercedes, picks her up, and seats her in a small chair at a table. Her mother sits across the table and says, "Come on, Sonja, let's find the toys." She goes on to explain that it is Sonja's job to find hidden objects today. To begin, she holds a small rattle for Sonja to see. Sonja looks at the rattle and then reaches for it. Without letting Sonja touch the rattle, her mother removes the rattle and, while Sonja is watching, places it under a small cloth and says, "Sonja, find the rattle." The toddler looks away, and her mother prompts a response by shaking the cloth. Sonja looks at the cloth, picks it up, and places it on her head to play Peekaboo. Her mother says, "Sonja, look for the rattle," and removes the cloth from her daughter's head. Sonja sweeps the rattle on the floor with her arm.

ALBERTO

Alberto, a 5-year-old with spina bifida and mild hyperactivity, is sitting in his father's lap. His father says, "Hey, it's time to work on naming colors." He has a set of small cards, each containing a swatch of color. He shows Alberto the first card and asks, "What color is this?"

Alberto looks at the card and says, "Red."

"Great," says his father, "That's right." Turning the next card, his father asks again, "What color is this?"

"Red," says Alberto.

"No," his father says, "This is green. Say green."

"Green," Alberto says as he looks at his dog across the room.

"Okay," says his father. He turns the next card and asks, "What color is this?"

Alberto looks at his father and, without conviction, says, "Green."

In contrast to the earlier scenarios, Sonja's and Alberto's caregivers initiated and directed the interactions. Although the caregivers' intent was understandable, and the children were responsive, repeated observation of such transactions raises questions about the effectiveness of intervention activities that do not appear to recognize the child's motivation or the relevance of the activities for the child.

Consider the following changed scenarios for Sonja and her mother and Alberto and his father.

SONJA

Sonja is crawling toward a small doll on the floor. Her mother knows that the doll is a favorite toy. As Sonja moves to the toy, her mother drops a towel over the doll. Sonja stops crawling, sits back, and looks at her mother who says, "Sonja, where is the doll?" Sonja looks at the towel, and her mother says, "Find the doll." Sonja lifts the towel, picks up and cuddles the doll, and smiles at her mother. Her mother says, "You found your doll. Can you say *doll?*" Sonja says, "Da," and points to her doll.

ALBERTO

Alberto tells his father he wants to play his favorite game "Candyland" and points to the location of the game box. As they open the box his father asks, "What color game piece do you want today?" Alberto does not respond, so his father pulls out two game pieces and asks as he points to each, "Do you want the red game piece or the green game piece?" Alberto points to the green one and says, "Green." Each time they turn over a card, Alberto's father encourages him to name the green and red colors and to find corresponding color spaces on the game board. The next morning as Alberto is getting dressed, his father says, "What color shirt do you want to wear today? You can wear a red one or a green one." Alberto points to the green shirt, and his father asks, "What color is this shirt?" Alberto looks at the shirt, then looks at his father and says, "Green!" His father says, "Sure is!" and helps him put on the shirt.

The previous examples described interactions between children and their caregivers that were either adult directed or child directed. The next two examples depict transactions that occur between groups of children and their interventionists: One provides an example of a child-directed program (Morehead Preschool), the other an example of an adult-directed program (Pleasant Hill Preschool).

MOREHEAD PRESCHOOL

Morehead Preschool is a child-directed program in which teachers follow children's lead, create multiple and varied learning opportunities, and attend to the various developmental levels of the children. For example, at opening group time the teacher asks the children, "What songs should we sing today?" The children offer a number of requests. The teacher lists the requested songs on the board and says, "You have selected six songs. How should we decide which songs to sing today?" The children and teacher discuss prioritizing the songs. They decide that because there are too many songs for one day, they will sing half of the songs that day and the other half the next day. As illustrated in Figure 4.2, the teacher encourages the children to suggest which songs to sing, thus building on their interests and following their lead. Furthermore, the teacher creates multiple learning opportunities to address literacy, mathematics, problem solving, social communication, and social goals. Finally, the teacher allows the children to participate at their developmental level (e.g., by maintaining proximity, watching others, holding song cards, answering questions, offering opinions).

PLEASANT HILL PRESCHOOL

Pleasant Hill Preschool uses an adult-directed approach. Group time begins with the teacher asking the children to sit quietly in their assigned places. When all of the children are seated, the teacher describes which centers are open that day and reminds students of classroom rules. The teacher then reviews the days of the week (e.g., children are asked what day of the week it is) and what the weather is like. One child is asked to select the correct "day" card and place it on the board. Another child is asked to select the correct "weather" card and do likewise. Then, the teacher says she would like everyone to sing a song about rainy weather. During the teacher-selected and teacher-directed activities, the children have little opportunity to indicate their interests.

These two examples are offered to demonstrate the differences between situations in which children's interests are followed and shaped into important learning opportunities and situations in which the adult selects and directs activities to enhance children's learning. Despite the move to "naturalistic" approaches as recommended practice (Noonan & McCormick, 2014), our observations of programs serving young children continue to suggest that much of the intervention work conducted with children with disabilities remains primarily adult selected and adult directed. One is likely to see scenarios such as those initially portrayed for Sonja, Alberto, and Pleasant Hill Preschool. The approach described in this volume offers an alternative to these scenarios.

ABI is designed to capture the essence of learning that was exemplified

Figure 4.2. Illustration of a group activity conducted at Morehead Preschool, a child-directed program.

in the vignettes for Tobia, Rashid, Maya, Carson, and Morehead Preschool—all of which demonstrated a child-directed approach. This approach capitalizes on children's motivation and the use of activities that are authentic (i.e., meaningful) and relevant to children.

The next section describes this approach, including its purpose, focus, elements, and underlying process, which result in a comprehensive approach for working with young children and their families.

ABI APPROACH TO INTERVENTION

The purpose of an ABI approach is to assist young children with disabilities or children who are at risk for disabilities to learn and to use important developmental skills. The foundation of the approach is the daily transactions that occur between infants and young children and their physical and social environments. These daily transactions account for the primary means by which children learn. Within an activity-based approach, learning opportunities that address children's educational and therapeutic goals and objectives are specifically embedded into authentic child-directed, routine, and planned activities. These authentic (i.e., meaningful) activities provide a range of practice opportunities for young children. Furthermore, an activity-based approach has a comprehensive framework that enables the user to capitalize on child–environment transactions and maximize development and learning. The ABI framework is presented in Figure 4.3, which includes descriptions of the purpose, focus, elements, and underlying process.

The purpose of ABI is to enhance children's learning and use of important developmental skills. To meet this purpose, the daily transactions that occur between young children and their physical and social environment are capitalized on to offer multiple and varied learning opportunities. Learning opportunities, in turn, elicit functional and generative responses from

Purpose:	To enhance children's learning and use of important developmental skills			
Focus:	Child-environment transactions during authentic activities			
Elements:	1	2	3	4
	Child-directed, routine, and planned activities	Multiple and varied learning opportunities	Functional and generative goals	Timely and integral feedback or consequences
Underlying process:	Embedding is a process that occurs across daily activities (child-directed, routine, and planned), offering multiple and varied learning opportunities that in turn elicit desired responses from children (i.e., demonstrating functional and generative skills) that are supported by timely and integral feedback or consequences that are directly related to or contingent on children's behaviors.			

Figure 4.3. Summary of the activity-based approach to intervention framework, including the purpose, focus, elements, and underlying process.

children, which are then supported by timely and integral feedback/consequences. The focus of an activity-based approach is on daily transactions. The approach is composed of four elements:

1. Child-directed, routine, and planned activities

2. Multiple and varied learning opportunities

3. Functional and generative goals

4. Timely and integral feedback or consequences

The underlying process associated with ABI includes embedding learning opportunities into authentic activities. Embedding refers to a process of addressing children's target goals and objectives during daily activities in a manner that expands, modifies, or is integral to the activity in a meaningful way.

Focus: Child–Environment Transactions

Understanding transactional exchanges between children and their environments is fundamental to the application of ABI. Transactional implies a bidirectionality of effect (Sameroff & Chandler, 1975; Sameroff & Fiese, 2000; Warren, Yoder, & Leew, 2002). For example, recall Maya from the beginning of the chapter. During another interaction with her brother, she waves her arms, and her brother responds by imitating her arm waving. Her brother's imitation may, in turn, affect the nature of her next motor response. The exchanges or transactions that occur between Maya and her brother are likely to change over time (e.g., they may become longer or more varied, a new element may be introduced).

Or, consider again Rashid and his father. Rashid points and says, "Dat?" His father looks at what he is pointing to and says, "That's your car. Do you want your car?" Rashid nods his head and says, "Ka." During the next transaction with his father, Rashid points and uses the new consonant–vowel combination *ka*.

The transactions between Rashid and his father illustrate the bi-directionality of effect and how the interaction is changed over time. Child–environment transactions are at the heart of learning and can be used to produce change in children's behavioral repertoires. To obtain desired change and growth, intervention efforts should focus on activities and events that are authentic to children. In this sense, *authentic* refers to transactions or exchanges that are salient and relevant for children, as well as integral to the ongoing flow of daily activities. The transactions that occurred between Maya and her brother and Rashid and his father offer examples of authentic transactions. Nonauthentic exchanges are contrived, artificial, isolated, and not meaningful for children. For example, asking a child to label flashcard pictures in an effort to teach him or her labels for objects is less authentic than answering a child's question about a toy of interest. Likewise, having a child practice walking on a balance beam to improve body awareness and balance is less authentic than encouraging the child to play on equipment at the park. Learning to produce vowel–consonant combinations in isolation is likely less authentic than learning to produce them in words that, when used, produce desired effects (e.g., a child says "mo" to get more juice). Learning about object permanence when a child drops toys from a high chair may be more meaningful (i.e., authentic) and relevant than having an adult move objects from a child's line of vision and instruct the child to find the object.

Whenever possible, caregivers and interventionists should strive to make child–environment transactions as authentic as possible. This often means learning about and designing intervention around individual children's strengths, interests, and needs, which is primarily accomplished by considering the four elements of an activity-based approach, each of which are described next. Note how the four elements build on one another into a comprehensive approach.

Element 1: Child-Directed, Routine, and Planned Activities

Within an activity-based approach, three general types of activities are used as the context for child–environment transactions: child-directed, routine, and planned activities. Each of the activities allows for multiple and varied learning opportunities. Learning opportunities (described in the next section), in turn, allow children to acquire and use functional and meaningful skills.

Child-Directed Activities   Child-directed actions, play, or activities refer to those that are initiated or guided by the child. For example, when a child chooses to ride his or her tricycle or chooses to play in the sandbox without prompting, the child is engaging in child-directed activities. Having children assemble for group time is generally an adult-directed rather than a child-directed activity; however, child-directed actions can occur during group time. For example, the children can select the number and types of songs they sing, or the children can be allowed to sit in places and positions that are comfortable for them rather than having all children sit in chairs. Allowing children to guide or direct the flow of activities or events is possible even when an adult is also involved in arranging and facilitating an activity.

Child-directed activities capitalize on children's motivation and interests and have been shown to enhance learning in a range of populations and environments (Bonawitz et al., 2011; Buchsbaum, Gopnik, Griffiths, & Shafto, 2011; Goetz, Gee, & Sailor, 1983; Griffin, 2000; Mahoney & Weller, 1980; Stremel-Campbell & Campbell, 1985; Wolery & Hemmeter, 2011). Adults who use child-directed activities 1) follow children's leads, 2) build on children's interests, and 3) match their responses or transactional exchanges to those initiated by children.

Child-directed activities are usually relevant and authentic for children. If children introduce and remain engaged in an activity, it is likely that they are motivated to do so because the activity is relevant, meaningful, and reinforcing to them (making the activity by definition authentic). Furthermore, when children are motivated and interested in a given activity, maintaining involvement does not require the use of primary or artificial rewards. For example, reaching for and grasping a desired toy is sufficiently rewarding for most children to practice and maintain their reaching and grasping behavior.

Following children's leads, in practice, translates into adults capitalizing on children's interests to guide the acquisition and generalization of important developmental skills. Transactions such as those initiated by Maya, Rashid, and Alberto permit parents to take advantage of their child's motivation and interests (e.g., Rashid's father took advantage of his son's interest in a ball to teach him a word, and Alberto's father agreed to play Alberto's favorite game and help him learn his colors). In the Morehead Preschool vignette and the illustration in Figure 4.2, child initiations were possible by permitting children to suggest songs or variations on usual songs. Using another example, Sonja's mother could have followed her child's direction by playing Peekaboo. The goal of working on object constancy would be maintained, but the activity choice would be child directed.

Not all child-directed activities necessarily move children toward the acquisition and use of target goals and objectives. For example, Eddie, a child with autism, may direct much of his activity to repetitive actions. The challenge for interventionists and caregivers is to gradually shift or expand Eddie's responses to address his target goal: *Eddie will use functionally appropriate actions with objects.* If Eddie's choice of activities is to repeatedly spin the wheels of a toy truck, his mother might prompt Eddie to place the toy's wheels on the floor and push the toy forward, producing a functional and appropriate response with the toy.

Routine Activities   A routine activity refers to the daily or regular occurrences of necessary events required to negotiate one's day-to-day existence. Eating, dressing, bathing, and traveling are all examples of routine activities. Everyone is faced with a daily or periodic regime of activities that must, for the most part, be accomplished. Using these routine activities to embed learning opportunities can significantly expand the potential number of opportunities for children to practice their goals and objectives. For example, Hayden's communication goal is to use two-word utterances to describe objects, people, and/or events. During his daily routines of meal and bath times, Hayden's caregivers can repeatedly address this functional and generative skill by modeling two-word utterances that describe (e.g., my towel, cold water, all done, wash more).

Another of Hayden's goals is to undress himself. The routine of getting ready for bed is likely an ideal time to address this goal by asking Hayden to take off his socks, shoes, shirt, and pants in order to undress for bed. Furthermore, this goal could be practiced each time Hayden removes his sweater or jacket when coming indoors.

In addition to increasing the number of practice opportunities, routine activities meet the definition of being authentic, and their use enhances the targeting of functional goals. The goals targeted for Hayden are functional and will assist him in becoming independent. Identifying opportunities for children to learn target goals in routine activities likely provides a significant increase in the number of available opportunities for the acquisition and maintenance of important developmental skills.

Planned Activities   Planned activities refer to designed events that occur with adult guidance; for example, 3-year-old Francine goes to the park with her mother to play, or Ms. Limon gathers the preschoolers around her to read them a story about a zebra. Thoughtfully designed planned activities can be used to provide multiple and varied learning opportunities for children to practice target goals. Successful planned activities require knowledge about individual children's present level of performance (including strengths and interests), advanced planning, and awareness of children's target goals. Planned activities should be constructed in such a manner as to create multiple and varied opportunities for children to practice target goals. Francine has two goals: Initiate and complete age-appropriate activities, and Manipulate objects with both hands. With advance planning, comprehensive information about Francine, and knowledge of her target goals, opportunities to practice these prioritized skills can be incorporated into a variety of activities, such as making cookie dough, conducting a science experiment on the playground, or engaging in an art project with other children. In addition, her parents can provide opportunities at home by encouraging her to color pictures in a coloring book or put puzzles together.

To the extent possible, planned activities should offer multiple and varied opportunities for children to engage in authentic activities. Planned activities should also be of interest to children and offered or structured in ways children find appealing while allowing interventionists to address target goals.

Element 2: Multiple and Varied Learning Opportunities

The nature and frequency of learning opportunities offered to children is important. Children must be able to practice new skills across a range of settings, people, and conditions. Events do not replicate exactly; therefore, children must learn how to adapt to changing conditions (Stokes & Baer, 1977). For example, one must be able to open doors that are small, large, or heavy when it is raining or the wind is blowing, and while talking or carrying a package. Such commonplace realities strongly mitigate against teaching children highly predictable routines conducted under static conditions if, indeed, the goal is to help children acquire flexible repertoires that assist them in adapting to changing environmental conditions. Thus, learning opportunities should be provided across child-directed, routine, and planned activities.

Adequate numbers of learning opportunities must also be available if children are to acquire and generalize important developmental skills. Unfortunately, a number of studies have reported that limited opportunities are provided for children to practice individual target goals (e.g., Pretti-Frontczak & Bricker, 2001; Schwartz, Carta, & Grant, 1996). The lack of practice opportunities to support children's acquisition of targeted new skills continues to be a concern in the field (e.g., Dinnebeil & McInerney, 2011; Dinnebeil, Spino & McInerney, 2011; Wolery & Hemmeter, 2011). Sufficient learning opportunities related to children's individual target goals are unlikely to occur incidentally or without adult intervention and advanced planning.

Learning opportunities need to be relevant or meaningful to children for them to benefit from the learning opportunity. Useful learning opportunities should match the child's current developmental abilities, be tailored to his or her interests, and prompt the child to practice target goals within the context of authentic activities or transactions. For example, if a child is learning to use both hands to manipulate objects, it is unlikely he or she will benefit from repeated attempts by an interventionist to cut out shapes unless 1) the child has the necessary prerequisite skills (e.g., ability to grasp, follow simple directions, sit upright), 2) the child is interested in cutting, and 3) joint attention is secured (e.g., having an adult assist the child in cutting using a hand-overhand teaching strategy while the child is looking out the window will likely not result in acquisition and use of both hands to manipulate objects). Ensuring meaningful opportunities requires teams to engage in ongoing observations of children.

Element 3: Functional and Generative Goals

Transactions and the learning opportunities embedded in them should focus on behaviors that expand children's communicative, motor, adaptive, social, and problem-solving skills. Learning opportunities that elicit critical developmental skills are likely to assist in improving and expanding children's repertoires. Fundamental to ABI is targeting educational and therapeutic goals and objectives that are functional and generative (i.e., represent broad classes of behavior and can be generalized across settings, conditions, and people).

Functional goals permit children to negotiate their physical and social environments in an independent manner satisfying to themselves and others. We use the term *functional* to refer to skills that are useful to children. For example, it is generally functional (i.e., useful) for children to learn how to open doors, turn on faucets, and flush toilets. Labeling days of the week may not have direct relevance to very young children's daily activities and, therefore, may not be a functional target (it may become more relevant as the children become older). Learning to name pictures in a book may be less useful to children than learning to label objects being used in play. Learning to initiate social interactions with peers (e.g., greeting, giving a peer a toy) is likely more useful for most children than learning to sing "I'm a Little Teapot." Engaging in fun activities such as singing songs should be encouraged; however, caregivers and interventionists should consider the value of an activity for expanding and enhancing children's development, in particular, as related to acquiring functional skills.

Goals should be generative as well as functional. *Generative* refers to two important dimensions. First, generative refers to selecting targets that can be used across settings, people, events, and objects. In most cases, children need to learn that the word *dog* refers to a class of objects, pictures, toys, and living animals rather than just the family pet. For the word *dog* to be generative, children must use it appropriately across a broad range of exemplars. For a pincer grasp to be generative, children must be able to use the response across settings (e.g., at the meal table, on the floor, at the bathroom sink), objects (e.g., Cheerios, beads, animal crackers, coins), and under a variety of conditions (e.g., when objects are hard, soft, wet, or dry).

Second, generative refers to the need to assist children in learning how to make response modifications as settings, objects, people, and conditions change. A functional goal is following directions; however, for a response to be generative, children should be able to vary their responses to follow directions offered by teachers and parents. Children should also have a range of substitutable responses. For example, when asked, "Where is Daddy?" the child might appropriately point to or go to Daddy (if he is in the room), say "daddy" while looking at his or her father, or indicate with a headshake that he or she does not know.

Overall, goals need to be a priority to the family, deemed developmentally and individually appropriate, and considered critical for the child's participation in daily activities. Goals targeted for intervention should also represent underlying processes that promote a child's access to and participation in the general curriculum and/or family routines. Furthermore, teams need to understand whether the goal of intervention centers on acquisition or use of the target skill(s)—both of which may require differentiated intervention efforts. Finally, teams should understand the differences between the targeting of general curricular outcomes for all children and individualized goals for particular children.

Goals targeted for individual children (often written on the IFSP or IEP) should be aligned with the child's present level of functioning and identified needs. The target goals should also promote independence and participation across a wide range of activities. In many instances, teams will identify more skills as potential intervention targets than can be reasonably addressed—thus, the need arises for teams to prioritize goals. When prioritizing, teams should select goals that 1) are not likely to develop without intervention, 2) significantly enhance a child's behavioral repertoire, 3) enable the child to be involved in the general curriculum/daily activities, and 4) match a child's developmental level of performance. For example, learning to make requests has the potential of enhancing a child's behavioral repertoire more than learning to label pictures on flashcards. By learning to make requests, children are able to get their needs met, interact with adults and peers, and engage in age-appropriate activities and play, whereas labeling pictures on flashcards is limited to a single activity that is not as likely to be interesting to the child or to promote independence and problem solving.

ABI is designed to help young children acquire and use functional and generative goals. This approach does not focus on teaching children to respond to specific cues under specific conditions; instead, the approach focuses on developing generalized motor, social, adaptive, communication, and problem-solving skills that children can modify or adapt across conditions.

Element 4: Timely and Integral Feedback or Consequences

Having children participate in child-directed, routine, and planned activities will not necessarily produce desired changes. Such activities and the provision of learning opportunities should provide a rich and meaningful context for intervention, but a final critical element is required. Without timely and appropriate feedback or consequences, children may not acquire or use target goals. The type of feedback or consequences, however, must meet two important criteria. First, the feedback/consequences provided to children should be timely, and second, the feedback/consequences should be, to the extent possible, associated with, connected to, or a logical outcome of the activity, action, or response.

Much has been written on the need for feedback/consequences to occur in a timely manner if efficient and effective learning is to occur (e.g.,

Duncan, Kemple, & Smith, 2000; Wolery & Hemmeter, 2011). The need to tie feedback/consequences to child behaviors may be particularly important for young children and for children with learning disabilities. If a toddler points at a cup, says "ju," and receives the cup with juice within a brief time span, he or she may quickly learn what response generally gets a cup of juice; however, if pointing and vocalizing never gets him or her juice, the toddler will likely try some other response (e.g., screaming). If considerable time passes between the child's response and receiving the juice, it may take many more transactions before the toddler learns that a point and a vocalization gets juice. To the extent possible, interventionists and caregivers should provide immediate feedback/consequences so that the child can discern the relationship between the response and subsequent feedback/consequences. As noted many years ago by Hart and Risley (1995), the quality of language input and the feedback received is significantly different based on socioeconomic level, and these differences produce outcomes that are often dramatically different for young children. This is likely true for young children with disabilities as well, thus emphasizing the importance of timely and relevant feedback to all children.

A second criteria associated with the delivery of feedback/consequences in an activity-based approach is to make it directly integral to or a logical outcome of the response. For example, the feedback/consequence associated with walking is that a child moves to a desired location or leaves an undesirable situation. The fact that the child can retrieve a desired toy by walking to it should negate the use of an artificial consequence (e.g., saying "Good walking"). Using or building in integral feedback/consequences also helps ensure it is timely. The action or connected feedback/consequences associated with turning a light switch in a dark room is that a person can see immediately, or turning a faucet generally produces water for a person to drink immediately. Using feedback or consequences that occur as a direct result of an action or response is greatly enhanced by using authentic transactions.

Tables 4.1 and 4.2 illustrate the fact that ABI is not designed to teach children specific responses in relation to specific cues. Rather, the approach is designed to offer children varied and multiple learning opportunities across activities. The main purpose of an activity-based approach is to have children associate classes of learning opportunities with classes of responses. So, too, with feedback/consequences, the goal is not to develop specific or one-to-one correspondences between responses and consequences but for children to effectively manage the range of feedback they may receive. The toddler who points for juice may receive his or her juice in a cup or glass, may be given a sip from someone else's glass, or may be given milk instead. Table 4.1 also illustrates the range and variety of feedback or consequences that can be provided. A second example of how the four elements build on one another into a comprehensive approach is provided in Table 4.2.

Table 4.1. Example of activities in which multiple and varied learning opportunities can be provided to address the functional and generative target goal of *Manipulating objects with both hands,* and examples of timely and integral feedback or consequences designed to enhance learning

Child-directed, routine, and planned activities	Multiple and varied learning opportunities	Functional and generative goals	Timely and integral feedback or consequences
Free play	Puzzles and blocks (favorite toys of the child) are made available in the classroom and at home.	Child fits puzzles pieces together or stacks blocks.	Child completes puzzle or tower.
Center time	Dress-up clothes, art aprons, and doll clothes with zippers, buttons, and ties are made available throughout the classroom.	Child buttons chef jacket and ties apron.	Child continues playing and wearing selected clothing.
Bath time	Caregiver asks the child to rub soap on a washcloth.	Child rubs soap onto washcloth.	Mom comments on how clean the child is getting.
Snack	Teacher gives the child a cup and a small pitcher of juice.	Child pours juice into cup.	Child drinks juice and is no longer thirsty.
Arrival	Upon arrival at school, the child is required to take off his coat and get lunch out of his backpack.	Child unzips coat and unzips backpack.	Teacher smiles and nods.
Small-group activity	Child joins a small group playing with playdough.	Child rolls, hammers, and cuts playdough.	Peer points to different shapes and labels.
After-school activity	Caregiver puts out coloring books, story-books, and art materials for an afternoon activity.	Child colors pages with crayons, turns pages in a book, and cuts out shapes.	Art project gets completed and shared with others.
Science and discovery table	Child is encouraged to transfer and measure different substances at the discovery table.	Child pours sand from a cup into a tub.	Tub gets filled with sand.

Underlying Process: Embedding Learning Opportunities

Embedding learning opportunities into authentic activities is the underlying process associated with ABI. Embedding refers to a process of addressing children's target goals during daily activities and events in a manner that expands, modifies, or is integral to the activity or event in a meaningful way. The process of embedding learning opportunities that address children's target goals is conceptually straightforward; however, the application of the process can be challenging (Grisham-Brown, Pretti-Frontczak, Hemmeter, & Ridgley, 2002; Macy & Bricker, 2006; Pretti-Frontczak & Bricker, 2000; Sandall & Schwartz, 2008; Wolery, Anthony, Caldwell, Snyder, & Morgante, 2002).

The successful creation and embedding of meaningful learning opportunities requires that interventionists and caregivers 1) conduct comprehensive

Table 4.2. Example of three activities in which multiple and varied learning opportunities can be provided to address the functional and generative target goal of *Initiating interaction with familiar adults* and examples of timely and integral feedback or consequences designed to enhance learning

Child-directed, routine, and planned activities	Multiple and varied learning opportunities	Functional and generative goals	Timely and integral feeback and consequences
Free play	Playing with toy in highchair and dropping it to the floor	Looks at caregiver, points to the toy on the floor	Caregiver retrieves toy.
Dressing/diapering	Getting diaper changed	Looks at caregiver and smiles	Caregiver smiles back.
Circle time	Sitting on caregiver's lap reading stories	Places caregiver's hands together to signify the desire to play Pat-a-cake	Caregiver sings and does hand motions.

and ongoing assessments; 2) create multiple and varied learning opportunities during child-directed, routine, and planned activities; 3) target functional and generative goals; and 4) systematically monitor the effects of intervention.

SUMMARY

Addressing important developmental targets, focusing on child–environment transactions, incorporating the four elements, and embedding learning opportunities provides the framework for ABI. This approach can be used in a variety of settings and under a variety of conditions by a range of direct services delivery personnel, specialists, and caregivers. The approach can be successfully used when working with individual children as well as groups of children with diverse repertoires and backgrounds. The flexibility of ABI permits broad application to infants and young children with disabilities or children who are at risk for mild, moderate, or severe disabilities. In addition, ABI can be successfully used with groups of children with varying developmental levels, economic backgrounds, experiences, values, and cultures.

An activity-based approach relies to a great extent on child-directed and routine activities that are not predetermined but rather instigated by children in particular environments. Child-directed activities allow children to engage in activities that are familiar and appealing and likely reflect the family's values (e.g., the types of toys and books available to the child in the home). So, too, the use of routine activities lends itself well to the incorporation of the child's learning into activities the family members have chosen as essential parts of their lives. Finally, planned activities can also be chosen or designed to reflect family experiences, cultures, and values. The introduction of a zoo activity might make little sense to young children who have never visited a zoo, whereas planning an activity focused on domestic animals may be more meaningful. Fundamental to the successful implementation of ABI is the tailoring of activities to the children and their goals that, in turn, permits respect for diversity.

REFERENCES

Bonawitz, E., Shafto, P., Gweon, H., Goodman, N., Spelke, E., & Schulz, L. (2011). The double-edged sword of pedagogy: Instruction limits spontaneous exploration and discovery. *Cognition, 120*(3), 322–330.

Bricker, D. (Series ed.). (2002). *Assessment, Evaluation, and Programming System (AEPS®) for Infants and Children* (2nd ed.). Baltimore, MD: Paul H. Brookes Publishing Co.

Buchsbaum, D., Goopnik, A., Griffiths, T., & Shafto, P. (2011). Children's imitation of causal action sequences is influenced by statistical and pedagogical evidence. *Cognition, 120*(3), 331–340.

Dinnebeil, L.A., & McInerney, W.F. (2011). *A guide to itinerant early childhood special education services.* Baltimore, MD: Paul H. Brookes Publishing Co.

Dinnebeil, L., Spino, M., & McInerney, W. (2011). Using implementation checklists to encourage the use of child-focused intervention strategies between itinerant visits. *Young Exceptional Children, 14*(4), 31–43.

Duncan, T., Kemple, K., & Smith, T. (2000). Reinforcement in developmentally appropriate early childhood classrooms. *Childhood Education, 76*(4), 194–203.

Goetz, L., Gee, K., & Sailor, W. (1983). Using a behavior chain interruption strategy to teach communication skills to students with severe disabilities. *Journal of The Association for Persons with Severe Handicaps, 10*(1), 21–30.

Griffin, E. (2000). *Narrowing the gap in reading: Instructional promise and peril.* Paper presented at the annual meeting of the American Educational Research Association, New Orleans, LA.

Grisham-Brown, J., Pretti-Frontczak, K., Hemmeter, M., & Ridgley, R. (2002). Teaching IEP goals and objectives in the context of classroom routines and activities. *Young Exceptional Children, 6*(1), 18–27.

Hart, B., & Risley, T.R, (1995). *Meaningful differences in the everyday experience of young American children.* Baltimore, MD: Paul H. Brookes Publishing Co.

Macy, M., & Bricker, D.(2006). Practical applications for using curriculum-based assessment to create embedded learning opportunities for young children. *Young Exceptional Children, 9*(4), 12–21.

Mahoney, G., & Weller, E. (1980). An ecological approach to language intervention. In D. Bricker (Ed.), *Language resource book* (pp. 17–32). San Francisco, CA: Jossey-Bass.

Noonan, M.J., & McCormick, L. (2014). *Teaching young children with disabilities in natural environments* (2nd ed.). Baltimore, MD: Paul H. Brookes Publishing Co.

Pretti-Frontczak, K., & Bricker, D. (2000). Enhancing the quality of IEP goals and objectives. *Journal of Early Intervention, 23*(2), 92–105.

Pretti-Frontczak, K., & Bricker, D. (2001). Use of embedding strategies during daily activities by early childhood education and early childhood special education teachers. *Infant-Toddler Intervention: The Transdisciplinary Journal, 11*(2), 111–128.

Sameroff, A., & Chandler, M. (1975). Reproductive risk and the continuum of caretaking casualty. In F. Horowitz, E. Hetherington, S. Scarr-Salapatek, & G. Siegel (Eds.), *Review of child development research* (Vol. 4, pp. 187–244). Chicago, IL: University of Chicago Press.

Sameroff, A., & Fiese, B. (2000). Transactional regulation: The developmental ecology of early intervention. In J. Skonkoff & S. Meisels (Eds.), *Handbook of early childhood intervention* (pp. 135–159). New York, NY: Cambridge University Press.

Sandall, S.R., & Schwartz, I.S. (2008). *Building blocks for teaching preschoolers with special needs* (2nd ed.). Baltimore, MD: Paul H. Brookes Publishing Co.

Schwartz, I., Carta, J., & Grant, S. (1996). Examining the use of recommended language intervention practices in early childhood special education classrooms. *Topics in Early Childhood Special Education, 16*(2), 251–272.

Stokes, T., & Baer, D. (1977). An implicit technology of generalization. *Journal of Applied Behavioral Analysis, 10,* 349–367.

Stremel-Campbell, K., & Campbell, R. (1985). Training techniques that may facilitate generalization. In S. Warren & A. Rogers-Warren (Eds.), *Teaching functional language* (pp. 251–285). Baltimore, MD: University Park Press.

Warren, S., Yoder, P., & Leew, S. (2002). Promoting social-communicative development in infants and toddlers. In S.F. Warren & J. Reichle (Series Eds.) & H. Goldstein, L.A. Kaczmarek, & K.M. English (Vol. Eds.), *Communication and language intervention series: Vol 10. Promoting social communication: Children with developmental disabilities from birth to adolescence* (pp. 121–149). Baltimore, MD: Paul H. Brookes Publishing Co.

Wolery, M., Anthony, L., Caldwell, N., Snyder, E., & Morgante, J. (2002). Embedding and distributing constant time delay in circle time and transitions. *Topics in Early Childhood Special Education, 22,* 14–25.

Wolery, M., & Hemmeter, M. (2011). Classroom instruction: Background, assumptions, and challenges. *Journal of Early Intervention, 33*(4), 371–380.

5

Conceptual Foundations
for Activity-Based Intervention

Throughout the evolution of ABI from its inception in the 1970s to its current iteration, the underlying conceptual framework or foundation has been instrumental in assisting developers in making decisions about what elements or procedures to include and how to introduce or embed those selected elements into educationally relevant activities. The conceptual underpinnings of ABI 1) provide the organizational framework for the approach and 2) ensure that essential facets of development and learning are addressed by the approach. Much of the value of ABI can be attributed to its robust conceptual framework.

Users of ABI should understand its conceptual framework and the importance of this framework to the elements that comprise ABI. Consequently, this chapter offers a discussion of the theoretical underpinnings of ABI. The chapter begins with a brief discussion of the changing perspectives associated with early experience and the historical foundation of services for young children with disabilities from institutionalized settings to the first community-based programs. This discussion complements the content presented in Chapter 2 and is offered as background for understanding the need to develop alternative intervention approaches such as ABI.

The remainder of the chapter describes the conceptual foundation for ABI—an approach that builds on the interests of children and is effective in producing desired growth and learning. In designing this approach from its inception to the current revision, we found that no single theory or perspective was adequate or suitably broad to generate a satisfactory, comprehensive intervention alternative. Rather, we found it necessary to adopt a number of theories or theoretical tenets. Our search for a conceptual foundation became paired with the need to synthesize a number of theoretical positions and assumptions in order to build a comprehensive and cohesive intervention approach. The adoption of a range of theoretical perspectives set the stage for changing, broadening, and making more appropriate intervention efforts with young children experiencing developmental and learning delays.

The changes and expansions of theoretical perspectives in concert with a growing body of knowledge focused on child development and learning served as the major catalysts for the creation of ABI. The chapter concludes by examining the indirect and direct links between the conceptual foundation and the elements of ABI.

HISTORICAL FOUNDATION

This section offers a brief historical perspective on the evolution of intervention efforts for young children with disabilities to provide background on the conceptual foundation that underlies ABI. This section first presents an overview of the shifting perspective on the importance of early experience for young children to assist in the appreciation of the significant theoretical change that preceded and likely accounts for, at least in part, the development of intervention efforts for young children with disabilities. This section then briefly reviews the evolution of intervention efforts with young children with disabilities in the United States.

Early Experience

To most professionals working with young children, the importance of early experience seems obvious; however, this has not always been the case, and delving into the early experience literature suggests that interpretation of the concept has shifted significantly over time. Before the 1950s, early experience was not considered a potentially important factor in determining developmental outcomes in children. Ramey and Baker-Ward (1982) noted that prior to World War II the predominant belief was that developmental outcomes were largely determined by genetics, and the rate of development was controlled by maturation. Environmental influences, and therefore early experiences, were seen as unimportant.

A dramatic shift occurred in the 1960s, however. The prevailing point of view changed from genetic predetermination to the primacy of environmental influences. This shifting position placed great importance on early experience (Hunt, 1961). Inherent in the initiation of early intervention programs in the 1960s for children from low-income families—and in the 1970s for children with disabilities—was the conviction by many researchers and interventionists that miracles could be accomplished. By providing stimulating and carefully orchestrated environmental input arranged to compensate for a genetic or biological impairment or a nonnurturing home, children could be made "normal." In addition, intervening early would inoculate children from future environmental failures. Early intervention could "fix" children, and they would stay "fixed" even when confronted with subsequent poor environments (Bricker, 1989).

Since those early optimistic days, information has been accumulating that has required yet another reinterpretation of the primacy of early experience and critical periods (Bailey, Bruer, Symons, & Lichtman, 2001). This new information and the reinterpretation of previous findings led to two important conclusions. First, early experience should be seen as but one link in the chain of growth and development. Although a good start is important and clearly desired, protective, supportive, stimulating, and appropriate early experiences do not necessarily shield children against future adversity (e.g., the development of a disability, subsequent neglectful or abusive environments, poor instruction). Early experiences are important but subsequent experiences are important as well.

Second, early experience is composed of an array of important, but often difficult to define and measure, internal and external variables that interact in complex ways. A simplistic view of early experience must be replaced by a complex view of the ongoing interaction among children's genetics, neurophysiological intactness, and their environmental contexts and interactions. For example, a growing body of research has made clear the significant and complex relationship between the brain and early experience (Bruer & Greenough, 2001; Schore, 1997). This complex relationship between the brain and behavior was well summarized by McCall and Plemons:

> Essentially all human behavior—looking, listening, speaking, thinking, loving, worshiping, imagining, and socializing—is governed by the brain. Therefore, it should not be surprising that any experience that changes the behavior of an infant, child, or adult also produces a change in the brain of that individual. (2001, p. 268)

Thus, it seems fair to conclude that initial concepts about early experience were simplistic and often inaccurate. The synergistic effects of genetics, biology, and environment are better understood; however, future research will likely provide an even more complete and accurate understanding of how the characteristics of individual children affect their behavior and how, in turn, neural functioning affects behavior.

Our understanding of early experience and its effect on children has changed since the 1950s. We have come to understand the need to place early experience in the larger context of lifelong development and learning. We have also come to understand, in all its surrounding complexity, that the types of early experiences offered to young children not only affect their current repertoires but also may be highly instrumental in shaping their futures. These findings provide significant impetus for the development of early intervention approaches that can offer the necessary supports for children whose early experience is insufficient to produce typical outcomes because of disability, environmental shortcomings, or both.

Evolution of Intervention

As noted in Chapter 2, after some limited attempts at community-based efforts, the beginning work with young children with significant disabilities was undertaken in residential settings (Bricker & Bricker, 1975). Prior to the 1970s, the majority of children with significant disabilities were institutionalized, often at very young ages. Because these children lived in environments that rarely reflected typical home settings (e.g., large hospital wards with little appropriate physical or social stimulation), they often learned to engage in an array of atypical, nonproductive, and often self-destructive behaviors. The only intervention that appeared to be effective was the experimental analysis of behavior that used carefully defined and controlled antecedents, responses, and consequences. With few exceptions, intervention efforts for young children with disabilities were highly structured and completely adult directed. In addition, these approaches took little account of children's developmental levels and often had children engage in nonrelevant and nonmeaningful activities (see Bricker & Bricker, 1975; Guess, Sailor, & Baer, 1974). To maintain children's interest and modify their behavior, children were offered tangible rewards. Although these highly structured approaches did not produce typical repertoires, they did produce significant changes in children's behavior. More important, these approaches reinvigorated the idea that young children with disabilities could learn and, therefore, should not be shut away in custodial facilities—a monumental accomplishment for the disability community (Wolfensberger, 1972).

In the early 1970s, the first community-based intervention programs for young children with learning and developmental disabilities and their families appeared (Tjossem, 1976). Initially, these programs were operated using the techniques found effective with children housed in residential settings; however, children living at home with their parents turned out to be resistive to highly structured, nonrelevant training activities, were uninterested in having teachers direct the majority of their daily activities, and generally did not change their behavior when offered food rewards (Bricker & Bricker, 1976). This negative feedback from children living in nurturing and interesting environments forced a reevaluation of what intervention approaches might prove to be engaging and produce desired changes in young children with disabilities.

One of the first community-based early intervention programs initiated at Peabody College in the early 1970s included children with and without disabilities (perhaps the first inclusive program for toddlers and preschoolers). The program provided staff the opportunity to observe the daily interactions of typically developing young children, as well as children with disabilities, with their peers, parents, and the physical environment (Bricker & Bricker,

1976). These observations made clear that the behavior of young children with disabilities being raised at home by their parents was more similar to typically developing young children than their peers living in institutions. Consequently, attention was turned to the array of new information on early development and learning as well as theories that attempted to explain how children typically learn and develop. This exploration, encompassing years of work, led to significant changes in the conceptualization and implementation of intervention efforts with young children with disabilities (Bricker, 1986, 1989; Bricker & Bricker, 1976).

As intervention efforts for young children and their families continued to evolve, it became clear that a single theory or conceptual framework was not able to offer an adequate explanation for the complex undertaking called early intervention. Some theories addressed cognitive learning, some addressed the integration of developmental processes, and others focused on the learning mechanisms of environmental feedback. Still others highlighted the impact of historical as well as contemporary contexts. Each of these perspectives addressed, at least in part, what appeared to be essential features of designing a comprehensive intervention approach. Consequently, the development of ABI came to be based on a range of diverse but complementary theoretical underpinnings.

THEORETICAL FOUNDATIONS

As Miller (1989) noted, no single developmental theory is up to the task of generating a comprehensive set of definitions, constructs, intervening variables, and hypotheses that adequately account for all learning and development across children. Nor has any one theory been able to explain or accommodate the array of existing empirical data generated around children's development and learning. Nonetheless, even given the current shortcomings of existing theory, theoretical frameworks to organize and give meaning to facts and to guide future research are of fundamental importance (Emde & Robinson, 2000). In addition to understanding and explaining development and learning, a theoretical foundation is necessary to the development of a coherent, cohesive, and effective intervention approach for young children with disabilities.

Most young children without genetic or biological complications appear to develop predictably. Expected behavioral patterns emerge when these children are exposed to "reasonable" environments, whereas children born with or who develop problems or who are raised in nonnurturing environments do not fare well without intervention (Farran, 2001; Guralnick, 1997, 2005; Shonkoff & Phillips, 2000). Crafting intervention approaches that assist children with disabilities and those who are at risk is essential to maximize their development, learning, and adjustment. The crafting of intervention approaches is likely to be more successful if based on solid theoretical foundations, rather than operating with a divergent set of guidelines and strategies that may not address the important facets of development and may not be consistent and complementary with each other.

As noted previously, the lack of a single comprehensive theory of development or intervention has required the creation of a conceptual foundation that has tapped a range of theoretical writings. Exploring and adopting a variety of theoretical tenets has been necessary in order to address the many facets associated with the enhancement of development and learning in young children with disabilities and those who are at risk.

The remainder of this chapter addresses the theoretical positions that have been used to fashion a set of conceptual tenets that underlie ABI. The discussion identifies major theoretical perspectives, and reviews theories of particular relevance. The concluding section of the chapter describes direct and indirect links among these theoretical perspectives and the elements of ABI.

Major Theoretical Perspectives

As indicated previously in this chapter, the formation of a comprehensive intervention approach for young children who have or are at risk for disabilities is a complex and challenging undertaking. Learning and development are more complex than many initial theories of human development proposed (Miller, 1989). Before describing the particular theories that are foundational to ABI, it is useful to present six important perspectives that can be extracted from prominent theories of learning and development. These tenets identify variables or dimensions that directly or indirectly underlie ABI.

1. Child characteristics (e.g., temperament, biological intactness, reactivity) and the integration of developmental processes affect development and learning.

2. The immediate environment and the larger historical and contemporary sociocultural context have a significant influence on development and learning.

3. Active, child-directed transactions across environmental settings shape development and learning.

4. Authentic environmental transactions promote learning and generalization.

5. The nature of environmental antecedents and learning opportunities affects development and learning.

6. The delivery of meaningful feedback is necessary for development and learning.

Because no one theory addresses the many facets of effective intervention efforts, we have found it necessary to create a conceptual framework for ABI by adopting perspectives from the written works of Vygotsky, Piaget, Dewey,

Cicchetti and his colleagues; social learning theorists such as Bandura; and situated cognitive theorists such as Brown. In addition, we have been heavily influenced by the work of behavior analysts who have repeatedly demonstrated that behavioral learning principles remain the most effective intervention strategies available.

Sociohistorical Theory

Sociohistorical theory and particularly the writings of Lev Vygotsky have greatly influenced other theorists and have helped draw the attention of practitioners and interventionists to the effects that the immediate and historical sociocultural surroundings have on the developing child (John-Steiner & Souberman, 1978; Moll, 1990). The dialectical approach, although admitting the influence of past cultural events and current society on the individual, asserts that the individual, in turn, influences his or her culture and society. These changes create new conditions that in turn continue to affect society and culture (Vygotsky, 1978). As Vygotsky noted, learning is a profoundly social process that is affected by the history of the child and the child's culture (Moll, 1990).

Vygotsky acknowledged the biological basis of development; however, he also argued that the interactions between a child and the social environment affect the development of the child as well as the larger social context. Hart and Risley (1995) noted this phenomenon while conducting their longitudinal study of language acquisition in young children. They observed that parental responses became more sophisticated as their children acquired more sophisticated language; this in turn led to the children's production of yet more complex language. Vygotsky's interactional perspective recognized the bidirectionality of effects between children and their immediate social environment. His position also addressed sociocultural change that results from the individual's action on and reaction to the sociocultural times, which may modify the sociocultural context for future generations. For example, the introduction of new words (e.g., *cyberspace*) or changes in word meaning (e.g., *cool*) reflect and may produce more cultural shifts.

Vygotsky's writings preceded ecological models (Bronfenbrenner, 1977) and interactional positions such as those described by Sameroff and Chandler (1975; Sameroff & Fiese, 2000). Transactional or interactional positions focus, in part, on child–environment exchanges as foundational to development and learning. The appreciation of cultural history and how it has shaped contemporary events and children's past and present environmental transactions underlies ABI. The ABI approach is built on the premise that the daily transactions between children and their social and physical environments provide the most useful, appropriate, and likely effective opportunities for producing desired change. Following on this premise is the importance placed on an appreciation for the child's, family's, and community's history and current values as critical to effective intervention efforts.

Developmental Theory

Theories of emerging development provide a rich resource for understanding and predicting the evolution of change in individual children and groups of children over time. A number of developmental theories offer perspectives and insights that, if not directly applicable to the design of effective intervention approaches, provide an important context from which to view children's growth and learning. The organizational perspective on developmental psychopathology proposed by Cicchetti and Cohen (1995) has particular relevance for ABI.

Cicchetti and Cohen's organizational perspective on development "focuses on the quality of integration both within and among the behavioral and biological systems of the individual . . . and specifies how development proceeds" (1995, p. 6). This theory postulates development as a series of "qualitative reorganizations" within and among biological and behavioral systems (e.g., cognitive, social, linguistic, emotional). Change occurs as earlier structures are incorporated into new levels of organization both within and across systems. For example, children acquire more advanced language skills by expanding, rearranging, or changing the syntactic rules that govern sentence production. These changes in language will likely also affect other major systems—that is, because of the interaction between developmental domains and their reciprocal impact, enhanced communications skills may also change the child's cognitive, social, and emotional behavior.

Aspects of the organizational perspective particularly relevant to intervention efforts include attention to the potential interactive effects between systems and the systematic reorganization of behavior into more complex behavioral skills. The belief that early developmental processes are interactional and synergistic has important implications for intervention approaches. Intervention efforts should be comprehensive (e.g., children with language delays are also likely to experience cognitive and social problems), taking into account all major systems or areas of development. A second implication for intervention is the need for accurate, ongoing, and in-depth assessment of a child's full repertoire across important behavioral systems. ABI is designed as a comprehensive approach that emphasizes targeting important skills across developmental areas. The approach requires that developmental targets be determined through in-depth, comprehensive, and functional assessment to ensure that all systems (i.e., behaviors) are addressed and that the behaviors are used appropriately and meaningfully.

Cognitive Theory

The influence of cognitive theory, specifically Jean Piaget's writings, on the formulation of an intervention approach for young children has been profound. Piagetian theory postulates that children act on their environment to construct an understanding of how the world operates (Piaget, 1952, 1967). Various interpretations of Piagetian theory have provided an important tenet underlying the ABI approach. His theory emphasizes the need for children to be actively involved in constructing knowledge of their physical environment. Children need to explore, experience, manipulate, and receive feedback from their actions on the physical world in order to move from the sensorimotor stage to representational and formal operations stages—that is, to manipulate symbols internally.

A critical aspect of children's active exploration of their environment is the relevant and direct feedback they receive. As young children examine objects within their reach, they find that a ball being thrown is different from a ball being squeezed. Children discover through systematic feedback from their actions that, for example, books are to look at, whereas hammers are better for pounding. These ongoing interactions between children and the environment help shape children's understanding of their physical surroundings and serve as the basis for higher cognitive functions.

Piaget's writings and his many interpreters have greatly enhanced appreciation for the development of higher mental functions in children. Piaget pointed out the importance of children's actions on their environment and the importance of subsequent feedback to the development of increasingly more sophisticated problem-solving behavior. His notion of acting on the environment and learning from these actions underlies ABI.

Piaget's theory of how children acquire knowledge was instrumental in shaping ABI, moving it from a singular focus on external behavior to thinking about internal constructions. His theory made clear the importance of the sensorimotor period as a foundation for the development of concrete and formal operations that are the hallmark of thinking beings. Furthermore, Piaget's focus on the importance of young children constructing their understanding of the world serves as a major impetus for the adoption of children's daily interactions with the physical environment as a basis for ABI.

Learning Theory

Most intervention approaches have been influenced, at least in part, by learning theory. The basic assumptions underlying ABI have been particularly affected by John Dewey's writings. Dewey's perspective, like those of Piaget and Vygotsky, rests in part on the idea that the interaction between children and their environments is fundamental to development and learning. For Dewey, genuine education comes about through experience. "Every experience is a moving force. Its value can be judged only on the grounds of what it moves toward and into" (1976, p. 38). According to Dewey, it is necessary for experiences to be interactive and have continuity to move children toward meaningful change.

As Dewey (1959) noted, children by nature are active, and the challenge is how to capture and direct their activity. Through thoughtful organization and planning, experiences (i.e., activities) can be arranged to meet children's interests and to address sound intervention goals. Activities should be meaningful and functional for children and not without focus or direction. "A succession of unrelated activities does not provide, of course, the opportunity or content of building up an organized subject-matter. But neither do they provide for the development of a coherent and integrated self" (Dewey, 1959, p. 122). Dewey's concept of continuity implied that the effective interventionist determines children's present levels of understanding and then arranges experiences in such a way as to move them efficiently toward a higher level of functioning.

Another aspect of Dewey's theory of particular relevance to the ABI approach is that children should be allowed to participate fully in activities. Full participation may include the selection of what to do and how to do it. The interventionist's role is to guide the children's selection of experiences (appropriate to their present levels of understanding) so that they become interactive and continuous. The interventionist's job, in effect, is to map relevant intervention goals onto the experiences that occur in children's lives— a hallmark of ABI.

In addition, as Dewey emphasized, learning occurs as a result of all experiences, not just those designated for formal training. Effective intervention approaches use the array of activities that occur in children's lives on a daily basis. The variety of activities available to young children can often be used to facilitate the acquisition of important knowledge and skills. The child's desire for an object, person, or event can be used to develop and expand communication skills. Playing in a sandbox can be arranged to develop motor and social skills. Rather than routinely having children wash their hands before snack time, adults can turn this task into an activity that demands problem solving (e.g., locate the soap, reach the sink, find the towel) and is relevant and meaningful to children. The effective use of child-directed, routine, and unanticipated activities is a fundamental part of ABI.

Social Learning Theory

Social learning theory is considered a version of learning theory and could, as well, be placed under the umbrella of developmental theories (Miller, 1989). Social learning theory offers important perspectives that have been essential to the development of ABI, in particular the tenet that learning results from the interaction between child and environmental factors. In Bandura's words, "behavior, cognitive and other personal factors, and environmental influences all operate interactively as determinants of each other" (1986, p. 23). Social learning theory emphasizes the importance of the social context, imitation, and observational learning (Miller, 1989). ABI has incorporated these important elements of social learning theory by emphasizing the social context for learning (e.g., using meaningful routines to embed learning opportunities), incorporating the insight that learning can occur indirectly through observation, and encouraging imitation of functional and generative behaviors that will enhance children's problem solving and independence.

The behavioral learning principles that have been distilled from operant learning theory with the addition of the more complex cognitive and personal features added by social learning theory continue to offer the most effective set of intervention principles available to interventionists (Meichenbaum, Bream, & Cohen, 1983). The primary principles can be conceptualized as a three-part sequence of antecedent, response, and consequence, or ARC unit.

Although the concept of antecedents, responses, and consequences can be presented in a simplistic fashion, in reality, as Bandura (1986) and others pointed out, the multiple conditions under which children and adults learn are more accurately viewed as a complex set of interactions and effects. That is, antecedents may be (and likely are) multifaceted and are influenced by the social context. For example, a mother might say, "Sit there," as she points to a chair. The antecedent "Sit there" may affect a child differently if it is said matter of factly or with great volume and force. The antecedent "Sit there" may be perceived differently if the child is alone or surrounded by several other children. The response, sitting, is also affected by numerous factors, for example, whether the child understands the words or if the child is able to move to the location. Understanding the effect of consequences on behavior is often difficult and complex because a range of historical and contemporary factors that may be hard to detect or appreciate combine to affect consequences.

ABI focuses on ARC units. That is, interventionists are encouraged to select antecedents that will ensure learning opportunities are embedded during child-directed, routine, and planned activities. Responses are operationalized as functional and generative skills targeted for children to acquire and use. Feedback or a consequence, to the extent possible, is the inherent or logical result of a child's response. Figure 5.1 demonstrates how ABI uses basic ARC units to enhance learning and development.

Situated Cognitive Learning Theory

The variation of learning and/or cognitive theory, often called situated learning or situated cognition, encompasses a broad range of perspectives (e.g., Greeno, Collins, & Resnick, 1996; Putnam & Borko, 2000) of relevance to ABI. In particular, ABI has adopted the situated cognitive perspective of Brown, Collins, and Duguid who argued that "activity and situations are integral to cognition and learning" and "different ideas of what is an appropriate learning activity produce very different results" (1989, p. 32). They also suggested that "by ignoring the situated nature of cognition, education defeats its own goal of providing useable, robust knowledge" (1989, p. 32).

By *situated nature,* Brown and his colleagues mean that learning is

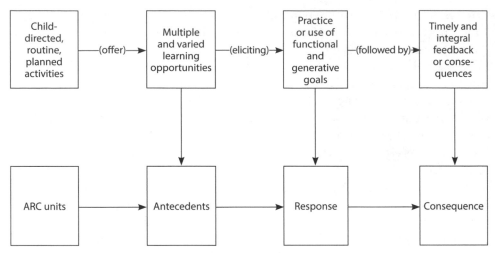

Figure 5.1. The relationship of activities, learning opportunities, goals and objectives, and feedback to antecedent, response, and consequence (ARC) units.

an integral part of the activity and situation in which it occurs. "Activity, concept, and culture are interdependent. No one can be totally understood without the other two. Learning must involve all three" (Brown et al., 1989, p. 33). These authors have blended logic and data into a case for what they call *authentic activity* and have argued that the acquisition of knowledge and learning of skills should occur under conditions that are authentic (i.e., the knowledge or skill is necessary, relevant, or useful to cope with real tasks or problems). This belief opposes training or education that employs abstract, fragmented strategies that do not reflect conditions found in nontraining environments. For example, attempting to enhance children's communication skills by conducting 10-minute drill sessions is likely less meaningful than assisting children to expand their communication skills as they need them to negotiate their daily environment.

The applicability of the situated perspective (Brown et al., 1989) is apparent for young children and provides additional conceptual support for ABI. If Brown and his colleagues are correct, then developing generative, functional, and adaptable response repertoires can be made efficient and effective by embedding learning opportunities and objectives in authentic situations. Authentic situations for young children should include activities that reflect the reality and demands of their daily living as well as play. Authentic activities have, from children's perspectives, a logical beginning, a sequence of events, and an ending. They are fundamental to young children's existence (e.g., requesting help), mirror conditions and demands the children face on a routine basis (e.g., dressing), or constitute play activities. Authentic activities permit children to learn and practice skills that will improve their abilities to cope with the many demands offered by their physical and social environments. Children view authentic activities as relevant, as evidenced by their interest and motivation to become involved. Such activities lead children to better understand and respond to their immediate sociocultural context. Furthermore, an authentic activity meets Dewey's criteria of sound educational practice because it "supplies the child with a genuine motive; it gives him experience at first hand; it brings him into contact with reality" (1959, p. 44).

LINKING THEORETICAL PERSPECTIVES TO ABI

The diverse and complex but complementary theories and perspectives briefly reviewed in this chapter provide the conceptual framework for ABI. Figure 5.2 offers a concrete illustration of the relationship between these important perspectives and ABI elements. The left side of the figure shows the relationship between two broad theoretical positions that provide the general foundation of ABI. The first set of boxes to the right list the theoretical guidelines and the set of four boxes to the far right list the four elements of an ABI approach that these guidelines underlie.

As noted the two theoretical or foundational principles are at the left of Figure 5.2:

- Child characteristics and the integration of developmental processes affect development and learning (Cicchetti & Cohen, 1995).

- The immediate environment and the larger historical and contemporary sociocultural context have a significant influence on development and learning (Vygotsky, 1978).

These two principles provide the broad conceptual framework for ABI as indicated by the connecting arrow. To the right of the conceptual foundations are listed four theoretically based guidelines:

- Active child-directed transactions across environmental contexts promote development and learning (Piaget, 1967; Sameroff & Chandler, 1975).

- The nature of environmental antecedents or learning opportunities affects development and learning (Bandura, 1986; Dewey, 1959).

- Authentic environmental transactions promote learning and generalization (Brown et al., 1989; Dewey, 1959).

- The delivery of meaningful feedback or consequences is necessary for development and learning (Bandura, 1986).

These guidelines underlie the four elements of ABI that are shown to the far right in Figure 5.2. The connecting arrows depict the relationship between the guidelines and ABI elements.

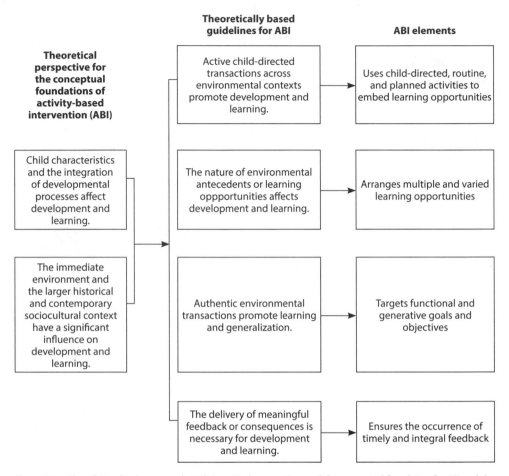

Figure 5.2.   The relationship between selected theoretical perspectives and the conceptual foundation for ABI and the theoretical guidelines for ABI elements.

SUMMARY

This chapter has provided a conceptual framework for understanding the formulation and application of ABI. The tenets distilled from the work of a variety of theorists and conceptual perspectives give strength to the positions that children are greatly influenced by their social and physical environments and their cultural context, that children need to be actively involved in the construction of higher mental processes, and that the nature of the environmental activities (i.e., experiences) children encounter are fundamental to their development and learning. Given these positions, an intervention approach such as ABI that uses authentic activities has great appeal.

As Dewey wrote, "There is no such thing as educational value in the abstract" (1976, p. 46). As he also noted, he believed that "the only true education comes through the stimulation of the child's powers by the demands of the social situation in which he finds himself" (Dewey, 1959, p. 20). The purpose of ABI is to create and use authentic activities in order to enhance children's development and learning.

REFERENCES

Bailey, D.B., Bruer, J.T., Jr., Symons, F.J., & Lichtman, J.W. (Eds.). (2001). *Critical thinking about critical periods*. Baltimore, MD: Paul H. Brookes Publishing Co.

Bandura, A. (1986). *Social foundations of thought and action: A social cognitive theory*. Upper Saddle River, NJ: Prentice-Hall.

Bricker, D. (1986). *Early education of at-risk and handicapped infants, toddlers and preschool children*. Glenview, IL: Scott Foresman.

Bricker, D. (1989). *Early intervention for at-risk and handicapped infants, toddlers and preschool children*. Palo Alto, CA: VORT Corp.

Bricker, W., & Bricker, D. (1975). Mental retardation and complex human behavior. In J. Kaufman & J. Payne (Eds.), *Mental retardation: Introduction and personal perspectives*. Columbus, OH: Charles E. Merrill.

Bricker, W., & Bricker, D. (1976). The infant, toddler, and preschool research and intervention project. In T. Tjossem (Ed.), *Intervention strategies for high risk infants and young children*. Baltimore, MD: University Park Press.

Bronfenbrenner, U. (1977). Toward an experimental ecology of human development. *American Psychologist, 32,* 513–531.

Brown, J., Collins, A., & Duguid, P. (1989). Situated cognition and the culture of learning. *Educational Researcher, 18*(1), 32–42.

Bruer, J.T., & Greenough, W. (2001). The subtle science of how experience affects the brain. In D.B. Bailey, Jr., J.T. Bruer, F.J. Symons, & J.W. Lichtman (Eds.), *Critical thinking about critical periods* (pp. 209–232). Baltimore, MD: Paul H. Brookes Publishing Co.

Cicchetti, D., & Cohen, D. (1995). Perspectives on developmental psychopathology. In D. Cicchetti & D. Cohen (Eds.), *Developmental psychopathology: Theory and methods* (pp. 3–20). New York, NY: John Wiley & Sons.

Dewey, J. (1959). *Dewey on education*. New York, NY: Columbia University, Bureau of Publications, Teachers College.

Dewey, J. (1976). *Experience and education*. New York, NY: Colliers.

Emde, R., & Robinson, J. (2000). Guiding principles for a theory of early intervention: A developmental-psychoanalytic perspective. In J.P. Shonkoff & S.J. Meisels (Eds.), *Handbook of early childhood intervention* (pp. 160–178). New York, NY: Cambridge University Press.

Farran, D.C. (2001). Critical periods and early intervention. In D.B. Bailey, Jr., J.T. Bruer, F.J. Symons, & J.W. Lichtman (Eds.), *Critical thinking about critical periods* (pp. 233–266). Baltimore, MD: Paul H. Brookes Publishing Co.

Greeno, J., Collins, A., & Resnick, L. (1996). Cognition and learning. In D. Berlinger & R. Calfre (Eds.), *Handbook of educational psychology* (pp. 15–46). New York, NY: MacMillan.

Guess, D., Sailor, W., & Baer, D. (1974). To teach language to retarded children. In R. Schiefelbusch & L. Lloyd (Eds.), *Language perspectives—acquisition, retardation, and intervention*. Baltimore, MD: University Park Press.

Guralnick, M.J. (Ed.). (1997). *The effectiveness of early intervention*. Baltimore, MD: Paul H. Brookes Publishing Co.

Guralnick, M. (Ed.). (2005). *The developmental systems approach to early intervention*. Baltimore, MD: Paul H. Brookes Publishing Co.

Hart, B., & Risley, T.R. (1995). *Meaningful differences in the everyday experience of young American children*. Baltimore, MD: Paul H. Brookes Publishing Co.

Hunt, J. (1961). *Intelligence and experience*. New York, NY: Ronald Press.

John-Steiner, V., & Souberman, E. (1978). Afterword. In M. Cole, V. John-Steiner, S. Scribner, & E. Souberman (Eds.), *L.S. Vygotsky—Mind in society* (pp. 121–133). Cambridge, MA: Harvard University Press.

McCall, R.B., & Plemons, B.W. (2001). The concept of critical periods and their implications for early childhood service. In D.B. Bailey, Jr., J.T. Bruer, F.J. Symons, & J.W. Lichtman (Eds.), *Critical thinking about critical periods* (pp. 267–288). Baltimore, MD: Paul H. Brookes Publishing Co.

Meichenbaum, D., Bream, L., & Cohen, J. (1983). A cognitive behavioral perspective of child psychopathology: Implications for assessment and training. In R. McMahon & R. DeV. Peters (Eds.), *Childhood disorders: Behavioral-development approaches.* New York, NY: Brunner/Mazel.

Miller, P. (1989). *Theories of developmental psychology.* New York, NY: W.H. Freeman.

Moll, L. (1990). *Vygotsky and education.* New York, NY: Cambridge University Press.

Piaget, J. (1952). *The origins of intelligence in children.* New York, NY: W. W. Norton.

Piaget, J. (1967). *Six psychological studies.* New York, NY: Random House.

Putnam, R., & Borko, H. (2000). What do new views of knowledge and thinking have to say about research on teacher learning? *Educational Researcher, 29*(1), 4–15.

Ramey, C., & Baker-Ward, L. (1982). Psychosocial retardation and the early experience paradigm. In D. Bricker (Ed.), *Intervention with at risk and handicapped infants.* Baltimore, MD: University Park Press.

Sameroff, A., & Chandler, M. (1975). Reproductive risk and the continuum of caretaking casualty. In F. Horowitz, E. Hetherington, S. Scarr-Salapatek, & G. Siegel (Eds.), *Review of child development research* (Vol. 4, pp. 187–244). Chicago, IL: University of Chicago Press.

Sameroff, A., & Fiese, B. (2000). Transactional regulation: The developmental ecology of early intervention. In J.P. Shonkoff & S.J. Meisels (Eds.), *Handbook of early childhood intervention* (pp.135–159). New York, NY: Cambridge University Press.

Schore, A. (1997). Early organization of the nonlinear right brain and development of a predisposition of psychiatric disorders. *Development and Psychopathology, 9,* 595–631.

Shonkoff, J.P., & Phillips, D.A. (Eds.). (2000). *From neurons to neighborhoods: The science of early childhood development.* Washington, DC: National Academy Press.

Tjossem, T. (Ed.). (1976). *Intervention strategies for high risk infants and young children.* Baltimore, MD: University Park Press.

Vygotsky, L. (1978). *Mind in society.* Cambridge, MA: Harvard University Press.

Wolfensberger, W. (1972). *The principle of normalization in human service.* Toronto, Ontario, Canada: National Institute on Mental Retardation.

6

Organizational Structure of Activity-Based Intervention

As discussed in Chapter 3, ABI is situated in a larger linked system framework that is composed of five components: screening, assessment, goal development, intervention, and progress monitoring. This chapter addresses in more detail the content and processes associated with the intervention component of the linked system. The content presented assumes that the previous components of the system, screening, assessment, and goal development, have been completed and the next step is to address the intervention component. Successful intervention does not occur without thought, planning, and a cohesive organizational structure that assists in guiding the team's behavior and using resources in ways that produce desired outcomes. Specifically this chapter discusses the organizational structure of ABI that provides the necessary guidance for successful intervention across a range of children with varied developmental and learning challenges.

Having an underlying organizational structure for ABI (as well as for other intervention approaches) is important for two reasons. First, federal legislation that mandates IFSPs and IEPs requires that they serve as a guide or map for intervention (Bricker, 2002; McLean, Wolery, & Bailey, 2004; Sandall, Hemmeter, Smith, & McLean, 2005). IFSPs/IEPs were not designed to serve as specific day-to-day treatment or lesson plans; rather, their purpose is to specify goals/objectives and offer broad intervention guidelines. Consequently, IFSPs/IEPs do not offer the necessary detail concerning how, when, and where training and practice opportunities should be employed to address children's individual needs within the context of child–environment transactions.

A second reason that ABI needs an organizational structure is that it may appear to rely on children's self-initiated activities or to only engage in "fun" activities. Using fun and interesting activities is only one aspect of an activity-based approach. It is important to recognize that activities in and of themselves, whether self-initiated or not, do not guarantee children will practice targeted skills or make desired progress toward their individual goals. Likewise, a child's active participation in an event may not lead to positive changes in development unless that activity is designed to address the child's needs. The arbitrary use of activities will likely not produce consistent child change; rather, a structure must be present that directs teams to develop activities that provide ample opportunities for children to practice and learn target goals and objectives.

Lack of specification in IEPs/IFSPs and the need for careful consideration of the type of activities used to address target goals requires that ABI have an underlying structure that directs the work of professional team members and caregivers. The organizational structure of ABI is composed of three major facets that are guided by three associated forms: intervention guides, embedding schedules, and activity plans. These forms are designed to assist team members in the selection of child-initiated, routine, and planned activities and to also ensure that sufficient practice opportunities are consistently available for successful intervention efforts resulting in progress toward targeted goals and objectives.

Intervention guides require teams to consider the major parameters that will direct their intervention efforts. When completed, intervention guides expand the information contained in the IFSP/IEP and ensure that a child's needs are addressed within daily activities. *Embedding schedules* alert teams to when, where, and how target goals can be addressed and ensure that multiple and varied learning opportunities are provided within and across play, daily routines, and planned activities. Finally, *activity plans* present more formal and detailed descriptions of activities planned by adults that can be used to embed multiple opportunities for children to practice their target goals and objectives.

The forms associated with the intervention guide, embedding schedule, and activity plan, or variations of them, provide the necessary organizational structure for ensuring that play, daily routines, and planned activities promote learning of important developmental skills and lead to positive changes in children. Each part of the organizational structure assists teams in moving from the overall guide for intervention (i.e., IFSP/IEP) to the day-to-day practices that will promote learning and development. Specifically, the intervention guide expands on the IFSP/IEP by identifying what to teach, how to teach, where to teach, and how to determine if teaching was effective. Embedding schedules take information from the intervention guide and integrate it into the context of daily activities or routines (e.g., how the team will embed learning opportunities for a target goal during dressing, travel, and meals). Finally, activity plans are a necessary supplement to ensure that multiple and varied learning opportunities are created for children on an ongoing basis.

The three facets of the organizational structure for ABI are described in the following sections. Completed examples of intervention guides, embedding schedules, and activity plans are also provided. The completed forms are designed to illustrate how the organizational structure ensures successful application of an activity-based approach in different service delivery models. Blank intervention guides, embedding schedules, and activity plans are contained in the chapter's appendix and are available for download. Implementers of ABI are encouraged to download, reproduce, and/or modify these forms.

INTERVENTION GUIDES

The first facet of ABI's organizational structure focuses on assisting team members to plan and execute intervention efforts and record child progress. Prior to beginning intervention efforts, the team should complete an intervention guide for each of the child's targeted goals. Intervention guides provide direction for addressing each target goal and for making data-driven decisions. Initially, intervention guides may appear to require considerable effort to complete; however, in practice, teams will discover the benefits of the organization and structure that intervention guides can provide.

Formats for intervention guides can vary but should address the following seven elements:

1. Identifying information

2. Target goals, objectives, and program steps

3. Core standards

4. Antecedents, targeted and nontargeted responses, and feedback or consequences

5. Teaching strategies

6. Monitoring progress

7. Decision rules

The intervention guide contains space for each of these elements. We encourage teams to modify this form to meet the needs of their program, children, and resources.

Identifying Information

This section of the intervention guide provides space for entering the child's name, team members' names, the dates when intervention was initiated on the goal, and when intervention is anticipated for completion. Dates for initiation and anticipated completion help teams devise realistic intervention efforts that are in line with existing resources. The anticipated date for completion will vary depending on the child and the number or type of objectives and program steps associated with a particular goal.

Target Goals, Objectives, and Program Steps

In this section teams can note the target goals and the associated objectives that come directly from a child's IFSP/IEP. Teams can also include program steps in this section. Program steps are simpler or smaller component skills of an objective. (AEPS [Bricker, 2002], for example, contains numerous examples of program steps as possible prerequisites to AEPS goals and objectives.) As discussed in Chapter 12, the development of program steps may be necessary when creating intervention guides for children with moderate to severe disabilities. For example, a program step for the objective of grasping objects might be extending the arm from the body and/or opening the palm. Typically, a separate intervention guide is created for each goal and its associated objectives (and program steps when applicable) that have been targeted for a child.

Core Standards

Federal accountability requirements have driven the need to align intervention efforts with the child's documented needs and subsequent services (IDEA 2004; U.S. Department of Education, n.d.). In the Core Standards section teams should list the state/local/agency standards aligned with a child's target goal, objectives, and program steps. For example, if the skill *Manipulates objects with both hands* is targeted, the team could indicate how this goal addresses or aligns with a state standard.

It is important to note that states and agencies are increasingly developing learning standards for young children that vary greatly in terms of content, organization, and numbers. Although it is beyond the scope of this book to show how various standards align with children's individual goals, teams should become familiar with their state's/program's/agency's standards and ensure that intervention efforts are aligned with broader outcomes for all children.

Antecedents, Targeted and Nontargeted Responses, and Feedback or Consequences

This section of the intervention guide is divided into three columns: antecedents, targeted and nontargeted responses, and feedback or consequences. These columns can be used to enter potential antecedents for the goal, objectives, and program steps; the expected targeted and nontargeted responses; and likely or recommended feedback or consequences following the child's response.

At the heart of ensuring multiple and varied learning opportunities is the selection of antecedents appropriate for the individual child. Antecedents refer to any event, action, or condition designed or selected to occur with the intent of providing learning opportunities. Adults (e.g., teachers, parents, caregivers, therapists), peers/siblings, or the physical environment (e.g., object, event, picture/sign/word) can serve as antecedents. At times, antecedents may also originate from within the child (e.g., hunger, interest in a toy). Antecedents range from simple (e.g., teacher provides hand-over-hand physical assistance, model of target skill) to more complex (e.g., progressive time delay, mand-model), and from nondirective (e.g., placing a toy out of reach) to directive (e.g., making a request, giving a direction). Multiple antecedents should be selected and used for each target goal (and associated objectives and program steps) and listed in the first column of this section. The purpose of noting antecedents on the intervention guide is to ensure that team members provide relevant and appropriate, as well as multiple and varied, learning opportunities consistently across daily activities.

The second column provides space for listing potential targeted and nontargeted responses. Targeted responses are specific skills associated with the goal (or objective or program step), whereas nontargeted responses refer to other potential responses that might occur following an antecedent but are not related directly to the goal, objective, or program step. For example, a teacher asks Arlo to take off his coat. Targeted responses may include taking off the coat or asking the teacher for help. Nontargeted responses may include no response from Arlo or his walking away without taking off the coat. It is important to consider both targeted and nontargeted child responses so that timely and integral feedback or consequences can be provided for all child responses (i.e., encouraging target behaviors to occur again or consistently and diminishing the occurrence of nontargeted behaviors).

The third column provides space for listing feedback and consequences that can follow the child's targeted or nontargeted response. Feedback or consequences can include adult (e.g., teacher, parent, caregiver, therapist) behaviors; peer/sibling behaviors; and/or physical environmental objects, events, pictures, signs, or words that support a child's responses (e.g., smiles, affirmations, getting needs or wants met). As discussed in Chapter 4, feedback and consequences should be timely and integral. Timeliness is important so that children can discern the relationship between their responses and subsequent consequences. In addition, there should be a logical or inherent relationship between the feedback or consequence and the outcome of the activity, action, or child's response (i.e., integral). Noting the type of feedback or consequence on the intervention guide for both targeted and nontargeted behaviors is important to ensure that team members are delivering consistent messages to the child.

Teaching Strategies

In this section of the intervention guide, teams can indicate the type of teaching strategies a child may require to participate in or benefit from interactions during daily routines, play, or planned activities. It is important that teams discuss and track the impact of different strategies on promoting children's practice, acquisition, and use of target skills. The intervention guide provides a means of team communication regarding strategies that may be effective and that can be used across activities.

ABI is designed for use with a variety of teaching strategies and relies heavily on the use of nondirective strategies. Although the use of massed trials and drills is not incompatible with ABI, this approach recommends interventionists and caregivers use, to the extent possible, intervention strategies that are responsive to a child's initiations and are compatible with daily routines and meaningful planned activities. The following sections provide brief descriptions of thirteen recommended teaching strategies. In addition to these strategies, team members may include other teaching ideas or modifications of the listed strategies in this section of the guide.

Forgetting   Interventionists and caregivers can use the strategy of forgetting to encourage action and problem solving by children. It can be an effective strategy for determining what children know and can do. Forgetting can occur when the adult fails to provide the necessary equipment or materials or overlooks a familiar or important component of a routine or activity. Examples include not having peanut butter available for making peanut butter and jelly sandwiches at snack time, not having paintbrushes available for a painting activity, or not recalling a word or phrase to a familiar story or song. When forgetting occurs, children should recognize the missing element and convey this information by asking questions, searching for materials, or engaging in other appropriate problem-solving actions.

Novelty   Children are generally enticed by new toys or activities. The careful introduction of novelty may stimulate desirable reactions from children. For infants and children with severe disabilities, this strategy may be more effective if the novelty is introduced within the context of a routine or familiar activity; for example, a new action or change in words could be added to a familiar song or game such as Duck, Duck, Goose. The game could be slightly altered by changing the words to Cat, Cat, Mouse. For older or more capable children, examples might include relocating activity centers to a new area of the room, bringing in a classroom pet, taking a new path from the bus to the classroom, or adding laminated shapes on the floor where children line up for transitions. For most infants and young children, the introduction of novelty is most effective if the change is not dramatically discrepant from their expectations. For example, adding new materials to a sensory table is an example of novelty that may stimulate children to respond and practice targeted goals.

Visible but Unreachable   Placing objects within children's sight but out of their reach is a strategy that requires simple environmental manipulation. Using this strategy can facilitate the development of social, communication, and problem-solving behaviors. Families often use this strategy by accident. For example, they may place a favorite food such as cookies or a favorite toy such as a talking doll on a shelf out of reach, which may motivate children to figure out how to obtain the food item or object. When using this strategy, it is important that the child is able to see the object and that a peer or adult is available to retrieve the object unless independent problem solving is the goal. Also, it is imperative that the child is in no danger in his or her pursuit of a desired out of reach object.

Placing objects out of reach is often an effective strategy to use with children who are learning early communication skills. A simple strategy that a team can use during mealtime in the classroom is to place food items in the center of the table before or after a serving is provided. Placement of foods in the center of the table before serving them allows the adult to name the items and wait for children to request them. Returning foods to the center of the table after one serving also allows children to see and request more of the food item.

Change in Expectations   Omitting or changing a familiar step or element in a well-practiced or routine activity is a strategy known as change in expectations. Many changes may appear comical to children. For example, an adult who tries to draw or write with an upside-down pencil using the eraser as the writing end may seem silly. The purpose of a change in expectations such as this is twofold: 1) children's recognition of change provides information about their discrimination and memory abilities, and 2) such changes provide ideal situations for evoking a variety of communication and problem-solving responses (e.g., the child verbalizes a protest, the child turns the pencil so that the pointed end is down). Children with severe disabilities can often recognize changes, such as putting a mitten on a foot, and communicate this recognition. Alert team members can often shape these communicative responses into functional behaviors.

Piece by Piece   Piece by piece is another easy-to-execute nondirective intervention strategy that can be used when activities require materials with many pieces. The interventionist can ration access to a multipiece project by retaining pieces so that the child must request materials repeatedly, piece by piece. For example, when working on a puzzle, pieces can be handed out as a child asks for them. Labeling the piece or action can be encouraged or required. This strategy may be used effectively when children use paint, glue, paper, crayons, blocks, or other small items. Meals with foods such as cereal, raisins, or fruit or vegetable slices/pieces also present opportunities for employing this strategy.

Team members should be alert, however, to the introduction of too many disruptions at the expense of participation in a desirable and useful activity. For example, having a child request each puzzle piece may interrupt the continuity of the activity and interfere with its being meaningful for the child. The interventionist should balance providing opportunities to practice skills with the child's needs to become actively and genuinely involved in an activity.

Assistance   Assistance is an effective strategy for teams to consider using. To get materials or to perform some part of the activity, the child will need some form of assistance from an adult or peer. The strategy of requesting assistance can be effective in the development of a range of skills in adaptive, fine motor, gross motor, and communication areas. For example, placing materials in a clear container with a lid the child cannot remove sets the stage for the child to seek assistance. Once the child has asked for help or presented the container to someone with an expectant look or request for help, the lid is loosened. The child can then practice grasping the lid and rotating his or her other wrist to complete the opening of the container and retrieve the material. Other examples include 1) wind-up toys that require an adult to start each time they cease their action; 2) tightening faucet knobs so that children must ask for assistance to turn them; 3) adding new dress-up clothes and accessories (e.g., purses, wallets) that have buttons, snaps, and laces that are too difficult for children to open.

Interruption or Delay   Interruption requires that a member of the team stop the child from continuing a chain of behaviors. For example, during a tooth-brushing routine, the caregiver interrupts the child when he or she starts to put toothpaste on the toothbrush. The caregiver holds the tube of toothpaste and asks, "What do you need?" The child will have to indicate what he or she needs to complete the behavior chain. This strategy has been effective with individuals with severe disabilities (Carter & Gurnsell, 2001; Roberts-Pennell & Sigafoos, 1999; Romer, Cullinan, & Schoenberg, 1994).

The delay strategy introduces a pause or short delay in an activity in order to prompt a response from the child. For example, an adult who is teaching a child to imitate a word may pause after saying the word and wait for the child to imitate the word. Delaying fits easily into many activities, and time delay has been shown to be effective in increasing the initiation of requests by children (e.g., Albert, Carbone, Murray, Hagerty, & Sweeney-Kerwin, 2012; Daugherty, Grisham-Brown, & Hemmeter, 2001; Schuster & Morse, 1998; Wolery, 1992; Wolery, Anthony, Caldwell, Snyder, & Morgante, 2002).

Physical Model   Using a physical model can provide an effective visual example for a child to imitate a targeted skill. This strategy capitalizes on children imitating a skill or behavior they observe someone else using. For this strategy to be effective the child must attend to or focus on the individual providing the physical model. For example, at the writing table the teacher sits beside Sean and models how to write a letter of his name. The teacher keeps the writing surface in front of both her and Sean so that the model is performed exactly as Sean will practice it. This strategy may be especially effective and reinforcing if the child observes a peer modeling a target behavior and then imitates it. For example, during snack Samuel observes a peer, Julia, opening the top of the pitcher and pouring juice in her glass without help. When Samuel obtains the pitcher he imitates the same skills used by Julia and pours his own juice without assistance.

Verbal Model   The verbal model is also called a mand model. This strategy requires the child's focused attention. The adult can ask the child a question requiring a short verbal response or request the child to respond verbally, then wait for a response. If the child does not produce the target behavior the teacher verbally models the target behavior for the child to imitate. For example, during circle/music time the teacher presents three cards illustrating three songs and asks Cheyenne which song she would like to sing. Cheyenne points to the card with the bumble bee without saying anything. The teacher asks, "What song is that?" When Cheyenne does not answer the teacher says, "Bumble Bee" and pauses to let Cheyenne imitate the response.

Self-Talk and Parallel Talk   Self-talk and parallel talk are related and similar strategies to support young children's language development. The essential element of these two strategies is the narration of actions. Self-talk can be used by the teacher or parent to talk about or describe what they are doing, seeing, eating, touching, or thinking in the presence of the child. If it is used in a routine such as changing a diaper, the caregiver narrates the routine as it occurs. For example, as the caregiver changes Elena's diaper she talks to her about what they are doing together: "Oh, yes, this diaper is wet and needs to come off. Let's take this wet one off and find you a dry one!" Self-talk can be used during a range of activities. A teacher could describe some of her actions during a play activity to a target child. For example, "I'm making a bridge. Here goes my car over the bridge."

Parallel talk, also uses narration. However, in parallel talk the adult provides the narrative of the child's actions as they occur; what he is doing, seeing, eating, or touching. For example, as Gabe plays with rubber stamps and makes colorful designs on paper, the teacher could say, "You picked the shell stamp with green and blue ink, and you are stamping it on yellow paper. What a great design, beautiful!"

Prompt Imitation   A prompt is defined as a hint or cue used to elicit a target behavior. The prompt imitation strategy provides both a cue and a model to be imitated by the child. This strategy is most often used to support children's language acquisition, and to be used successfully it is critical that the prompt relates to something on which the child is already focused. For example, in using a prompt imitation strategy to encourage a child's use of the word cracker, the teacher would wait until the child is focused on the crackers, wanting more, and tell the child, "Say 'more cracker.'"

Expansion or Restatement   This combination of similar strategies is used when children are beginning to communicate with spoken language. The strategies capitalize on the child's current use of language, reinforcing and supporting his or her efforts in two ways: 1) as an expansion that enhances the child's comment with additional description, or 2) as a restatement of the child's comment using a correction in the statement. Using expansion, for example, upon hearing Charlotte correctly identify a "doggie," the caregiver replies, "Yes, it's a big doggie" providing additional description about the doggie. In a restatement example, upon hearing Herbie describe his friend's cookie acquisition, saying, "He got cookies!" the teacher would answer, repeat, and correct Herbie's comment to, "Yes, he has cookies."

Directions   Providing directions is a strategy frequently used and consists of offering simple suggestions to a child that helps expand or extend the content of self-directed activities. The strategy is useful in presenting new ideas that the child can incorporate into play or work without interrupting or derailing the activity. The direction strategy can also be used to provide opportunities for children to practice targeted skills. Directions should be compatible with the play context, related to the child's interests, and directly linked to the current activity while adding to the play. For example, the teacher joins Carmel and Maddie as they play with baby dolls. Thus far the baby dolls are eating, crying, and being held. The teacher says to the girls, "The babies are tired. Can you put your babies in the bed?" Using a targeted skill, for example, if a child is learning the concept under, the teacher might suggest that the girls put the babies under the blankets.

Two points should be emphasized when using these and similar teaching strategies. First, as discussed previously, children's goals should guide teams. The strategies should be used only when they assist in helping children reach their targeted goals. Employing these strategies without careful integration with a child's overall plan contained in the intervention guide will likely yield unsatisfactory outcomes. Second, teaching strategies should be used in a thoughtful and sensitive manner. The overuse of any strategy may produce an undesired outcome. For example, if interruptions or delays are overused, children may experience frustration that leads to lost interest or the onset of an emotional outburst. ABI encourages the use of these strategies with careful monitoring of their effectiveness.

Monitoring Progress

This section of the intervention guide provides space for entering information on monitoring progress procedures including who should collect the data and where, when, and how it should be collected. To begin, teams should decide who is going to collect data on the target goal (or objective or program step). Next, teams should decide where to collect data (i.e., in which settings or during which activities). For example, will data be collected at home or at the center? If necessary, the team may want to specify the activity during which data will be collected. For example, data may be collected in the classroom during snack, circle time or small learning group activities, or outside on the playground. Once the location is selected, teams should determine when to collect data based on the criteria portion of the child's goals, objectives, and program steps. When to collect data includes how often the data will be collected (e.g., daily, weekly, monthly) and/or the specific days. Finally, teams should discuss how to monitor progress on the child's goal, objective, and/or program step. Three general methods are available for teams to use when monitoring progress: written descriptions, permanent records, and counts or tallies.

Decision Rules

The final section on the intervention guides provides space for entering decision rules associated with monitoring child progress. Having such rules is necessary to ensure that children are making adequate progress toward target goals (Bricker, 2002; Miller & Chapman, 1980; Romski & Sevcik, 2005). When children are not making expected progress, teams should consider changing 1) targeted goals; 2) antecedents and/or feedback/consequences; 3) teaching strategies; and 4) frequency, type and/or locations of learning opportunities provided. A section is also provided on the form for other changes that don't fit into one of the above categories. Depending on the team's decision, the change or changes to be made can be indicated on the form.

The development of quality intervention guides requires thought and time; consequently, making their development efficient is important for most teams. Team members can adopt several strategies that make the creation of intervention guides efficient. For example, when children have similar target goals, the same or a slightly modified intervention guide can be used with multiple children. If minor to moderate variations are required for children, the team may be able to use portions of an intervention guide for several children. For example, two children may have the same goal, but the antecedents, consequences, or evaluation procedures will be individualized for each child. We recommend downloading the intervention guide form so it can be completed electronically. Previously developed intervention guides can then be used as prototypes, and general information can be transferred electronically to new intervention guides.

As noted, the main purpose of an intervention guide is to bridge the gap between the goal development process and the intervention process. Because IFSPs/IEPs are not treatment or intervention plans, it is important for teams to add a step of creating intervention guides. Figures 6.1 and 6.2 offer examples of completed intervention guides. Figure 6.1 provides an example of a completed intervention guide for 2-year-old Karis Cumberbatch. The goal of walking independently is addressed in the intervention guide. Each section is completed for this target goal.

Figure 6.2 provides a completed intervention guide for Leo Riesa. His IEP goal is using a variety of two- and three-word phrases. Specifically, how the target goal aligns with standards for preschoolers is addressed, as are the individualized interventions, ongoing monitoring procedures, and decision rules.

As we have emphasized, intervention guides are important to the successful implementation of an activity-based approach because they provide the structure to assist teams in planning the specific intervention necessary to promote children's progress toward targeted goals, objectives, and program steps. Once intervention guides are completed for each priority goal, the team is ready to develop embedding schedules for addressing target goals during a variety of daily activities.

EMBEDDING SCHEDULES

The second facet of ABI's organizational structure focuses on assisting team members embed practice opportunities into daily activities to ensure that children have ample time to address their priority goals. Given that ABI is designed to use play, child-initiations, daily routines, and planned activities as major teaching vehicles, it is critically important that these activities be used to offer children repeated and appropriate learning opportunities. We have discovered that without careful planning children are not given adequate opportunities to practice targeted skills, and many ideal teaching moments are missed. Embedding schedules are designed to assist team members in identifying learning opportunities and highlighting possible practice opportunities throughout the day.

Embedding schedules should be designed to meet the needs of the program, children, setting, and available resources—this may mean significant variation in embedding schedule formats. However, in most cases embedding schedules will need to address at least two dimensions: focus (i.e., individual or groups of children) and setting (i.e., home or center), as well as indicating when potential practice opportunities may occur.

Regardless of the setting for which the schedule is created (e.g., home, school, community), the focus (i.e., number of children), or the information to be included on the form, embedding schedules should contain identifying information regarding the child or children's names, team members responsible for embedding learning opportunities, and the dates the schedule will

---

ABI Intervention Guide

1. Identifying information

Child's name: Karis Cumberbatch

Team members: Parents, Early Head Start teacher, early intervention specialist, and physical therapist

Date intervention initiated: September 2013   Date intervention completed: May 2014

2. Target goal, objectives, and program steps

Goal:

1.0   At home, at school, and in the community, Karis will walk independently for 15 feet across three different surfaces (e.g., grass, carpet, tile), each day for 1 week.

Objectives:

1.1   At home, at school, and in the community, Karis will walk with one hand support for 15 feet across two different surfaces (e.g., grass, carpet, tile), each day for 2 weeks.
1.2   At home, school, and in the community, Karis will move around by holding onto furniture or other stationary objects. She will move her feet, taking at least two steps in any direction, three times a day for 2 weeks.

Program steps:

1.3.1   At home, school, and in the community, Karis will pull herself up from a squatting position to a standing position two times a day for 2 weeks.

---

3. Core standards

Develops motor control and balance for a range of physical activities, such as walking, rolling a wheelchair or mobility device, skipping, running, climbing, and hopping.

Figure 6.1.   Completed ABI Intervention Guide for targeted goal of walking independently.

(continued)

Figure 6.1.   *(continued)*

ABI Intervention Guide *(continued)*

4. Antecedents, targeted and nontargeted responses, and feedback or consequences

Antecedents designed to provide learning opportunities	List of possible child responses: targeted (+) and nontargeted (-)	Feedback or consequences
Program step 1.3.1: Provide physical assistance by placing hands on her trunk. Caregiver sitting above Karis pats her knees and says, "Come see Mama!" Place desired toy/object in visible but out of reach position above her.	Pulls to a stand. (+) Remains sitting. (-)	Provide praise and smiles. (+) She gets to sit on caregiver's lap. (+) She gets the toy/object wanted. (+) Wait a few seconds and then encourage Karis to try again. (-)
Objective 1.2: Place interesting objects out of reach, at standing shoulder height. Caregiver sits 6–10" away from where Karis is standing.	Holds onto furniture or stationary objects and takes two or more steps in the direction of the object. (+) Reaches for and takes two steps toward caregiver. (+) Points to desired object. (-) Crawls toward object. (-)	Gets object or toy. (+) Moves closer to caregiver. (+) Adult prompts/encourages Karis to walk to get the toy. (-)
Objective 1.1: Provide verbal cue (e.g., "Let's go see Dad," or "Let's go outside") and one-hand assistance. As Karis stands, offer her a hand so she can control the direction of her walking.	Takes steps holding an adult's or peer's hand for support. (+) Sits down and wants to be picked up. (-) Uses two hands for support. (-) Stays where she is and continues playing. (-)	Adult or peer encourages her to take additional steps. (+) Receives praise from Dad. (+) Plays outside. (+) Takes additional steps, and adult tries to remove hand for support. (-) Encourage Karis to walk again later. (-)
Goal 1.0: Provide verbal cue (e.g., "Should we check out the swings over there?" or "Where did you leave your book? Can you find it?").	Karis walks independently, at least 15 feet, to get to the playground swings. (+) Karis walks independently, at least 15 feet, getting her book and bringing it back. (+) Karis waits without movement. (-)	She gets to the swing and caregiver helps her to get in it. (+) She finds the book and caregiver reads it to her. (+) Caregiver waits a little while then makes the suggestion again. (-)

5. Teaching strategies

- Show Karis which furniture or stationary objects she can use for support (physical modeling strategy).
- Integrate therapeutic exercise techniques into daily activities to improve Karis's joint range of motion (including continuous passive motion), increase her strength and endurance (isotonic and isometric), and improve her balance and coordination.
- Include Karis in small-group play with peers with more advanced walking skills.

ABI Intervention Guide *(continued)*   *page 3 of 3*

6. Monitoring progress

Who (person responsible for collecting the data)	Where (which activities or locations)	When (how often or on which days)	How (which methods)
Early Head Start teacher	During classroom transitions (e.g., from outside to inside, from carpet area to tile in snack area)	Daily (Monday through Friday)	Probe
Physical therapist	During classroom transitions	Weekly (Mondays and Wednesdays)	Probe
Early intervention specialist and parents	Home and at Grandma's house	Weekly home visit and weekends	Probe

7. Decision rules

If adequate progress does not occur in _____2 weeks_____ (specify time frame for when the team will review the data), consider changing:

___X___ Targeted goal

___X___ Antecedents or feedback/consequences

_____ Teaching strategies

_____ Frequency, type, and/or locations of learning opportunities provided

_____ Other (describe) _____

_____

_____

ABI Intervention Guide

1. Identifying information

Child's name: Leo Reisa

Team members: Teacher: Mary Lynn; speech-language pathologist: Jeanetta; parents: Carlos and Isabel Reisa

Date intervention initiated: September 2013   Date intervention completed: September 2014

2. Target goal, objectives, and program steps

Goal:

1.0   Using a variety of two and three words, Leo will request objects, people, or materials three times a day, inform others three times a day, and greet others two times a day, for 2 weeks.

Objectives:

1.1   Using a variety of two and three words, Leo will request objects, people, or materials from others (adults or peers) three times a day for 2 weeks.
1.2   Using a variety of two and three words, Leo will inform others (adults or peers) about daily activities three times a day for 2 weeks.

Program steps:

1.3   Using a variety of two and three words, Leo will say greetings/goodbyes to others (adults or peers) two times a day for 2 weeks.

3. Core standards

- Engages in communication and conversation with others.
- Uses language to express ideas and needs.
- Uses increasingly complex and varied vocabulary.
- Uses different forms of language.
- Uses different grammatical structures for a variety of purposes.
- Engages in storytelling.
- Engages in conversations with peers and adults.

Figure 6.2.   Completed ABI Intervention Guide for goal of using a variety of two- and three-word phrases.

ABI Intervention Guide *(continued)*

4. Antecedents, targeted and nontargeted responses, and feedback or consequences

Antecedents designed to provide learning opportunities	List of possible child responses: targeted (+) and nontargeted (-)	Feedback or consequences
Objective 1.3: Provide verbal prompt (e.g., "Tell Sadie Good Morning"). Prompt turn taking (e.g., "Your turn to greet your friend"). Provide verbal prompt (e.g., "Tell your friends goodbye").	Leo says, "Hi Sadie." (+) Leo says, "I'm Leo." (+) Leo says, "See you tomorrow." (+) Leo says, "Bye." (-)	Leo's friend, Sadie, says, "Hi Leo." (+) Leo's friend says, "I'm Garth." (+) Leo's friends say goodbye to him. (+) Ask Leo what he would like to say to his friends. (-) Model using greeting/goodbye to other children. "Bye, Sadie." (-)
Objective 1.2: Ask Leo to tell about what he is doing or what he is playing.	Uses 2–3 words to describe his activity. (+) Uses a single word. (-)	Use and expand Leo's comment to follow up or respond indicating he was understood. (+) Model two- or three-word utterance. (-)
Objective 1.1: Model request (e.g., "More juice please"). Ask Leo, "Is there something else you would like? Tell me."	Uses two- or three-word utterances to make a request for more juice. (+) Asks if there are any cheese and crackers left. (+) Asks, "Juice?" (-)	Comment on what he is doing. (+) Other children respond to his request. (+) Provide or fulfill request. (+) Model two- or three-word utterance. (-)
Goal 1: Say, "Leo, tell me three things you would like for snack today." Ask, "Who are the members of your family?" Say, "Today Leo is our announcer. He will tell the class when it is time to clean up and go to another activity."	Leo says, "Juice, crackers, and cheese." (+) Leo names his Papa, Mama, and dog, Pepe. (+) Leo announces to the class "Clean up." (-)	Leo gets juice, crackers, and cheese for snack. (+) Leo participates in a social interaction with others. (+) Caregiver whispers to Leo, "Say time to clean up." (-)

5. Teaching strategies

- In favorite activities include peers who can provide two- to three-word models.
- Use milieu language strategies including incidental teaching, mand-model, and time delay.
- Use nondirected strategies such as visible but unreachable and piece by piece.
- Use a variety of buddy activities.
- Provide "snack talk" topics.
- Select "favorite topics" conversation starters.

(continued)

Figure 6.2.   *(continued)*

ABI Intervention Guide *(continued)*

6. Monitoring progress

Who (person responsible for collecting the data)	Where (which activities or locations)	When (how often or on which days)	How (which methods)
Teacher, Mary Lynn	Snack, outside time, and free play	Mondays, Wednesdays, and Fridays	Probes
Speech-language pathologist, Jeanetta	Circle time and small group time	Monthly	Language sample

7. Decision rules

If adequate progress does not occur in _____2 weeks_____ (specify time frame for when the team will review the data), consider changing:

_____ Targeted goal

__X__ Antecedents or feedback/consequences

_____ Teaching strategies

__X__ Frequency, type, and/or locations of learning opportunities provided

_____ Other (describe) _____

_____

_____

be used. Once the identifying information has been noted, the team can create the embedding schedule, which usually consists of a simple grid or series of rows and columns that can be used and reused as children's target goals and teaching strategies change.

Teams should transfer selected information from the intervention guide (i.e., target goals, objectives, and/or program steps), as appropriate, onto the embedding form. Embedding schedules are usually created with the child or children's goals listed across the top of the schedule and the sequence of daily activities listed down the left hand column. After the grid is created, teams determine what information to place in the intersect boxes. For example, if a child's target goal is *Manipulate objects with both hands,* that would be entered on the form under the target goal. The team would then select antecedents (e.g., placing objects to be manipulated within the child's reach, prompting the child to manipulate objects, modeling how to manipulate objects) and feedback or consequences (e.g., access to the object) appropriate to the child's activities across the day and enter the information in the intersect boxes. When deciding which activity to use as the context for embedding learning opportunities, teams should consider which activities can provide authentic situations for the child to practice/perform target goals (e.g., arrival, snack, art, discovery table). Therefore, in this example, the antecedent *Model how to manipulate objects* could occur at arrival as peers and adults model how to unzip coats and backpacks.

For illustration, three types of embedding schedules are presented in this chapter. The first was developed for an individual child in the home setting. The second was created for a group of children in a center-based program. The third was written for two children in learning centers.

Figure 6.3 provides an example of an embedding schedule for Maddox, a child receiving home-based services, and highlights when learning opportunities can be embedded across different daily routines. The schedule provides multiple appropriate and varied antecedent examples to help Maddox practice his targeted goals. Using the grid permits the antecedent examples within the intersect boxes to serve as visual reminders of where and when learning opportunities can be embedded. Teams are encouraged to discuss with caregivers which routines offer the best opportunities for addressing children's target goals in the home. In this example, the family identified the routines of dressing, eating, playing, traveling, and bathing as times when learning opportunities could be provided to address Maddox's target goals of using two-word utterances and using objects as intended or designed.

The embedding schedule contained in Figure 6.4 is designed for multiple children. This embedding schedule notes when learning opportunities can be embedded across daily classroom activities for three children—Leo Reisa (see Figure 6.2 for his completed intervention guide), Quinn, and Akeelah—who attend a center-based program. The children have multiple target goals, and this variation of the embedding schedule allows the team to identify

ABI Embedding Schedule

Focus: Individual **Setting:** Home

page 1 of 2

Child's name: Maddox

Team members: Parents: Ginny and John; early intervention specialist: Jean; speech-language pathologist: Pattie

Dates schedule will be used: October 2014

Routine	Target goal	Target goal
	Maddox will use two-word utterances to describe or express possession and negation.	Maddox will use objects as intended or designed.
Dressing	Ask Maddox questions about his clothes related to possession, or ask nonsense questions that he can negate because they are wrong. Give him opportunities to verbalize choices and decisions in dressing routines or clothes choices.	
Eating	Give Maddox choices that require putting words together (e.g., "More milk, more spaghetti?" "Are you still eating or all done?"). Use strategies that require him to claim possession or negate something out of place.	Provide Maddox with dining utensils, a plate/bowl, and a cup for liquids. Adults model the appropriate use of objects.

Figure 6.3. Completed ABI Embedding Schedule for an individual child in a home setting.

ABI Embedding Schedule *(continued)* **Focus:** Individual **Setting:** Home   *page 2 of 2*

Routine	Target goal	Target goal
	Maddox will use two-word utterances to describe or express possession and negation.	Maddox will use objects as intended or designed.
Playing	Give Maddox choices of games or activities to play (e.g., "We can play Hide and Seek or Treasure Hunt, you choose"), or select a game/activity he does not like and won't play, giving him the opportunity to decline.	Provide objects used in specific play activities (e.g., shovel and bucket with sand play, balls and croquet mallets). Adult/peer/sibling models the appropriate use of objects.
Traveling	Plan activities or games during travel that can involve the environment outside or inside the travel vehicle (e.g., colors of vehicles, trains, signs, cards) with rules; need to use your name before naming colors (e.g., "Maddox sees blue").	
Bathing		Introduce bath toys one at a time, making sure Maddox is using the toy for its intended purpose (adult model) before a new toy appears.

ABI Embedding Schedule

Focus: Group   **Setting:** Classroom

Children's names: Leo Reisa, Quinn Brewster, Akeelah Belle

Team members: Parents: Leeza and Leo Sr.; ECSE teacher: Ramona; speech-language pathologist: Jean

Dates schedule will be used: September 2014

Daily classroom activities and opportunities for practice

Children and target skills	Arrival	Circle activities/music	Free play	Snack	Art and discovery	Outside play
Child's name: Leo						
1. Uses two- and three-word utterances to request objects, people, or materials from others.		When it is Leo's turn to choose he can select by naming song and instruments.	Provide puzzles for Leo to work on and ask him to describe the pieces and say where they belong.	Give Leo small portions of everything. He can use his words to ask for more (e.g., "more juice," "I want more").	While reading a book ask Leo to describe or tell the story.	
2. Shares or exchanges objects.	Ask Leo to show a classmate a toy or favorite object from home that they can play with together.		Pair Leo with a classmate who also likes to build. Suggest they build something together.		Pair Leo with child who has slightly more advanced social skills as they play together with water and things that float.	
3. Demonstrates understanding of size concepts.		Introduce water music with different sized jars and tools to tap. Leo can work with class to name and fill containers based on size.		Snack can offer a variety of foods of different sizes (e.g., crackers, cookies, fruit sections). Snack talk conversations between children can discuss sizes of food items.	Leo plays with blocks of a variety of sizes. Adult can play with him and ask for only short blocks for a job. At clean up Leo can verbally label each size as he puts them away.	

Figure 6.4.   Completed ABI Embedding Schedule for multiple children in a center-based setting.

Daily classroom activities and opportunities for practice

Child's name: Quinn				
1. Initiates toileting.	As Quinn arrives to class ask him if he needs to use the toilet.	As children transition to snack they can get in line to go to the bathroom.		As Quinn comes inside after play he can be reminded to use the toilet.
2. Demonstrates understanding of color concepts.		Read books about colors with Quinn. As colors are identified Quinn can match them with his or classmate's clothes.	After snack as Quinn brushes his teeth he can name all the toothbrush colors of his classmates.	During art have play dough and LEGOs accessible. Quinn can sort, build, and put away by colors.
3. Uses two- and three-word utterances to request objects, people, or materials from others.	As Quinn arrives ask him to name something he wants to do and who he would like to play with.	As Quinn and Leo play with puzzles and shape sorters they can tell each other about the pieces and shapes and where they belong.		As Quinn plays beach party with two other children he can name the toys found and the classmate who found it.

Child's name: Akeelah				
1. Walks with walker at least 15 feet.	At transition to circle, offer Akeelah walker and wait for her to transition to circle.	During buddy dance party ask Akeelah who she would like to dance with. Encourage her participation in dancing.	At transition to snack offer Akeelah her walker and wait for her to transition to the snack table.	Offer Akeelah choices for the activity she wants to participate in (e.g., beach party, grocery store). Wait for her to make her choice.	Plan activities that support Akeelah's participation and use of her walker (e.g., Bear Hunt, Red Rover).
2. Uses words to request objects.		Ask Akeelah to choose and name a song she wants to sing.	Arrange materials with integral pieces missing to encourage Akeelah to request them.	Make sure Akeelah gets small portions of snack food so she can request more of the food items.	Show Akeelah the art activity choices, and ask her to name the items she wants to use.

which daily classroom activities provide the best opportunities to address each child's target skills. In Figure 6.4, the daily classroom activities are listed across the top row of the page, with the children's names and target skills listed in the lefthand side column. This form lists the daily schedule for the classroom, and it lists multiple children with multiple targeted skills for each child. Each target skill listed can be linked to provide learning opportunities with any of the daily activities, and each target behavior linked with a daily activity lists at least one antecedent to help team members provide embedded learning opportunities to practice target skills.

Figure 6.5 is an embedding schedule that illustrates how the individual goals of two children, Lupita and Cooper, can be addressed (i.e., embedded) across three classroom learning centers (e.g., housekeeping, book corner, art and discovery). Additional variations and procedures for creating embedding schedules (also called *activity schedules* or *activity matrices*) are found throughout the literature (e.g., Grisham-Brown, Hemmeter, & Pretti-Frontczak, 2005; Raver, 2003; Sandall & Schwartz, 2008).

The creation of embedding schedules should not preclude variations and spontaneity in the type and sequence of activities used for intervention. If, for example, children introduce a change, or an unplanned event occurs that can be used to foster development of target goals and objectives, then team members should not be reluctant to deviate from the schedule. When developing and using embedding schedules, it is critical that all team members be familiar with children's target goals. Knowledge of target goals allows interventionists to follow children's leads and interests, even when these actions deviate from planned events, to ensure multiple practice opportunities. Teams implementing ABI are encouraged to experiment with the embedding schedule forms and adapt them to fit their needs.

The appendix to this chapter contains blank examples of each type of embedding schedule form, and blank versions are also available for download. As with intervention guides, we encourage teams to modify the forms to meet their program, children, setting, and resource needs.

ACTIVITY PLANS

The third facet of ABI's organizational structure is the use of activity plans. Activity plans represent a more formal mechanism for ensuring that antecedents and consequences related to target goals are embedded within activities in order to maximize learning experiences. Activity plans are created for routine (e.g., snack, dressing, bathing) and planned events (i.e., designed events that require adult planning, preparation, and guidance). Planned activities can include taking field trips, completing art or science projects, preparing special recipes, and participating in circle time events.

Activity plans are more generally and frequently created for children receiving services in community-based or center-based programs that include groups of children. However, planned activities can also be created

ABI Embedding Schedule

Focus: Group   **Setting:** Learning centers   *page 1 of 2*

Child's name: _____ Lupita and Cooper _____

Team members: _____ Speech-language pathologist and occupational therapist _____

Dates schedule will be used: _____ Mondays and Thursdays _____

Routine	Target goal	Target goal
Classroom centers	Lupita Uses word phrases and sentences to inform, direct, and greet/depart	Cooper Uses two hands to manipulate objects, toys, and materials
Housekeeping	Tells others (adults or peers) about her play in the housekeeping area, or greets/ says "goodbye" to peers as they enter/ leave the center.	Holds container with one hand and something to stir with the other; or he can button or zip clothing on self or baby dolls.
Book corner	Tells others (adults or peers) about what she is reading and tells who the main characters are.	Practices holding books/magazines with one hand and turning the pages with the other hand.

Figure 6.5.   Completed ABI Embedding Schedule for multiple children across learning centers.

(continued)

Figure 6.5. *(continued)*

ABI Embedding Schedule *(continued)* **Focus:** Group	**Setting:** Learning centers	*page 2 of 2*
Routine	**Target goal**	**Target goal**
Classroom centers	Lupita Uses word phrases and sentences to inform, direct, and greet/depart	Cooper Uses two hands to manipulate objects, toys, and materials
Art and discovery	Asks the teacher to look at her artwork or to help obtain desired materials/objects. Tells the teacher when she is finished and ready to clean up and try something else.	Paints at the easel and holds the paint in one hand while using the paintbrush with the other. Pours different liquids from one container to another at the discovery table.

for children receiving home-based services. Whether used in a center or at home, activity plans should be helpful in identifying increased opportunities to practice target behaviors not typically used in a routine or to give caregivers increased examples of language they can use to engage their child.

Activity plans benefit teams in at least two ways. First, a team that plans activities may discover opportunities to address children's target skills that were not obvious or apparent prior to the planning. Second, teams may enhance their cooperation, collaboration, and use of limited resources. The activity plan form we recommend contains seven sections: 1) activity name, 2) materials, 3) environmental arrangement, 4) sequence of steps, 5) embedded learning opportunities, 6) planned variations, and 7) other. The last section provides space for noting supplemental parameters that may be important to the targeted skills such as vocabulary or peer interactions. It should be emphasized that all sections do not have to be completed for every activity plan. For some children the team may find every element useful in planning to carry out an activity, based on the children, their characteristics, other group members, the environment, the activity's purpose, and so forth. For others, teams will find they do not need the same depth or detail and will select fewer elements needed to carry out the activity. Activity plans developed for home-based services frequently may not need to address each of the seven sections.

Activity Name

The name of the activity should be noted on each plan (e.g., blocks, dinosaur eggs, butterfly blot prints, puzzles, meals, pet store). Ideas for activities can be selected from curricula or curricular guides—such as the AEPS (Bricker, 2002); The Carolina Curriculum for Infants and Toddlers with Special Needs (Johnson-Martin, Attermeier, & Hacker, 2004a) and the Carolina Curriculum for Preschoolers with Special Needs (Johnson-Martin, Haker & Attermeier, 2004b); HighScope COR (HighScope Educational Research Foundation, 2003); the Infant-Toddler Developmental Assessment (Provence, Erikson, Vater, & Palmeri, 1995); the New Portage Guide, Birth to Six (Larson et al., 2003); Transdisciplinary Play Based Assessment (Linder, 2008); and the SCERTS Models (Prizant, Weatherby, Rubin, Laurent, & Rydell, 2006a, 2006b).

Materials

An important consideration when planning activities is the selection of materials. Four criteria can assist teams in selecting materials:

1. Materials should be relevant to daily activities

2. Materials should be multidimensional

3. Materials should be developmentally appropriate

4. Materials should enhance learning opportunities and generalization of skills

Materials that are relevant to daily activities are accessible and part of the child's environment (e.g., when in the kitchen, use bowls, pots, and pans). They should acknowledge children's interests and life experiences. For children living near the ocean, for example, using sand, seashells, rocks, beach grass, or driftwood sticks can provide practice with counting, categorizing objects, and printing names in the sand.

Multidimensional materials are those that can be used in a variety of ways. Balls are an excellent example because they come in a variety of sizes and textures and can be used to kick, roll, throw, or bounce. Materials such as balls often spark a child's interest to use the material in both predictable and unexpected ways. Popsicle sticks are another example of a multidimensional material because children can use them as a tool, to make a picture frame, to count, to color, and to spread glue, to name but a few applications.

Teams should be aware of individual developmental abilities when selecting materials so that children are able to interact with the materials successfully. Knowing the general developmental stages through which children progress is important in selecting materials that will challenge and assist them at each stage. For example, knowing that children start with sensory exploration of materials and progress to functional and imaginary use of materials will help teams select materials that allow children to safely explore the materials/objects with their senses (i.e., using their eyes, ears, mouth, hands, and nose). For example, 12- to 18-month-old babies will likely remove pieces of a simple three-piece puzzle and taste them or clap two of the pieces together before putting the pieces back in the puzzle. Returning the pieces may require adult modeling, direction, or assistance. Older children may remove and replace the pieces in the puzzle and may advance to imaginary play with the puzzle pieces. They may remove the fire truck puzzle piece and pretend to drive it to a fire before returning it to the puzzle. Another child may take out an animal puzzle piece and make animal sounds, feed the animal, and pretend to brush its hair. An entire scenario of taking care of the animal may occur before the child inserts the piece back into the puzzle. Finally, materials should be chosen that increase learning opportunities and facilitate generalization. The use of materials that are incorporated into a variety of activities, situations, and settings offers slightly different learning experiences with the use of the same or similar skills.

Environmental Arrangement

Arranging the environment for an activity is important for several reasons. First, some activities may require the team to assemble or secure materials ahead of time. For example, a team may want to collect a large appliance-size box for children to reenact one of their favorite stories. The team will need to find the box and possibly alter the room to accommodate it. Second, some activities may require extensive shifts in the physical environment (e.g., arranging an obstacle course, changing a dramatic play area from housekeeping to a winter sports shop). Third, appropriate amounts of materials and sufficient space should be available to accommodate children during specific activities. Teams must decide how many children can reasonably and safely play in each activity area. Teams must also ensure children's equipment (e.g., wheelchairs, walkers, orthopedic chairs, communication devices) can be accommodated easily in the area and available for those who rely on the equipment to participate. Finally, consideration of the arrangement of the environment before the activity begins will hold transitions and children's wait time to a minimum.

Sequence of Steps

Most activities follow a sequence of steps and contain events associated with a beginning (e.g., transitioning from another area or event, getting materials, moving to a particular location, describing what to do), middle (e.g., manipulating of objects, accomplishing a task, participating in a project), and end (e.g., cleaning up materials, a finished product, reviewing what was accomplished, transitioning to another area or event). Children need opportunities to participate in both the beginning and ending of activities to increase their independence, to learn to anticipate transition cues, and to increase their participation during transitions. Teams need to understand how to maximize and use each part of an activity to create learning opportunities that address children's target skills. The beginning of an activity can create numerous opportunities to address children's target skills. For example, having children obtain needed materials creates opportunities for children to practice such skills as 1) following multiple-step directions, 2) finding objects in usual locations, 3) walking across different surfaces, 4) problem solving, and 5) demonstrating an understanding of spatial relations such as behind and next to. Once materials have been obtained, discussing directions associated with the activity and moving to the location where the activity will be conducted can create additional learning opportunities.

The middle portion of an activity often provides the most obvious and varied learning opportunities for target skills. This portion of an activity reviews the primary events expected to occur, including actions initiated by the children leading to the completion of the activity. Thinking through the actual steps of an activity should help teams ensure a match among children's interests, abilities, and needs, and provide opportunities to practice target skills.

The ending of an activity, like the beginning and middle, can provide numerous learning opportunities to practice different skills. Well-planned clean-up procedures and a recall or summarization of the activity can provide practice on skills from different developmental areas (e.g., fine motor, gross motor, social, cognitive). Recalling or summarizing the activity involves a discussion between children and adults about what happened or what was learned during the activity.

Embedded Learning Opportunities

As stated in Chapter 2, the purpose of activity-based intervention is to pro-mote the acquisition and generalization of functional and developmentally appropriate skills in young children. To meet this purpose, the daily trans-actions that occur between young children and their physical and social environment are used to offer multiple and varied learning opportunities. Embedding refers to a process of addressing children's target skills during daily activities in a manner that expands, modifies, or is integral to the activity in a meaningful way. Activity plans help to ensure teams consider all the skills that can be addressed during a particular activity and help to ensure sufficient learning opportunities are created when they design activi-ties.

This section of the activity plan allows teams to highlight goals targeted for individual children as well as broader outcomes targeted for all children. Individual goals can be taken directly from intervention guides, and broader outcomes can be taken from agency (e.g., Head Start Outcomes Framework) or core standards.

After reviewing the materials, environmental arrangement, and sequence of events, teams should be able to note specific and general goals/ outcomes that will be addressed by children's participation within the activ-ity. For example, in an activity that involves several children singing famil-iar songs and playing musical instruments, teams can address skills from across the curriculum, target individual children's goals, and ensure that multiple children participate differently within the same activity. In this example, some children may participate by watching and listening, whereas others participate by singing, asking questions verbally or using sign lan-guage, dancing, or playing a musical instrument. It is critical, particularly in center-based programs, that children with a wide variety of skills and abilities are able to participate fully in the activity.

Planned Variations

Activities can easily be reused and enhanced through variations. Variations seek to build on the basic structure of an activity by introducing one or more changes that can be used if children display little interest in the original planned activity or to expand the activity in a meaningful way. Many vari-ables affect children's interest, and any well-planned or favorite activity may become unappealing on a particular day. Variations also allow for enhancing the number and type of opportunities available to embed learning opportuni-ties related to individual goals or broader curricular outcomes. For example, if a teacher plans an obstacle course and the children do not show interest in the activity, the teacher can try a planned variation of a musical parade that would support embedding similar learning opportunities (e.g., both activities address mobility, balance, coordination, following directions, participation with others, opportunities to inform/request, opportunities to express ideas, anticipation).

Other

This section is included to provide space for information that may be particularly important for specific goals of participating children. For example, it may be important to address vocabulary associated with the targeted communication goals for some of the participating children. The vocabulary to be targeted can be noted in this section.

Another dimension that may be important for some goals is to address peer interactions or responses or caregiver involvement. Again this section can be used to indicate the range of peer interactions that can be targeted and encouraged during this planned activity. Depending on the children's goals, other dimensions (e.g., problem-solving strategies) may need to be addressed. Team members should give careful consideration to which other dimensions may be usefully addressed during the activity.

Figure 6.6 provides an example of an activity plan for children receiving center-based services. When groups of children are served, teams need to consider how the individual needs of children will be accommodated within the same activity. How will children be expected to behave and perform differently? How will they be allowed to participate in different ways? The activity plan for a snack illustrates the wide range of skills that can be addressed in a single planned activity.

The main purpose of activity plans is to create additional learning opportunities during planned activities. Many times teams find they are able to generate numerous ideas for activity planning but have difficulty embedding practice opportunities for children's target behaviors within the activities. Using activity plans can prompt teams to consider more novel or unconventional approaches to embedding multiple learning opportunities related to target skills and/or broader curricular outcomes within an activity. Activity planning also helps teams create "reusable" activities that are fun and interesting to children and can include numerous planned variations. Activity plans can be created for individual children or for groups of children. For example, Figure 6.7 offers an activity plan for play/blanket time in which a single child is the focus of intervention efforts.

The activity plan examples provided in Figures 6.6 and 6.7 illustrate how multiple and varied learning opportunities can be embedded across all steps of an activity. Additional activity plans can be found in the AEPS (Bricker, 2002). Blank forms can be found in the chapter appendix or as downloads. As with intervention guides and embedding schedules, we encourage teams to make modifications to meet their needs.

ABI Activity Plan

1. Activity name   Snack

Target child(ren) and objectives:

Leo:
- Uses 2–3 words to request objects, people, or materials from others.
- Shares or exchanges objects.
- Demonstrates understanding of size concepts.

Quinn:
- Demonstrates understanding of color concepts.
- Uses 2–3 words to request objects, people, or materials from others.

Akeelah:
- Walks with walker.
- Uses words to request objects (food).

2. Materials

Food (fruits, vegetables, drinks, grain items, cheese or other spread)
Dining materials (cups, bowls, child-size pitcher, napkins, placemats, utensils)
2–3 tables
15–20 child-size chairs
2 large storage containers for snack materials
Tables are arranged about 3 feet from sink, counter, and garbage (or a table can be set up as clean-up area).

3. Environmental arrangement

During the transition to snack tables, one interventionist assists the children with hand washing while another sits at the snack table to welcome the children as they arrive. The children can sit at the tables with one adult per table. All food and materials are prepared and placed in a large plastic container with a lid prior to the beginning of snack. The interventionist brings a container with the snack to the table and sits with the children to serve and eat the snack.

Figure 6.6.   Snack activity plan for a group of children.

4. Sequence of steps

Beginning

- The interventionist welcomes the children to the snack table and hands the children their place mats.
- One child per table is selected to distribute the place mats and napkins. Another child distributes bowls, cups, and utensils. These roles are rotated among children for each snack/meal. If this is a targeted objective, the identified child should have this role more frequently.
- Instruct children to get the food container, take what they are permitted, and pass it on to next child.
- Instruct children to ask for more food if they finish first serving.

Middle

- The interventionist brings out containers with the food in them and passes a container to a child and asks the child to open it. All containers should have lift lids. All children should have an opportunity to open a container.
- As containers are opened, ask children to identify the food, its color, and, if possible, the food group.
- Pass food containers around the table for children to serve themselves.
- Ask the children to take a specified amount of food (e.g., five grapes, three crackers).
- The children pour the water/juice from the pitcher into their cups.
- The children eat and engage in "snack talk" with each other or talk about topics provided.
- The children request more food.

End

- As children finish their snacks they can tell the interventionist and carry their eating items to the clean-up area.
- Remind the children still sitting at the table that snack time is ending in a certain amount of time (e.g., 5 minutes).
- Children place the materials in appropriate location (e.g., dishes, utensils, cups in sink; uneaten food and napkins in garbage).
- Children transition to next activity.

5. Embedded learning opportunities

Fine motor skills
- Grasping cylindrical items
- Grasping pea-sized items
- Stacking items
- Rotates wrist to manipulate
- Holds objects with one hand and manipulates with the other

Gross motor skills
- Moving around the room with balance and coordination
- Getting into and out of chair at table
- Sitting for 15 minutes

Adaptive skills
- Washes and dries hands
- Opens containers
- Serves self
- Eats and drinks independently
- Spreads cheese or butter on cracker with knife
- Pours water or juice into cup
- Transfers food from container to eating dish
- Carries materials from table to clean-up

Cognitive skills
- Uses object to obtain another object
- Solves problems using multiple strategies
- Follows multistep directions without contextual cues
- Identifies colors

Social-communication skills
- Responds to comprehension questions of "why," "how," "when"
- Produces multiple-word sentences to communicate
- Uses plural forms of pronouns
- Uses language to initiate and sustain interaction
- Provides and seeks information when talking with others
- Uses conversational rules

Social-emotional skills
- Explains or shows others how to do tasks they have mastered
- Maintains interaction with a peer

(continued)

Figure 6.6. *(continued)*

ABI Activity Plan *(continued)*

6. Planned variations

The children help prepare the snack before they eat it.

Snack takes place in a different location (e.g., picnic table outside, in the circle).

Prepared snacks are in paper bags (with children's names on them) for picnic.

---

7. Other (e.g., vocabulary, peer interactions, caregiver response)

Vocabulary
- Use peers' names.
- Use interventionists' names.
- Identifies textures of food (e.g., chewy, crunchy, smooth, hard)
- Uses numbers 1–10 to count out food items or children

Peer Interactions
- Pair/seat children together who are matched to work on conversations.
- Provide conversation starters (snack talk) for children to get started.
- Encourage children to help each other if needed.

ABI Activity Plan

1. Activity name   Floor time/blanket play

Target child(ren) and objectives: Jemma

Target skills:
- Uses index finger to activate
- Rises from sitting to standing position
- Searches for object in usual location
- Carries out two-step directions

2. Materials

Large blanket and an open space (indoors)
Containers of toys that make sounds and light up when activated
Small blanket
Light snack (e.g., Cheerios, crackers) and drink in a sippy cup

3. Environmental arrangement

Place large blanket in an open space, and place toys in different locations on the blanket. Place the snacks and the small blanket within your reach, where the child cannot reach.

Figure 6.7.   Blanket play activity plan for home setting.

(continued)

Figure 6.7.   *(continued)*

ABI Activity Plan *(continued)*

4. Sequence of steps

Beginning

When Jemma is alert and engaged with you, have her select additional interesting toys. Carry the toys to the blanket while maintaining joint attention with Jemma. Encourage Jemma to crawl/walk over to the large blanket by calling her name and/or activating one of the toys.

Middle

Jemma moves around the blanket independently or at your request to activate and manipulate different toys. Hide different toys under the small blanket, and encourage her to find the hidden toy. You can also sing familiar songs and rhymes such as "Row, Row, Row Your Boat"; "Head, Shoulders, Knees, and Toes"; and "Pat-a Cake." Offer her something to eat or drink as a break from playing with the toys. During the activity, see if she is hungry or thirsty, or respond to her initiations for food/drink.

End

Give a reminder to Jemma that it is almost time to clean up and begin placing one toy at a time into a large container. You can ask her to hand you toys to put away and/or to say "Bye-bye" to the toys as they go into the container. Encourage her to crawl/walk away from the blanket so that it can be folded.

---

5. Embedded learning opportunities

Fine motor skills
- Transfers object from one hand to the other
- Releases hand-held object onto and/or into a larger target with either hand
- Turns object over using wrist and arm rotation with each hand
- Uses either hand to activate objects

Adaptive skills
- Bites and chews soft and crisp foods
- Drinks from cup and/or glass held by adult
- Meets internal physical needs of hunger, thirst, and rest

Cognitive skills
- Visually follows object and/or person to point of disappearance
- Reproduces part of interactive game and/or action in order to continue game and/or action
- Imitates motor action that is commonly used
- Imitates words that are frequently used
- Retains one object when second object is obtained

Gross motor skills
- Moves barrier or goes around barrier to obtain object
- Uses simple motor actions on different objects

Social-communication skills
- Says nursery rhymes along with familiar adult
- Follows person's gaze to establish joint attention
- Responds with a vocalization and gesture to simple questions
- Uses consistent consonant-vowel combinations
- Uses descriptive words
- Initiates simple social game with familiar adult

6. Planned variations

Invite a playmate to join you and the child on the blanket to play with toys and sing songs.

Place blanket and toys outside.

Include books and read stories.

7. Other (e.g., vocabulary, peer interactions, caregiver response)

Colors (red, blue, green, yellow)

Attributes (big, little, bright, flash)

Actions (pat, bang, pull)

Words to songs/rhymes (row, boat, bake, cake, man, head, shoulders, knees, toes)

Other single words (on, off, more, me)

Playmate or sibling shows child how to activate different toys.

Playmate or sibling lies beside child and they look in the mirror together, making faces and hiding behind objects that they can peek around.

SUMMARY

An activity-based approach requires an underlying organizational structure to direct the work of professional team members and caregivers. This organizational structure is composed of three facets and their associated forms including intervention guides, embedding schedules, and activity plans.

We believe that ABI cannot be used successfully without adherence to an underlying organizational structure. However, programs may differ significantly in terms of children, staff, and resources; consequently, variations in the formats and use of these forms may be in order. We encouraged staff to make the necessary adaptations to ensure the forms meet their program's needs. The essential message of this chapter is not the adoption of a specific organizational structure but that teams who use ABI must have some rigorous framework that provides direction and guidance to their activities with young children and their families.

REFERENCES

Albert, K., Carbone, V., Murray, D., Hagerty, M., & Sweeney-Kerwin, E. (2012). Increasing the mand repertoire of children with autism through the use of an interrupted chain procedure. *Behavior Analysis in Practice, 5*(2), 65–76.

Bricker, D. (Series Ed.). (2002). *Assessment, Evaluation, and Programming System (AEPS®) for Infants and Children* (2nd ed., Vols. 1–4). Baltimore, MD: Paul H. Brookes Publishing Co.

Carter, M., & Gurnsell, J. (2001). The behavior chain interrupted strategy: A review of research and discussion of future directions. *Journal of The Association for Persons with Severe Handicaps, 26,* 37–49.

Daugherty, S., Grisham-Brown, J., & Hemmeter, M. (2001). The effects of embedded skill instruction on the acquisition of target and non-target skills with preschoolers with developmental delays. *Topics in Early Childhood Special Education, 21,* 231–221.

Grisham-Brown, J., Hemmeter, M.L., & Pretti-Frontczak, K. (2005). *Blended practices for teaching young children in inclusive settings.* Baltimore, MD: Paul H. Brookes Publishing Co.

HighScope Educational Research Foundation. (2003). Preschool COR development and validation. In *User guide: Preschool Child Observation Record.* Ypsilanti, MI: High/Scope Press.

Individuals with Disabilities Education Improvement Act (IDEA) of 2004, PL 108-446, 20 U.S.C. §§ 1400 *et seq.*

Johnson-Martin, N.M., Attermeier, S.M., & Hacker, B.J. (2004). *The Carolina Curriculum for Infants and Toddlers with Special Needs (CCITSN)* (3rd ed.). Baltimore, MD: Paul H. Brookes Publishing Co.

Johnson-Martin, N.M., Hacker, B.J., & Attermeier, S.M. (2004). *The Carolina Curriculum for Preschoolers with Special Needs (CCPSN)* (2nd ed.). Baltimore, MD: Paul H. Brookes Publishing Co.

Larson, N., Herwig, J., Wollenburt, K., Olsen, E., Bowe, W., Chvojicek, R., & Copa, A. (2003). *New Portage Guide, Birth to Six.* Portage, WI: Educational Service Agency.

Linder, T. (2008). *Transdisciplinary play-based assessment* (2nd ed.) Baltimore, MD: Paul H. Brookes Publishing Co.

McLean, M., Wolery, M., & Bailey, D. (2004). *Assessing Infants and Preschoolers with Special Needs* (3rd ed.). Upper Saddle River, NJ: Pearson.

Miller, J., & Chapman, R. (1980). Analyzing language and communication in the child. In R. Schiefelbusch (Ed.), *Nonspeech language, and communication: Acquisition and intervention* (pp. 159–196). Baltimore, MD: University Park Press.

Prizant, B.M., Wetherby, A.M., Rubin, E., Laurent, A.C., & Rydell, P.J. (2006a). *The*

SCERTS Model: A comprehensive educational approach for children with autism spectrum disorders: Volume I: Assessment. Baltimore, MD: Paul H. Brookes Publishing Co.

Prizant, B.M., Wetherby, A.M., Rubin, E., Laurent, A.C., & Rydell, P.J. (2006b). *The SCERTS Model: A comprehensive educational approach for children with autism spectrum disorders: Volume II: Intervention.* Baltimore, MD: Paul H. Brookes Publishing Co.

Provence, S., Erikson, J., Vater, S., & Palmeri, S. (1995). *Infant-Toddler Developmental Assessment (IDA).* Austin, TX: PRO-ED.

Raver, S. (2003). Keeping track: Using routine-based instruction and monitoring. *Young Exceptional Children, 6*(3), 12–20.

Roberts-Pennell, D., & Sigafoos, J. (1999). Teaching young children with developmental disabilities to request more play using the behaviour chain interruption strategy. *Journal of Applied Research in Intellectual Disabilities, 12,* 100–112.

Romer, L.T., Cullinan, T., & Schoenberg, B. (1994). General case training of requesting: A demonstration and analysis. *Education and Training in Mental Retardation, 29,* 57–68.

Romski, M., & Sevcik, R. (2005). Augmentative communication and early intervention: Myths and realities. *Infants & Young Children, 18*(3), 174–185.

Sandall, S., Hemmeter, M., Smith, B., & McLean, M. (2005). *DEC recommended practices: A comprehensive guide for practical application in early intervention/early childhood special education.* Longmont, CO: Sopris West.

Sandall, S.R., & Schwartz, I.S. (2008). *Building blocks for teaching preschoolers with special needs* (2nd ed.). Baltimore, MD: Paul H. Brookes Publishing Co.

Schuster, J., & Morse, T. (1998). Constant time delay with chained tasks: A review of the literature. *Education and Treatment of Children, 21*(1), 74–107.

U.S. Department of Education. (n.d.). *OSEP Part B and C state monitoring and formula grants.* Retrieved from http://www2.ed.gov/policy/speced/guid/idea/monitor/index.html

Wolery, M. (1992). Constant time delay with discrete responses: A review of effectiveness and demographic, procedural, and methodological parameters. *Research in Developmental Disabilities, 13*(3), 239–266.

Wolery, M., Anthony, L., Caldwell, N., Snyder, E., & Morgante, J. (2002). Embedding and distributing constant time delay in circle time and transitions. *Topics in Early Childhood Special Education, 22*(1), 14–26.

Appendix 6

Blank Forms

This appendix contains blank examples of the ABI intervention guide, embedding schedules, and activity plan forms. Teams are encouraged to copy these blank forms or to download blank forms to assist in the implementation of the approach.

1. Identifying information

Child's name: _____

Team members: _____

Date intervention initiated: _____ Date intervention completed: _____

2. Target goal, objectives, and program steps

Goal:

Objectives:

Program steps:

3. Core standards

4. Antecedents, targeted and nontargeted responses, and feedback or consequences

Antecedents designed to provide learning opportunities	List of possible child responses: targeted (+) and nontargeted (-)	Feedback or consequences

5. Teaching strategies

6. Monitoring progress

Who (person responsible for collecting the data)	Where (which activities or locations)	When (how often or on which days)	How (which methods)

7. Decision rules

If adequate progress does not occur in _____ (specify time frame for when the team will review the data), consider changing:

_____ Targeted goal

_____ Antecedents or feedback/consequences

_____ Teaching strategies

_____ Frequency, type, and/or locations of learning opportunities provided

_____ Other (describe) _____

_____

_____

ABI Embedding Schedule

Focus: Group   **Setting:** Classroom

Children's names: _____

Team members: _____

Dates schedule will be used: _____

	Daily classroom activities and opportunities for practice				
Children and target skills					
Child's name:					
1.					
2.					
3.					

ABI Embedding Schedule *(continued)*

Focus: Group   **Setting:** Classroom

Daily classroom activities and opportunities for practice

Child's name:

1.

2.

3.

Child's name:

1.

2.

3.

An Activity-Based Approach to Early Intervention, Fourth Edition, by JoAnn (JJ) Johnson, Naomi L. Rahn, and Diane Bricker.

ABI Embedding Schedule

Child's name: _____

Team members: _____

Dates schedule will be used: _____

Routine	Target goal	Target goal

Routine	Target goal	Target goal

1. Activity name

Target child(ren) and objectives:

2. Materials

3. Environmental arrangement

4. Sequence of steps

Beginning

Middle

End

5. Embedded learning opportunities

6. Planned variations

7. Other (e.g., vocabulary, peer interactions, caregiver response)

7

Issues Associated
with the Use of
Activity-Based Intervention

ABI is built on straightforward principles that are grounded in theory and research. The application of the approach, however, as with any comprehensive approach, is associated with a number of issues. Any intervention approach must confront an array of challenges or associated issues that will arise as personnel go about implementing the approach. These issues arise because of the complexities associated with human learning and the intervention process. It is likely that adult-directed teaching in which multiple sequential trials are presented is easier to use than more naturalistic approaches that require monitoring children's play and daily routines. In adult-directed approaches, activities are generally chosen and directed by an adult with little attention to a child's input or interest. Such approaches may be effective for some children; however, for many children, disregarding their motivation and interests results in poor attention and lack of focus resulting in little progress toward targeted goals and objectives. We grant that an approach such as ABI is more challenging to use across activities, but we believe more rapid, efficient, and effective learning—particularly for children with disabilities and those at risk—offsets this challenge.

This new edition makes a number of changes from previous editions that are intended to make ABI more effective and more easily understood, but it is likely that the reader will still confront important issues associated with the implementation of the approach. To anticipate the reader's questions and concerns, this chapter discusses the more salient issues that have been identified by professionals and caregivers using or thinking of using ABI.

These issues include 1) following children's leads, 2) adult control, 3) practice opportunities, 4) children with severe disabilities, 5) community-based programs, 6) team collaboration, and 7) monitoring progress. It should be emphasized that these issues are present, at least in part, with most intervention approaches used with young children.

FOLLOWING CHILDREN'S LEADS

Capitalizing on activities that are of interest to children is an important element of ABI. Following children's leads and initiations or using activities that children find inherently motivating keeps interest high and usually alleviates the need for artificial feedback (e.g., "Good talking!" "Good eating!" "Good sitting!") and nonrelated consequences (e.g., stickers). Furthermore, following children's leads and interests allows many child–environment transactions to focus on learning from the adult's perspective while remaining fun from the child's perspective. For example, if an interventionist wants a child to practice articulation skills (e.g., s-blend sounds) and knows the child likes Scooby Doo, the interventionist can create multiple learning opportunities by introducing several Scooby Doo books. As a result of the child's interest in Scooby Doo, he or she is likely to respond to questions and cues that prompt him or her to make s-blend sounds (e.g., Scooby, snack, stone, stick, start, scary, stretch) while looking at the books. The child is also able to share information with peers about the characters and actions in the book, providing additional opportunities to practice s-blend sounds during authentic child–environment transactions.

Following children's leads and interests raises an issue of whether children will direct their initiations or interests to activities that will necessarily address their particular cognitive, social, communicative, adaptive, or motor delays. It may be unrealistic to expect children, especially those with challenging physical, mental, or emotional needs, or a combination of needs, to consistently select activities that would enhance or expand their current repertoires. For example, a child with a serious articulation problem may find it both unproductive and unrewarding to ask for desired objects. The child who walks with difficulty may not be inclined to engage in actions that require walking. Furthermore, a child who has difficulty interacting with others may be unlikely to seek out peers and engage in cooperative play activities. These examples make it evident that team members cannot always wait for children to initiate activities that will necessarily lead to practicing target skills in areas of need.

Children's play and initiations should not be permitted to unfold without careful analysis of their contributions to the acquisition of targeted goals and objectives. The use of child initiations needs to meet two important criteria. First, they need to be complemented by routines and planned activities, and second, the child initiations need to address, at least in part, priority goals and objectives.

Successful application of ABI requires that play and child-directed activities be complemented or supplemented with routine and planned activities to ensure that the intervention process provides multiple and varied learning opportunities that address children's priority goals and objectives. Children are encouraged to initiate and direct activities; however, supplemental activities should be introduced as necessary to ensure practice on their targeted goals and objectives. For example, children may indicate the desire to sing the same songs repeatedly at group time. The interventionist may be able to adapt the children's requests by adding new target words or actions to the songs, by introducing new songs containing similar components of desired songs, or by interspersing other activities between songs into which practice opportunities for target skills can be embedded.

Successful application of ABI also requires the careful scrutiny of child initiations to ensure that practice on target skills occurs within that activity and, if it does not occur, to shape child-directed activities so that they incorporate target goals. For example, Keith has a motor impairment that requires the use of a wheelchair. A priority goal for Keith is to move to avoid obstacles (e.g., toys, furniture, people), go up and down inclines, and travel across different surfaces (e.g., cement, carpet) when operating his wheelchair. Not surprisingly, this 5-year-old would rather play computer games with his friends than practice maneuvering his wheelchair. Thus, when implementing an activity-based approach, the teacher arranges multiple situations for Keith to maneuver his wheelchair during daily activities (e.g., moving around other peers to get to the computer, moving around play equipment to get to where his friends wait). These examples of authentic opportunities capitalize on Keith's interests (i.e., playing computer games and being with his friends) to practice the target skill of using and maneuvering his wheelchair. With thought and planning, embedding learning opportunities that may initially appear incompatible with high-interest activities can be accomplished while still respecting children's choices and reinforcing their initiations.

Efficient child change will not occur unless children's needs are frequently and systematically addressed; consequently, in the activity-based approach, caregivers are an integral part of the team whether they engage in intervention efforts in a center-based program, at home, or both. The inclusion of caregivers is essential if multiple and varied opportunities are provided for children whatever the setting. Caregivers should understand that to adequately address targeted goals and objectives, it may be necessary to supplement child-initiated activities with routines and planned activities designed to address target goals and objectives.

To reiterate, ABI is not a laissez-faire approach that is directed totally by children and their interests. The approach is designed, when possible, to use the activities initiated and enjoyed by children. The use of child initiations, however, does not preclude the introduction of planned activities or the use of routine activities, nor does it preclude the redirection of child-directed activities.

The balance among child-directed, routine, and planned activities ensures that children's targeted goals and objectives are systematically addressed.

ADULT CONTROL

Direct services delivery personnel, consultants, and caregivers who have typically scripted and directed children's activities have reported feeling uncomfortable when first employing child-directed approaches such as ABI. Team members who have traditionally chosen the intervention activities may be uneasy using an approach that responds to and encourages child initiations. Furthermore, the training that many professionals have experienced—particularly those working with individuals who have disabilities—has taught them the importance of structure and the need to occupy children with productive tasks often using multiple sequential trials. Many teachers, interventionists, and specialists such as speech-language pathologists have been taught that they need to control the flow and content of intervention to ensure that children learn or acquire targeted individual behavioral or general curriculum goals. Consequently, these professionals feel a responsibility to totally organize the day or home intervention time, and often this organization leaves little time for child initiations or play. We believe that such adult control results in poor outcomes because children's motivations and interests are overlooked or are not used as vehicles for incorporating children's targeted goals and objectives.

Clearly adults need to control the overall framework of children's days. ABI does not relinquish adult control; rather it reorients how adults interact with children and what activities are introduced to reach goals and objectives. The effective user of ABI becomes attuned to what children like and do and, to the extent possible, uses those activities to practice targeted skills.

Interventionists may feel they are not actively teaching when children are permitted to reshape an activity or introduce an unanticipated action; however, if that activity is directed toward the children's goals and objectives, then the lack of predictability for the interventionist is likely not important. Furthermore, the role of the interventionist is actually more critical within this approach given the need to ensure frequent and meaningful practice opportunities to ensure target skills are provided within child-directed, routine, and planned activities. In other words, ABI offers team members additional ways of encouraging children's learning of important target skills.

In addition, some professionals have voiced concern that following children's leads or initiations may result in children's engagement in nonproductive activities or in moving from activity to activity without sustained interest or involvement. Most professionals have encountered children whose attention span is short and who, if permitted, cycle quickly through many activities, apparently without learning new skills. Is ABI appropriate for such children? Does this approach encourage and intensify their inability to focus and sustain attention? If team members are following children's leads and encouraging self-initiated activities, will children learn they can control the situation and shift activities at the expense of learning new skills or expanding their behavioral repertoires? We believe the use of ABI and in particular following children's leads or responding to their interests does not necessarily result in loss of control. In fact, the appropriate application of ABI does not permit children to engage in nonproductive or inappropriate actions. Rather, the approach provides an underlying structure that we believe enhances children's learning and use of functional and generative skills. The following example and subsequent discussion illustrate how interventionists might shape a child's nonproductive initiations into productive outcomes.

BAILEY

Bailey is 2 years old and has a moderate developmental delay. She frequently initiates action but rarely spends more than a few minutes involved in any single activity. Bailey might look at a book for a few seconds, then usually puts down the book to pick up a toy that, in turn, is quickly dropped in order to snatch another toy from her brother.

Although her activities are child directed, to permit Bailey to continue such behavior does not represent an appropriate application of ABI, as the approach does not require that interventionists and caregivers relinquish total control over children and their activities.

When employing ABI with a child like Bailey, an initial step would be for the team to document patterns in Bailey's behavior through ongoing observations. Such observations are critical for 1) understanding what motivates and interests Bailey, 2) determining Bailey's present level of performance to ensure adult expectations are consistent with her current skill level, and 3) creating daily activities and interactions that provide sufficient structure and guidance to support Bailey's acquisition of target skills. Such observations and systematic exploration by varying activities and feedback should culminate in the team learning how to use Bailey's initiated actions in ways that are appropriate and sustained. Effective use of ABI should permit Bailey to initiate a variety of actions while simultaneously permitting the interventionists/caregivers to shape and guide these initiations into productive behavior.

To repeat, use of ABI does not require that interventionists or caregivers follow child initiations when they do not lead to productive outcomes. *Productive outcome* refers to improvement in children's skills associated with their IFSP/IEP goals and objectives. This aim emphasizes the importance of selecting functional and generative goals for children. The selection of meaningful intervention targets provides the necessary guidance for selecting meaningful antecedents and activities and for monitoring change over time. Child-directed, routine, or planned activities should always address the acquisition of children's goals and objectives. If goals for Bailey include those that address her interactions with toys and others in her environment, then the interventionist would prompt activities or support child-directed activities that provide opportunities to work on these goals. Caregivers could use a variety of strategies to encourage sustained interactions with Bailey's favorite materials or toys. For example, if Bailey gets a book from her bedroom, adults may encourage her to select books that allow her to perform an action (e.g., *Pat the Bunny,* or peek-and-lift tab books), thereby increasing the likelihood that she will remain with the activity for a longer period of time but still building on her interest or initiations.

Underlying this discussion of adult control is the need for advanced planning by interventionists, preferably with other team members. Without advanced planning, interventionists may struggle in terms of selecting appropriate intervention targets or strategies and interpreting outcomes correctly. Furthermore, without advanced planning, interventionists may not capitalize on learning opportunities found in child-directed, routine, or planned activities. The framework underlying ABI and organizational strategies that require advanced and ongoing planning are discussed in Chapters 4 and 6.

PRACTICE OPPORTUNITIES

How many and what type of practice opportunities should be presented to children are important issues for those using ABI as well as any other intervention approach. Providing multiple opportunities to practice and thus learn target goals and objectives seems particularly important for young children with disabilities, and it is likely that the magnitude or severity of the disability is correlated with the amount of practice necessary for children to learn target skills. Unfortunately, there is little empirical work to permit drawing firm conclusions about how frequently opportunities should be presented, how much contextual conditions should vary, and what type of opportunities should be presented (Guralnick, 2006). Finding empirical answers to these important questions should become part of the EI/ECSE research agenda; however, until there are objective findings, practitioners must rely on guidelines derived from their collective experience.

How frequently should learning opportunities be presented? Because empirical evidence is lacking, we can surmise that in general the more practice the faster the acquisition of skills. It is likely that the number of opportunities needed to learn is also tied to such factors as child characteristics, nature of the target skills, and available resources. Nonetheless, offering multiple opportunities to practice important skills appears necessary to promote the acquisition of new skills and the strengthening and generalization of existing skills. In general, interventionists and caregivers are encouraged to provide or create many authentic learning opportunities. The axiom "more is better" is likely accurate for practice opportunities.

CAMERON

Cameron is 5 years old and has developmental delays. His team is planning intervention activities to address his IEP goals. During the process, team members consider each of Cameron's target goals, his interests, and the possible authentic activities that occur during the school day into which opportunities to address specific goals could be embedded. In this case, the team addresses Cameron's goal to print his name. They use Cameron's interest in computers to arrange authentic opportunities to practice printing his name. The interventionist places a sign-up sheet next to the computer and asks all children to print their names on the list if they wish to use the computer. The interventionist uses this same sign-up strategy for children to gain access to other desired activities (e.g., the sand table).

The team also targets creating nametags to hang on various objects that belong to Cameron (e.g., his lunch bag) and in various places (e.g., his bedroom door) as another activity to provide opportunities for Cameron to print his name. A planned letter-writing activity may also offer a number of opportunities for Cameron to print his name (e.g., signing letters, adding a return address to the envelope). Finally, Cameron's goal could be addressed by making sure pencils, pens, or crayons are available so that he can write his name on any art project. Choosing activities to embed learning opportunities for Cameron to address his goal is largely directed by his interests.

When offering children opportunities to practice target goals, how much should conditions and settings vary? For skills to be maximally useful, children need to be able to execute them across a variety of settings and conditions rather than being tied to specific antecedents or activities. For example, if a child is learning the names of common objects, then she can work on labeling objects many times throughout the day. The caregiver or interventionist should examine the child's daily schedule and note the different settings and conditions where the child could potentially practice target object names. For example, opportunities might be available to practice object-naming skills during reading time, snack time, and bath time. Such activities may provide numerous authentic opportunities in which labeling an object is meaningful and useful to the child. The example provided next illustrates how Karlee's intervention team systematically varied settings and conditions to reach a skill targeted on her IFSP.

KARLEE

Karlee is 18 months old and not yet walking; consequently, an important IFSP outcome is to walk independently across a variety of surfaces using alternating steps so that her family will not have to carry her. Because Karlee has low muscle tone in her legs and is hypersensitive to touch, the team decides the initial opportunities to address her walking goal should occur with her mother in the living room. In this setting, Karlee's mother provides her with hip support, and the carpeted floor is less offensive to touch. Over time, Karlee's mother reduces the amount of physical assistance she provides her daughter. Once Karlee is able to take a few independent steps on the rug, her mother encourages her to walk on the kitchen's tile floor and across the hallway to look out the window. In addition, opportunities to walk to her father, the neighbor, and her siblings are offered across settings. Eventually, Karlee's mother takes her to the park to provide her with opportunities to use her walking skills in a new setting that offers different conditions.

Within an activity-based approach, interventionists are encouraged to use variety when creating learning opportunities. Specifically, ABI does "not attempt to teach children to respond to specific cues under specific conditions, rather, [it] attempts to teach generative and functional skills across development domains" (Losardo & Bricker, 1994, p. 745). The important aspect to consider is the need to vary the opportunities (i.e., vary the setting, people, materials, and strategies), not only to ensure the initial acquisition of critical skills but also to ensure the eventual generalization of skills. As shown in the example with Karlee, conditions, settings, and people gradually changed to ensure that she was able to successfully walk in more challenging environments.

What type of learning opportunities should be presented? We believe that learning opportunities should be meaningful and relevant to children to the extent possible. Our underlying belief is that when antecedents and feedback are matched to children's interests and developmental level and integrated into authentic activities, positive outcomes are likely to occur.

The skills targeted for intervention should be taken from children's IFSP/IEPs; therefore, it is essential that program staff develop high-quality IFSPs/IEPs. To serve as the primary source for targeting intervention efforts, target skills should be developmentally appropriate, address important behaviors, and produce genuine functional outcomes for children and families (Hemmeter & Grisham-Brown, 1998; Pretti-Frontczak & Bricker, 2000; Wolery, 2005).

Interventionists and caregivers should ensure that children acquire and generalize important response classes that include problem solving, communication, physical manipulation of objects, mobility, and adaptive and social interaction skills. Targeting the response class of mobility, for example, does not mean that all children will learn to walk, but it does mean that independent mobility should be a goal for most children, whether mobility is accomplished by foot, walker, wheelchair, or other adapted system. The comprehensive and pervasive nature of response classes provides numerous opportunities for thoughtful and innovative caregivers and interventionists to use child initiations or to embed practice opportunities into routine and planned activities.

ANDRE

Andre is 4 years old and meets his needs by pointing and vocalizing. After a comprehensive assessment, his intervention team targets two important social communication goals: Andre will use consistent word approximations, and Andre will locate objects, people, and/or events without contextual cues. These goals were taken from the AEPS (Bricker, 2002) and meet the criteria specified previously for meaningful goals. That is, these two goals are developmentally appropriate, address important developmental skills, and should produce functional outcomes for Andre and his family. In addition, the type of social communication goals selected for Andre permits the team to identify numerous activities in which learning opportunities targeting these goals can be embedded. These goals also permit the use of a wide range of authentic activities. For example, Andre's access to desired objects or events can be made contingent on his use of consistent word approximations. A range of events and games can be structured around having Andre locate named objects or people. Adults can even provide Andre with choices between different objects to give additional opportunities to practice the target skill of using word approximations.

The selection of appropriate and useful goals will do much to ensure intervention efforts with children are effective and produce desired outcomes.

CHILDREN WITH SEVERE DISABILITIES

Another important issue when implementing ABI is its applicability to infants, toddlers, and young children with severe disabilities. Typically developing children and those who have or who are at risk for mild to moderate disabilities tend to engage in many more diverse activities than do children with more severe disabilities. In addition, children with less severe disabilities are often more easily engaged, and their attention may be maintained longer. And children with less severe disabilities tend to initiate action and respond more frequently than do children with more severe disabilities. In fact, a major characteristic of many people with severe disabilities is the lack of appropriate self-initiated activity (e.g., Koegel, Koegel, Frea, & Smith, 1995).

An important question is whether the lack of initiation—or at least appropriate initiation—in individuals with severe disabilities is physiologically based or is systematically fostered by their being ignored or punished by the social environment. We believe that the low frequency of useful initiations by children with severe disabilities stems from a combination of biological problems and previous experience. As Drasgow, Halle, Ostrosky, and Harbers (1996) pointed out, many young children with severe disabilities have a number of subtle or idiosyncratic behaviors that could be used or shaped into useful responses. Our experience suggests, however, that often these responses are overlooked or ignored, and instruction is directed toward adult imposition of the response to be performed by the child.

For children without disabilities, play and self-initiated activities provide essential vehicles for learning increasingly more complex social, communicative, cognitive, and motor skills. We believe that play and child initiations are equally important ways for children with severe disabilities to learn new skills. ABI supports this form of learning by emphasizing the importance of child-directed interactions within daily caregiving routines, play, and planned activities. Caregivers and interventionists need to carefully observe and respond to the occurrence of children's signals and actions, however minimal and idiosyncratic, and build on these responses or redirect them into more useful and meaningful response forms.

DENZEL

Denzel is in preschool and has a severe cognitive disability. One of his IEP goals is initiating and responding to communicative interactions. He spends much of his day sitting and gazing around his environment without initiating interactions with others; however, the staff have noticed that he often responds to music and singing by turning to the source of the sound, smiling, and initiating small body movements. The intervention team decides to introduce the song, "Row, Row, Row Your Boat" in an interactive manner. An interventionist sits on the floor across from Denzel and holds both of his hands. While singing, she moves Denzel's body gently back and forth. Denzel responds to the action/song by rocking back and forth with the interventionist. The interventionist ceases singing and rocking and waits for Denzel to initiate some communicative action (e.g., pulling on her hands) that results in continued singing and rocking. In addition, the interventionist prompts the use of the sign for more.

We believe that increased attention to enhancing appropriate child-directed activity (not self-destructive or stereotypical behavior) may enhance the ability of children with severe disabilities to show caregivers and interventionists what they like and what interests them. In fact, some treatment by level of development analyses (i.e., aptitude) finds that younger children with fewer skills benefit more from child-driven interventions than from adult-driven approaches (e.g., Cole, Dale, & Mills, 1991; Yoder et al., 1995). These findings, however, do not negate the need for structure and careful programming for children with severe disabilities.

The adequacy of instruction across areas of need requires coordination and joint planning by team members involved in a child's intervention program. This coordination and planning is especially important for children with severe disabilities if they are to develop functional and generalizable skills that, as indicated previously, have consistently been identified as serious problems for this population (e.g., Drasgow et al., 1996). Furthermore, a primary challenge of working with young children with severe disabilities stems from medical issues and conditions that affect learning and may interrupt team members' plans. Such interruptions (e.g., hospitalization) may result in significant regression that may require retargeting previously learned skills. Teams should remain flexible in order to adapt to changes in the children's environments or conditions.

ABI uses behavior analytic techniques known to be successful in helping individuals with severe disabilities acquire useful and meaningful skills. The approach incorporates the people and places important to children by intervening in daily routines, and it emphasizes skills with immediate utility by providing something helpful or desirable for children as needs arise (e.g., getting the child a cup of juice when he vocalizes and points to the juice pitcher). Intervention targets are addressed across activities to ensure that learning opportunities occur under different conditions to increase the generalizability of skills.

An activity-based approach does not preclude, nor is it incompatible with, the use of adult-directed strategies or a massed-trial format (i.e., asking the child to repeat the same response across several sequential trials). The magnitude and number of problems presented by children with severe disabilities will likely require team members to employ a variety of teaching strategies if they are to ensure systematic child progress. The successful use of ABI requires the thoughtful balancing of planned activities with child initiations and the balancing of learning opportunities across activities. (For more detail on the use of ABI with children with severe disabilities, see Chapter 12.)

COMMUNITY-BASED PROGRAMS

Increasing numbers of children with disabilities are being placed in community-based child care, educational, and recreational programs (Grisham-Brown, Hemmeter, & Pretti-Frontzcak, 2005; Odom, Favazza, Brown, & Horn, 2000). Most of these programs were designed to accommodate typically developing children. Furthermore, these staff members generally have training and experience focused on typically developing children and their families. Thus, the placement of children with disabilities into community-based programs presents a number of challenges (Bricker, 2001; Grisham-Brown, Pretti-Frontczak, Hemmeter, & Ridgley, 2002). Community staff need to be prepared to offer children with disabilities specialized instruction and to manage the children's behavior successfully. Community staff members often operate with limited budgets, which may not permit individualized attention to participating children. The use of ABI cannot solve all of these problems; however, the approach's reliance on routine activities and child initiations makes it compatible with how most community-based programs function and, therefore, applicable for use in these programs.

Significant compatibility exists between ABI and the philosophy and operation of many community-based programs. This compatibility comes, in part, from the reliance on child development and early education literature and practice by both ABI and many community-based programs. ABI did not evolve primarily from special education but rather it is a hybrid that incorporates principles and premises from early education and psychology as well as special education. Encouraging child initiations and child-directed actions within the context of routine and play activities is familiar to most child care workers and early childhood teachers.

In addition, ABI is compatible with developmentally appropriate practice (DAP), which guides quality child care and early education programs (Grisham-Brown et al., 2005). Both ABI and DAP encourage child exploration and initiation, embed consequences into child activity, target tasks that are developmentally appropriate for children, and view adults as supporters of children's actions and interests.

ABI encourages the physical, social, and instructional inclusion of children with disabilities in all activities rather than relocating children into isolated settings for specific instruction. The activity-based approach emphasizes the use of antecedents and consequences that can be provided in child-directed as well as teacher-directed activities. These emphases blend well with most approaches used in community-based programs; however, the application of ABI in community-based settings will likely require some adaptation.

The successful use of ABI in community-based programs depends on whether mechanisms are in place to ensure that children with disabilities are assessed, appropriate IFSP/IEP goals are developed, ample opportunities to practice target skills are provided, and progress is monitored. Most child care workers and early education personnel are not prepared or trained to conduct these activities. Consequently, the use of ABI will likely require that training and support be provided to the staff of community-based programs. The philosophical congruence between ABI and DAP, however, as well as the compatibility between ABI and the previous experiences of early childhood workers should enhance the understanding and openness to this training.

TEAM COLLABORATION

Implementation of an activity-based approach depends on linking key processes including assessment, goal development, intervention, and evaluation. Procedures and rationale for linking processes are described in Chapter 3. Due to the interrelatedness of processes and many of the issues described previously, we have found that when adults work collaboratively, implementation of ABI is more likely to be successful. However, we also understand the reality in which interventionists are expected to deliver services, and we recognize the challenges collaboration presents. For information on team collaboration, refer to Bricker and Widerstrom (1996); Dinnebeil, Hale, and Rule (1999); King et al. (2009); or Snell and Janney (2005). This section addresses why team collaboration is important to the implementation of

ABI. Chapter 13 also provides a number of suggestions for implementing an activity-based approach as a team.

ABI lends itself well to an integrated and collaborative team approach, primarily because participating children and families need support from professionals with different expertise. Thus, a primary reason for promoting collaboration among team members (e.g., caregivers, teachers, therapists) is to address the complex needs of young children who experience problems, young children with severe disabilities, and young children who are at risk— all of whom often require a cadre of personnel to meet their needs (e.g., educational, therapeutic, social, and medical professionals). It is vital that these personnel work together in addressing the needs of the child within the context of the child's family and larger community.

A second, though no less important, reason for team collaboration within an activity-based approach is to ensure the targeting of functional and generative skills across environments. Recommended practice suggests that prioritized skills targeted for intervention address children's needs for participation in daily activities (e.g., feeding, playing) and participation in family routines (e.g., eating at restaurants, going to the grocery store). Thus, team members often need to cross over traditional disciplinary boundaries to address target skills, rather than relocating children into isolated settings for specific instruction. For example, a speech-language pathologist or another team member assigned to a preschool classroom does not need to request separate space away from classmates to practice a child's target language skills. The specialist can join the child in the classroom and observe and embed opportunities to practice language skills in classroom activities. Specialists can also observe ongoing activities, and then give the preschool teacher feedback regarding the opportunities he or she could create for the child and how to build on these opportunities. Intervention is likely to be more effective if used across settings and conditions more available to the preschool teacher than to a specialist who visits infrequently.

Finally, as noted throughout this text, a key aspect of an activity-based approach is the provision of multiple and varied learning opportunities. In order to provide these necessary learning opportunities, all members of the child's team need to understand and participate in the intentional and individualized instruction deemed necessary to meet target skills. Thus, caregivers, therapists, and other interventionists need to work together in designing, implementing, and evaluating the effects of intervention.

MONITORING PROGRESS

Assessing or measuring the effects of intervention efforts on children is an essential part of any approach; consequently, tracking child progress toward targeted goals and objectives is required. In addition, federal education acts (e.g., the No Child Left Behind Act of 2001 [PL 107-110]) have emphasized the need to document program effects and require that states receiving federal dollars report accountability data on a regular basis. No matter the service delivery program or intervention approach, ensuring that children are making progress toward their goals and objectives is essential; thus, the issue of monitoring progress permeates the field of EI/ECSE.

This issue can be examined from two perspectives. The first is the commitment by program personnel to the practice of progress monitoring, and the second is the strategy adopted for conducting the evaluation. Each of these perspectives is important and significantly affects program staff's willingness and success in conducting progress monitoring.

One hears from many teachers, interventionists, and specialists that they lack the time to evaluate children's progress. They argue that heavy case loads, multiple responsibilities, and attention to the many small crises (e.g., skinned knee, parental need to share information) that arise when working with young children interferes with efforts to evaluate child progress or program impact. Such factors often lead personnel to eschew regular evaluation of child change. Although one may be sympathetic to these realities, it is unacceptable both from a federal requirement perspective as well as a best practices perspective to not engage in regular efforts to monitor child progress (Grisham-Brown & Pretti-Frontzcak, 2011; Losardo & Notari-Syverson, 2011; Neisworth & Bagnato, 2005). The issue becomes not whether to monitor progress but how to create systems that can be successfully used by busy staff.

The second perspective is the creation of progress monitoring systems that respect the realities of service delivery program staff but that also produce objective information on the effectiveness of the ongoing intervention efforts. Unfortunately, collecting and aggregating program monitoring data on young children at risk and with disabilities is far more challenging than collecting similar data on children for whom standardized procedures and tests exist to measure their progress toward state standards. However, the linked system framework described in Chapter 3 makes clear that monitoring progress is an essential element in comprehensive, coordinated service delivery systems. Therefore, ABI (as should be other intervention approaches) is committed to monitoring progress to ensure that staff and caregivers' time is being used productively and, as children acquire targeted skills, intervention efforts are adjusted accordingly. Without this information, one is flying blind—a strategy we can ill afford with young children in need of serious intervention efforts.

As noted, we believe the first step to successful progress monitoring is that program staff be committed to collecting progress monitoring information; with the next step being the need to find strategies that permit them to routinely assess children's progress. We recommend a three-phase strategy. First, it is necessary to gather information on children's initial developmental repertoires (i.e., initial or baseline assessment). Second, it is necessary to collect, at least weekly, one or two instances of children performing a targeted skill. Third, it is necessary to reassess progress toward all targeted goals at least two or three times a year.

Often gathering baseline data is the easy phase in the process because of state eligibility requirements and federal IFSP/IEP requirements. That is, most states require 1) some objective substantiation for determining eligibility (e.g., norm-referenced or curriculum-based assessment test outcomes) and 2) some bases for selecting IFSP/IEP goals and objectives. Consequently, before entry into a program, a comprehensive evaluation is usually completed on a child that offers data for establishing eligibility and for deriving initial IFSP/IEP goals and objectives. As we note elsewhere (e.g., Chapter 3), we strongly recommend the use of curriculum-based measures for these purposes because they yield more useful information for intervention goals and content.

The second phase focuses on collecting weekly data that provides objective feedback on the success or effectiveness of the intervention efforts. This phase often offers the greatest challenge to program staff because it requires systematic effort to document children's weekly progress toward targeted goals and objectives. Unfortunately many personnel believe this necessitates administering a mini-test to all children on a regular basis—which we agree is likely to be time prohibitive. Rather we recommend that staff learn to collect probe data that can be acquired as children engage in child initiations, daily routines, and planned activities. Probes refer to brief or quick (i.e., one or two instances) assessments of children's progress toward specific goals or objectives. For example, if walking without support is a child's goal, the interventionist could observe over the week the child's progress by creating a play situation that requires that the child take unsupported steps. The interventionist can note and quickly record the number and quality of steps taken. These data can then be aggregated across weeks to determine the child's progress. The probe takes little time but provides essential feedback on the impact of intervention efforts.

The use of probe systems should permit useful data collection without burdening busy staff, and there are multiple ways to gather probe data on children's progress toward goals and objectives. Teams will have to evaluate and select the type of probe data to be collected for each child. For example, at the end of a planned activity, the teacher could ask children with language goals to recount parts of the activity and note on paper the accuracies of their responses. At group time, the interventionist could ask several specific questions that directly target selected children's goals and quickly check on a clipboard *ok, partly ok,* or *not ok.* On the playground the physical therapist could set up an obstacle course for several children to assess progress on their motor skills and quickly note on her tablet the children's responses.

The idea behind the collection of probe data is two fold. First, find ways to gather objective and valid information on a child's performance of a target skill, and second, find ways to quickly record the information. At the end of the day the collected information will need to be transcribed into some other format for better understanding and display.

The third phase is the completion of a more global assessment on the children at quarterly intervals. If using a measure such as the AEPS, it is not necessary to complete the entire test but to focus only on the selected goals and objectives and to reassess child progress on these items. This focus greatly reduces the time investment for quarterly assessment yet provides essential information on child progress toward all targeted goals and objectives.

The following example illustrates this three-part progress monitoring strategy.

KELLY

Kelly is 30 months old, and she goes to a child care program 5 days a week. The staff have concerns about her lack of language. Kelly's parents are referred to a local clinic for an evaluation. The clinic team completes the AEPS test by observing Kelly at her program on 3 different days. Her parents are asked to complete the Family Assessment section of the AEPS as well. After collecting this initial assessment information, the team meets with Kelly's parents to discuss the findings. The outcomes make clear that Kelly is eligible for EI/ECSE services. Kelly's parents ask that she remain in her present child care program, and fortunately EI/ECSE providers have the flexibility to deliver itinerant services in community-based child care programs.

Once eligibility is determined, the next step is to select IEP goals and objectives for Kelly. The AEPS test results yield the necessary information for the team (including Kelly's parents) to select and prioritize goals. Once goals are selected for Kelly, the itinerant EI/ECSE staff assists both her parents and child care staff in finding opportunities to embed her priority goal of producing two-word utterances in play, daily routines, and planned activities. The speech-language pathologist visits once a week and collects brief probe data on progress toward her use of two words while talking with Kelly and when looking at a book of Kelly's choice. In addition, the itinerant and child care staff work together to assess Kelly's progress on all targeted goals and objectives at 4-month intervals.

SUMMARY

This chapter highlighted the more challenging issues associated with the application of ABI, including following children's leads, adult control, practice opportunities, children with severe disabilities, community-based program use, team collaboration, and monitoring progress. These issues are not unique to ABI but are inherent in any of the intervention approaches used with young children. Using the activity-based approach requires users to carefully consider these issues and in many cases institute change in how they interact with children during play, routines, and planned activities.

The issues addressed in this chapter are important as they represent some of the more serious challenges facing the field of EI/ECSE. For example, finding effective strategies to increase practice opportunities with groups of children with diverse abilities and needs has and will continue to be a significant issue because of the relationship between practice and skill acquisition. Integrating progress monitoring into programs is a growing requirement that must be met in a way that produces valid information but also can be accomplished by busy program personnel. Researchers and practitioners need to continue to confront these issues and search for alternatives that may prove to be more effective.

We believe that ABI can be successfully employed with a range of children in a variety of settings. However, no current approach is completely successful with all children. This reality requires the continued refinement of existing approaches as well as the introduction of yet untried strategies that may enhance intervention efforts. Professionals who resist exploring alternatives should, we believe, weigh the challenges of change, which are real, against the potential for improved outcomes for young children and their families.

REFERENCES

Bricker, D. (2001). The natural environment: A useful construct? *Infants and Young Children, 13*(4), 21–31.

Bricker, D. (Series Ed.). (2002). *Assessment, Evaluation and Programming System (AEPS®) for Infants and Children* (2nd ed.). Baltimore, MD: Paul H. Brookes Publishing Co.

Bricker, D., & Widerstrom, A. (Eds.). (1996). *Preparing personnel to work with infants and young children and their families: A team approach.* Baltimore, MD: Paul H. Brookes Publishing Co.

Cole, K., Dale, P., & Mills, P. (1991). Individual differences in language delayed children's responses to direct and interactive preschool instruction. *Topics in Early Childhood Special Education, 11*(1), 99–124.

Dinnebeil, L., Hale, L., & Rule, S. (1999). Early intervention program practices that support collaboration. *Topics in Early Childhood Special Education, 19*(4), 225–235.

Drasgow, E., Halle, J., Ostrosky, M., & Harbers, H. (1996). Using behavioral indication and functional communication training to establish an initial sign repertoire with a young child with severe disabilities. *Topics in Early Childhood Special Education, 16*(4), 500–521.

Grisham-Brown, J., Hemmeter, M.L., & Pretti-Frontczak, K. (2005). *Blended practices for teaching young children in inclusive settings.* Baltimore, MD: Paul H. Brookes Publishing Co.

Grisham-Brown, J., & Pretti-Frontczak, K., (2011). *Assessing young children in inclusive settings.* Baltimore, MD: Paul H. Brookes Publishing Co.

Grisham-Brown, J., Pretti-Frontczak, K., Hemmeter, M., & Ridgley, R. (2002). Teaching IEP goals and objectives in the context of classroom routines and activities. *Young Exceptional Children, 6*(1), 18–27.

Guralnick, M. (2006). The system of early intervention for children with developmental disabilities: Current status and challenges for the future. In J. Jacobson, J. Mulick, & J. Rojahn (Eds.), *Handbook of mental retardation and developmental disabilities* (pp. 465–480). New York, NY: Plenum.

Hemmeter, M., & Grisham-Brown, J. (1998). Developing children's language skills in inclusive early childhood classroom. *Dimensions in Early Childhood Classrooms, 25*(3), 6–13.

King, G., Strachan, D., Tucker, M., Duwyn, B., Desserud, S., & Shillington, M. (2009). The application of a transdisciplinary model for early intervention services. *Infants & Young Children, 22*(3), 211–223.

Koegel, R., Koegel, L., Frea, W., & Smith, A.E. (1995). Emerging interventions for children with autism: Longitudinal and lifestyle implications. In R. Koegel & L. Koegel (Eds.), *Teaching children with autism: Strategies for initiating positive interactions and improving learning opportunities* (pp. 1–15). Baltimore, MD: Paul H. Brookes Publishing Co.

Losardo, A., & Bricker, D. (1994). Activity-based intervention and direct instruction: A comparison study. *American Journal on Mental Retardation, 98*(6), 744–765.

Losardo, A., & Notari-Syverson, A. (2011). *Alternative approaches to assessing young children* (2nd ed.). Baltimore, MD: Paul H. Brookes Publishing Co.

Neisworth, J., & Bagnato, S. (2005). DEC recommended practices: Assessment. In S. Sandall, M. McLean, & B. Smith (Eds.), *DEC recommended practices:* A comprehensive guide for practice application in early intervention/early childhood special education (pp. 45-69). Longmont, CO: Sopris West.

No Child Left Behind Act of 2001, PL 107-110, 115 Stat. 1425, 20 U.S.C. §§ 6301 *et seq.*

Odom, S., Favazza, P., Brown, W., & Horn, E. (2000). Approaches to understanding the ecology of early childhood environments for children with disabilities. In T. Thompson, D. Felce, & F. Symons (Eds.), *Behavioral observation: Technology and applications in developmental disabilities* (pp. 193–214). Baltimore, MD: Paul H. Brookes Publishing Co.

Pretti-Frontczak, K., & Bricker, D. (2000). Enhancing the quality of Individualized Education Plan (IEP) goals and objectives. *Journal of Early Intervention, 23*(2), 92–105. doi:10.1177/105381510002300204

Snell, M., & Janney, R. (2005). *Teachers' guides to inclusive practices: Collaborative teaming.* Baltimore, MD: Paul H. Brookes Publishing Co.

Wolery, M. (2005). DEC recommended practices: Child-focused practices. In S. Sandall, M.L. Hemmeter, B.J. Smith, & M.E. McLean (Eds.), *DEC recommended practices: A comprehensive guide for practice application in early intervention/early childhood special education* (pp. 71–106). Longmont, CO: Sopris West.

Yoder, P., Kaiser, A., Goldstein, H., Alpert, C., Mousetis, L., Kaczmarek, L., & Fisher, R. (1995). An exploratory comparison of milieu teaching and responsive interaction in classroom applications. *Journal of Early Intervention, 19*(3), 218–242.

8

The Challenges of Intervention Research and the Empirical Bases for an Activity-Based Approach

As discussed in Chapter 2, approaches to EI/ECSE and specific strategies and procedures have gradually shifted from highly structured, adult-directed procedures (Bricker & Bricker, 1976) to those that are child initiated and make use of play and daily activities. Early programs employed teacher-directed, one-to-one instruction, and dispensed tangible rewards. Later intervention efforts mapped instruction onto routines and child initiations and used social feedback or consequences associated with the action or activity. When possible, these important shifts in intervention procedures were based on empirical findings (e.g., Bricker & Sheehan, 1981; Pretti-Frontczak & Bricker, 2001); however, as noted by Baer (1981) and others (e.g., Gast, 2010; Gersten et al., 2005), collecting objective data verifying the effects of intervention efforts is a complex undertaking.

A contemporary focus in the field of special education has been on establishing evidence-based practices (EBPs; Cook & Cook, 2013). Cook and Cook defined EBPs as, "practices that are supported by multiple, high-quality studies that utilize research designs from which causality can be inferred and that demonstrate meaningful effects on student outcomes" (p. 73). Current challenges in research on EBPs include too few studies to determine which practices are indeed evidence-based, refinement of intervention approaches to examine what works for which children and under what conditions, and how to ensure implementation of these practices in real-world settings once their evidence base is established (Cook & Cook, 2013; Odom, 2009; Odom & Wolery, 2003; Wolery & Hemmeter, 2011). In the field of EI/

ECSE, EBPs and value-based practices form the foundation for implementation of intervention services (Odom, 2009; Odom & Wolery, 2003). These practices based on both research evidence and professional knowledge and experience are reflected in the Division for Early Childhood (DEC) Recommended Practices (DEC, 2014).

THE CHALLENGE OF INTERVENTION RESEARCH

Research in assessing the effects of intervention on young children presents a unique set of challenges. Studies focused on risk groups generally have larger samples and have better controls in place than studies using disability groups (e.g., see Farran, 2000; Raver, 2002); however, even in methodologically sophisticated studies, careful delineation between the treatment and reliability or fidelity of treatment is often not addressed (Gersten, Baker, & Lloyd, 2000; Swanson, Wanzek, Haring, Ciullo, & McCulley, 2011) or does not provide information about the degree of fidelity necessary to produce intervention effects (Wolery & Hemmeter, 2011). Indeed, fidelity of treatment is an issue at the forefront of EI/ECSE research (see, e.g., the 2013 special issue of the *Journal of Early Intervention*, Vol. 35, No. 2).

The complex process of intervention that must account for multiple effects, or more likely interactional effects of multiple variables on children and families, often is not addressed in intervention studies for at least three important reasons: 1) methodological constraints, 2) the target population, and 3) prohibitive costs.

Methodological Constraints

A number of methodological constraints confront investigators who are interested in conducting intervention research (Shonkoff & Phillips, 2000) and research in special education specifically (Odom et al., 2005). Children, unlike genes, germs, or chemical reactions, cannot be usefully examined in isolation (Lerner, Hauser-Cram, & Miller, 1998). The phenomena of children's learning, in other words, cannot be placed in a petri dish and watched as it unfolds. It is also difficult to parse the intervention efforts into manageable pieces to determine what constellation of factors accounts for change in children. For example, it would be difficult, if not impossible, to tease out the effects of a child's parents or the child's health on learning or performance apart from the effects of intervention content and procedures (Sameroff, 1994).

Equally frustrating from a scientific viewpoint is the inability to exercise laboratory control when conducting intervention research in real-world settings. When in the laboratory, investigators may carefully regulate, for example, the presentation of materials, the number of trials, and the consequences following a child's response, whereas research conducted in children's homes or classrooms makes controlling such variables much more complicated

(Scruggs & Mastropieri, 1994). Intervention research must contend with a multitude of variables that likely affect the manner in which children learn and respond (Baer, 1981; Gersten et al., 2000), and the study of ABI is no exception (Rahn, 2013).

When researchers conduct carefully controlled laboratory experiments with children, a major question arises as to how well conditions reflect circumstances that children are likely to encounter outside the laboratory. In other words, how relevant are the findings, or what is the external validity of the outcomes? The relevance of results is an important question for interventionists/teachers and parents (Kennedy, 1997). Findings that have little or no relevance to a child's daily interactions may be of questionable use (or validity) when trying to formulate effective interventions that should take into account an array of conditions and variables. For example, will an experimental procedure (e.g., one teacher following specific guidelines) found to expand vocabulary hold up, or replicate, when this procedure is used under less well-controlled conditions (e.g., with multiple children, by more than one teacher)?

The methodological complexities facing anyone attempting to examine the effects of a particular intervention, whether the focus is one isolated procedure or a mix of multiple procedures and factors, are indeed daunting. To date, no satisfactory paradigm or controls have been forthcoming. Consequently, the intervention researcher is faced with a series of necessary decisions that clearly compromise the findings.

Target Population

Children with disabilities and children exposed to unhealthy or even toxic environments pose a second set of challenges to determining the effectiveness of intervention approaches. Children at risk and with disabilities are by definition different from typically developing children in at least one respect, and often in many others. The variability within children who have or are at risk for disabilities may exceed that which is found in groups of typically developing children (Lewis & Wehren, 1982), which poses a challenge in special education research (Odom et al., 2005). An intervention approach or strategy found to be successful with a child with a visual and motor impairment, for example, might not be successful with a child with a language or behavioral disorder. An approach found effective with a group of children with general developmental delays may be less effective with children with behavioral problems. In addition, children who come to a center hungry, tired, or in emotional turmoil may benefit little from any intervention approach until their basic needs are addressed (Maslow, 1954, Raver, 2002).

Economic, cultural, and/or linguistic differences of the target population may also introduce significant challenges. For decades researchers have noted that an intervention found to be effective with a group of children with well-educated, middle-class parents may not be appropriate or effective with children whose backgrounds or learning styles differ (Gersten et al., 2000; Vincent, Salisbury, Strain, McCormick, & Tessier, 1990). In response to this challenge, researchers have begun investigating individual children's responses to intervention approaches within multitiered systems of support or response to intervention (RTI) frameworks (e.g., Buysse & Peisner-Fein-burg, 2010; Greenwood et al., 2013). These systems entail beginning with the least intrusive, most universal strategies (e.g., a high-quality early learning environment and curriculum) and adding more specialized, intensive strate-gies as children demonstrate the need for more structure to make progress. Within this model, interventionists monitor children's progress regularly and make data-based decisions regarding changes to intervention for indi-vidual children. Such multitiered approaches may yield valuable information on effects of specific interventions on individual children; however, we must wait for further verification on multitiered models as to their usefulness (e.g., can they be implemented reliably by teachers?) and effectiveness (e.g., do they produce consistent progress in children?) across populations of children with disabilities or those who are at risk.

The population challenges described have led many special education investigators, including EI/ECSE, to select single-subject designs to exam-ine the effects of intervention procedures on individual children or small groups of children (Horner et al., 2005). Single-subject designs are experi-mental in nature and allow the researcher to examine individual changes in a child's behavior in response to an intervention (Horner et al., 2005). Single-subject studies require a smaller number of participants (generally at least 3), making them more feasible for studying interventions with low-incidence populations (e.g., children with autism, children with vision impairments). However, generalizability of findings continues to be a problem for this experimental design.

As with methodological challenges, population size and diversity con-tinue to be major problems for individuals interested in documenting the effects of specific or more broad-based interventions such as ABI. Some prog-ress has occurred with the use of single-subject approaches and with multi-tiered models; however, these approaches do not yet offer totally acceptable solutions to the vexing problem of population diversity inherent in children with disabilities.

Prohibitive Costs

The third challenge that faces intervention researchers is cost. Delivering comprehensive interventions to children under experimental conditions can be an extraordinarily expensive undertaking if investigators are to control even the major relevant variables thought to affect intervention outcomes (e.g., size and constitution of sample, effect of parents/caregivers, teacher com-parability, comparison of intervention features). As Baer pointed out long ago:

> The sociological incredibility of analytic research to untangle the separate effects of the components of [curricular] packages is identical to the sociological incredibility of the research necessary to compare one package from a certain theoretical orientation to another package from a different theoretical orientation . . . getting to that point is incredibly expensive. (1981, p. 572)

And, we might add, highly unlikely. The cost of collecting an array of critical information on intervention effects is magnified by other costs. For example, most group design intervention research requires a sizeable investment in order to prepare the intervention staff, parents, and other caregivers who may be involved in delivering the intervention content (Escobar, Barnett, & Geotze, 1994; Tarr & Barnett, 2001). Once prepared to deliver the intervention content, researchers should ensure the continued fidelity of treatment by intervention agents to prevent the occurrence of unacceptable drift. Another important cost is the potential disruption the delivery of the intervention and data collection may impose on a program. For example, administering child performance measures, accommodating observers, or video recording teaching sessions may produce conditions that interfere with program operation.

The costs of examining the various features or components of an intervention approach, preparing personnel, and ensuring fidelity of treatment might be acceptable if there were adequate resources available. The cost, however, of evaluating the effectiveness of an intervention approach, not to mention evaluations of comparisons between approaches, is greater than state or federal government agencies appear willing to support on a sustained basis, except in rare cases such as the Infant Health and Development Program (1990) and the National Early Intervention Longitudinal Study (Bailey, Scarborough, & Hebbeler, 2003).

Single-subject research is likely the least expensive intervention research methodology; however, the requirement for systematic replication to examine generalization of effects to other subjects can drive up costs of this approach as well. Studies of discrete or focused intervention procedures (e.g., Sewell, Collins, Hemmeter, & Schuster, 1998) are much less costly than attempting to examine broad approaches such as ABI (Bricker & Gumerlock, 1988). Comprehensive intervention approaches are composed of multiple components or features. Attempting to measure the intensity and frequency of each intervention feature as well as examining child and family effects can be, to use Baer's word choice, *incredibly* expensive (Baer, 1981; Barnett & Escobar, 1990; Casto & White, 1993) and methodologically challenging (Gersten et al., 2000; Losardo & Bricker, 1994). The time and resources necessary for investigators to conduct comprehensive intervention research and for intervention staff to accommodate this research is generally unavailable to most intervention programs on a sustained basis.

Genuine cost constraints make it important for researchers to have available a variety of research methods (i.e., experimental and quasi-experimental, single subject, correlational, and qualitative designs) to answer research questions at different stages of research (e.g., early stage exploratory research vs. later randomized control trials; Odom et al., 2005). Even so it is likely that cost will impose a variety of constraints on intervention researchers that will make it important to carefully qualify their findings. The field of EI/ECSE as well as all of special education is in dire need of new more reality-based paradigms to study intervention effects. These paradigms must take into account population diversity and the multiple factors that likely affect children's progress, and they must do so at a cost society is willing to bear.

The discussion to this point on the current challenges to determining the effects of intervention is offered to set the stage for an appreciation of the material covered in the remainder of this chapter, to remind readers of the challenges inherent in intervention research, and to temper criticism of the methodological weaknesses that pervade much of the work to date.

The remainder of this chapter summarizes findings that illuminate directly or indirectly the effectiveness of EI/ECSE, in general, and ABI, in particular. In this review, two types of intervention research are examined. First, the text highlights findings from extensive reviews in the literature on general program effects with populations of young children with disabilities and children who are at risk for disabilities (and augment the discussion contained in Chapter 2). Second, the text reviews studies that have focused directly on evaluating the effects of ABI.

EFFECTS OF EARLY INTERVENTION/
EARLY CHILDHOOD SPECIAL EDUCATION

The Effectiveness of Early Intervention (Guralnick, 1997) contains a series of comprehensive reviews of intervention efforts conducted during the 1970s, 1980s, and 1990s. These reviews offer insightful analyses of the efficacy studies conducted on children with disabilities and children who are at risk. In most cases, the authors of these chapters concluded that high-quality programs delivered early in children's lives, and in some cases for extended periods, produce better immediate outcomes for children and families than if they had not participated in these programs:

- "High-quality, intensive programs that last for some years are the most likely to result in children's improvements in school or later real-life activities, but they are not a guarantee" (Bryant & Maxwell, 1997, p. 43).

- "There is, however, increasing recognition that both parent- and child-focused interventions can have beneficial impact" (Feldman, 1997, p. 188).

- "Early intervention for all types of communication disorders can be effective and almost certainly more efficient than intervention provided at later ages" (McLean & Woods Cripe, 1997, p. 418).

Most contributors to the book were careful to note the methodological flaws of the reviewed studies, to qualify outcomes (e.g., initial differences in experimental and control groups that "washed out" over time), and to acknowledge the variability in study features that made drawing conclusions across investigations difficult. It is also interesting to note that most contributors to the book concluded that research addressing the effects of specific intervention features had just begun (second-generation research [Guralnick, 1997]) and that considerable work remained before interventionists could arrive at reliable conclusions about the effectiveness of carefully defined and described intervention content and procedures across populations of children and their families.

Since 1997, other comprehensive reviews that address the effectiveness of EI/ECSE have been published. Authors and contributors to these volumes have reviewed the effects of intervention on young children with disabilities and children who are at risk for disabilities. Conclusions from two influential volumes (i.e., *From Neurons to Neighborhoods* [Shonkoff & Phillips, 2000] and *Handbook of Early Childhood Intervention* [Shonkoff & Meisels, 2000]) reflect the comprehensive knowledge base about the effects of EI/ECSE.

From Neurons to Neighborhoods contains the findings from a 2½-year project dedicated to the evaluation of the "current science of early childhood development" (Shonkoff & Phillips, 2000, p. ix). The project committee summarized findings supported by more than 3 decades of research and program evaluation. Several findings directly address the effectiveness of EI (pp. 342–343):

- "Well-designed and successfully implemented interventions can enhance the short-term performance of children living in poverty...

- "Well-designed and successfully implemented interventions can promote significant short-term gains on standardized cognitive and social measures for young children with documented developmental delays or disabilities....

- "Short-term impacts on cognitive development of young children living in high risk environments are greater when intervention is goal-directed and child-focused....

- "Measured short-term impacts on cognitive and social development of young children with developmental disabilities are greater when the intervention is more structured and focused on the child–caregiver relationship....

- "Analyses of the economic costs and benefits of early childhood interventions for low-income children have demonstrated medium- and long-term benefits to families as well as savings in public expenditures..."

The specific qualifications that accompanied these conclusions (e.g., effects are short-term, focus is on specific behaviors, programs are well-designed and executed), as well as the general limitations of EI research (e.g., basic problems in research designs, significant variability across programs, focus is primarily on cognitive performance) are discussed by Shonkoff and Phillips (2000).

The stated purpose of a second influential volume, *Handbook of Early Childhood Intervention* (Shonkoff & Meisels, 2000), "is to provide a scholarly overview of the knowledge base and practice of early childhood intervention" (p. ix). In particular, the chapter by Farran (2000) provided a comprehensive analysis of the effects of intervention on vulnerable populations. Farran drew a number of sobering and well-supported conclusions based on her careful analysis of individual studies. For example,

- "Abecedarian and Project Care programs are perhaps the most scientifically controlled and thoroughly reported early intervention efforts in social science . . . Overall, their findings show modest success . . ." (2000, p. 515).

- High/Scope Perry Preschool Project's follow-up of the target children at age 27 years suggested, "In many categories, there are significant differences favoring the program group as well as a fairly consistent trend in their favor" (2000, p. 517).

However, Farran also identified concerns about the type of analyses used to arrive at these conclusions.

- The Infant Health and Development Program's initial findings on children reported mixed outcomes before age 3. By the fifth-year follow-up, the experimental and control groups were not different on most measures. "The lack of effect for such an ambitious, well-run, and expensive program was unanticipated and troubling" (2000, p. 521).

Farran summarized the corpus of work on intervention treatment effects with risk groups suggesting that the intervention programs have not been shown to be better than doing nothing at all, and that the more disadvantaged the children and families, the more compromised the intervention effects. She further suggested that intervention attempts have likely not been effective with low-income groups because the treatments do not take into account the ecological context of the families, as well as how to better prepare children for their subsequent public school experiences.

Farran also addressed intervention programs for children with disabilities. Again, her careful analysis led her to several troubling conclusions. First, there has been little attention given to the impact of programs on young children supported by the Individuals with Disabilities Education Act (IDEA) of 1990 (PL 101-476) and the Individuals with Disabilities Education Act Amendments (IDEA) of 1997 (PL 105-17). "This review makes clear that the largest intervention effort for children with disabilities and their families [IDEA programs] has received little systematic attention concerning its effectiveness" (2000, p. 539). Second, the diversity across studies (e.g., population, design, and measurement variability) makes it difficult to arrive at general conclusions. "These studies [efficacy studies focused on children with disabilities] are so disparate that general conclusions are somewhat difficult to derive" (2000, p. 533). Third, future research should direct more of its attention to "determining when in the developmental sequence it is appropriate and facilitating to administer certain forms of intervention" (2000, p. 540). Farran continued with the observation that "A more reasonable conclusion may be that we must look to the specific form of the intervention delivered at a particular time frame" (2000, p. 541).

Since the publication of *From Neurons to Neighborhoods* (Shonkoff & Phillips, 2000) and *Handbook of Early Childhood Intervention* (Shonkoff & Meisels, 2000), additional studies have been published documenting the effects of EI. Although a comprehensive review of these publications is beyond the scope of the work presented in this chapter, results from later longitudinal studies of prominent and well-researched EI programs (e.g., Chicago Longitudinal Study [Reynolds, Temple, White, Ou, & Robertson, 2011]; Abecedarian Project [Campbell et al., 2012]; Perry Preschool Study [Schweinhart et al., 2005]) have continued to demonstrate outcomes consistent with earlier findings.

What conclusions can be drawn from these investigations? First, quality intervention efforts have produced short-term effects, but most of these reported effects appear to dissipate over time. The dissipation may be, in part, the result of poor intervention received once children enter the public schools or, as Farran suggested, the lack of attention to children's and families' ecological contexts. Second, flaws in design and analyses have compromised the results obtained from many of these investigations. The most current scientific template, however, may be inappropriate to use to determine the effects of intervention efforts. Future success may be dependent on developing scientifically defensible but different standards for intervention research. Third, the diversity in populations, designs, measures, and intervention/treatments makes drawing general conclusions difficult. An important task for researchers is to examine which evidence-based interventions work for whom and under what conditions (Cook & Cook, 2013). The results would not be general conclusions but rather would establish specific relationships among children, their developmental trajectories, environmental context, and intervention/treatment efforts.

EFFECTS OF ABI

Our attempts to study the effectiveness of ABI have faced the same problems (i.e., methodological constraints, target population, prohibitive costs). In particular, we have had little opportunity for random assignment to groups and significant difficulty in finding ways to establish legitimate control or comparison groups against which we can evaluate the effects of ABI. Even when locating contrast groups, their comparability as well as the comparability of other intervention approaches often cannot be established (e.g., Losardo & Bricker, 1994). Although confronted with these realities, we have collected information on child progress, parent satisfaction, and the general effectiveness of the approach since the early 1980s.

Although much of the collected information was formative and has been used internally to refine and improve the approach, we have published a series of outcome studies. These studies are reviewed next with an eye toward examining the effectiveness of ABI. It should be mentioned that the early studies were primarily designed as evaluation studies, and descriptions of the intervention content and procedures are brief. The label *activity-based* was not used until the 1988 study; however, from the early 1980s the approach employed at the University of Oregon's Early Intervention Program was activity-based (see Bricker, 1986). Consequently, the evaluation studies described next were focused on determining the effectiveness of the activity-based approach.

Bricker and Sheehan (1981)

Bricker and Sheehan (1981) published the first study addressing the effects of ABI in 1981. The article presented 2 years of program evaluation data on 63 children. The children ranged in age from 5 to 69 months and spanned the continuum from children without disabilities to those with severe disabilities. Children attended a center-based classroom 5 days per week; however, attendance varied across children. The intervention program focused on the children's IEP goals and objectives by embedding learning opportunities into routine, child-initiated, and planned activities. Parental involvement and participation were encouraged.

Standardized and criterion-referenced tests (i.e., the Bayley Scales of Infant Development [Bayley, 1969], the McCarthy Scales of Children's Abilities [McCarthy, 1972], and the Uniform Performance Assessment System [White, Edgar, & Haring, 1978]) were administered at the beginning and end of each school year. During both years, almost all pretest and posttest comparisons on standardized and criterion-referenced tests indicated that children's performances were significantly improved at posttest and that most changes were educationally significant (i.e., exceeded 1 standard deviation). The fidelity of treatment was not monitored; therefore, we cannot be sure how faithfully the intervention staff implemented the elements of the activity-based approach. The program was, however, a field site for teaching graduate students, so there is reason to believe that the intervention closely adhered to the tenets of the activity-based approach. There were no control or comparison groups; however, the consistent findings of change across groups and tests suggest the intervention program had an impact. Nonetheless, the effects of maturation cannot be ruled out.

Bricker, Bruder, and Bailey (1982)

Bricker, Bruder, and Bailey (1982) reported an evaluation of the effects of developmental integration on 41 young children with disabilities assigned to three different classrooms that operated using the ABI approach. The children ranged in age from 10 months to 5 years and included typically developing children and those with a variety of disabilities. This study also used standardized and criterion-referenced measures (i.e., the Bayley Scales of Infant Development [Bayley, 1969], the McCarthy Scales of Children's Abilities [McCarthy, 1972], the Uniform Performance Assessment System [White et al., 1978], and the Student Progress Record [Oregon State Mental Health Division, 1977]) and a pretest and posttest design. The study had no comparison group; however, standardized tests were included to provide some control through the use of the general cognitive index that is designed to examine performance change in proportion to chronological age. Interventionists were taught to embed learning opportunities related to children's goals and objectives into child-directed, routine, and planned activities—a key element of ABI. Parental involvement was a priority, although the form of involvement varied by family and child need.

The evaluation data reported on a subsample of the participating children indicated that statistically and educationally significant gains from pretest to posttest were made on the criterion-referenced tests. With the exception that no significant shift in the general cognitive index occurred for one of the groups, all other comparisons on the standardized tests were significant as well. These findings replicate the initial 1981 study outcomes but also suffer from the same limitations—no measures of treatment fidelity and no control group. Comparisons on the general cognitive index were used in lieu of control groups, and although better than no controls, these comparisons fall far short of accepted standards necessary for the objective demonstration of an intervention effort.

Bailey and Bricker (1985)

Similar to the previous study, Bailey and Bricker (1985) examined the effects of ABI on more than 80 children with mild to severe disabilities from infancy to 3 years old. Children attended either a home-based or center-based program that employed an activity-based approach by embedding learning opportunities into a variety of meaningful activities, targeting functional responses, and providing contingent feedback to children. Family participation remained a priority, although, as before, the nature of the participation varied across families. Standardized and criterion-referenced tests were administered at the beginning and end of the school year (i.e., the revised Gesell and Amatruda Developmental and Neurologic Examination [Knobloch, Stevens, & Malone, 1980] and the Comprehensive Early Evaluation and Programming System [Bailey, 1983], the forerunner to the AEPS [Bricker, 2002]).

An analysis of the pretest and posttest comparisons found significant gains for all children on the criterion-referenced measure. On the standardized measure, significant differences were found using maturity scores; however, no differences were found when using developmental quotients. This latter finding suggests that child change in proportion to age was not affected even if the children had gained a significant number of new skills over the year as indicated by the change on the criterion-referenced instrument and change in the maturity scores. Parent satisfaction with the program was reported to be high. This study did not have a comparison group nor were treatment fidelity data collected; however, once again this program served as a teaching site for graduate students learning to use ABI. There is little doubt that changes were introduced to the activity-based approach over time that may or may not have produced differential outcomes. Unfortunately, there is no objective documentation of how the approach changed over time and how that change might, in turn, have been related to child change.

Bricker and Gumerlock (1988)

In a fourth study on the impact of ABI on child performance, Bricker and Gumerlock (1988) reported 2 years of outcome data on a sample of 46 infants and toddlers. These children had disabilities that ranged from mild to severe, and they attended a center-based program operated by trained interventionists. The elements of ABI were employed, and intervention content was determined by the children's IEP goals and objectives. As in previous studies, the effects of ABI were measured using a pretest and posttest comparison of scores on criterion-referenced and standardized measures (i.e., the Bayley Scales of Infant Development [Bayley, 1969], the revised Stanford-Binet Intelligence Scale [Thorndike, Hagen, & Sattler, 1986], the revised Gesell and Amatruda Developmental and Neurologic Examination [Knobloch et al., 1980], and the Evaluation and Programming System [Bricker, Gentry, & Bailey, 1985], also a forerunner of the AEPS). As in the previous studies, the analysis showed that the children's performance in general improved significantly from pretest to posttest on the standardized and criterion-referenced measures. In addition, this study reported children's progress on specific short-term and long-term educational goals. Again, this study did not measure treatment fidelity or provide controls.

In these four investigations, only limited attention was given to which treatments worked for children with differing characteristics. The Bricker and Sheehan (1981) study reported subgroup analysis for typically developing, at-risk, mild, moderate, and severe disability groups. And the Bricker and colleagues (1982) study reported separate findings for the groups of children with and without disabilities. These findings indicate that the intervention appears to have had a relatively positive effect across subgroups of children.

Bricker and Colleagues (1997)

From 1991 through 1996, funds provided by the U.S. Department of Education's Office of Special Education Programs and awarded to the Early Intervention Program at the University of Oregon were used to develop a model demonstration program (Bricker et al., 1997). This model demonstration program had two phases. Phase one was designed to demonstrate the positive impact of ABI on young children with disabilities, and phase two was a replication to verify that the findings reported for phase one could be reproduced at different sites. Phase one lasted 2 years and included three sites. Staff at each site were taught to use the four elements of ABI with the participating children. A total of 52 children participated, and they ranged in age from 7 to 27 months at the beginning of the project. Children at one site were classified as at risk (i.e., had teenage mothers), whereas the children at the other two sites had a range of disabilities. Fidelity of treatment data were collected for the duration of the project. Interventionists were found to consistently use the four elements of the approach. The revised Gesell and Amatruda Developmental and Neurologic Examination (Knobloch et al., 1980) and the first iteration of AEPS (Bricker, 1993) were administered at the beginning, middle, and end of the school year.

A Proportional Change Index (PCI) is a numerical statement of the relationship between a child's rate of development during intervention and the rate of development at the time intervention began, and it is used to compare developmental change over time. Use of the PCI controls for differences between developmental age and chronological age at pretest. PCI data in this study suggested that children progressed at their expected or better rate as measured by the revised Gesell and Amatruda Developmental and Neurologic Examination (Knobloch et al., 1980). A within-group analysis of covariance was performed on participants' posttest AEPS scores (Bricker, 1993). The variate was the type of goals (i.e., target and nontarget). The covariate used was pretest scores on the AEPS. The analysis revealed that the greatest gains were made in target areas as compared with nontarget areas for both years of phase one. Parents were asked to complete a satisfaction questionnaire, and the results indicated high satisfaction with the program for both years.

Phase two was conducted over a 2-year period and involved eight replication sites in two states. Staff at each site were provided instruction on implementation of the four elements of the activity-based approach; however, the amount of instruction varied across sites. A total of 52 staff members participated. Fidelity of treatment data were collected on 36 teachers, and their performance did not vary over time. Children's performances were compared using the AEPS. The pretest–posttest comparisons indicated that children ($N = 145$) made significant gains on all six domains of the test.

In April 1994, an external site visit of this demonstration project was conducted. Observations of the classrooms, interviews with staff, and reviews of the outcome data were undertaken. The site team's report stated the following:

> We view this project as having substantial national significance to the field of early intervention. The project staff has done an excellent job of implementing the model in community programs that represent quite diverse populations served by early childhood programs. (Peck, Schwartz, & Warren, 1994)

The site team listed several project strengths and concluded with a set of recommendations that urged project staff to expand the current evaluation model to include examination of the potential range of contextual factors that may affect the implementation of activity-based intervention.

The first phase of this model demonstration project was designed to examine the effects of ABI by collecting extensive child progress data. The second phase was designed to determine if outcomes could be replicated at other sites following training on the activity-based approach. Child progress data from phase one and phase two were robust from the perspective of the large sample size and that participants spanned the early childhood age range and disability continuum from children at risk to children with severe disabilities. Participants also came from different geographic sites and programs. In addition, phase two was able to demonstrate that interventionists can learn to use the activity-based approach with training. As noted by the site team, however, the outcomes from the project did little to clarify the contextual factors that may affect implementation of the approach.

Losardo and Bricker (1994)

In 1994, Losardo and Bricker published a well-controlled single-subject study that compared the effects of ABI with a direct instruction approach. Six children who ranged in age from 47 to 66 months participated in this study. All children were attending a center-based intervention program for young children with disabilities. Experimental control was established through the use of an alternating treatment design so that the effects of direct instruction and ABI on vocabulary acquisition and generalization could be compared across the children. Vocabulary items were matched and then randomly assigned to either the activity-based or direct instruction treatment conditions. The procedure was divided into a baseline and treatment phase for each child. Treatments were counterbalanced daily. During instruction, interventionists worked with the children following the stipulated elements of each approach. Fidelity of treatment data were collected and indicated that teachers systematically implemented the treatments over time. Study outcomes suggested that acquisition of vocabulary items occurred more quickly under the direct instruction condition but that generalization was significantly better for vocabulary items learned under the ABI condition. In addition, subsequent maintenance of the gains was significantly greater for the activity-based condition than for the direct instruction condition. In many ways the outcomes of this study make intuitive sense. That is, massed trials will produce more rapid acquisition, but meaningful embedded learning opportunities produce better generalization.

Pretti-Frontczak and Bricker (2001)

Pretti-Frontczak and Bricker (2001) conducted an exploratory study of teachers' use of embedding, the underlying process of ABI. Participants included seven classroom teachers and one child with an identified disability in each classroom with whom the teacher provided the intervention, all from two early childhood/ECSE programs. Teachers were trained in administering the AEPS, writing quality goals and objectives, and the embedding strategy. After training, teachers administered the AEPS, wrote goals and objectives, and delivered intervention to the focus child. During classroom observations, researchers coded teachers' use of the embedding strategy during 15-second intervals using a partial-interval response coding system. Results suggested teachers used the embedding strategy during only 9.7% of intervals, indicating a low rate of implementation of the embedding approach. Teachers were most likely to use the embedding strategy during one-to-one activities, and during language and preacademic activities using instructional materials (e.g., flashcards) or manipulatives (e.g., blocks). The embedding strategies most commonly used were asking questions and providing models.

McBride and Schwartz (2003)

In this study researchers used a single-subject multiple-probe design to compare the rate of three ECSE teachers' presentation of instructional strategies in four conditions: baseline (i.e., usual classroom intervention), teacher training on ABI, teacher training on ABI with discrete trials intervention (i.e., instructional cue, child response, teacher consequence), and generalization. Results suggested that although teachers increased their rate of use of instructional strategies in the ABI condition, the rate increased substantially when teachers were taught to use instructional trials within the ABI framework. Children showed a higher rate of correct responding in the ABI with discrete trials condition over other conditions. The researchers concluded that it might be important for teachers to understand how to conduct instructional trials within an ABI framework.

Rahn (2013)

A single-subject adapted alternating treatments design was used to compare vocabulary learning in ABI and Dialogic Reading. Participants included three 3-year-olds attending a preschool program for children whose families were living in poverty. Vocabulary items were randomly assigned to conditions (ABI, Dialogic Reading, control) and taught within alternating 10-minute intervention sessions three times per week. Results suggested that both

interventions were superior to control. ABI was more effective for one partici-
pant, although results were mixed for the remaining two participants with
both interventions having similar effects on vocabulary acquisition.

With the exception of the last four studies, the investigations of ABI
reviewed in this section are representative of first-generation EI efficacy
research (Guralnick & Bennett, 1987). That is, the findings from such
studies produced global outcomes that indicated EI, or in this case, ABI, is
effective in producing short-term change in children. The last four studies
reviewed move closer to what Guralnick (1997) has called second-generation
research. This type of research is designed to study the effects of specific
features rather than global effects. If one accepts the significant constraints
facing intervention researchers discussed earlier in this chapter, we believe
the general efficacy of ABI has been demonstrated. The early work based primarily on program evaluation data, however, can be criticized for its design
and methodological flaws.

A major role of interventionists, specialists, and caregivers is to provide opportunities for children to learn target goals and objectives as well as
general curricular goals often associated with state standards. A major feature of ABI and other naturalistic approaches is embedding learning opportunities into a range of authentic and therefore meaningful activities. The
study of this important underlying process of ABI is an example of second-
generation research and, therefore, is a step forward in beginning to bring
better understanding to what specific parts, or portions, of global approaches
produce change in children. An analysis of the work related to embedding of
learning opportunities is beyond the scope of this chapter, and many of the
studies focused on this instructional process and other instructional strategies have been reviewed elsewhere (e.g., Pretti-Frontczak, Barr, Macy, &
Carter, 2003; Winton, Buysse, Turnbull, Rous, & Hollingsworth, 2010).

The research on embedding and other similar strategies has been
conducted by a variety of research teams—all of whom report similar outcomes. Overall findings have suggested that naturalistic methods in which
interventionists embed learning opportunities produce consistent positive
change in children (e.g., Daugherty, Grisham-Brown, & Hemmeter, 2001;
Grisham-Brown, Schuster, Hemmeter, & Collins, 2000; Horn, Lieber, Li,
Sandall, & Schwartz, 2000; Kohler, Anthony, Steighner, & Hoyson, 2001;
Kohler, Strain, Hoyson, & Jamieson, 1997; Rahn, 2013; Sewell et al., 1998;
Wolery, 1994; Wolery, Anthony, Caldwell, Snyder, & Morgante, 2002; Wolery,
Anthony, & Heckathorn, 1998). Additional studies are needed, however, that
focus on other elements of ABI.

SUMMARY

Significant methodological, population, and cost constraints face investigators interested in studying the effects of intervention for children with special
needs in real-world settings. As we noted, the barriers to the demonstration

of intervention effects, particularly long-term effects, are sufficient to dissuade any but the most determined investigators. Intervention researchers face a serious dilemma between establishing sufficient experimental control to make the outcomes defensible (i.e., internal validity) and conducting the work in ways that at least minimally match what teachers, interventionists, and caregivers face on a daily basis (i.e., external validity). One of the most significant challenges facing intervention researchers is the discovery or development of procedures that permit establishing sufficient scientific control but also accommodate the reality of field-based work.

Studies of global intervention efforts focused on populations of children at risk and with disabilities have suggested that quality intervention efforts do produce at least short-term positive effects. As one might expect, both the nature of the population and lack of resources have resulted in work that has serious methodological flaws. We believe that future studies are needed in four areas to move the field toward a better understanding of the effects of ABI as well as other intervention approaches: 1) implementation of specific components of ABI (i.e., second-generation research; Guralnick, 1997), 2) implementation of ABI under ideal conditions (i.e., efficacy research; Odom, 2009), 3) implementation of ABI under typical classroom conditions by interventionists (i.e., effectiveness research; Odom, 2009), and 4) methods for bridging the research-to-practice gap through effective training for interventionists (e.g., "enlightened professional development" [Odom, 2009, pp. 58–59]). Results from such research will provide valuable information to improve the activity-based approach and enhance its effects on young children with special needs and their families.

REFERENCES

Baer, D. (1981). The nature of intervention research. In R. Schiefelbusch & D. Bricker (Eds.), *Early language: Acquisition and intervention*. Baltimore, MD: University Park Press.

Bailey, D., Scarborough, A., & Hebbeler, K. (2003). *National early intervention longitudinal study: Executive summary. NEILS Data Report No. 2*. Menlo Park, CA: SRI International.

Bailey, E. (1983). *Psychometric evaluation of the Comprehensive Early Evaluation and Programming System*. Unpublished doctoral dissertation, University of Oregon, Eugene.

Bailey, E., & Bricker, D. (1985). Evaluation of a three-year early intervention demonstration project. *Topics in Early Childhood Special Education, 5*, 52–65.

Barnett, S.J., & Escobar, C.P. (1990). Economic costs and benefits of early intervention. In S.J. Meisels & J.P. Shonkoff (Eds.), *Handbook of early childhood intervention*. Cambridge, United Kingdom: Cambridge University Press.

Bayley, N. (1969). *Bayley Scales of Infant Development*. New York, NY: Psychological Corp.

Bricker, D. (1986). *Early education of at-risk and handicapped infants, toddlers, and preschool children*. Glenview, IL: Scott Foresman.

Bricker, D. (Ed.). (1993). *Assessment, Evaluation, and Programming System for Infants and Children*. Baltimore, MD: Paul H. Brookes Publishing Co.

Bricker, D. (Series Ed.). (2002). *Assessment, Evaluation and Programming System (AEPS®) for Infants and Children* (2nd ed.). Baltimore, MD: Paul H. Brookes Publishing Co.

Bricker, D., Bruder, M., & Bailey, E. (1982). Developmental integration of preschool children. *Analysis and Intervention in Developmental Disabilities, 2,* 207–222.

Bricker, D., Gentry, D., & Bailey, E. (1985). *Evaluation and Programming System: For Infants and Young Children—Assessment Level 1: Developmentally 1 Month to 3 Years.* Eugene, OR: University of Oregon.

Bricker, D., & Gumerlock, S. (1988). Application of a three-level evaluation plan for monitoring child progress and program effects. *Journal of Special Education, 22,* 66–81.

Bricker, D., McComas, N., Pretti-Frontczak, K., Leve, C., Stieber, S., Losardo, A., & Scanlon, J. (1997). *Activity-based collaboration project: A nondirected model demonstration program for children who are at-risk and disabled and their families.* Unpublished report, University of Oregon, Center on Human Development, Early Intervention Program, Eugene, OR.

Bricker, D., & Sheehan, R. (1981). Effectiveness of an early intervention program as indexed by measures of child change. *Journal of the Division for Early Childhood, 4,* 11–28.

Bricker, W., & Bricker, D. (1976). The infant, toddler, and preschool research and intervention project. In T. Tjossem (Ed.), *Intervention strategies for high-risk infants and young children.* Baltimore, MD: University Park Press.

Bryant, D., & Maxwell, K. (1997). The effectiveness of early intervention for disadvantaged children. In M.J. Guralnick (Ed.), *The effectiveness of early intervention* (pp. 23–46). Baltimore, MD: Paul H. Brookes Publishing Co.

Buysse, V., & Peisner-Feinberg, E. (2010). Recognition & response: RTI for pre-k. *Young Exceptional Children, 13*(4), 2–13.

Campbell, F.A., Pungello, E.P., Burchinal, M., Kainz, K., Pan, Y., Wasik, B.,...Ramey, C.T. (2012). Adult outcomes as a function of an early childhood educational program: An Abecedarian project follow-up. *Developmental Psychology, 48*(4), 1033–1043. doi:10.1037/a0026644

Casto, G., & White, K. (1993). Longitudinal studies of alternative types of early intervention: Rationale and design. *Early Education and Development, 4,* 224–237.

Cook, B.G., & Cook, S.C. (2013). Unraveling evidence-based practices in special education. *Journal of Special Education, 47*(2), 71–82. doi:10.1177/0022466911420877

Daugherty, S., Grisham-Brown, J., & Hemmeter, M.L. (2001). The effects of embedded instruction on the acquisition of target and nontarget skills in preschoolers with developmental delays. *Topics in Early Childhood Special Education, 21,* 213–221.

Division for Early Childhood. (2014). *DEC recommended practices in early intervention/ early childhood special education 2014.* Retrieved from http://www.dec-sped.org/recommendedpractices

Escobar, C., Barnett, W., & Goetze, L. (1994). Cost analysis in early intervention. *Journal of Early Intervention, 18,* 48–63.

Farran, D. (2000). Another decade of intervention for children who are low income or disabled: What do we know now? In J.P. Shonkoff & S.J. Meisels (Eds.), *Handbook of early childhood intervention* (2nd ed.). Cambridge, United Kingdom: Cambridge University Press.

Feldman, M. (1997). The effectiveness of early intervention for children of parents with mental retardation. In M.J. Guralnick (Ed.), *The effectiveness of early intervention* (pp. 171–192). Baltimore, MD: Paul H. Brookes Publishing Co.

Gast, D.L. (2010). General factors in measurement and evaluation. In Gast, D.L. (Ed.), *Single subject research methodology in behavioral sciences* (pp. 91–109). New York, NY: Routledge.

Gersten, R., Baker, S., & Lloyd, J. (2000). Designing high-quality research in special education: Group experimental design. *Journal of Special Education, 34,* 2–18.

Gersten, R., Fuchs, L.S., Compton, D., Coyne, M., Greenwood, C., & Innocenti, M.S. (2005). Quality indicators for group experimental and quasi-experimental research in special education. *Exceptional Children, 71*(2), 149–164.

Greenwood, C.R., Carta, J.J., Atwater, J., Goldstein, H., Kaminski, R., & McConnell, S. (2013). Is a response to intervention approach to preschool language and literacy instruction needed? *Topics in Early Childhood Special Education, 33*(1), 48–64. doi:10.1177/0271121412455438

Grisham-Brown, J., Schuster, J.W., Hemmeter, M.L., & Collins, B.C. (2000). Using an embedded strategy to teach preschoolers with significant disabilities. *Journal of Behavioral Education, 10,* 139–162.

Guralnick, M.J. (Ed.). (1997). *The effectiveness of early intervention.* Baltimore, MD: Paul H. Brookes Publishing Co.

Guralnick, M.J. (1997). Second-generation research in the field of early intervention. In M.J. Guralnick (Ed.), *The effectiveness of early intervention* (pp. 3–20). Baltimore, MD: Paul H. Brookes Publishing Co.

Guralnick, M., & Bennett, F. (Eds.). (1987). *The effectiveness of early intervention for at-risk and handicapped children.* San Diego, CA: Academic Press.

Horn, E., Lieber, J., Li, S.M., Sandall, S., & Schwartz, I. (2000). Supporting young children's IEP goals in inclusive settings through embedded learning opportunities. *Topics in Early Childhood Special Education, 20,* 208–223.

Horner, R.H., Carr, E.G., Halle, J., McGee, G., Odom, S., & Wolery, M. (2005). The use of single-subject research to identify evidence-based practice in special education. *Exceptional Children, 71*(2), 165–179.

Individuals with Disabilities Education Act Amendments (IDEA) of 1997, PL 105-17, 20 U.S.C. §§ 1400 *et seq.*

Individuals with Disabilities Education Act (IDEA) of 1990, PL 101-476, 20 U.S.C. §§ 1400 *et seq.*

Infant Health and Development Program. (1990). Enhancing the outcomes of low-birth-weight, premature infants. *Journal of the American Medical Association, 263,* 3035–3042.

Kaiser, A., & Hemmeter, M.L. (Eds.) (2013). Treatment fidelity [Special issue]. *Journal of Early Intervention, 35*(2).

Kennedy, M. (1997). The connection between research and practice. *Educational Researcher, 26,* 4–12.

Knobloch, H., Stevens, F., & Malone, A. (1980). *Manual of developmental diagnosis: The administration and interpretation of the revised Gesell and Amatruda developmental and neurologic examination.* Hagerstown, MD: Harper & Row.

Kohler, F., Anthony, L., Steighner, S., & Hoyson, M. (2001). Teaching social interaction skills in integrated preschool: An examination of naturalistic tactics. *Topics in Early Childhood Special Education, 21,* 93–103, 113.

Kohler, F., Strain, P., Hoyson, M., & Jamieson, B. (1997). Merging naturalistic teaching and peer-based strategies to address the IEP objectives of preschoolers with autism: An examination of structural and child behavior outcomes. *Focus on Autism and Other Developmental Disabilities, 12,* 196–206.

Lerner, P., Hauser-Cram, P., & Miller, E. (1998). Assumptions and features of longitudinal designs. In B. Spodek, O. Saracho, & A. Pellegrini (Eds.), *Issues in early childhood educational research.* New York, NY: Teachers College Press.

Lewis, M., & Wehren, A. (1982). The central tendency in study of the handicapped child. In D. Bricker (Ed.), *Intervention with at-risk and handicapped infants.* Baltimore, MD: University Park Press.

Losardo, A., & Bricker, D. (1994). Activity-based intervention and direct instruction: A comparison study. *American Journal on Mental Retardation, 98,* 744–765.

Maslow, A. (1954). *Motivation and personality.* New York, NY: Harpers.

McBride, B., & Schwartz, I.S. (2003). Effects of teaching early interventionists to use discrete trials during ongoing classroom activities. *Topics in Early Childhood Special Education, 23,* 5–17. doi:10.1177/027112140302300102

McCarthy, D. (1972). *McCarthy Scales of Children's Abilities.* New York, NY: Psychological Corp.

McLean, L.K., & Woods Cripe, J. (1997). The effectiveness of early intervention for children with communication disorders. In M.J. Guralnick (Ed.), *The effectiveness of early intervention* (pp. 349–428). Baltimore, MD: Paul H. Brookes Publishing Co.

Odom, S.L. (2009). The tie that binds: Evidence-based practice, implementation science, and outcomes for children. *Topics in Early Childhood Special Education, 29*(1), 53–61. doi:10.1177/0271121408329171

Odom, S.L., Brantlinger, E., Gersten, R., Horner, R.H., Thompson, B., & Harris, K.R. (2005). Research in special education: Scientific methods and evidence-based practices. *Exceptional Children, 71*(2), 137–148.

Odom, S.L., & Wolery, M. (2003). A unified theory of practice in early intervention/early childhood special education: Evidence-based practices. *Journal of Special Education, 37*(3), 164–173. doi:10.1177/00224669030370030601

Oregon State Mental Health Division. (1977). *The student progress record.* Salem, OR: Author.

Peck, C., Schwartz, I., & Warren, S. (1994). *Site Visit Report–April 27–28, 1994. A non-directed model demonstration program: Activity-based intervention.* Eugene, OR: University of Oregon.

Pretti-Frontczak, K., Barr, D., Macy, M., & Carter, A. (2003). An annotated bibliography of research and resources related to activity-based intervention, embedded learning opportunities, and routines-based instruction. *Topics in Early Childhood Special Education, 23,* 29–39.

Pretti-Frontczak, K., & Bricker, D. (2001). Use of the embedding strategy by early childhood education and early childhood special education teachers. *Infants-Toddlers Intervention: The Transdisciplinary Journal, 11,* 111–128.

Rahn, N.L. (2013). *A comparison of word learning in 3-year-old children at-risk for language and literacy difficulties in dialogic reading and activity-based intervention* (Doctoral dissertation). Retrieved from Proquest Dissertations and Theses (Publication No. 3567464).

Raver, C. (2002). Emotions matter: Making the case for the role of young children's emotional development for early school readiness. *Social Policy Report, XVI,* 3–18.

Reynolds, A.J., Temple, J.A., White, B.A., Ou, S.R., & Robertson, D.L. (2011). Age 26 cost-benefit analysis of the child-parent center early education program. *Child Development, 82*(1), 379–404. doi:10.1111/j.1467-8624.2010.01563.x

Sameroff, A. (1994). Ecological perspectives on longitudinal follow-up studies. In S. Friedman & H. Haywood (Eds.), *Concepts, domains, and methods.* San Diego, CA: Academic Press.

Schweinhart, L.J., Montie, J., Xiang, Z., Barnett, W.S., Belfield, C.R., & Nores, M. (2005). *The High/Scope Perry Preschool Study through age 40: Summary, conclusions, and frequently asked questions.* Ypsilanti, MI: High/Scope Press.

Scruggs, T., & Mastropieri, M. (1994). Issues in conducting intervention research: Secondary students. In S. Vaughn & C. Bos (Eds.), *Research issues in learning disabilities: Theory, methodology, assessment, and ethics.* New York, NY: Springer Verlag.

Sewell, T., Collins, B., Hemmeter, M., & Schuster, J. (1998). Using simultaneous prompting within an activity-based format to teach dressing skills to preschoolers with developmental disabilities. *Journal of Early Intervention, 21,* 132–145.

Shonkoff, J.P., & Meisels, S.J. (2000). *Handbook of early childhood intervention* (2nd ed.). Cambridge, United Kingdom: Cambridge University Press.

Shonkoff, J.P., & Phillips, D.A. (Eds.). (2000). *From neurons to neighborhoods.* Washington, DC: The National Academies Press.

Swanson, E., Wansek, J., Haring, C., Ciullo, S., & McCulley, L. (2011). Intervention fidelity in special and general education research journals. *Journal of Special Education, 47*(1), 3–13. doi:10.1177/0022466911419516

Tarr, J., & Barnett, W. (2001). A cost analysis of Part C early intervention services in New Jersey. *Journal of Early Intervention, 24,* 45–54.

Thorndike, R., Hagen, E., & Sattler, J. (1986). *The Stanford-Binet Intelligence Scale* (4th ed.). Chicago, IL: Riverside.

Vincent, L., Salisbury, C., Strain, P., McCormick, C., & Tessier, A. (1990). A behavioral ecological approach to early intervention: Focus on cultural diversity. In S.J. Meisels & J.P. Shonkoff (Eds.), *Handbook of early childhood intervention.* Cambridge, United Kingdom: Cambridge University Press.

White, O., Edgar, E., & Haring, N. (1978). *Uniform performance assessment system.* Seattle, WA: University of Washington, College of Education, Experimental Education Unit, Child Development and Mental Retardation Center.

Winton, P.J., Buysse, V., Turnbull, A., Rous, B., & Hollingsworth, H. (2010). *CONNECT Module 1: Embedded Interventions.* Chapel Hill, NC: University of North Carolina, FPG Child Development Institute, CONNECT: The Center to Mobilize Early Childhood Knowledge. Retrieved from http://community.fpg.unc.edu/connect-modules/learners/module-1

Wolery, M. (1994). Implementing instruction for young children with special needs in early childhood classrooms. In M. Wolery & J.S. Wilbers (Eds.), *Including children with special needs in early childhood programs* (pp. 151–166). Washington, DC: National Association for the Education of Young Children.

Wolery, M., Anthony, L., Caldwell, N., Snyder, E., & Morgante, J. (2002). Embedding and distributing constant time delay in circle time and transitions. *Topics in Early Childhood Special Education, 22,* 14–25.

Wolery, M., Anthony, L., & Heckathorn, J. (1998). Transition-based teaching: Effects on transitions, teachers' behavior, and children's learning. *Journal of Early Intervention, 21,* 117–131.

Wolery, M., & Hemmeter, M.L. (2011). Classroom instruction: Background, assumptions, and challenges. *Journal of Early Intervention, 33*(4), 371–380. doi:10.1177/1053815111429119

III

Application of Activity-Based Intervention

9

Observation Skills

The Foundation of Activity-Based Intervention

"Observation goes hand in hand with teaching; neither yields the optimal result by itself."
(Halle & Sindelar, 1982, pp. 44–45)

Accurate and directed observation is essential to the delivery of quality intervention. ABI is no exception, and consequently, gathering critical data through either structured or unstructured observation on what children do and how they do it is essential to this approach. Observation prior to intervention is necessary to determine what to teach and how to teach it. During intervention, observation is necessary to determine the child's response to the intervention provided. Observation of the child's responses allows the interventionist to make changes to the teaching methods and strategies when the child does not make expected gains or to move on to teaching new skills when the child meets the established criterion for targeted goals or objectives.

Observation has been an integral part of ABI from its inception in the 1970s. While developing one of the first community-based inclusive EI programs, Bricker and colleagues found that observing how typically developing children responded to each other, to adults, and to instructional activities provided enormous insight into how children learn. These observations enabled the change from using a highly structured approach to an approach that took into account children's interests and motivations. To move to more authentic approaches, child-directed activities, daily routines, and play became the primary vehicle for the delivery of intervention (Bricker, 2000). Even as the ABI approach has evolved over the years, observation continues to be critical to its implementation.

The act of observation can be defined as a process of regarding attentively or watching while the verb *observe* means to regard with attention to see or learn from the act of watching. These definitions are important because they emphasize the directed nature of the regarding or watching. In this chapter *observation* refers to the purposeful and careful watching and listening to gather accurate and useful information on children's behavioral repertoires. For our purposes it is useful to dissect observation into critical elements that should be considered when using observation in ABI. These elements include observer(s), purpose, structured or unstructured, physical and social setting and objects, data gathering, and analysis.

Observer(s) refers to the individual or individuals who are assigned the task of observing a child or children. To be an accurate observer generally requires training and experience in order to separate important data from information that may not enhance understanding. At the very least an observer needs to be present, able to focus on the purpose of the observation, and take notes or complete a form that accumulates relevant information.

Purpose refers to why the observation is being undertaken. Most children engage in a myriad of actions and activity—usually too many for any observer to take in and record. Consequently, most observers require that some focus or purpose direct their watching and listening.

Structured and *unstructured* refer to whether the observer has the freedom to record any and all observations (e.g., on blank paper, during video recording), or whether the observer is using a form that guides the focus and content of the observation. For example, a structured observation might be recording a language sample that entails entering all sounds and words uttered by a child but not include recording social interactions or motor movements. An unstructured observation might require recording all of a child's responses during 20 minutes of free play time.

Physical and social setting and *objects* refer to reporting information on where the child was observed and who and what was present during the observation. Even in structured observations such as entering data on a form that tracks peer interactions during group time, it is usually important for the observer to note information about the child's physical and social environment. Who and what is present may have significant effects on children's behavior.

Data gathering refers to what the observer actually records during the period of the observation(s). For some structured observations, observers may note the number of times a response occurs. For unstructured observations, observers may keep a running record of the child's behavior during outdoor playtime and the conditions under which the response occurs. The type of data collected is largely determined by the purpose of the observation.

Finally, *analysis* refers to how the data or information gathered are aggregated or assembled for presentation and use. If numbers of responses by conditions are recorded, the analysis may entail a count of responses by condition (e.g., "The child interacted with peer 1 by snatching a toy three times over a 15-minute observation, interacted with peer 2 by answering her communicative request five times, and did not interact with peer 3.").

Consideration of these elements assists in understanding that quality observation demands careful and accurate watching and listening with a clear purpose in mind. Each of these elements is described in the following example.

Observers: Katie's team members

Purpose: To gather information on Katie's developmental repertoire

Structured observation: The team was specifically concerned with gathering information on Katie's responses while at school during child-directed, routine, and planned activities using the ABI Observation Form (Figure 9.1)

Setting: Classroom with other children and staff

Data gathering: Observation of Katie while she engaged in daily routines and play

Analysis: Consideration of multiple observations and consolidation of findings into an intervention plan

Katie's team (the observers) conducted a series of 30-minute observations. The purpose of the observations was to gather information on what she did during classroom routines and activities (physical and social setting). The team used the ABI Observation Form to structure the observations during the 30-minute sessions (data gathering). After 2 weeks, the team aggregated the data from the forms (analysis). These aggregated data gave the team members a clear picture of what Katie did during classroom activities and under what conditions. These findings were used to begin an IEP for Katie. The team planned to complete Katie's IEP after the baseline assessment was completed by staff and by parents using a family friendly measure.

Carefully planned observations such as those conducted by Katie's team are essential to the application of authentic intervention approaches such as ABI. The remainder of this chapter offers an overview of high-quality observations and describes how observation can be used with each component of the linked system, which serves as the framework for ABI.

CHARACTERISTICS OF HIGH-QUALITY OBSERVATIONS

High-quality observations of young children with special needs within an ABI approach need to meet several important criteria—criteria that reflect the elements of observation discussed in the previous section. First, the team should determine the purpose of the observation before collecting information. The purpose needs to be decided in advance as it will have an impact on how the observation is conducted, including the setting and length of the

ABI Observation Form

Child's name: Katie

Observer: Shawna (ECSE teacher)

Date: January 4, 2014

Time: 8:55–9:40 am

			Child's skill level (check)	
Activities observed	**Observations**	**Skills required for successful participation**	**Can do**	**Needs to learn**
Child-directed activities				
Sensory table, book area (9:30–9:40)	Katie was playing with two other children at the sensory table. She picked up a scoop and attempted to pour rice in a strainer, missing the opening. She handed a measuring cup to another child without saying anything. The other child took the cup and said, "Thanks." Katie put her hands in the sensory table and moved them around in the rice. Another child put a cupcake tin in front of Katie and said, "You can have this." Katie moved her hands around in the table for about 30 seconds more and then walked to the book area of the classroom and picked up a board book. She sat on the floor and began turning pages in the book. It took her several attempts to turn pages. She held the book in her lap and used both hands to separate the cardboard pages. She talked to herself while "reading" the book but the words were not understandable.	Functional play with toys		√
		Playing near peers	√	
		Taking turns	√	
		Using phrases and sentences to communicate with others		√
		Using both hands for manipulating objects		√
Routine activities				
Breakfast (9:10–9:30)	The teacher dismissed children by calling their names one at a time. When Katie's name was called she didn't immediately get up, but did stand up and go to the table when prompted by another child. Katie walked to the table and found the placemat with her picture on it. Katie waited quietly until all of the children and teachers were at the tables. The meal was served family style. Katie needed assistance to scoop applesauce from the larger bowl into her bowl. She took a bagel from a basket and held it up to the teacher, but didn't say anything. The teacher said, "Do you want cream cheese?" and Katie nodded. Katie drank from a cup without a lid with minimal spilling. Katie spilled about half of the applesauce off of the spoon, but ate independently throughout the meal. Katie said very few words during the meal. She said, "uh huh" in response to a question, and said "more juice" when her cup was empty. Katie talked only with adults during the meal, but she watched and smiled at her peers. At the end of the meal, Katie threw away her garbage and brought her dishes to the sink when given a verbal reminder.	Following routine directions independently		√
		Identifying her picture	√	
		Waiting	√	
		Scooping foods		√
		Selecting preferred foods and eating independently	√	
		Using a spoon with minimal spilling		√
		Using phrases and sentences to communicate with others		√

Figure 9.1. Example of a completed ABI Observation Form.

ABI Observation Form *(continued)*   *page 2 of 2*

			Child's skill level (check)	
Activities observed	**Observations**	**Skills required for successful participation**	**Can do**	**Needs to learn**

Planned activities

Circle time (8:55–9:10)	The teacher began circle time by singing a song encouraging children to join the circle. Katie watched other children go to the circle and then independently walked over and sat down. The teacher led a hello song. Katie did some of the actions to the song (e.g., clapping, tapping her hands on her knees), and said her name when it was her turn. She smiled frequently during the song. The teacher then led the children through calendar and weather activities. During both activities, Katie watched the teacher or appropriate person/object. She occasionally said a single word in imitation (e.g., "ten" for the date during the calendar activity). During the weather activity, Katie was asked to indicate if it was sunny or cloudy. She correctly answered "sunny." Then the teacher read a book that was about the seasons. Katie watched and listened during the book reading. She did not raise her hand to answer questions posed by the teacher during the book reading and did not respond to questions that the teacher posed to the whole group.	Sitting and attending during large-group activities	√	
		Imitating actions during songs or fingerplays	√	
		Using phrases and sentences to comment and respond to questions		√

observation, as well as the type of information or data collected during the observation. Child-related factors need to be considered as well. For example, an observation of a child with significant behavior challenges may require a different set of observation tools and methods than an observation of a child with expressive communication delays.

The second criterion is that observations should be conducted within familiar, typical environments (Bagnato, 2005; Bagnato, McClean, Macy, & Neisworth, 2011). For example, when determining eligibility, the team should observe the child in authentic environments (e.g., home, child care setting, community preschool classroom) rather than in unfamiliar settings (e.g., clinic, testing room). Observers should be as unobtrusive as possible to avoid affecting the child's behavior. Ideally, the observer should be familiar to the child and setting (e.g., classroom teacher) to minimize disruptions to the typical routines and activities being observed.

Third, observations should be of sufficient length to provide accurate or valid information about the child's skills. The length of the observation will depend on the purpose of the observation. For example, if the purpose is to observe a toddler's self-feeding skills, it may be appropriate to observe for 20–30 minutes during the family's mealtime. If, however, the purpose is to observe how a preschooler with autism manages transitions between class-room activities, it may be necessary to observe several 5–10 minute periods during an entire school day.

A fourth criterion requires team members to conduct multiple, ongoing observations (Bagnato et al., 2011). One observation may provide an accu-rate glimpse of the child's typical behavior, or it may not. Children have vari-able patterns of behavior dependent on a variety of factors including setting events (e.g., whether they are hungry or tired), time of day (e.g., early morn-ing may be better than late afternoon), the activity itself (e.g., structured vs. unstructured, teacher-directed vs. child-initiated, familiar vs. unfamiliar), the child's interest in the activity, and people involved in the activity (e.g., preferred peers, familiar vs. unfamiliar adults). Thus, it is generally impor-tant that team members conduct multiple observations in and across differ-ent settings, at different times of day, in a variety of activities, and during interactions with adults and children.

Fifth, observations should be recorded according to predetermined direc-tions and rules. The observer should be clear about information relevant to the observation given its purpose and should record this information in an organized fashion that can be subsequently interpreted by the team. The recording method should match the purpose of the observation. Although observational recording methods are beyond the scope of this book, these methods might include anecdotal notes, video recordings, checklists (stan-dardized or informal), or more specific behavioral data collection methods (e.g., interval, duration, latency). Good sources of information on these meth-ods include *Assessing Infants and Preschoolers with Special Needs* (McLean,

Wolery, & Bailey, 2003) and *Applied Behavior Analysis for Teachers* (Alberto & Troutman, 2012).

A final criterion is that observation results should be summarized and interpreted in combination with other relevant information (e.g., parent report, results from a curriculum-based measure, weekly data collection). Data gathered should be viewed in concert with other information available to the team. Combining data and information from multiple sources will likely provide the most accurate and complete picture of the child's behavioral repertoire.

The intent of this section is to emphasize that quality observation takes thought and effort that, in turn, requires an expenditure of time by team members to plan, execute, and subsequently use the collected information to understand what children can do and determine what developmental targets should be addressed by intervention efforts.

Time expenditure raises an issue that often dominates EI/ECSE staff concerns. One of the more frequent problems noted by interventionists and specialists is the lack of time to engage in observation and data collection or in group discussions about how to proceed with a child. The dilemma faced often by staff is that the daily requirements of service delivery (e.g., conducting group time, attending to a sick or hurt child, logistics for activities, speaking with parents) preclude spending time on observation as well as holding frequent and predictable team meetings. We appreciate the need to attend to multiple and complex factors of service delivery; however, we would argue strongly that accurate information on what children can and cannot do, when and how they do it, and with whom or what is *essential information* that forms the basis of effective intervention. In addition, regular staff meetings are essential to share information, combine input, and arrive at a plan that all personnel can implement. Without such information and organized staff effort, intervention may be haphazard, inefficient, and not produce desired outcomes. We believe that observation provides the very foundation of effective intervention, and quality programs must include it as a critical piece of what they do on an ongoing basis.

The next section offers a range of strategies for including observation in each of the components of the linked system.

OBSERVATION WITHIN A LINKED SYSTEM FRAMEWORK

As we have highlighted throughout this chapter, observation is critically important to the delivery of intervention services for young children with disabilities. Thus, observation is a fundamental part of the ABI approach and each of the components that comprises the linked system framework (see Chapter 3). The framework includes five components: screening, assessment, goal development, intervention, and monitoring progress. The following sections describe the manner in which observation is integrated into each component, specifically addressing the goal, importance, application, and outcomes for each.

Screening

Observation skills and an understanding of typical and atypical development are particularly important during the screening component of the linked system framework. We define screening as the completion of a brief, formal procedure or measure of a child's developmental status. The child's performance on the measure is compared with a normative group (i.e., children of the same chronological age). This comparison provides information as to whether the child should be referred for further assessment or appears to be typically developing; however, screening results should be qualified by observation of the child during the screening process (e.g., if the child was upset or ill) and/or paired with other observational information (e.g., teacher reports of behavioral outbursts that require intervention) to ensure the most accurate picture of the child.

Goal   The goal of observation during screening is to collect information that will help team members make accurate decisions about whether the child is developing as expected or if the child's development may be delayed or different from what is typically expected.

Importance   Screening is the first step for securing services for most children. Consequently, accurate and reliable screening results are essential to ensure access to needed services as early as possible. Careful observation by individuals knowledgeable about typical and atypical child development is critical to ensure that children with potential delays are not missed, thus delaying potentially beneficial services.

Application   Screening is often conducted by professionals (e.g., the Battelle Developmental Inventory Screening Test; Newborg, 2004), but increasingly programs are adopting parent-completed screening tools (e.g., ASQ-3 [Squires & Bricker, 2009]). When children are identified for services, whether by professionals or parents, follow-up activities should include observing the child in typical routines and activities (e.g., playing with caregiver, participating in free play in child care setting). In addition to formal screening results, caregivers and teachers may have cause for concern based on their observations of the child's skills and behaviors compared with other children of the same chronological age in their care. Concerns may also be raised by other professionals such as physicians referring their young patients for developmental-behavioral screening based on their observations within clinical settings.

Outcomes   Screening results paired with observations from primary caregivers, teachers, and other professionals should provide adequate information to determine if further assessment is warranted.

Katie's family completed the ASQ-3 (Squires & Bricker, 2009) online prior to Katie's 36-month well child visit. Results from the ASQ-3 suggested potential delays in fine motor, cognitive, and social-communication skills. Katie's pediatrician, Dr. Andrews, asked Katie's mom some additional questions about her observations of Katie's skills in these areas. Katie's mom reported Katie used only a small number of phrases and sentences. She also said Katie wasn't yet drawing or coloring and had difficulty grasping and holding onto objects. For example, she said Katie had a hard time using a spoon to scoop food. Finally she noted that Katie did not play with many of her toys like other children her age. Dr. Andrews noted that Katie was very quiet during the visit and used simple schemes to examine toys in the office (e.g., banging, mouthing). Although some children were shy during office visits, Katie's behavior appeared different than what Dr. Andrews observed during most visits with children who were about the same age. Based on the results of the ASQ-3 and informal (but directed and accurate) parent and physician observations, Dr. Andrews referred Katie to the EI/ECSE community-based team for an evaluation.

Assessment

Assessment—the second component in the linked system—refers to the collection of in-depth information on children's developmental repertoires, and in addition should provide critical information on the next intervention targets and potentially effective intervention methods. During an initial assessment, interventionists need to determine 1) whether or not a child is eligible for EI or special education services, 2) the skills that are required for the child to be successful in various environments (e.g., home, classroom, child care setting), 3) which of these skills the child already has, and 4) which skills the child needs to learn. As noted in Chapter 3, collecting assessment information usually requires administration of a standardized, norm-based developmental inventory or a curriculum-based measure. However, observation of the child during the assessment process as well as information garnered from other sources is essential to augment the formal test findings.

Goal   In addition to completing a formal assessment on a child, it is often necessary to observe the child in familiar settings to identify the functional and generalizable skills the child uses during everyday routines and activities. These formal findings and observational data are vital to making decisions about eligibility and selecting appropriate intervention targets.

Importance   Observation is essential to team members' understanding of how the child functions across typical activities and settings. Bagnato and colleagues (Bagnato, 2005; Bagnato et al., 2011) described ongoing observation across functional routines and activities as authentic assessment and argued for its centrality in the assessment process. Rather than observing a child performing a skill in isolated tasks (e.g., picking up small cubes on a tray), team members should observe these skills in authentic situations (e.g., picking up cereal while eating breakfast). These observations provide essential information about which skills should be selected as intervention targets to increase the child's functioning across daily routines and activities.

Application   The intervention team uses observation during initial assessment to complement other information-gathering activities (e.g., completion of a curriculum-based measure). Two applications are essential for assessment. First, the acquired test information augmented by observation should make clear the child's need for referral to intervention services. Second, the initial assessment information in concert with observational data should provide concrete information on what the child is able to do and what might be the next developmental skills to target.

During assessment observations can be structured or unstructured. Unless a reason exists to conduct unstructured observations during assessment, we strongly recommend observations be structured using a procedure or form such as the ABI Observation Form (see Figure 9.1). The interventionist might also combine the use of this form with one or more areas from a curriculum-based measure (e.g., AEPS [Bricker, 2002]). For example, while observing a 4-year-old child eating breakfast in a Head Start classroom, the interventionist might complete the Routine Activity portion of the ABI Observation Form while also taking notes on items from the Adaptive area of the AEPS for later scoring.

To assist team members in collecting useful and important observational data, the ABI Observation Form aligns with the primary types of ABI activities: 1) child-directed activities, 2) routine activities, and 3) planned activities.

Child-Directed Activities   Interventionists should observe children engaging in activities that the child initiates. In a classroom, child-directed activities are most often observed during free play. For example, children might choose to play with blocks, at the sensory table, or in the housekeeping area. In the home, interventionists should observe children playing with available toys and materials. Of particular interest during these observations is how children interact with the materials and with others during play. For example, does the child line up cars rather than drive them on the ramp? Does the child use a spoon to pretend to stir soup in the kitchen area? Does the child use a block as a pretend telephone? Each of these observations leads to a better understanding of the child's cognitive development and functional play skills. When observing the child's interactions with others, interventionists should consider whether the child primarily plays alone, with adults, or with other children, as well as the nature of these play interactions. For example, does the child play alongside other children rather than playing with them?

Routine Activities Routine activities in the classroom include, for example, arrival, portions of circle time that are repeated regularly, meals, outdoor play, bathroom, and departure. Transitions between classroom activities should also be considered when observing routines. During observation of routine activities, the observer should identify what teachers expect children to do at particular times of the day, especially during transitions (e.g., going from circle time to lining up to go outside). In the home, routine activities include dressing, bathing, and mealtimes. Other routine activities might be observed in the community, including going for rides in the car, grocery shopping, and going to the park. Interventionists should discuss routines with caregivers to identify primary family routines, including which routines may present challenges and opportunities for intervention. Whether in the home, classroom, or community, the observer should identify key skills children need to function successfully in the environment either independently or with minimal assistance. This then allows for an assessment of skills the child has and skills that need to be learned.

Planned Activities Planned activities in the classroom include stories read by adults, art activities, planned motor activities (e.g., obstacle course), and more content-focused small-group activities (e.g., a sink or float science activity). The focus of the observation should be on skills required for successful participation in the activities with an assessment of which of these skills the child already has and which need to be learned. Foundational skills needed for successful participation in planned activities are often related to attention (e.g., being able to sit, look, and listen to the teacher during large-group book reading) and self-regulation (e.g., being able to wait for a turn during a board game, being able to listen to and follow multistep directions during an art activity). A child who is able to sit and pay attention during a large-group book reading activity is more likely to learn key concepts from the book than a child whose attention is focused on other events that are irrelevant to the activity (e.g., pulling lint from the carpet). Thus, these foundational skills should be considered in addition to skills that are the more obvious focus of the planned activity (e.g., counting with one-to-one correspondence, rhyming).

Outcomes The primary outcome of observation within the assessment component of the linked system is acquiring complementary information that can be used to determine eligibility for special education services and to target next skills for children eligible for services.

During their initial assessment, the intervention team completed the AEPS (Bricker, 2002), and Katie's parents completed portions of the AEPS Family Report. In addition, team members conducted observations of Katie at home and in her preschool classroom. The purpose of these observations was to see if Katie qualified for early childhood special education services and, assuming she was found eligible, identify the most important skills for the team to address to meet Katie's unique needs. They recorded their observations using anecdotal notes on the ABI Observation Form. These data, combined with the information recorded on the AEPS's Child Observation Data Recording Forms (CODRFs) and data from the Family Report, were used to guide the development of goals for Katie and subsequent intervention efforts.

During the observations, the team noticed Katie had difficulty completing art activities at the same time as peers, and required adult assistance when drawing and grasping some objects. In addition, the team noticed Katie rarely chose to go to the writing and art centers in the classroom. She sometimes painted at the easel, however, and participated at circle time by drawing a line on the computerized board when given physical assistance. At home and at preschool, she had difficulty using a spoon during meals, sometimes spilling applesauce and cereal, and needed assistance with dressing and undressing (e.g., zipping and unzipping her jacket, unbuttoning her sweater). They also observed that although Katie had typical receptive language (e.g., she could follow routine and novel multistep directions), she had significant delays in expressive language, using only 2–3 word phrases, many of which were the same general phrases (e.g., "That's mine."). This made it challenging for Katie's parents and teachers to understand what she wanted. In addition, while she played in the same classroom areas with friends and played with her sister at home, she had difficulty communicating with other children. The team also observed that Katie played with a relatively limited number of toys and was not yet engaging in functional play (e.g., "talking" on a pretend phone) or representational play (e.g., "talking" on a block that is being used to represent a phone).

Following each observation, team members collaborated to write narrative summaries for inclusion in Katie's evaluation report. They also used information gathered during the observations along with the AEPS Family Report and information from informal discussions with Katie's classroom interventionist to score items on the AEPS (Bricker, 2002).

Based on observation, family input, and AEPS Test results, the team determined Katie was eligible for services. She demonstrated delays in three areas that affected her participation in typical preschool activities: fine motor, cognitive, and social-communication. The team then used this information to develop Katie's IEP goals and objectives.

Goal Development

Goal development is the process of identifying a child's most important needs and formulating goals to address reaching those goals. Separate observation generally does not take place during goal development, rather the team uses information gathered during assessment to select and write functional IFSP outcomes for children ages birth to three, or IEP goals and objectives for children ages three and older.

Goal   During this component the aim is for teams to use information from observations to select and write functional, meaningful outcomes or goals and objectives. The quality of the goals selected will be highly dependent upon previously completed assessments and complementary observational data that were collected and analyzed.

Importance   Because IFSP outcomes or IEP goals and objectives drive instructional planning and intervention efforts (or should), it is essential that teams choose the right intervention targets. Identifying the appropriate targets is challenging, particularly when the child has many areas of needs. Therefore, it is essential that quality information be collected during assessment and then used appropriately to develop goals and subsequent intervention content.

Application   The team should reflect on assessment data and their complementary observations of the child's participation within daily routines and activities. In particular, the team should identify those skills most critical to the child's functioning during activities and interactions with others across environments. Skills that will do the most to enhance the child's independence and expand his/her developmental repertoire should be chosen.

Outcomes   The primary outcome of assessment findings and supplemental observations gathered during this component is to provide information that can inform the team's selection and writing of functional and meaningful IFSP outcomes or IEP goals/objectives.

Katie's IEP team, including Katie's family, discussed the results of their observations and used this information combined with the AEPS test and Family Report (Bricker, 2002) results to select target skills most important to improve Katie's functioning and participation in the classroom, home, and community. The team agreed they wanted Katie to learn to use a variety of 3- to 4-word phrases to communicate her wants and needs. In addition, the team wanted Katie to be able to play with a variety of toys using functional and representational play skills. They also wanted Katie to be able to use both hands to manipulate a variety of objects (e.g., pencil, spoon, zippers). The team wrote IEP goals and objectives in these three areas following the guidelines for developing high-quality goals and objectives presented in Chapter 3. Because the team used observations of Katie across her typical environments, they knew the skills they selected would increase Katie's participation in important everyday activities.

Intervention

Intervention entails those activities used to assist children in acquiring selected goals and objectives. Being an accurate and reliable observer is essential to the success of intervention. Once the intervention team has a thorough understanding of the environments in which the child participates (e.g., home, school, child care), the requirements for successful participation in those environments, and which skills the child needs to learn, they can turn their attention to planning and delivering intervention that will help the child learn the targeted skills.

Goal   The goal of observation during intervention is to identify times during child-directed, routine, and planned activities when interventionists can thoughtfully and intentionally use or embed naturalistic teaching strategies to provide opportunities for children to practice targeted skills.

Importance   Careful observation is critical to identifying multiple, varied, functional, and relevant opportunities within the child's environment as vehicles for embedding selected goals and objectives. Without careful observation, prime opportunities (i.e., teachable moments) might be overlooked, missing valuable practice time on critical skills.

Given the need for multiple opportunities to learn new skills, it is important to note that research suggests interventionists generally provide relatively few opportunities for children with special needs to practice targeted IEP skills (Pretti-Frontczak & Bricker, 2001). One potential reason for fewer practice opportunities may be that interventionists have difficulty *identifying* multiple opportunities for practice within routines and across activities. Accurate observation is essential in helping interventionists recognize opportunities throughout the day for embedding practice on IFSP or IEP goals.

Application   The intervention team should carefully observe all types of activities that occur in the child's environment (i.e., child-initiated, routine, and planned activities) to identify optimal times for embedding practice on goals and objectives. The more familiar team members are with expectations and necessary skills for participation in activities, the easier this process becomes. For example, determining opportunities for embedding in one's own classroom or one's co-teaching classroom may be easier than identifying practice opportunities as a visiting classroom consultant.

Opportunities to embed should be identified by the team through an ongoing process of observation, identification, and modification based on the success of implementation. This process requires teams to spend time up front planning to ensure that multiple opportunities are provided to each child. It also requires effective communication and collaboration among team members to ensure they are providing opportunities for the child to practice skills. For example, although the speech-language pathologist may take the lead in developing an IEP objective for a child using a communication device to make requests, it is critical that the entire team identify and then provide sufficient opportunities for the child to make requests (e.g., to request food items at meals, paint colors during art, songs during circle time, what center to go to during choice time). This may be accomplished by using the information gathered on the ABI Observation Form to brainstorm multiple practice opportunities and which team members/staff might be responsible for providing those opportunities. Early childhood teachers, paraprofessionals, and other staff members should be included in this process so that everyone understands their role in helping the child reach desired outcomes.

Fidelity of implementation is another important component of intervention delivery. *Fidelity* can be described as the degree to which an intervention is carried out as originally designed (O'Donnell, 2008). It is important that the key components of an intervention are implemented as intended. If only some key components are present and others are omitted, the intervention may be less effective than when all core components are addressed. For example, one important component of ABI is that the interventionist delivers the intervention within the context of typical routines and activities. If the intervention is only delivered in a therapy room outside of the classroom, this important component of ABI would be missing, likely compromising the intervention effort and child's progress. That is, the child can perform the skill in an isolated setting (e.g., labeling food items on flashcards) but is unable to use the skills functionally (e.g., labeling food items to make requests during meals). Thus, it is important that the team observe an intervention while it is being delivered to determine if the necessary elements of the planned interventions are present. If elements are missing, it is important to determine how to make changes to ensure that all elements of the intervention are present. The ABI Fidelity Checklist is included in the appendix for this chapter and can be used to determine the extent to which all elements of ABI are being used. This checklist can be completed by interventionists after video recording their teaching, or it can be completed by another interventionist or a supervisor. Ideally, the checklist would be used over multiple days and activities.

Outcomes The primary outcomes of observation during intervention are to identify multiple and varied opportunities for teaching functional and generalizable skills and to deliver the intervention with the necessary fidelity to ensure all elements of ABI are being used.

Katie's team identified times of the day when they could address Katie's IEP goals/objectives. They considered each goal/objective currently being targeted (e.g., uses a variety of 3- to 4-word phrases for requesting in a variety of activities, uses two hands to manipulate objects during a variety of activities, uses functional play with a variety of toys) and how they could embed practice opportunities across activities. The team identified opportunities, the team member/staff responsible, and how progress monitoring data would be collected. The team implemented their intervention plan, providing Katie with several opportunities each day to make requests, use both hands in manipulating toys and materials, and play with toys in functional ways. As part of their professional development plan, Katie's intervention team used the ABI Fidelity Checklist to observe each other embedding practice opportunities. They found that although they were providing Katie with several opportunities throughout the day to practice targeted skills, most of those opportunities were adult-directed. The team agreed they needed to observe Katie more closely to identify child-initiated activities during which they could embed practice on Katie's IEP goals/objectives.

Monitoring Progress

Monitoring progress refers to the evaluation of a child's progress toward selected goals and objectives. Ongoing observation and recording the child's use of targeted skills within everyday routines and activities are keys to measuring child progress. Without monitoring child progress, team members might continue to use intervention strategies that are ineffective. Teams might also provide intervention for unnecessary lengths of time on skills the child has already acquired. In both cases, failing to measure progress can lead to inefficient use of intervention time—a valuable and limited resource.

Goal   The goal of observation when monitoring progress is to determine to what extent the child is making progress toward mastering targeted goals and objectives and whether or not the intervention procedures need to be modified to ensure steady progress toward skill acquisition.

Importance   Observation within this phase is critical because our interest lies in whether or not the child can use the targeted skill across settings and conditions. This requires observing the child using (or not using) the skill in a variety of daily routines and activities. For example, if the team is interested in whether a child can complete hand washing independently, the team might observe the child washing hands after using the bathroom and before meals. This skill needs to be observed within the typical course of classroom or home activities to see how the child completes the task when required and appropriate. For example, if the child has not yet learned to complete the hand washing routine independently based on observation and weekly data collection, the team would want to consider using a more intensive intervention method to teach the skill (e.g., backward chaining, mini visual schedule with sequence of steps in hand washing routine).

Application   Observation during this component involves ongoing weekly and sometimes daily observations of the child as he or she participates in child-initiated, routine, and planned activities. These observations are often brief (3–5 minutes or less) and should become integrated into the interventionist's daily practice. Data on targeted skills should be recorded during observations for later analysis. It may be helpful for intervention teams to develop forms for recording data that are kept in a central location (e.g., on a clipboard, posted around the room) for easy access. Recorded observations provide objective information to support team decisions about intervention efforts.

For example, if a team plans to introduce a communication device to a child during classroom routines and planned activities as a strategy for increasing requests, they should first collect data on the number of requests the child makes before the device is introduced. Then the team should introduce the device and collect additional data to determine if there is a change in the child's use of the targeted skill, requesting. If the team finds that the child is using the device consistently to make requests and has met the stated criteria on the IEP (e.g., makes requests in four out of five opportunities across three different activities), they would then move on to provide intervention on other related IEP goals (e.g., increasing the length of phrases made on the device from "crackers" to "I want crackers."). If through observation the team finds that the child is not using the device or is inconsistently using the device to make requests, collaborative problem solving would be needed to determine the next steps for revising intervention efforts. For example, the team might hypothesize the child was not using the device because the buttons were difficult to push or the device was too heavy to carry around, in which case they might try a new device. The team might also decide that more intensive teaching strategies are needed to assist the child in using the device (e.g., hand-over-hand assistance). All of these decisions should be based on accurate observations of the child as he or she participates in daily activities.

Outcomes   The primary outcomes of observation during progress monitoring are a determination of the extent to which the child has met criteria for the targeted goal, and whether or not intervention should be modified to try to improve the rate of learning.

Katie's team monitored her progress toward her IEP goals through observation. They used a data collection form that allowed them to track whether or not Katie responded with a correct or incorrect response to opportunities to practice her targeted skills. During observations of Katie's communication skills, they found Katie was beginning to use 3-word phrases but only during structured activities (e.g., circle time, art, meals). These data suggested that additional opportunities for Katie to use 3- to 4-word phrases during child-directed activities (e.g., sensory table, dress-up area) were needed. The team also observed that Katie wasn't yet using 3-word phrases with peers. The team then modified routine activities to encourage Katie to talk more with peers. For example, the team enlisted a favorite friend to greet Katie when she arrived at school each day, and they had a snack helper, rather than the teacher, offer Katie a choice of snack items so that she could communicate her requests to another child. The team also brainstormed strategies to teach Katie to play functionally with toys. For example, they had observed that Katie often chose to play in the dress-up area. The speech-language pathologist and ECSE teacher joined Katie in the dress-up area on alternating days and provided language models (e.g., "I want the dress."). The team also found that their previous attempts to help Katie learn how to play more functionally with toys were not successful. They needed to increase the level of support for Katie during play activities. The team decided to use physical prompts (e.g., providing hand-over-hand support to help Katie stir the pretend cake batter) in addition to models and verbal prompts. The team continued to observe Katie and systematically record data on a weekly basis so that they could determine objectively if their revised intervention plan was producing desired outcomes.

SUMMARY

Accurate and reliable observation of children is necessary for effective intervention. Gathering relevant information about children's behavior across the day and settings is fundamental to valid assessment. Assessment data in turn provide the basis for developing goals and subsequent intervention efforts. Without accurate and reliable data on children's developmental repertoires, goal setting and intervention likely will not produce desired outcomes. If goals and intervention are based on information that does not adequately or accurately reflect what children are currently doing, it will be only by luck that intervention goals and content hit their mark. Young children and their families cannot afford to waste precious time on efforts that will not optimally affect their development, providing a strong need for conducting preliminary and ongoing accurate and reliable observation.

REFERENCES

Alberto, P.A., & Troutman, A.C. (2012). *Applied behavior analysis for teachers* (9th ed.). Upper Saddle River, NJ: Pearson.

Bagnato, S.J. (2005). The authentic alternative for assessment in early intervention: An emerging evidence-based practice. *Journal of Early Intervention, 28*(1), 17–22. doi:10.1177/105381510502800102

Bagnato, S.J., McLean, M., Macy, M., & Neisworth, J.T. (2011). Identifying instructional targets for early childhood via authentic assessment: Alignment of professional standards and practice-based evidence. *Journal of Early Intervention, 33*(4), 243–253. doi:10.1177/1053815111427565

Bricker, D. (2000). Inclusion: How the scene has changed. *Topics in Early Childhood Special Education, 20*(1), 14.

Bricker, D. (Series Ed.). (2002). *Assessment, Evaluation and Programming System*

(AEPS®) for Infants and Children (2nd ed.). Baltimore, MD: Paul H. Brookes Publishing Co.

Halle, J.W., & Sindelar, P.T. (1982). Behavioral observation methodologies for early childhood education. *Topics in Early Childhood Special Education, 2*(1), 43–54. doi:10.1177/027112148200200109

McLean, M., Wolery, M., & Bailey, D.B., Jr. (2003). *Assessing infants and preschoolers with special needs* (3rd ed.). Upper Saddle River, NJ: Pearson.

Newborg, J. (2004). *Battelle Developmental Inventory–Second Edition (BDI-2)*. Itasca, IL: Riverside.

O'Donnell, C.L. (2008). Defining, conceptualizing, and measuring fidelity of implementation and its relationship to outcomes in k-12 curriculum intervention research. *Review of Educational Research, 78*(1), 33–84. doi:10.3102/0034654307313793

Pretti-Frontczak, K., & Bricker, D. (2001). Use of the embedding strategy during daily activities by early childhood education and early childhood special education teachers. *Infant-Toddler Intervention, 11*(2), 111–128.

Squires, J., & Bricker, D. (with Twombly, E., Nickel, R., Clifford, J., Murphy, K., Hoselton, R., Potter, L., Mounts, L., & Farrel, M.S.). (2009). *Ages & Stages Questionnaires®, Third Edition (ASQ-3™): A parent-completed child monitoring system* (3rd ed.). Baltimore, MD: Paul H. Brookes Publishing Co.

Appendix 9

Blank Forms

This appendix contains blank examples of the ABI observation and fidelity checklist forms. Teams are encouraged to copy these blank forms or to download blank forms to assist in the implementation of the approach.

Child's name: _____ Observer: _____

Date: _____ Time: _____

| Activities observed | Observations | Skills required for successful participation | Child's skill level (check) | |
| --- | --- | --- | Can do | Needs to learn |

Child-directed activities

Routine activities

			Child's skill level (check)	
Activities observed	Observations	Skills required for successful participation	Can do	Needs to learn

Planned activities

ABI Fidelity Checklist

Interventionist: _____   Observer: _____

Date: _____   Time: _____

Child: _____

Activities observed: _____

IEP goal/objective(s) targeted for intervention: _____

Directions: Observe for 20–30 minutes in two or more routines. Circle *yes*, *no*, or when appropriate, *NA* (not applicable) for each question. Calculate fidelity of implementation on page 3.

Intervention component	Yes No NA
Opportunities	
Are opportunities embedded within child-directed activities?	Yes No
Are opportunities embedded within routine activities?	Yes No
Are opportunities embedded within planned activities?	Yes No
Do the activities match the child's developmental level?	Yes No
Are the opportunities provided authentic (i.e., relevant for child and a part of natural ongoing activities)?	Yes No
Does the interventionist capitalize on the child's interests (e.g., offering toys and materials that appeal to the child)?	Yes No
When the child initiates an interaction, does the interventionist follow the child's lead (e.g., child says, "I want to play with the cash register"; adult responds, "Sure, you can work at the grocery store, and I'll be the shopper")?	Yes No
Does the interventionist provide multiple (at least 3) opportunities for the child to practice each targeted skill?	Yes No
Are opportunities varied allowing the child to practice targeted skills within different situations and conditions (e.g., walking up different sets of stairs; writing with pencils, crayons, with a stylus on a tablet)?	Yes No
Are the skills being targeted functional (i.e., useful) and generative (i.e., represent broad classes of behavior and can be used across settings, people, objects and conditions)?	Yes No
Are the skills being targeted critical to the child's successful participation in activities?	Yes No

Intervention component	Yes	No	NA

Intervention strategies

	Yes	No	NA
Does the interventionist use at least three or more of the following intervention strategies? Circle strategies used.	Yes	No	
Forgetfulness (e.g., "forgetting" to put out spoons for applesauce)	Yes	No	
Novelty (e.g., changing the words to a familiar song)	Yes	No	
Visible but unreachable (e.g., putting favorite toys out of reach to encourage requesting)	Yes	No	
Change in expectations (e.g., putting a sock on the child's hand instead of his foot during dressing)	Yes	No	
Piece by piece (e.g., holding blocks and encouraging child to request each block)	Yes	No	
Assistance (e.g., putting blocks in a container that is difficult to open to encourage requesting)	Yes	No	
Interruption (e.g., when child is playing grocery store and is ready to "pay" for groceries, interventionist holds up wallet and says, "What do you need?")	Yes	No	
Delay (e.g., holding up crackers and waiting for child to request them before giving cracker)	Yes	No	
Physical model (e.g., interventionist shows child how to write letters)	Yes	No	
Verbal model (e.g., interventionist points to dog and says, "doggy")	Yes	No	
Self-talk (e.g., interventionist says, "I'm making a bridge. Here goes my car over the bridge.")	Yes	No	
Prompt imitation (e.g., interventionist says, "Say more crackers.")?	Yes	No	
Expand or recast/correction (e.g., child says, "doggy" and interventionist says, "Yes, that's a big doggy!" or child says, "He got cookies" and adult says, "Yes, he has cookies.")?	Yes	No	
Directions (e.g., playing with a doll house, the interventionist says, "The baby is tired. Can you put the baby in the bed?")	Yes	No	

Feedback/consequences

	Yes	No	NA
Is feedback to the child/consequences timely (i.e., delivered immediately following the child's behavior)? For example, when the child requests crackers, are crackers given to child immediately?	Yes	No	
Are consequences almost always an inherent part of the interaction or a logical outcome of the interaction (e.g., when the child asks for crackers, interventionist gives the child more crackers) rather than artificial (e.g., adult says, "Good job asking for crackers.")?	Yes	No	NA
When the child makes an error or provides a response other than the desired behavior (e.g., when teaching 2-word utterances, adult says, "What do you want?" while holding up a picture of crackers; child says, "more") does the interventionist provide a correction by modeling the correct response or providing a prompt or other additional support (e.g., "This is a cracker. Say more cracker.")?	Yes	No	NA

Total yes responses from pages 1 & 2 _____ /

Total yes + no responses (i.e., do not include NA responses) from pages 1 & 2 _____

X 100 = _____% fidelity of implementation

Comments:

This form is a modified version of a Fidelity Checklist developed by Losardo and Bricker at the University of Oregon.

10

Activity-Based Intervention in Center-Based Programs

As we have noted in previous chapters, the ABI approach is flexible in that it can be used with individuals or groups of children; can be used across settings, objects, events, and people; and can be easily integrated into ongoing daily activities. This chapter addresses the application of ABI in center-based programs. By center-based we refer to any program that is operated apart from a child's home and includes multiple children. These settings may include preschools, kindergartens, Head Start programs, EI/ECSE classes, recreation programs, and both public and home child care programs.

Successful application of ABI in center-based settings does not occur without planning and thoughtful execution. The content of this chapter is designed to assist center-based personnel to first appreciate the necessary practices to be employed and then to apply those practices. This chapter begins with a general description of the four phases essential to intervention to successfully employ ABI (or any intervention approach) in center-based programs. Each phase is operationalized, and examples are provided. The second part of the chapter discusses how to use ABI in center-based settings and includes two examples—one in an inclusive EI/ECSE class and one in a Head Start program.

PHASES OF INTERVENTION

The phases of intervention differ from the components of the linked systems approach by being more focused and include: 1) conducting comprehensive and ongoing assessments; 2) targeting functional and generative goals; 3) providing multiple and varied learning opportunities; and 4) monitoring children's progress.

Phase 1: Conducting Comprehensive and Ongoing Assessments

The first phase directly applicable to intervention is the completion of a curriculum-based measure designed to assist teams in gathering comprehensive and ongoing information about young children. Results from curriculum-based measures such as the AEPS (Bricker, 2002), along with observations of the children engaging in a variety of activities across settings, should be used to provide a detailed description of children's strengths, interests, and emerging skills. This summary is often referred to as a present level of performance and serves as a guide for identifying needs as well as a baseline for comparing progress over time. For preschool children, the present level of performance, which is included in the IEP, must include a description of how the child's disability has an impact on his or her participation in typical preschool activities (IDEA 2004). Assessment summaries should also focus on the child's strengths, not just on areas of need (Neisworth & Bagnato, 2005). In addition, professionals should limit the use of discipline-specific jargon and provide definitions of technical terms when necessary so that families can understand and use the information summarized (Neisworth & Bagnato, 2005).

Amina's family recently immigrated to the United States from Somalia. Amina, who is 3 years old, was diagnosed with autism shortly after arriving in the United States. Following the diagnosis, Amina's family contacted the local school district to request services. After an initial eligibility determination—which included collecting information from the family about Amina's development, observing Amina in her home, reviewing the diagnostic tests already completed (e.g., Autism Diagnostic Observation Schedule [Lord, Rutter, DiLavore, & Risi, 2000]), and completing the AEPS test and Family Report (Bricker, 2002)—the team summarized Amina's skills in the present level of performance section on her IEP.

   Guided by the recommended criteria, the team described Amina's current skills in the areas of social-communication, social skills, cognitive skills, and adaptive skills in language all team members could understand. They identified her strengths, noting the skills she had already mastered. They included examples from their observations, the AEPS test, and the AEPS Family Report. They also described how Amina's special needs affected her participation in daily activities. From this initial summary, the team prioritized which skills were most important for Amina to learn over the next school year. The team also determined that Amina's needs would best be met in an inclusive center-based program that was co-taught by an early childhood teacher and an ECSE teacher with expertise in autism. In addition, the team asked a speech-language pathologist who works with the program to be a member of Amina's intervention team.

Phase 2: Targeting Functional and Generative Goals

Targeting functional and generative goals is the second phase essential to implementing the ABI approach. As we have noted, creating and embedding multiple learning opportunities related to targeted goals is at the heart of this approach. When functional and generative goals are targeted, interventionists and caregivers should be able to address them across child-directed, routine, and planned activities. For example, the goals of manipulating objects, walking across different surfaces, taking care of physical needs, playing with objects/toys, expressing wants and needs, and interacting with familiar adults and peers can be addressed in a range of center-based program activities (e.g., center time, free play, outdoor time), family routines (e.g., meals, dressing, watching television, driving, bath time), and community activities (e.g., visiting grandparents, shopping, going to the park).

Conversely, finding multiple ways to address goals that are *not* functional and generative can force interventionists and caregivers to rely on highly structured and contrived situations. For example, the goals of stacking 1-inch cubes, walking on a balance beam, pushing numbers on a play phone, and labeling pictures on flashcards may limit the number and types of activities in which interventionists and caregivers can effectively create and embed learning opportunities leading to meaningful skills. That is, most daily activities do not involve balance beams, play telephones, or flashcards or readily lend themselves to stacking 1-inch cubes. Likewise, targeting a specific skill such as one particular game played with one particular person limits opportunities for the child to practice a more generative skill such as initiating social games with familiar adults. Teams are encouraged to select goals that will address children's needs and that are functional and generative; however, they also need to ensure that the number of goals targeted can be reasonably addressed and monitored. Therefore, teams are encouraged to select a small number of critical skills, focusing intervention efforts on highly functional skills that can be used across people, settings, and activities. If teams select too many goals, intervention efforts may become diluted, leading to little child progress on any identified skills.

Amina's team identified four functional and generative goals for her (Table 10.1; associated objectives are not listed). The goals identified were chosen because they could be used across multiple settings (i.e., at home and at the center-based program) and were essential to Amina's successful and independent participation in these environments.

Table 10.1.   Amina's individualized education program goals

Area	Goal
Social-communication	Amina will use three-word utterances.
Social-emotional	Amina will respond appropriately to peers' social behavior.
Cognitive	Amina will watch, listen, and participate during small-group activities.
Adaptive	Amina will carry out all toileting functions independently.

AEPS® items adapted by permission from Bricker, D. (2002). *Assessment, evaluation, and programming system for infants and children* (2nd ed., Vols. 1–4). Baltimore, MD: Paul H. Brookes Publishing Co.

Phase 3: Providing Multiple and Varied Learning Opportunities

The third phase necessary for the successful use of the activity-based approach is providing multiple and varied learning opportunities for children. A learning opportunity is created when an antecedent is presented or occurs that encourages the child to practice, perform, or attempt to produce a target skill. For example, if targeting the skill of signing MORE correctly, a variety of antecedents could be provided to elicit the target response, such as asking the child if he or she wants more, modeling how to sign MORE, withholding an object or placing an object out of the child's reach, or providing hand-over-hand assistance to make the sign MORE. In this example, a learning opportunity is created by the occurrence of any of the above-mentioned antecedents as long as the antecedents encourage/allow the child to practice, perform, or attempt to make the sign MORE.

Furthermore, in ABI a learning opportunity is only created when an antecedent is presented/occurs that allows the child to continue an action or maintains the child's intent or interest within the activity. If the antecedent modifies or extends the child's action or attention, it must not shift the child's behavior or attention away from the activity in which he or she is interested or engaged. Continuing with the example of a child learning to sign MORE, a learning opportunity is not created if the child is not looking or attending when the adult models the sign, the child is uninterested in the withheld object, or the child does not require full assistance and withdraws from the interaction as a result.

Initially, selecting antecedents to create learning opportunities can appear to be a simple and straightforward process; however, selecting appropriate antecedents is quite complex. First, teams need to understand the potential array of existing antecedents. Chapter 6 also includes a description of intervention strategies (e.g., interruption or time delay, visible but unreachable, physical model) that involve presenting an antecedent (e.g., placing a favorite toy out of reach) to occasion a desired behavior (e.g., the child requesting the toy). A number of additional resources define and describe various antecedents and prompting procedures (e.g., Barnett, Bell, & Carey, 2002; Grisham-Brown, Hemmeter, & Pretti-Frontczak, 2005; Grygas Coogle, Floyd,

Hanline, & Kellner-Hiczewski, 2013; Meadan, Ostrosky, Milagros Santos, & Snodgrass, 2013; Noonan & McCormick, 2014; Sandall & Schwartz, 2008). Second, teams must know each child's individual target goals to select antecedents that will create learning opportunities. Third, teams need to deliver multiple and varied antecedents across activities when children are interested and motivated to ensure adequate practice opportunities.

In addition to selecting antecedents that will provide multiple and varied learning opportunities, teams need to be diligent in their selection of feedback or consequences provided to children. As with antecedents, a continuum of types of feedback or consequences exists (e.g., praise; attention; rewards such as stickers, gaining a desired toy, completing a puzzle, or getting to eat or drink). Feedback/consequences can include adult (e.g., teacher, caregiver, therapist) responses; peer/sibling responses; and/or environmental objects, events, pictures, signs, or words that follow a child's responses. The appropriateness of the feedback/consequence selected can only be determined by its effect on the child. To be effective, feedback/consequences should be timely (i.e., immediate) and integral (i.e., directly related to or contingent on children's behaviors or associated with, connected to, or a logical outcome of the activity, action, or response). Timely feedback is necessary so that the child can discern the relationship between the response and subsequent consequences. Integral feedback is necessary so that children will learn that responses produce related and meaningful outcomes.

Amina's team completed an ABI Intervention Guide (described in Chapter 6) to determine antecedents they could deliver throughout the day to provide a variety of opportunities for her to practice the targeted IEP goals. For example, they determined they would use a series of antecedents, arranged from those providing the least support to those providing the most support, during classroom activities to help Amina learn to use a communication device to produce three-word utterances. The device was equipped with four words/phrases (e.g., "I," "want," and two favorite songs—"Wheels on the Bus," and "No More Monkeys Jumping on the Bed") to permit Amina to make requests. The antecedents from least to most support were: 1) offer the device along with a question asking which of two items she wants, 2) pause to allow her to respond, 3) provide a visual cue by pointing at the two picture choices, and 4) provide hand-over-hand assistance to help Amina make a request. The team used these antecedents during circle time to provide an opportunity for Amina to request favorite songs, during meals to request favorite foods, and during free play to choose highly preferred activities. After delivering an antecedent, Amina's team varied their responses (i.e., feedback/consequences) based on Amina's behavior. When Amina made a request (i.e., performed the desired behavior), the team promptly delivered what she had requested (e.g., beginning to sing "Wheels on the Bus") to help her associate requests with receiving what she wanted.

Phase 4: Monitoring Children's Progress

The final phase for successful implementation of ABI is systematically monitoring children's progress toward priority goals and objectives. A variety of methods exist for doing this. No universal data collection system is appropriate for use with all children, all goals, or all programs. Teams will likely function more effectively if they adopt a decision-based model that guides how and when data are collected. Decision-based models are useful because they 1) emphasize the cyclic nature of the evaluation process, 2) begin and end with the purpose or reason for collecting data, and 3) require teams to collect ongoing data (i.e., daily or weekly child progress data) and impact data (i.e., quarterly or annual child progress data) (e.g., McAfee & Leong, 2008).

Teams will likely need to use a variety of methods to collect sufficient data to make accurate decisions. Gathering data on children's performance on IEP goals/objectives should inform teams about

1. What progress has been made toward target goals/objectives (i.e., the effectiveness of interventions)

2. Which antecedents and/or consequences produce change

3. What accommodations, modifications, or intervention strategies are used

4. How often learning opportunities are provided

5. Within what types of activities learning opportunities occur

Gathering more global data on children's developmental progress (e.g., reassessing using the AEPS [Bricker, 2002] or other curriculum-based measures) and/or their progress in the general curriculum helps teams make program-level decisions and increases the link between intervention efforts and accountability requirements. Although beyond the scope of this text, a number of resources exist for helping teams create data collection systems for collecting daily/weekly data, quarterly data, and annual data on child progress. For example, Alberto and Troutman (2012) and McLean, Wolery, and Bailey (2004) provided detailed examples of how to collect ongoing data regarding children's performance on target goals, as well as strategies for collecting data on children's overall developmental progress and progress in the general curriculum. The following section discusses data collection methods particularly useful within an ABI framework.

When implementing an activity-based approach, teams need to gather data related to children's performance on target goals as well as their overall developmental progress and progress in the general curriculum. Data regarding children's performance on target goals can be gathered using three methods: written descriptions (e.g., running records, anecdotal notes, jottings), permanent records (e.g., diagrams, writing samples, pictures), and counts and tallies (e.g., sampling procedures, rating scales, probes). Regardless of the method, teams should ensure the following:

- Data collection procedures are directly linked to the criterion written for a target skill (e.g., if the criterion states that the child will manipulate three different objects with both hands performing different movements, then information regarding the number and type of objects and how a child manipulates them should be collected).

- Data collection procedures are flexible and applicable across settings, events, and people.

- Data collection procedures yield valid and reliable data.

- Data collection responsibilities are shared by team members (e.g., direct and related services personnel, consultants, caregivers).

- Data collection procedures are compatible with available resources (e.g., time, skills, materials).

Data regarding children's overall developmental progress and their progress in the general curriculum are often gathered through quarterly administrations of curriculum-based measures (e.g., AEPS [Bricker, 2002]). These data are useful for gauging the effects of intervention on individual children as well as groups of children. Information from quarterly evaluations, in particular, provides feedback about the child's developmental progress and helps clarify where intervention modifications or revisions may be necessary. In addition, administrations at the beginning and end of the year of standardized norm-referenced (e.g., Battelle Developmental Inventory [Newborg, 2005]) or curriculum-based measures (e.g., AEPS) allow programs to evaluate general effects for groups of children and for providing accountability information.

Amina's team created data collection forms that allowed them to collect data on progress toward her IEP goals and associated objectives. Team members were assigned to collect data on the number of opportunities provided for Amina to use her communication device within each targeted activity. For example, a paraprofessional collected data during circle time, the ECSE teacher collected data during meals, and the ECSE teacher and speech-language pathologist shared the responsibility for collecting data during free play. The team used these data to make decisions about the effectiveness of their intervention methods, including whether or not they were giving Amina adequate opportunities to make requests using the communication device and if the antecedents and consequences provided were effective in eliciting and reinforcing the target skill. Based on their data, Amina's team concluded they needed to provide additional and more varied opportunities to make requests. The speech-language pathologist and ECSE teacher met to discuss ways to increase these opportunities throughout the school day.

APPLICATION OF ABI IN CENTER-BASED PROGRAMS

This section includes practical strategies for using ABI in center-based programs. It includes two examples with different children who participate in different types of center-based programs. The first example describes a preschool-age child, Jaden, who attends an inclusive classroom co-taught by an early childhood teacher and an ECSE teacher. The services provided are designed to assist Jaden in developing play skills, intelligible communication, and fine motor manipulation skills. The second example describes the application of ABI in a Head Start program with special itinerant service for designated children. In this example, the preschool-age child, Cooper, participates in a Head Start program and is visited weekly by an ECSE teacher to address the target goals of manipulating objects with both hands; using words, phrases, or sentences to express anticipated outcomes; and participating in group activities.

Before undertaking intervention with any child, staff should 1) develop a plan, 2) designate team responsibilities, 3) determine practice opportunities, 4) organize materials, and 5) design strategies to involve family members.

Develop a Plan

Prior to implementing ABI, the ECSE teacher or teaching team need to determine when learning opportunities will be provided for individual children. This requires planning time dedicated to brainstorming and recording ideas for when and how children's goals/objectives can be addressed. Teams should use a group embedding schedule (see Appendix to Chapter 6 for a blank form) to help organize this process. In using this form, it is important for teams to identify the antecedent (i.e., what the adult will say or do, what environmental arrangement will be made) for each opportunity that will be provided.

Designate Team Responsibilities

Once opportunities are identified, teams need to decide which team members are responsible for providing each opportunity. The embedding schedule should be posted or made otherwise easily accessible (with only children's initials used to maintain privacy) so that all team members can remind themselves of their assigned responsibilities quickly and easily. For example, if Amina's goal is to use multiple word phrases to greet others, an assistant and an early childhood teacher might be responsible for providing an antecedent (e.g., giving an expectant look and then waiting) for the child to initiate a greeting. As opportunities are provided, assigned team members should engage in ongoing data collection to help teams determine if the intervention is effective or if changes to intervention are needed.

Determine Practice Opportunities

Because they occur with regularity, we recommend the frequent use of routine activities for embedding targeted goals and objectives. This allows all team members to get into a habit of providing consistent opportunities for children to practice skills. For example, if the assistant and early childhood teacher know they are responsible for providing Amina with an opportunity to greet them, they will get into the habit of greeting her daily, providing her with multiple opportunities to practice this skill each week.

Organize Materials

Providing consistent opportunities, whether in routine, child-initiated, or planned activities, requires organization and daily set up of materials needed for providing embedded learning opportunities. For example, if Amina's team is going to use a communication device to allow her to make requests, they need to have the device properly programmed and available for her prior to the start of the school day. This might include having a board ready for requesting food at snack time, a board for requesting favorite toys during free play, and a board for requesting paint colors and other materials (e.g., scissors, glue) during an art activity. All of this requires clear communication with other team members (e.g., assistants) who are also responsible for preparing materials. Having a daily checklist associated with these responsibilities can be helpful in making sure materials are ready before the beginning of the school day.

Design Strategies to Involve Family Members

Finally, teams should communicate with families to encourage caregivers to provide opportunities for the child to practice targeted skills in the home setting. First, interventionists need to let families know what skills their child is practicing at school. This can be accomplished in a variety of ways including sending home daily notes describing the child's day, sending home photos showing the child practicing targeted skills, or emailing families with updates. Second, interventionists might share ideas for ways families can work on targeted skills at home along with any necessary materials. For example, Amina's team might send home a communication board with Amina's favorite foods so that the family can provide opportunities for Amina to request foods at mealtimes.

In the examples provided next, these steps are addressed in the larger context of the four phases of intervention: 1) conducting comprehensive and ongoing assessments, 2) targeting generative and functional goals, 3) providing multiple and varied practice opportunities, and 4) monitoring children's progress. In addition, the organizational structure described in Chapter 6 is used to guide the intervention efforts of the staff and caregivers.

Example 1: Early Intervention/Early Childhood
Special Education Inclusive Center-Based Program

Jaden Johnson is 4 years old and is eligible for ECSE services for developmental delay. Jaden lives with her parents and her 6-year-old brother. Jaden attends a neighborhood preschool program 3 days per week where she receives ECSE services including occupational and speech-language therapies. Information related to Jaden's present level of performance was gathered through a comprehensive assessment conducted by her parents (Marcia and Don), ECSE teacher (Gwen), EC teacher (Jennifer), classroom assistant (Tashana), occupational therapist (Denise), and speech-language pathologist (Debra). Assessment observations are based on daily interactions with Jaden and guided by the AEPS activities (Bricker, 2002).

The intervention plan for Jaden addresses the four phases of intervention.

Phase 1: Conducting Comprehensive and Ongoing Assessments   Most days begin with Jaden taking a bath followed by selecting the clothes she will wear for the day. She can pull her pajama bottoms off after her mother gives her some initial assistance by pushing them down. She raises her arms up, and her mother pulls the pajama top over her head. In the bathtub, she will point to the toy bag hanging on the shower rack. She likes to reach in and get her containers for filling and pouring. She uses small hand-sized containers with one hand to scoop water and pour it over her body and hair. After a few minutes of play, she rubs soap over her body parts as her mother names them. Then, she rinses off by scooping and pouring water on herself again.

After her mother assists her with drying off, she joins her mother at the dresser and pulls out a matching shirt and short set. Jaden identifies her favorite color as pink (e.g., /I/ /wī/ /pin/ for *I like pink*). She is able to match red, yellow, and green shirt and short combinations. She consistently follows the routine directions that go with taking a bath and getting dressed. Jaden is starting to follow new directions that include location concepts (e.g., in, on, behind, up, down). For example, when her mother or father point to an object on her shirt, she finds it and points or imitates the name of the object, or when asked to hang her pajamas on the hook behind the door, she complies with the request. When asked, Jaden is able to inform others of an object's/person's location.

Jaden can be difficult to understand when she answers questions or makes comments. Specifically, Jaden consistently substitutes the initial consonant sounds in words that are more difficult to produce (e.g., /ch/ or /j/) with initial consonant sounds that are easier to produce (e.g., /p/ and /d/). For example, she will say /tă / for *cat,* /dō/ for *go,* /poo/ for *food,* and /dā/ for *grape.* Specifically, Jaden substitutes /t/ for /k/, /w/, or /l/; /d/ for /g/ or /j/; /p/ for /f/; /b/ for /v/; and /f/ for /th/. Jaden can also be difficult to understand because she consistently deletes (i.e., does not produce) the final consonants /p/, /b/, /t/, /d/, /k/, or /g/. In other words, she deletes the final consonant sounds in words ending with these particular sounds, two-syllable words with these sounds ending a syllable, and words ending with two consonants. For example, she will say /tuh/ for *tub* (deleting the final consonant sound), /bah-um/ for *bottom* (deleting the consonant sound in a word with two syllables), or /wan/ for *want* (deleting final consonant sound for a word with two consonants at the end).

After getting dressed, Jaden walks independently to the kitchen. She likes to stand on a stool next to her mother and help prepare breakfast. Her mother offers her choices of foods (e.g., different kinds of cereal, fruit, bread, toaster waffle, pancake). To make a selection Jaden points to food items she desires. She sometimes imitates the name of the food offered but, again, has difficulty being understood by adults when the words end in particular consonants or when she makes substitutions for consonants at the beginning of words. For example, Jaden will say /poo/ for *fruit,* /mil/ for *milk,* /tōs/ for *toast,* and /dā/ /deh wy/ for *grape jelly.*

Jaden also assists with getting her breakfast by shaking cereal into a bowl, stirring batter, or putting bread in the toaster. Jaden is starting to use a plastic knife to cut soft fruits such as bananas, kiwi, and watermelon but requires adult assistance to peel fruit. Jaden usually eats the same food for a few days before switching to a new one, but she eats a variety of foods across the week. She is able to grasp a spoon or fork but needs help from an adult to scoop/spear food. She is able to bring the food to her mouth and remove the food from the utensil with her lips with little spilling. She drinks from a cup without assistance. She is starting to use a large serving spoon to scoop food from a larger bowl to her bowl or plate when she wants more of a particular food. Jaden usually moves toward or points to the food if she wants more and will only request food verbally if prompted by an adult (e.g., "What do you want, Jaden?").

Once breakfast is finished, Jaden throws a small ball or dog toy for her dog, Charlie. She is starting to help take care of Charlie by assisting with feeding, watering, and taking him for walks. She puts the dog's bowl in the sink and lifts the faucet lever to fill the dish with water. She pushes the button on the electric can opener to start opening the dog food, and she gets the leash from the closet when it is time to walk Charlie. Often, she brings the leash to her father when he gets home from work to indicate that she is ready to take Charlie for a walk. If it's raining outside, she will also bring her jacket and wait for her father to assist her with putting it on and zipping it. Her mother and father report that she is most talkative around Charlie. She imitates a few two- and three-word phrases including /Nī/ /Tawy/ for *Nice Charlie;* /Dǔ/ /dǒ-ie/ for *Good doggie;* /Weh/ /dō/ for *Let's go;* /tum/ /on/ /Tawy/ for *Come on, Charlie;* /Dō/ /deh/ /ǐ/ *Go get it;* and /Tawy/ /poo/ for *Charlie's food.*

At school, Jaden frequently selects activities in the art and dramatic play areas. She is starting to draw and paint simple shapes (e.g., circles, horizontal and vertical lines that intersect). She can hold different writing instruments (e.g., crayons, markers, pencils, paint brushes) by grasping them with her whole hand (i.e., four fingers wrapped around the instrument). She also makes the letters of her name with hand-over-hand assistance when asked to put her name on an art project.

She is observant at school and follows routine directions. She is beginning to sing along to music and can complete movements associated with songs during circle time activities (e.g., act out animal movements, shake hands with friends when prompted). When given a choice of instruments, she will choose to shake a tambourine during music time. In the dramatic play area, she wears a puppet on her hand and, along with one or two other children, will move the puppets across a puppet stage and make them dance and talk with the other puppets through gestures and animal sounds. Jaden will also exchange her puppet with other children and follow along in the games they make up with the puppets. Jaden often selects the big dog puppet but will trade for the smaller puppy puppet. At home, her mother also reports that Jaden shares her toys with her brother.

When changing from inside to outside activities, Jaden joins the teacher and other children counting the laminated footprints on the floor. She is starting to count from 1 to 10 in correct sequence with the group. Outside, Jaden watches the other children run, jump, and play with a ball. She often requests an adult to put her on the swing (e.g., Me /pin/? for *Me swing?* or /Wan/ /uh/ for *Want up*). She will sit on a tricycle and squeeze the horn. She will also gesture to other children that she wants to sit in the taxi tricycle and have them pedal.

Both at home and at school, Jaden demonstrates that she understands concepts related to size, shape, and color when reading books. She responds to questions such as, "Where is the circle?" "Where is the blue ball?" and "Where is the big chair?" by pointing to or retrieving an object. After pointing to or retrieving the object, she will sometimes imitate the target concept word but has difficulty being understood because she will often not produce the final consonant. She can tell others the names of people in family photos or framed pictures of family members in the house. Sometimes, she is also able to recall some information about the person or event (e.g., /My/ /pah-y/ for *My party,* /My/ /hă/ for *My hat,* /Nana/ /tă/ for *Nana's cat,* and /Tawy/ /beh/ for *Charlie's bed*). At school, she also has learned the names of a few children. When children's pictures are individually held up by the teacher to dismiss the children from circle to an activity, she listens to the other children call out the child's name.

Phase 2: Targeting Functional and Generative Goals   Based on the comprehensive assessment information and the resulting present level of performance, the team selects a number of priority goals and associated objectives/benchmarks to target for intervention. Skills targeted within Jaden's goals include manipulates a variety of objects, says a variety of one and two words, and uses one object to represent another object. The team uses the revised version of the Goal and Objective Rating Inventory (Notari-Syverson & Shuster, 1995) to ensure that the goals and associated objectives/benchmarks are functional and generative. The team then takes steps to ensure that daily activities promote learning and use of target goals.

Phase 3: Providing Multiple and Varied Learning Opportunities   The team uses the three forms (i.e., ABI intervention guides, embedding schedules, and activity plans) described in Chapter 6 to assist in creating and embedding multiple and varied learning opportunities. Jaden's team reviews her present level of performance and target goals, and then considers how to individualize intervention. They create an ABI intervention guide for each prioritized IEP goal outlining specific antecedents and consequences as well as needed accommodations and modifications and possible intervention strategies. Figure 10.1 contains an ABI intervention guide for the target goal, says a variety of one and two words. Because Jaden receives services at a community preschool, the team considers the daily classroom activities in which she is likely to participate (e.g., arrival, free play, snack). They then develop an embedding schedule that reminds adults which antecedents to provide and when to embed learning opportunities across daily classroom activities. The team creates an embedding schedule for multiple children (i.e., Jaden, Marley, and Grace) to help streamline efforts when serving groups of children. Figure 10.2 contains an embedding schedule for Jaden and two other children in the class. Finally, the team develops several weekly planned activities that address Jaden's and other children's target goals. Figure 10.3 contains an activity plan that can be incorporated into classroom activities.

Phase 4: Monitoring Children's Progress   The team reviews the intervention guide to develop a data collection system to monitor Jaden's performance on target goals. The team discusses how to create a data collection system that 1) is accessible and usable by everyone on the team, 2) keeps writing to a minimum, and 3) includes situational information and performance information. After reviewing the intervention guide, the team makes a number of decisions:

- The parents will record the number of times Jaden uses one- and two-word phrases several times each week (e.g., during various family routines, at relatives' homes, at the park, during dance class) and whether they could understand words with the target final consonants.

- When Jaden attends class, Gwen (ECSE teacher), Denise (occupational therapist), and Tashana (classroom assistant) will record the number of one- and two-word phrases Jaden uses, the function of the utterances (i.e., to request, inform, or greet), and whether they can understand those

ABI Intervention Guide

1. Identifying information

Child's name: Jaden Johnson

Team members: Parents: Marcia and Don; ECSE teacher: Gwen; classroom assistant: Tashana; speech-language pathologist: Debra; occupational therapist: Denise

Date intervention initiated: September 2013   Date intervention completed: May 2014

2. Target goal, objectives, and program steps

Goal:

1.0 Using a variety of one and two words, Jaden will request objects, people, or materials three times a day, inform others, and greet others during daily activities. Two different adults will understand what she says three times a day for 2 weeks.

In Goal 1.0 and associated objectives, to be understood by other adults means that when Jaden says words to request, inform, and/or greet, adults will hear Jaden produce target final consonant sounds and/or produce target first consonant sounds without making substitutions. The final consonant target sounds are /p, b, t, d, k/, and the first consonant target sounds are /k, l, g, f, v, ch, j, th/.

Objectives:

1.1 Using a variety of one and two words, Jaden will request objects, people, or materials from others (adults or peers) during daily activities. Two different adults will understand what she says three times a day for 2 weeks. For example, Jaden will say words/phrases such as "Up," "Give toy," or "More food."

1.2 Using a variety of one and two words, Jaden will inform others (adults or peers) about daily activities. Two different adults will understand what she says three times a day for 2 weeks. For example, Jaden will say words/phrases such as "cat," "milk," and "big book."

1.3 Using a variety of one and two words, Jaden will greet others (adults or peers). Two different adults will understand what she says three times a day for 2 weeks. For example, Jaden will say "Hey," "Hi Marley," "Hi Beth," "Hi Kate," or "Good morning."

Program steps:

3. Core standards

Links to Head Start Child Development and Early Learning Framework (U.S. Department of Health and Human Services, 2011)

Expressive Language
- Engages in communication and conversation with others
- Uses language to express ideas and needs
- Uses increasingly complex and varied vocabulary
- Uses different grammatical structures for a variety of purposes

Figure 10.1. Completed ABI Intervention Guide for Jaden.

ABI Intervention Guide *(continued)*

4. Antecedents, targeted and nontargeted responses, and feedback or consequences

Antecedents designed to provide learning opportunities	List of possible child responses: targeted (+) and nontargeted (-)	Feedback or consequences
1.1 Place/hold desired object/person/ material with the first consonant sounds of /k, l, g, f, v, ch, j, th/ or the final consonant sounds of /p, b, t, d, k/ within view but out of Jaden's reach. Ask Jaden questions that require a one- or two-word response/request with the first consonant sounds of /k, l, g, f, v, ch, j, th/ or the final consonant sounds of /p, b, t, d, k/ (e.g., Ask, "Do you have any pets?" or when playing outside, ask, "What do you want to do?")	Uses one or two words to request objects, people, or materials by producing/ saying the first consonant sounds of /k, l, g, f, v, ch, j, th/ or producing/saying the final consonant sounds of /p, b, t, d, k/ in words (+) Uses one and two words to request objects, people, or materials but substitutes the first target consonant sound or does not produce final target consonant sounds (-) Points or looks at the desired object/ person/material (-) Answers question nonverbally (e.g., shakes her head, goes to get an object) (-)	Give her requested item or comply with request. (+) Affirm and repeat what Jaden says. (+) Model one- or two-word response with final target consonant sounds. (-) Wait and look expectantly for a response, or wait and repeat the question. (-)
1.2 Ask Jaden to inform others (e.g., "Who would you like to sit with?" "What do you have for lunch?") Model one and two words with first or final target consonant sounds (e.g., "Food," "Dog," "Come on," "Let's go").	Uses one or two words to inform others by producing/saying the first consonant sounds of /k, l, g, f, v, ch, j, th/ or producing/saying the final consonant sounds of /p, b, t, d, k/ , in words (+) Uses one and two words to inform others but substitutes the first target consonant sound or does not produce final target consonant sounds (-) Answers question nonverbally (e.g., by pointing) (-)	Ask a follow-up question. (+) Comment on what Jaden says. (+) Correctly model the one or two words Jaden says. (-) Tell Jaden to answer your question and provide a model of response. (-)
1.3 Peer or adult says, "Hi." Peer or adult models, "Hi Leo," and then waits for Jaden to imitate. Peer or adult waves. Adult asks Jaden, "What do you say to your friend?" Sing the Good Morning song at circle time or other greeting song.	Uses one or two words to greet others by producing/saying the first consonant sounds of /k, l, g, f, v, ch, j, th/ or producing/saying the final consonant sounds of /p, b, t, d, k/ , in words. (+) Uses one and two words to greet others but substitutes the first target consonant sound or does not produce final target consonant sounds. (-) Looks at person but does not respond. (-) Waves or smiles at person. (-) Remains with the group, but does not say the words to the song. (-)	Peer or adult smiles. (+) Peer says hi in response. (+) Affirm and repeat what Jaden says (e.g., "Yes it is good to see Leo this morning."). (+) Correctly model the one- or two-word greeting. (-) Ask Jaden to say one- or two-word greeting. (-) Sing another greeting song and encourage Jaden to sing along. (-)

5. Teaching strategies

Ensure joint attention and then provide several massed trials for Jaden to produce targeted final consonant sounds.

Use milieu strategies including incidental teaching, mand-model, and time delay.

Use nondirected strategies including novelty (present new and interesting objects with target first or final consonants) and forgetfulness (forget how to say words with target or final consonants and ask Jaden to help you say them).

(continued)

Figure 10.1. *(continued)*

ABI Intervention Guide *(continued)*   *page 3 of 3*

6. Monitoring progress

Who (person responsible for collecting the data)	Where (which activities or locations)	When (how often or on which days)	How (which methods)
ECSE teacher (Gwen), occupational therapist (Denise), and classroom assistant (Tashana)	Daily classroom activities and monthly home visit	Three times per day on Mondays and Wednesdays	Record what Jaden says (written descriptions) and the function of her utterances, and note which target consonant sounds were understandable (counts/tallies).
Speech-language pathologist (Debra)	Circle time	Monthly	Record a language sample (written descriptions) to document utterances, length of utterances, function, and intelligibility.
Parents (Marcia and Don)	Home, relatives' homes, the park, and dance class	3 or 4 times per month	Record what Jaden says (written descriptions) and note whether she was understandable (counts/tallies).

7. Decision rules

If adequate progress does not occur in _____1 month_____ (specify time frame for when the team will review the data), consider changing:

_____ Targeted goal

_____ Antecedents or feedback/consequences

_____ Teaching strategies

__X__ Frequency, type, and/or locations of learning opportunities provided

__X__ Other (describe) _Team will consider narrowing focus to one or two earlier developing sounds or only sounds in_

initial position, and then gradually add in additional sounds and sounds in final position.

_____

ABI Embedding Schedule

Children's names: Jaden, Marley, and Grace

Focus: Group   **Setting:** Classroom

Team members: Classroom staff and therapists

Dates schedule will be used: First quarter (Sept. to Nov.)

Children and target skills	Daily classroom activities and opportunities for practice					Practice opportunities per day
Child's name: Jaden	Arrival	Free play	Circle activities	Snack	Centers	
1. Manipulates objects	Ask Jaden to unzip her coat.	Encourage Jaden to play with blocks, puzzles, and art materials.		Provide a spoon or a fork to eat with, foods to prepare, and a knife for spreading or cutting.	Place objects to manipulate in writing center (e.g., pencils, scissors) and science center (e.g., tweezers, microscope with slides).	4
2. Uses one- and two-words to request, inform, and greet	Model saying, "Good morning." Ask Jaden to greet peers.		Sing the Good Morning song. Ask Jaden to request a song. Ask Jaden to tell the class what color shoes she has on (including black, pink, gray as targets).	Ask Jaden what she is having for lunch. Label words related to snack/eating that end with target consonants (e.g., milk, nut, fruit, last).	Model greeting peers as they enter the different centers. Ask Jaden what she is doing. Ask Jaden where she wants to play or what toys she wants.	6
3. Uses one object to represent another		Model how to use different sized blocks as food or a shoe for a doll's car.			Use a small dust pan or a ladle as a shovel in the discovery table. Use sticks as paintbrushes in the art area.	3

Figure 10.2. Completed ABI Embedding Schedule for Jaden and two other children in her class.

(continued)

Figure 10.2. (continued)

ABI Embedding Schedule (continued) Focus: Group Setting: Classroom

	Daily classroom activities and opportunities for practice					
Child's name: Marley						
1. Expresses likes and dislikes	Present song options for Marley to choose.		Ask Marley which activities she likes and does not like.			2
2. Sorts like objects		Ask Marley to put all of the books together and all of the puppets together.		Encourage Marley to put all cups on one table and all snack food on another.		2
3. Uses spoon to feed self				Provide food requiring spoon use.		1
Child's name: Grace						
1. Uses toilet	Ask Grace if she has to use the bathroom.			Ask Grace if she has to use the bathroom.		2
2. Follows routine directions	Remind Grace to hang up her coat and put away her lunch.	Ask Grace to put the blocks away.		Prompt Grace to take one and pass to her friends.		3

ABI Activity Plan

1. Activity name   Action books

Target child(ren): Jaden, Marley, Grace

Target skills: Manipulates objects; uses one and two words to request, inform, and greet; expresses likes and dislikes; sorts like objects; follows routine directions

2. Materials

8 ½" x 11" construction paper

Scissors, hole punch, brads, markers, glue sticks, cotton swabs, and plastic lids

Precut action figures from magazines or coloring books

Smocks, sponges, and towels

Several examples of complete action books

3. Environmental arrangement

A flat surface is needed for children to sit or stand on to reach materials. Set up the activity near a sink if possible and near other art materials that can be incorporated into the activity as it progresses. Materials in labeled containers make it easy for children to identify them and clean them up. Hang smocks on coat hooks low enough for children to get and return smocks independently.

Figure 10.3. Completed ABI Activity Plan for Jaden and two other children in her class.

(continued)

Figure 10.3. *(continued)*

ABI Activity Plan *(continued)*   *page 2 of 3*

4. Sequence of steps

Beginning

Ask children about their favorite book, movie, or television characters. After they respond with a variety of characters, tell them your favorite character, and show them a completed action book you created about that character. Other completed action books made by children should be available to serve as examples and encourage creativity. Read one or two of the action book stories and, when finished, ask children if they can guess how the book was made. As children guess, write down the materials they will need to create their own action book. Once the list is complete, instruct children to help find the needed items, get a smock, and come to the table to make their own action book.

Middle

Have children select the colors of the paper for their books. Then, have them cut the paper to the size book they desire. Next, children select several character pictures from magazines or old coloring books and glue the pictures on their pages. Children can select and glue other objects onto the pages with their character. Ask children to tell what their character is doing, and write phrases or sentences on the page. Then, children punch three holes on the side of the front page to insert brads.

End

Children return materials to their labeled containers and wipe tables with sponges. Then, they remove their smocks. Children transition to the circle area with their books. Invite children to read their book to another child or adult.

5. Embedded learning opportunities

Learns/practices fine motor skills
- Uses hands to manipulate objects
- Uses scissors to cut
- Holds and uses writing instruments
- Copies/prints letters

Learns/practices cognitive skills
- Demonstrates understanding of color, shape, size, quantity, and quality concepts
- Follows directions
- Evaluates solutions to problems
- Plans and acts out recognizable event, theme, or storyline
- Counts objects

Learns/practices social skills
- Initiates preferred activities
- Participates in small-group activities (remains, watches, follows directions)
- Initiates and completes activities

Learns/practices social-communication skills
- Requests materials to make action book
- Informs others about action book and who the characters are and what they are doing
- Reads book to a peer

ABI Activity Plan *(continued)*

6. Planned variations

1. Children make family books with pictures of family members.
2. Children use stamps and ink pads for pictures.
3. Children make favorite animal action books.

7. Other (e.g., vocabulary, peer interactions, caregiver response)

Pronouns (e.g., he, she, mine, my, they, him)

Present progressive verbs with "ing" (e.g., flying, climbing, running, jumping)

Nouns (e.g., hole punch, marker, paper, book, glue stick, Q-tip, lid, chalk)

Adjectives (e.g., colors: pink, black, gray; sizes: tiny, big, long, short, fat; quantity: many, any; quality: hot, soft, light, heavy, dry, wet, quiet, fast, dirty)

Position words (e.g., back, front, last, bottom, first)

Children help find pictures/objects for one another's action books.

Children share materials (e.g., magazines, glue sticks).

Children read finished action books to one another.

Children work in pairs to clean up area and return materials.

with the target consonants. Each person will collect data during three different classroom activities. Gwen will also collect data on her monthly home visits. Every month, Gwen and Tashana will collect and summarize the total number of words used and the percentage understood by others.

- Debra (speech-language pathologist) will collect a monthly language sample during visits to the classroom.

- All team members will review data monthly to make decisions regarding changes to how often learning opportunities are provided, the manner in which opportunities are provided (i.e., antecedents and consequences), and the activities during which opportunities are embedded.

The team develops two forms to accomplish these data collection activities, one form for parent use (Figure 10.4) and one for classroom personnel (Figure 10.5). Both forms allow team members to indicate what they hear Jaden say, either by writing it phonetically or by writing what they know she was saying and then determining whether her utterances were intelligible based on criterion stated in her target goal and associated objectives. As the team collects data, they meet regularly to discuss Jaden's progress and make decisions regarding intervention efforts.

Example 2: Head Start Center-Based Program with Itinerant Services

Cooper is 5 years old and eligible for Head Start services. As a preschooler with a disability, he also qualifies for ECSE services. Cooper attends a local Head Start program 4 days per week. The ECSE itinerant teacher visits the classroom weekly to consult with the Head Start teacher and work with Cooper. Information related to Cooper's present level of performance was gathered through a comprehensive assessment conducted by his mother (Shawna) and grandmother (Teresa), Head Start teacher (Marlene), occupational therapist (Amy), and ECSE itinerant teacher (Nicole). Assessment observations were based on Cooper's interactions with others in the Head Start program and guided by the AEPS (Bricker, 2002). Similar to Jaden, Cooper's intervention plan addresses the four phases of intervention: 1) conducting comprehensive and ongoing assessments, 2) targeting functional and generative goals, 3) providing multiple and varied learning opportunities, and 4) monitoring children's progress.

Phase 1: Conducting Comprehensive and Ongoing Assessments In the morning, Cooper tells his mother what he wants to eat using three- to four-word phrases such as, "I want cereal, please." He feeds himself with an adaptive fork, spoon, and a suctioned bowl and plate. He spears or scoops the food and brings it to his mouth with minimal spilling. He drinks from a cup by bringing it to his mouth and returning it to the table without spilling. After eating, he places his utensils in the sink and pushes in his chair.

To prepare for school, Cooper selects his own clothing that matches the

ABI Data Collection Form

page 1 of 1

Child's name: _____Jaden_____   Family routine: _____Going to the park_____

Date: _____Week of November 3, 2013_____

One or two words Jaden uses (write how it sounds)	Does she correctly produce target sounds?	
Ni Tawy (Nice Charlie)	Yes	(No)
Du doie (Good doggie)	Yes	(No)
Tum on Tawy (Come on, Charlie)	Yes	(No)
Dō! (Go!)	Yes	(No)
Want (Want)	(Yes)	No
Want uh (Want up) Note: Dad modeled "want."	Yes	(No)

Child's name: _____Jaden_____   Family routine: _____Dance class_____

Date: _____Week of November 10, 2013_____

One or two words Jaden uses (write how it sounds)	Does she correctly produce target sounds?	
Want pin (Want pink)	Yes	(No)
Pink (Pink)	(Yes)	No
I want pink Note: Dad modeled "pink."	(Yes)	No
Wan turn (Want turn)	Yes	(No)
My turn	(Yes)	No

Figure 10.4. ABI Data Collection Form completed by Jaden's parents.

ABI Data Collection Form

Child's name: _____Jaden_____   Date: _____October 24, 2013_____

Person collecting data: _____Gwen_____

Activity	Utterances	Request	Inform	Greet	Intelligible
Activity name: Circle	Up, please.	X			No
	Good morning.			X	Yes
Start time: 10:00	Hi, Beth.			X	Yes
Stop time: 10:05	Wheels on the bus		X		No
	Monday, Tuesday…		X		No
	My turn.		X		No
	I help.		X		Yes
	Today	X			Yes
Activity name: Snack	More juice, please.	X			No
Start time: 11:15	Grape jelly		X		No
Stop time: 11:25	Cats like milk.		X		No
	More, please.	X			Yes
	Mine?	X			No
	Hungry		X		No
Activity name: Centers	Give me toy.	X			No
	Hi Kate.			X	Yes
Start time: 11:30	Big book.		X		Yes
Stop time: 11:45	Let's go.		X		Yes
	Want help?		X		Yes
	Mine		X		Yes
	My hat.		X		No

Figure 10.5. ABI Data Collection Form completed by Jaden's teacher.

day's weather (e.g., long pants when it is cold, shorts when it is hot) and is able to dress himself. For example, he can pull long pants over both feet and pull them up to his waist. He can put on a pullover garment and a front opening garment. He requires adult assistance when zipping or buttoning clothing and tying his shoes. He completes a toileting routine: pulls down pants, uses toilet paper after using the toilet, pulls up pants, flushes toilet, and washes hands. Cooper uses a tissue to clean his nose and brushes his teeth with minimal assistance from his mother or grandmother.

When Cooper arrives at his Head Start program, he gets off the bus with the other students but needs adult reminders to stay with the group. He places his coat and book bag in his area but requires assistance to unzip his clothing. During free play, Cooper will initiate context-relevant topics and respond to the topic initiations of other children in one-to-one situations and small groups (i.e., less than four other children). He engages in conversational turn taking and topical discussions using three- to four-word phrases. Cooper asks peers if he can join them in play (e.g., "Can I play?"), answers their questions usually with one-word responses (e.g., "Yes"), makes requests to peers (e.g., "Can I have that?"), and responds to their requests (e.g., saying "Sure" while handing toy to peer).

During circle time when most of the children in the class join the adults to sing songs, read stories, and talk about the day's events, Cooper is able to remain with the large group for a limited amount of time (usually less than 5 minutes). He is able to remain with the group (i.e., walks around the perimeter of the group or sits near one or two other children) with visual and verbal prompts (e.g., picture symbol of "sit" paired with the word *sit*). He is beginning to look at objects and people that are the focus of the activity (e.g., books being read, person singing a song). Cooper sings songs he has heard many times that contain repeating phrases (e.g., "Five Little Monkeys," "Old MacDonald"). He answers routine questions during circle about concrete topics (e.g., "What is the weather outside?"), but he is not yet answering questions or participating in discussions about anticipated outcomes (e.g., predicting the end to a story, talking about what he will do this weekend).

Cooper greets, informs, and requests objects/materials from adults and peers in one-to-one situations and small-group activities. He initiates and completes age-appropriate activities, such as getting puzzles out, putting them together, and then putting them away. He is able to assemble toys by putting the pieces together (e.g., puts LEGO pieces together). Cooper plans and acts out recognizable events and themes, such as playing restaurant and grocery store.

During adult-created and -led one-to-one activities, Cooper consistently demonstrates an understanding of colors, shapes, and sizes. For example, during block play, book reading, and art, Cooper matches like colors, follows directions related to colors, and names objects' colors. At snack, he demonstrates one-to-one correspondence by passing out utensils to other classmates. He is able to categorize like toys/objects in the housekeeping area (e.g., puts utensils, food together).

On the playground, Cooper is able to jump forward with two feet together from surface to surface (e.g., from grass to cement). He plays games with balls (e.g., bounces it to another peer, catches the ball when it is thrown, kicks and throws overhand).

Phase 2: Targeting Functional and Generative Goals   Based on the comprehensive assessment information and the resulting present level of performance (i.e., assessment summary), the team selects a number of priority goals and associated objectives to target for intervention. Cooper's goals include manipulates objects with both hands; uses words, phrases, or sentences to express anticipated outcomes; and participates in group activities by remaining with the group, looking at people talking, and following group directions. The team uses the revised version of the Goal and Objective Rating Inventory (Notari-Syverson & Shuster, 1995) to ensure that the goals and associated objectives are functional and generative. The team then takes steps to ensure daily activities promote learning and use of target goals.

Phase 3: Providing Multiple and Varied Learning Opportunities   The three forms (i.e., intervention guides, embedding schedules, and activity plans) described in Chapter 6 are used to assist the team in creating and embedding multiple and varied learning opportunities. Cooper's team reviews his present level of performance and target goals, and then considers how to individualize his intervention. They create an intervention guide for each target goal and associated objective outlining specific antecedents and consequences as well as needed accommodations and modifications and possible intervention strategies. Figure 10.6 contains an intervention guide for the target goal of manipulates objects with both hands.

Because Cooper receives services at the Head Start preschool and from the itinerant teacher, the team considers the daily classroom activities in which he is likely to participate (e.g., arrival, free play, small group, snack). The itinerant teacher then assists the Head Start teacher to identify times in the day to embed learning opportunities. The occupational therapist offers suggestions for appropriate antecedents and necessary accommodations and modifications that need to be made throughout classroom activities as well as possible intervention strategies. Figure 10.7 contains an embedding schedule for Cooper in which opportunities to embed practice on his target skills are noted across five classroom activities. Finally, the team develops several planned activities for each week that address Cooper's target goals. Figure 10.8 contains an activity plan that can be incorporated by the itinerant teacher into the classroom routine during her weekly visits.

Phase 4: Monitoring Children's Progress   The team reviews the intervention guide to develop a data collection system to monitor Cooper's performance

---

ABI Intervention Guide

1. Identifying information

Child's name: Cooper Reynolds
_____

Team members: Mother: Shawna; grandmother: Teresa; Head Start teacher: Marlene; occupational therapist: Amy; ECSE
_____ itinerant teacher: Nicole
_____

Date intervention initiated: September 2013   Date intervention completed: September 2014

---

2. Target goal, objectives, and program steps

Goal:

1.0 During daily activities, Cooper will manipulate a variety of objects, toys, or materials that require use of both hands at the same time, while performing different movements. He will manipulate three different objects, toys, or materials once a day for 2 weeks. For example, Cooper will tie shoes, button clothing, thread and zip a zipper, and/or cut out shapes with curved lines.

Objectives:

1.1 During daily activities, Cooper will perform any two-handed task using one hand to hold or steady an object, toy, or material while using the other hand to manipulate the object, toy, or material or perform a movement. He will perform three different two-handed tasks per day for 2 weeks. For example, Cooper will hold a piece of paper and draw with a crayon, hold paper and cut paper in half, hold a bowl and spoon up food or liquid, spread food with a knife, zip a zipper, or turn the pages of a book.

Program steps:

---

3. Core standards

Links to Head Start Child Development and Early Learning Framework (2011)

Physical Development and Health
- Develops hand strength and dexterity.
- Develops eye–hand coordination to use everyday tools, such as pitchers for pouring or utensils for eating.
- Manipulates a range of objects such as blocks or books.
- Manipulates writing, drawing, and art tools.

Figure 10.6.   Completed ABI Intervention Guide for Cooper.

(continued)

Figure 10.6.   *(continued)*

ABI Intervention Guide *(continued)*

4. Antecedents, targeted and nontargeted responses, and feedback or consequences

Antecedents designed to provide learning opportunities	List of possible child responses: targeted (+) and nontargeted (-)	Feedback or consequences
1.1 Present Cooper with an object that requires one hand to hold and steady and the other to manipulate (e.g., bowl and spoon, books, pasta shells, shoelace strings). Adult models how to manipulate objects that require one hand to hold and steady and the other to manipulate (e.g., pouring juice into a cup, holding a paper and drawing a line). Ask Cooper to complete a task that requires one hand to hold and steady and the other to manipulate (e.g., "Cooper, zip up your coat.").	Cooper manipulates objects that require one hand to hold and steady and the other to manipulate. (+) Cooper requires assistance to hold or manipulate object. (-) Cooper does not respond to the object, model, or request. (-)	Comment on what he is doing. (+) Smile at Cooper. (+) Cooper successfully completes the task. (+) Wait for a few seconds and then encourage Cooper to try again. (-) Provide hand-over-hand assistance to help Cooper either hold or manipulate object. (-) Redirect Cooper back to the object, model, or request. (-)
1.0 Present Cooper with an object that requires the use of both hands while performing different movements (e.g., pictures with curved lines and a pair of scissors). Model how to manipulate objects with both hands performing different movements (e.g., thread and zip zipper, cut out shapes). Ask Cooper to complete a task that requires use of both hands performing different movements (e.g., ask Cooper to hang laundry on clothesline with clothespins in housekeeping).	Cooper manipulates objects that require use of both hands at the same time while performing different movements. (+) Cooper manipulates object using one hand to hold and steady and the other to manipulate. (-) Cooper does not respond to the object, model. (-)	Comment on what he is doing. (+) Smile at Cooper. (+) Cooper successfully completes the task. (+) Wait for a few seconds and then encourage Cooper to try again. (-) Redirect Cooper back to the object, model, or request. (-) Provide hand-over-hand assistance. (-)

5. Teaching strategies

Provide toys or materials that will help Cooper strengthen and control his fine motor movements (e.g., jacks and marbles, spring-type clothespins, hole punch, clay/play dough, garlic press, rolling pin, cookie cutters, plastic rolling pizza slicer).

Place spray bottles in the housekeeping area and near the sink for use when washing.

Create snacks with foods that are difficult to spread and take strength (e.g., cream cheese).

Use the directive strategy of assistance only with novel toys, materials, or objects.

Use the nondirective strategies of piece-by-piece and delay.

ABI Intervention Guide *(continued)*

6. Monitoring progress

Who (person responsible for collecting the data)	Where (which activities or locations)	When (how often or on which days)	How (which methods)
Early Head Start teacher (Marlene)	Arrival, free play, outdoor play	Twice a week (Monday and Wednesday)	Probes—prior to, during, or at the end of an activity to see which toys, materials, or objects Cooper can manipulate
Occupational therapist (Amy)	Snack	Weekly (Tuesdays)	Probes
ECSE itinerant teacher (Nicole)	Center time or free play	Weekly (Wednesdays)	Probes

7. Decision rules

If adequate progress does not occur in _____1 month_____ (specify time frame for when the team will review the data), consider changing:

__X__ Targeted goal

_____ Antecedents or feedback/consequences

__X__ Teaching strategies

_____ Frequency, type, and/or locations of learning opportunities provided

_____ Other (describe) _____

_____

_____

ABI Embedding Schedule

Child's name: _____Cooper_____

Team members: _____Mother: Shawna; grandmother: Teresa; Head Start teacher: Marlene; occupational therapist: Amy; ECSE
   itinerant teacher: Nicole_____

Dates schedule will be used: _____First quarter_____

Daily classroom activity	**Target goal** Manipulates objects/toys/materials	**Target goal** Uses words, phrases, or sentences to express anticipated outcomes	**Target goal** Participates in group activities (remains, looks, responds to directions)
Arrival	Wait for Cooper to unzip and remove his coat, unzip his book bag, and remove his notebook.	Ask Cooper what he thinks will happen at school today when he gets off the bus.	When getting off the bus remind Cooper to remain with the group. Give Cooper directions (e.g., hold hands with peer).
Free play	Make available and encourage Cooper to play with blocks, LEGOs, toy cars, and small figures.	When transitioning to free play, ask Cooper what he wants to do during free play time.	Invite Cooper to play game with peers; encourage Cooper to take at least four turns in game before moving to new activity.
Circle time	Ask Cooper to pull apart felt pieces and put them on the storyboard; hold basket and pass out instruments; use rhythm sticks during songs.	Before reading book, show the cover and ask Cooper what he thinks will happen in the story.	Seat Cooper near front of circle; sing songs that require following directions (e.g., putting rhythm sticks on floor, then on lap).

Figure 10.7. Completed ABI Embedding Schedule for Cooper.

(continued)

ABI Embedding Schedule *(continued)* **Focus:** Individual **Setting:** Classroom *page 2 of 2*

Daily classroom activity	**Target goal** Manipulates objects/toys/materials	**Target goal** Uses words, phrases, or sentences to express anticipated outcomes	**Target goal** Participates in-group activities (remains, looks, responds to directions)
Meals	Ask Cooper to hold container and pass out eating utensils. Ask Cooper to print name cards to use for seating arrangements. Serve foods that require fork, spoon (e.g., hold bowl and spoon).	While Cooper is helping set the table, ask Cooper to tell you what he thinks will be served for lunch. Ask Cooper what he thinks they will do outside or in gym after lunch.	At the beginning of the meal, remind Cooper to stay at the table until clean-up time. Give him directions to clean up plate, utensils, and so forth when finished. Remind Cooper to look at friends when they are talking to him.
Center time	Encourage Cooper to paint at easel steadying paper while using paintbrush. Provide funnels and containers for pouring in the discovery table. Encourage Cooper to hang clothes using clothespins and clothesline in the dress-up area.	When introducing a new game, show pieces and ask Cooper to tell what he thinks children will do to play game. At easel, ask Cooper to tell you what he is going to paint.	Set visual sand timer and ask Cooper to stay in the center he chooses (e.g. at easel) until the sand is gone. For pretend areas, provide visual schedule of steps in activity (e.g., doing laundry) and ask Cooper to do each step before leaving center.

ABI Activity Plan

1. Activity name   Blocks, ramps, and small vehicles

Target child(ren): Cooper

Target skills: Manipulates objects with both hands; uses words, phrases, or sentences to express anticipated outcomes; participates in group activities

2. Materials

Variety of sizes and shapes of soft foam blocks

Picture labels of small vehicles

Long, soft foam boards for ramps

Variety of small vehicles (e.g., cars, trucks, buses, vans, motorcycles)

One rectangular child-size table

Variety of road sign displays

3. Environmental arrangement

Place rectangular, child-size table on carpet in block area. Encourage children to build roads/garages with soft foam blocks on top of the table. Children can prop long, sanded wooden boards against the table to create ramps.

Figure 10.8.   Completed ABI Activity Plan for Cooper.

4. Sequence of steps

Beginning
Introduce the activity by showing children the baskets that contain a variety of vehicles. Prompt children to label the vehicles they would like, and have them hold the basket with one hand and remove the vehicles with the other hand. Show children the blocks and road signs and ask them how they could use these materials to make roads and garages for the cars.

Middle
Have children use blocks and boards on the table in the block area. Children create roads, ramps, and garages. They place vehicles on the roads and move the vehicles. They also place road signs at various locations on the roads.

End
Give a 5-minute warning to signal clean up and the end of the activity. Ask children to return their vehicles to the basket with matching picture labels. Instruct children to place blocks on the shelves and carry long boards to the storage area. Ask children to recall one thing they did during the activity, and record the statements.

5. Embedded learning opportunities

Learns/practices fine motor skills
- Manipulates a variety of vehicles to provide different sensory experiences
- Stacks blocks to create garages or buildings
- Places vehicles in a row on long boards
- Opens bucket with lid using two hands

Learns/practices cognitive skills
- Groups vehicles by categories (e.g., colors, size, transportation mode)
- Counts vehicles
- Counts peers who are playing the game
- Sorts like vehicles when cleaning up
- Demonstrates one-to-one correspondence by handing out vehicles
- Demonstrates understanding of spatial concepts (e.g., in, next to)
- Explains directions to peers (recalls information)

Learns/practices social-communication skills
- Labels the vehicles using descriptors
- Uses conversational turn-taking (asks questions about the vehicles)
- Asks peers their color preference of vehicle
- Uses names of peers to tell them it is their turn

Learns/practices social skills
- Passes out vehicles to peers
- Takes turns with a desired vehicle
- Greets and invites new peers to join in and play the game
- Assists with clean up

(continued)

Figure 10.8.   *(continued)*

ABI Activity Plan *(continued)*   *page 3 of 3*

6. Planned variations

1. Add large vehicles.

2. Add props such as a Fisher-Price gas station with people.

3. Tape a large sheet of paper on the table, and let children draw roads.

4. Place materials in the sandbox outside.

5. Provide hats for children to wear that correspond with vehicles (e.g., firefighter hat, police officer hat, chauffeur hat).

---

7. Other (e.g., vocabulary, peer interactions, caregiver response)

Colors (e.g., blue, yellow, red, black, green, orange, lavender, lime, gold, purple)

Sizes (e.g., big, small, long, short, wide, narrow, tall, large, little)

Names of vehicles (e.g., plane, bulldozer, balloon, tricycle, bicycle, car, sailboat, helicopter, mail, truck, police car, motorcycle, fire truck, jet plane)

Speed (e.g., fast, slow)

Locations (e.g., up, down, around, in, out, beside, next to, on, under, below)

Names of signs (e.g., stop, yield, curve, railroad crossing, school bus stop, one way, no U-turn)

Use long boards that require two children to pick up and move them.

Direct children's attention to peers' actions in activity.

Prompt children to imitate a particular action of peer.

Encourage children to plan together roads they will lay out on the floor with boards and blocks.

on target goals. After reviewing the intervention guide, the team makes a number of decisions:

- Marlene (Head Start teacher) will record the objects/toys/materials Cooper manipulates prior to, during, or at the end of three different activities (i.e., arrival, free play, and outdoor play) two times a week. Marlene will also contact Cooper's mother and grandmother each month to see how he is doing at home, then summarize the total number of different objects/toys/materials manipulated each month.

- Amy (occupational therapist) will record the objects/materials Cooper manipulates prior to, during, or at the end of snack one time a week.

- Nicole (itinerant teacher) will record the objects/toys/materials Cooper manipulates prior to, during, or at the end of either center time or free play one time a week.

- Based on Cooper's mom Shawna's request that the family be involved in monitoring his progress, Shawna and Teresa (Cooper's grandmother) will collect data on how he manipulates objects with both hands at home.

- All team members will review data monthly to make decisions regarding changes to how goals are targeted and the accommodations, modifications, and intervention strategies provided.

The team also discusses how to create a data collection system that 1) is accessible and usable by everyone on the team, 2) keeps writing to a minimum, and 3) includes situational information and performance information. To create such a form, the team brainstorms the different objects that can be manipulated as Cooper participates across classroom activities. They consider objects and materials present within the different planned and routine activities (e.g., during snack time). The occupational therapist helps the team order the list from materials that are more difficult to manipulate (examples of the target goal) to materials that are easier to manipulate (examples of target benchmarks). The form is completed by noting or checking which objects he manipulates independently, with assistance, or does not yet manipulate. Figure 10.9 contains a data collection form the team uses to collect data on Cooper's target goal of manipulating objects. After talking with Cooper's mom, Nicole (itinerant teacher) creates a family friendly version of the data collection form so that Cooper's parents can record objects/toys/materials he manipulates at home each week. The team then meets regularly to discuss Cooper's progress and make intervention decisions.

SUMMARY

This chapter addresses the application of ABI in center-based settings. The successful application of ABI in center-based settings requires that interventionists conduct comprehensive and ongoing assessments, target functional

ABI Data Collection Form

page 1 of 1

Child's name: __Cooper_____   Date: __Week of September 8, 2013_____

Person collecting data: __Head Start teacher: Marlene; occupational therapist: Amy; ECSE itinerant teacher: Nicole__

Examples of target behavior	Activity	Cooper's performance
Tie shoes	Arrival	-
Button clothing	Housekeeping	-
Thread and zip a zipper	Housekeeping	-
Cut out shapes with curved lines	Art	-
Hold a piece of paper and draw with a crayon, paintbrush, pencil, or marker	Free play	A
Hold a bowl and spoon up food or liquid	Snack/lunch	X
Hold container and pour substance (e.g., hold glass and pour juice, hold beaker and pour water, hold bucket and pour beans)	Discovery	X
Hold a container and dispense items (e.g., hold container and pass out napkins or utensils)	Snack/science	A
Hold a marker in one hand and push cap on with the other, or hold onto LEGO and connect another LEGO	Art	X
Spread food with a knife (e.g., put cream cheese on bagel)	Snack/lunch	A
Zip a zipper	Bathroom	A
Stack blocks	Free play	X
Turn pages of a book	Centers	X

Performance scoring key:
X = manipulated the object without assistance
A = manipulated the object with physical assistance
- = made no attempt to manipulate the object even after prompts by an adult

Figure 10.9.   Completed Data Collection Form for Cooper arranged from more difficult to easier to manipulate materials.

and generative goals, provide multiple and varied practice opportunities, and monitor children's progress. When each phase is implemented consistently and with high quality, children are given multiple opportunities to practice important skills, thereby maximizing developmental outcomes.

REFERENCES

Alberto, P.A., & Troutman, A.C. (2012). *Applied behavior analysis for teachers* (9th ed.). Upper Saddle River, NJ: Pearson.

Barnett, D., Bell, S., & Carey, K. (2002). *Designing preschool interventions: A practitioner's guide.* New York, NY: The Guilford Press.

Bricker, D. (Series Ed.). (2002). *Assessment, Evaluation, and Programming System (AEPS®) for Infants and Children* (2nd ed., Vols. 1–4). Baltimore, MD: Paul H. Brookes Publishing Co.

Grisham-Brown, J., Hemmeter, M.L., & Pretti-Frontczak, K. (2005). *Blended practices for teaching young children in inclusive settings.* Baltimore, MD: Paul H. Brookes Publishing Co.

Grygas Coogle, C., Floyd, K., Hanline, M.F., & Kellner-Hiczewski, J. (2013). Strategies used in natural environments to promote communication development in young children at risk for autism spectrum disorder. *Young Exceptional Children, 16,* 11–23. doi:10.1177/1096250612473126

Individuals with Disabilities Education Improvement Act (IDEA) of 2004, PL 108-446, 20 U.S.C. §§ 1400 *et seq.*

Lord, C., Rutter, M., DiLavore, P.C., & Risi, S. (2000). *Autism Diagnostic Observation Schedule* (2nd ed.; ADOS-2). Torrance, CA: Western Psychological Service.

McAfee, R., & Leong, D. (2008). *Assessing and guiding young children's development and learning* (5th ed.). Upper Saddle River, NJ: Pearson.

McLean, M., Wolery, M., & Bailey, D. (2004). *Assessing infants and preschoolers with special needs* (3rd ed.). Columbus, OH: Charles E. Merrill.

Meadan, H., Ostrosky, M.M., Milagros Santos, R., & Snodgrass, M.R. (2013). How can I help? Prompting procedures to support children's learning. *Young Exceptional Children, 16,* 31–39. doi:10.1177/1096250613505099

Neisworth, J.T., & Bagnato, S.J. (2005). DEC recommended practices: Assessment. In S. Sandall, M.L. Hemmeter, B.J. Smith, & M.E. McLean, *DEC recommended practices: A comprehensive guide for practice application in early intervention/early childhood special education* (pp. 45–69). Longmont, CO: Sopris West.

Newborg, J. (2005). *Battelle Developmental Inventory* (2nd ed.; BDI-2). Rolling Meadows, IL: Riverside.

Notari-Syverson, A., & Shuster, S. (1995). Putting real life skills into IEP/IFSPs for infants and young children. *Teaching Exceptional Children, 27*(2), 29–32.

Noonan, M.J., & McCormick, L. (2014). *Teaching young children with disabilities in natural environments* (2nd ed.). Baltimore, MD: Paul H. Brookes Publishing Co.

Sandall, S.R., & Schwartz, I.S. (with Chou, H.-Y., Horn, E.M., Joseph, G.E., Lieber, J., Odom S.L., & Wolery, R.). (2008). *Building blocks for teaching preschoolers with special needs* (2nd ed.). Baltimore, MD: Paul H. Brookes Publishing Co.

U.S. Department of Health and Human Services. (2011). *Head Start child development and early learning framework.* Washington, DC: Office of Head Start.

11

Activity-Based Intervention
and Home-Based Programs

ABI can be used in various settings. Whereas Chapter 10 described the use of ABI in center-based programs, this chapter describes the use of ABI in home-based settings. In addition, this chapter offers a range of background information on the involvement of parents in their child's intervention planning and delivery. By home-based we refer to the services usually delivered in the home that are offered by professionals to a family of a child with a disability or at risk for a disability (Wasik & Bryant, 2001). These services are usually provided to families whose child is younger than 2 years of age and consequently in this chapter we refer primarily to EI services.

The conceptual framework for use of ABI in home settings does not differ from use in center-based settings; however, there are differences in the application of the approach. This chapter begins with a discussion of important federal legislation and service coordination. The second part of the chapter discusses theoretical models designed to help understand family dynamics. The third part of the chapter addresses the evolution of home-based services. And the last part of the chapter discusses the four intervention phases of the ABI approach when used in the home setting.

FEDERAL LEGISLATION AND SERVICE COORDINATION

In 1986, legislation mandating EI services for infants and toddlers with disabilities and their families (PL 99-457) was signed into law. Now known as the Individuals with Disabilities Education Improvement Act (IDEA) of 2004 (PL 108-446), EI is a federal grant program designed to assist states in providing comprehensive statewide programs to infants and toddlers with disabilities and their families. EI has four primary goals: 1) to enhance the development of infants and toddlers with disabilities, 2) to reduce educational costs by minimizing the need for special education through EI, 3) to minimize the likelihood of institutionalization and maximize independent living, and 4) to enhance the capacity of families to meet their child's needs (Early Childhood Technical Assistance Center [ECTAC], 2014). In order for states to participate in the program, they must 1) appoint a lead agency (e.g., Health, Education, Child Development, Rehabilitation, Developmental Services) to receive the grant and administer the program, 2) assemble an Interagency Coordinating Council (ICC) that includes parents of young children with disabilities designated to advise and assist the lead agency, and 3) ensure EI is available to all qualifying infants and toddlers with disabilities and their families.

Under the IDEA (34 Code of Federal Regulations 303.16), infants and toddlers with disabilities are defined as

> Individuals under three years of age who need early intervention services because they 1) are experiencing developmental delays, as measured by appropriate diagnostic instruments and procedures, in one or more of the following areas: cognitive, physical, communication, social or emotional, and adaptive; or 2) have a diagnosed physical or mental condition that has a high probability of resulting in developmental delay. The term may also include, if a state chooses, children under three years of age who would be *at risk* of experiencing a substantial developmental delay if early intervention services were not provided.

Child eligibility criteria are determined by each state, and, as a result, definitions of eligibility differ across states. Once a child is determined eligible according to a state's criteria, the lead agency responsible for EI appoints a service coordinator. The service coordinator assembles a team and begins developing the child's IFSP.

Service Coordination

As noted, IDEA requires that a service coordinator be appointed for each eligible child and family receiving EI services. The implementation of service coordination is determined by each state and may vary considerably; however, three basic models of service coordination are generally used (Roberts, 2005):

1. A dedicated (or independent) model of service coordination in which the service coordinator provides no other EI services and is not housed/ employed by an EI direct service provider

2. A combined roles model in which a primary EI program provides the service coordinator and most therapeutic services, with the service coordinator serving as the family's primary contact

3. A one-stop shopping model in which the center serves as a single point of entry for multiple programs, providing service coordination as well as multiagency coordinated services in an integrated infrastructure

Regardless of the model used, the service coordinator's role is to be a supportive and knowledgeable advocate, responsible for assisting families in understanding and exercising their rights and ensuring procedural safeguards. The relationship established between families and their service coordinators has been found to be important to successful EI efforts (Bruder & Dunst, 2008; Guralnick, 1997; Park & Turnbull, 2003).

The service coordinator also facilitates the EI services needed by families, required under the law. These services may include assistive technology services/devices, audiology, family training (including counseling, home visits, and other support), health services, medical services, nursing services, nutrition services, occupational therapy, physical therapy, psychological services, respite care, social work services, special instruction, speech-language pathology, transportation and related costs, vision services, and sign language and cued language services.

Individualized Family Service Plan

In addition to coordinating services for families, the service coordinator plays an important role in the development and implementation of the child's IFSP. The IFSP is required by IDEA legislation to assist families in development of outcomes for their child and family. The IFSP functions as both a written plan and a process to guide supports and services for each infant or toddler. The written plan, developed by the family and other team members (who can include other family members, an advocate, service coordinator, professionals who have assessed the child, and professionals likely to provide services to the child), serves to convey information that is specific to the child and family, and must include a number of elements individualized to the child and family. These elements include written statements of 1) the child's present levels of physical, cognitive, communication, social or emotional, and adaptive development (i.e., present level of development); 2) family information that details resources and priorities and concerns relating to the child's development; 3) the major outcomes expected to be achieved for the child and the family, and the criteria, procedures, and timelines used to determine the degree to which progress toward achieving the outcomes is being made and whether modifications or revisions of the outcomes or services are necessary; 4) specific EI services necessary to meet the unique needs of the child and the family, including the frequency, intensity, and method of delivering services; 5) the natural environments in which EI services will be provided, including a justification if services will not be provided in a natural environment; 6) the services; 7) the identification of the service coordinator from the profession most immediately relevant to the child's or family's needs who will be responsible for the implementation of the plan and coordination with other agencies and people; and 8) the steps to be taken to support the child's transition to preschool or other appropriate services (Friend & Cook, 2013; Hanson & Lynch, 2004).

members feel within the family. In highly cohesive families, the child with disabilities may have significant emotional support and friendships from other family members. However, highly cohesive families can also be overly protective of the child with special needs. Other less-cohesive families may find it easy to adapt to a child with a disability but may also make frequent changes in a manner that produces confusion and lack of support for the child with disabilities.

Family flexibility describes the amount of change in family leadership, role relationships, and relationship rules, with the focus on how the family system balances stability versus change. Four levels of family flexibility are used to assess a family's abilities to adjust to change: rigid, structured, flexible, and chaotic. Ultimately families go through many changes, and both stability and change, and the ability to change when needed, are considered necessary for families to remain functional.

Family communication is considered critical to help families in the dimensions of cohesion and flexibility. Family communication is measured by focusing on the family as a group with regards to their listening skills, speaking skills, self-disclosure, clarity, continuity-tracking, and respect and regard. Finally, in the interaction component of the Family Systems framework it is also important to determine who makes the decisions and rules for the family. That individual's inclusion in all decision making for the family is critical, and the success or failure of natural outcomes will depend on that individual's participation.

Turnbull and Turnbull (2001) proposed that families exist to meet the needs of individuals within the family unit, as well as the overall needs of the family itself. Families provide for family member needs through their interactions and by using their available resources, such as shifting roles and relationships. Family interactions fulfill family needs through what are referred to as *family functions* and include affection, self-esteem, spiritual, economics, daily care, socialization, recreation, and education. The main tenet of Family Systems is that family functions are interrelated and problems in one area have implications for other family functions.

Finally the family life cycle component addresses the developmental and nondevelopmental changes that affect all families over time. These life cycle changes include births, deaths, divorce, and alterations in employment and in residence. Knowledge of family systems theory also has major implications for professionals in being able to recognize and identify family roles and relationship patterns. Professionals can use this information to better support families, making EI services more successful.

Ecological Systems Theory

A third theory that has significantly influenced the field of EI is Ecological Systems Theory (Bronfenbrenner, 1979). Bronfenbrenner proposed this theory as a way to explain the relationship between the child with a disability and the environment. This theory helps explain the array of systems and their relationships to the developing child and family. Bronfenbrenner proposed a schema consisting of four concentric circles, each nested in the next larger circle. The circles represent four systems of relationship—microsystem, mesosystem, exosystem, and macrosystem—and their importance to the child and family. Hanson and Lynch (2004) believed this model to be particularly appealing when studying families of children who have disabilities because it describes the range of influences on families and interactions among each system over time.

At the microsystem level, the primary component is the child and family; however, other microsystems may include the child's relationships with grandparents, child care, and EI programs, for example. These close relationships comprise the mesosystem, made up of microsystems with which the child and family are most closely associated. The exosystem level is composed of settings that do not directly involve the child and family but have some effect on them. For example, the exosystem could include a parent company of a child care program, the family's social networks, parents' employers, neighborhoods, and other entities outside of the family's immediate circle that can have direct influence on the child and family. Finally, at the macrosystem level are systems that may influence family values, culture, and beliefs or policies, such as early education and disability services, federal health care coverage, federal immigration policy, and benefits to veterans.

The key tenet of the Ecological Systems model is that there is interaction both within and among levels so that events that occur in one system have an impact on what occurs in another. Influencing the child's development are the interactions between various components in the child's family/community environment, as well as in the government and society. Changes or conflicts in any one system may affect other systems, and changes in any of the subsystems can affect a child's development as much as the child's immediate system (Bronfenbrenner, 1979).

To study a child's development requires looking at the child and the immediate environment, as well as the interaction of the larger environment that includes these other systems. Bronfenbrenner's Ecological Systems theory focuses on the quality and context of the child's environment. A parent's network of local friends and acquaintances who all move hundreds of miles away for employment is an example of how a child may not be directly involved in a particular unit within the nested systems, but certainly feels the positive or negative impact of such an influence. Within these environments or systems, several factors such as financial status, work satisfaction, self-concept, and basic needs have an impact on the types of support required for a family. The ecological framework helps EI programs recognize the strengths of each family's influences and resources. This framework also provides insights into families' broader social networks and environments.

The common connection in these foundational theories (Bronfenbrenner,

1979; Maslow, 1954; Turnbull & Turnbull, 2001) is the recognition of family roles, interests, and needs as both important and relevant. This knowledge contributes to the identification and provision of functional and necessary supports that enhance the family's ability to promote their child's development. Without careful consideration of the important characteristics of a family, the success of EI is likely diminished.

EVOLUTION OF HOME VISITING

The role of families in EI has changed since language involving families was first introduced in federal legislation (PL 99-457, Part H). Families became a primary focus of federal legislation for young children with disabilities when the phrase "infants and toddlers with disabilities and their families" began being used throughout the law. By emphasizing the family in recognition of their critical role in a child's development, legislation redefined the family to be more than recipients of services. Over time EI has progressed in its view of families, moving from a professional-centered approach, to family focused, and finally to family centered. Now legislation, policy, and professional practices recognize the importance of parents and family especially in the early years.

EI, much like ECSE, began with more discipline-based, normative perspectives in determining eligibility for services. Likewise adult-directed interventions were focused on acquisition of developmental milestones and outcomes that were expected to increase children's skills based on norm- and criterion-referenced tests. Professionals focused on their own disciplines as experts providing separate interventions, and teams with multiple service providers then determined the needs of the family from a multidiscipline perspective. Families were not considered active participants or capable of contributing to their own child's intervention.

In the 1990s, the role of the family began to change, with increased family involvement believed to be the key to greater intervention success (Hart & Risley, 1995; Ketelaar, Vermeer, Helders, & Hart, 1998; Kontos & Diamond, 2002; Warfield, Hauser-Cram, Krauss, Shonkoff, & Upshur, 2000). The family focused approach considered families an integral part of the intervention team, and professionals and families collaborated to determine what was needed to enhance the child's development (Jung, 2010). For many professionals, the shift from professional-centered to family focused services challenged their training, intervention methods, and expertise, but the need for families to be involved in the planning of goals and objectives in their children's intervention plans gradually began to be more widely accepted (Dunst, Johanson, Trivette, & Hamby, 1991).

The field of EI gradually evolved toward implementation of a family centered approach as recommended practice (Division for Early Childhood [DEC] Task Force on Recommended Practices, 2007, 2014). The family centered approach involves beliefs, values, principles, and practices designed to support and strengthen a family's capacity to promote and enhance their child's development (Dunst, 2000). Essentially, family centered care is defined as a philosophy of care in which the fundamental role of the family is recognized and respected, in which families are supported in their natural caregiving and decision-making roles, and in which parents and professionals are equals (Brewer, McPherson, Magrab, & Hutchin, 1989).

Baird and Peterson (1997) identified seven tenets of family centered philosophy, including recognition that the family is the 1) child expert; 2) ultimate decision maker for the child and family; 3) constant in the child's life, with professionals being a temporary relationship; 4) determiner of priorities for goals and services; 5) determiner of amount of participation; 6) collaborator with service providers; and 7) repository of cultural identity, beliefs, values, and coping styles. These practices are driven by the priorities and concerns of the family, with the professional's role being that of agent to promote the strengths, capabilities, and decision making of the family (Dunst et al., 1991).

Research conducted using family centered approaches suggests better outcomes for children than when using the traditional child-centered approach (Kaiser et al., 1996; Kashinath, Woods, & Goldstein, 2006; Mahoney & Perales, 2005; Peterson, Carta, & Greenwood, 2005). Family-centered approaches are focused on the child in everyday settings, activities, and relationships. Additional research has shown that family-centered practices increase parent impressions of well-being (Dunst, Bruder, Trivette, & Hamby, 2006; Trivette, Dunst, & Hamby, 2010), which positively affects child outcomes. Additional studies show that families consider quality of the support more important than quantity of supports, with informal supports such as family, friends, and relatives having an equal or greater impact on them than more formal supports provided by professionals (Cook & Sparks, 2008; Epley, Summers, & Turnbull, 2011; Paulsell, Boller, Hollgren & Esposito, 2010; Wasik & Bryant, 2001).

As transitions in EI occurred, moving from more to less therapeutic types of interventions and services and from professional-directed to family-centered services, significant transitions in where interventions took place and who met with the family also underwent changes. The next section begins with information about the history of the home visit and its purposes. It then charts significant contemporary changes in the roles and activities of family service coordinators and caregivers during home visits.

History of Home Visiting

The practice of using home visits as an EI service and support to families is not a contemporary strategy. Since the 1870s in the United States and Europe, and possibly earlier, midwives, doctors, and religious leaders made house calls to their patients and parishioners. Over the years, home visiting was found to be helpful in providing social services to families in need as a result of poverty, risk for social isolation, unequal access to health care, family violence, and pregnancy outcomes (Johnson, 2009). Home visits provided support to these families as well as information about the importance of education (Cook & Sparks, 2008).

Contemporary home visiting as a service for EI officially began in 1986 when programs were established by Congress under Part C under IDEA (Part H in 1986) (Astuto & Allen, 2009). Home visiting, in its most recent iteration, is the process by which a professional provides direct support and coordination of family services to families of children with disabilities in home-based settings (The California Evidence-Based Clearinghouse for Child Welfare, n.d.; Wasik & Bryant, 2001).

In 2011, the most recent data reported by the federal government, EI services were provided to a total of 336,895 eligible infants and toddlers and their families (U.S. Department of Education, 2014). Campbell and Sawyer (2007) noted that in 1993, 47% of young children participating in EI Part C received services in the home. In the 19 years up until 2011, that number grew to 87% of infants and toddlers with disabilities receiving home-based services. Campbell and Sawyer also noted that infants and toddlers not served in the home were primarily served in child care settings (5.5% were served in family and community-based child care settings where children without disabilities were served; 9% were served in other settings that included anything other than home or community-based, such as hospital, residential setting, clinic, or EI program for young children with disabilities).

When PL 99-457 was passed by Congress in 1986, it was offered as an incentive program. At this time most states began the process of developing EI programs for families and their infants and toddlers with disabilities, and eventually all states chose to participate. Although much of the law specified state requirements, each state was also given authority for a number of decisions as they developed their own programs. A major decision left up to the states included where services would be provided. Due to the nature of the law's requirement that services be provided to young children in "those natural or normal settings as their same age peers without disabilities" (PL 99-457), all states developed new programs and expanded existing programs that offered home based EI services (Campbell & Sawyer, 2007). Home-based services now are offered in every state to families with children younger than age 3 with disabilities.

Although the practice of home visiting is not a modern 21st-century concept in the human services field, the EI field's adoption of the practice and the evolution of services for families and their infants and toddlers with disabilities has been transformative. Most of this transformation has taken place since the enactment of PL 99-457.

Many home visiting programs began as extensions of more therapeutic-type services found in centers or clinics, focusing primarily on intervention-ist-planned activities and direct work with the child as the caregiver learned by watching (McWilliam, 2006). The expectation then was for the caregiver to provide follow-up practice for the child during the week on strategies modeled and used in direct intervention by the home visitor. Gradually information regarding the primacy and importance of the parent–child and family relationships, recognition of the association between young children's routine participation in everyday activities and their acquisition of new skills, and the more accurate interpretation of the legislation led to a significant shift in the structure and focus of home visits.

The first change in home visit strategies began with the kinds and types of intervention activities the home visitor introduced. For years the home visit was associated with the professional arriving for the visit with an intervention plan and several toys selected to help the child practice targeted skills. Gradually the intervention plan developed by the professional gave way to asking the caregiver to talk about the child's participation in the home and considering the child's daily activities as the impetus for practicing new skills. For many home-visiting programs, the bag of toys disappeared and was replaced by toys and materials found in the home. The second, more significant change began as professionals shifted their focus of intervention strategies from the child to the caregiver, realizing the remaining 23 hours of the day and 6 days of the week were more important for the child's acquisition of new skills than 1 hour of work with the home visitor.

This shift in focus led to a new need for home visitors to provide information, strategies, and practice to the child's caregiver, who would be able to provide intervention to the child across the routine activities engaged in every day. This new practice in home visiting was termed *coaching* by Peterson, Luze, Eshbaugh, Hyun, and Ross (2007). Coaching caregivers of infants and toddlers changes the role of the EI home visitor from working directly with the infant or toddler to supporting the caregiver's *and* the infant's or toddler's interactions. The home visitor uses a number of strategies as well as verbal coaching to help the caregiver learn to engage the child in activities throughout the day to learn new skills. As the coach, the home visitor uses modeling and demonstration, guiding the caregiver through new intervention strategies, discussions, observations, and problem-solving techniques. Several excellent coaching strategy practices have been developed and are being used by a number of home visiting programs with considerable success (Friedman, Woods, & Salisbury, 2012; Marvin & Yates, 2007; Sawyer & Campbell, 2012). Coaching can be easily combined with the ABI approach to produce efficient and effective outcomes for both caregivers and children.

Adult Learning Theory

Because the focus of EI shifted from the child to the broader context of family, the home providers' adult interactions became as important as their interactions with children. In order to coach effectively, the home visiting professional needs to understand how adults learn new skills, too. Designed to better understand the education of adults, Adult Learning Theory (Knowles, 1990) was introduced in the 1970s and is based on the following assumptions: 1) adults are internally motivated and self-directed learners, 2) adults have life experiences and knowledge that they bring to new learning experiences, 3) adults are goal oriented and practical, 4) adults learn when they recognize a need to know something, and 5) adults need respect.

Knowles suggested that as self-directed learners, adults are uninterested in decisions and strategies determined by others without their participation. Furthermore, life experiences, including work-related activities, family, education, and social relationships are assumed to contribute to their learning. As a person matures, a growing number of experiences influence his or her resources for learning. These past experiences help adults become open to learning when they believe the new knowledge will support and enhance their current life situations. Adult Learning Theory assumes learners are internally motivated based on what is important to them at that particular time in life (Knowles et al., 1984).

Given the unique nature of home visiting, home visiting professionals' responsibilities are different from those needed to teach in the preschool classroom. Instead of practicing the knowledge and skills acquired in EI/ECSE personnel preparation programs on preschoolers, these professionals are now required to have skills in collaborating and coaching to transfer knowledge, skills, intervention techniques, and strategies to the parent/caregiver who will work with the infant or toddler. Like the preschool classroom teacher, the home visitor administers curriculum-based assessments and documents changes and acquisition of the infant's/toddler's new skills. The home visitor also works with the caregiver, monitoring progress on interventions being used with the child and working closely with the caregiver to help identify activities throughout the day when learning opportunities can be provided.

Home Visit Guidelines

Various authors have identified guidelines associated with home visiting in EI (Cook & Sparks, 2008; McWilliam, 2010; Wasik & Bryant, 2001). The guidelines are important and should be adopted by home visiting professionals:

1. The family has the greatest influence on the child.

2. Children are able to practice new skills and learn throughout the day when they are engaged and active participants in familiar daily activities.

3. No intervention is effective if it cannot fit into the family's daily routine.

4. All intervention occurs between visits. A visitor's presence in the home changes the dynamics of the family relationship.

5. Ongoing and continual evaluation of family strengths, limitations, and progress is used to modify intervention.

6. Attention to future needs for the family is critical.

7. Collaboration is essential.

Many changes have come about in the more than 25 years since legislation mandated services to infants and toddlers with disabilities. These include changes in our understanding of the importance of family in the life of the child and changes in how EI services are provided to families and their infants and toddlers with disabilities. The last part of this chapter describes the four phases of the ABI approach with families of infants and toddlers with disabilities.

PHASES OF INTERVENTION IN THE HOME SETTING

Chapter 10 described how to apply the ABI approach to center-based programs. In this chapter the same four intervention phases are revisited in relationship to children and their families participating in home visiting programs: 1) conducting comprehensive and ongoing assessments, 2) targeting functional and generative goals, 3) providing multiple and varied learning opportunities, and 4) monitoring children's progress.

Phase 1: Conducting Comprehensive and Ongoing Assessments

The first phase begins the process leading to intervention using an ABI approach. The completion of a curriculum-based measure designed to assist teams in gathering comprehensive information about a young child's development is a critical first step. The results obtained from a curriculum-based measure such as the AEPS (Bricker, 2002), a parent-completed assessment such as the AEPS Family Report, and the direct observations of the child as he or she participates in a variety of activities in familiar environments provide a detailed description of the child's strengths, interests, and emerging skills that will be included in the IFSP. The summary on the IFSP, termed present level of development for children younger than age 3 and served by part C, serves as the starting point or baseline. This baseline is used to compare the child's progress over time, as well as to guide the identification of new skills linked with the family's interests, concerns, and needs. The summary initiates the development of the rest of the IFSP.

Immediately after Owen's birth, a pediatrician met with his parents to discuss the results of his initial observation and assessments. The pediatrician reported that Owen had decreased muscle tone, a condition that kept him from keeping his knees and elbows tucked close to his body. He showed Owen's parents how when he stretched Owen's limbs they appeared limp, very flexible, and stayed outstretched rather than flexed back to his body. The pediatrician explained to Owen's parents that his decreased muscle tone or hypotonia was a condition that made him eligible for EI services and that he strongly recommended they begin getting services as soon as possible. He also talked with them about how Owen's decreased muscle tone could affect his mobility development such as crawling, fine motor skills such as grasping, head control, self-care skills such as eating and dressing, and possibly his ability to communicate. Owen's family was referred to the local EI program, and a staff member visited the family before discharge from the hospital. Arrangements were made for an initial home visit to conduct an initial developmental-behavioral assessment, make appropriate referrals, and begin intervention planning.

The initial assessment required reviewing the diagnostic tests already completed (e.g., Test of Infant Motor Performance Scale [TIMP], 1995) as well as completing the AEPS test and AEPS Family Report (Bricker, 2002). The team summarized Owen's skills in the present level of development section of his IFSP. They identified Owen's strengths, noting his mastered skills, and included examples taken from observations of Owen in his home with his parents and from the assessment tests. The team described how Owen's special needs affected his participation in daily activities. From this summary, the most important skills for Owen to learn over the next 6 months were prioritized. The team also determined that Owen's needs would best be met by beginning weekly home visits. The focus of the visits was to coach his mom and dad in developing strategies to address Owen's goals and build his functional skills, through his participation in family activities and routines.

After the first 6 months, the AEPS was re-administered to determine the status of Owen's development in all areas, along with the AEPS Family Report. Owen's IFSP was updated with family and child outcomes focused on strengthening Owen's muscle tone in all areas and moving his body to help him build strength needed to roll, move his limbs, and improve his head control.

Phase 2: Targeting Functional and Generative Goals

Targeting functional and generative goals is initiated after the child's present level of development is determined during Phase 1 when an initial IFSP is developed and whenever new outcomes are written. As noted in Chapter 10, functional refers to outcomes that serve to enhance the child's ability to address environmental demands, and generative refers to goals that can be addressed across many activities, objects, and people.

When targeted goals are functional and generative, addressing them across child-directed, routine, and planned activities is possible. Functional and generative goals are intended to increase children's independence and participation in family activities and routines throughout the day. For example the goals of grasping objects, moving into a sitting position, drinking from a cup, putting food in the mouth, imitating actions or words, locating familiar objects, and participating in an established social routine can be addressed throughout an infant's/toddler's day while participating in typical family activities and engaging in play at home.

When targeted goals are not functional and generative, it is difficult for interventionists and caregivers to address them in child-directed, routine, and planned activities because the skills likely are not useful, necessary, or do not lead to greater independence. If targeted goals are not functional and generative, they are unlikely to be used across a variety of activities and will not support response modifications as settings, objects, people, and conditions change. For example, the goals of stacking blocks, raising hands above head, uncovering a covered toy/object, and pushing buttons on a play phone may limit the number and types of activities in which interventionists and caregivers can effectively create and embed learning opportunities leading to meaningful skills. Even reinforcement of such skills may not lead to expanding the child's functional repertoire.

With some consideration, most daily activities can be used to target functional skills. The ABI approach capitalizes on linking development of new targeted skills as part of the daily activities in which children are already engaged. Likewise, targeted repetitive practice on a skill with little function or generative use limits opportunities for a child to generalize his or her skill repertoire. Teams are encouraged to select functional and generative goals that will address the child's needs, and to ensure the number of goals targeted can be reasonably addressed and monitored. Therefore teams are encouraged to focus intervention efforts by prioritizing selection of a small number of highly functional critical skills that can be used across people, activities, and time.

At 14 months, Owen's family relocated to a different city and initiated contact with a new EI program. The family connected with the EI services and arranged for a first home visit in their new location. The purpose of this first visit was to schedule subsequent home visits, conduct new assessments (re-administration of the AEPS test and AEPS Family Report), and begin intervention planning. From the recent assessment information, Owen's new team identified five functional and generative, concurrent goals in four developmental areas. These goals, listed in Table 11.1, were chosen because Owen's parents were very interested in his acquisition of the skills and knew they would lead to greater independence for their son. The goals could be used throughout the day in several activities and routines and were essential to Owen's acquisition of motor, adaptive, and social-communication skills (i.e., functional and generative).

Owen's home visitor was an EI professional. Owen's team consisted of his parents, the home visitor, an occupational therapist, a physical therapist, and a

Table 11.1.   Owen's individualized family service plan goals

Developmental area	Goal
Fine motor	Grasps hand-sized objects with either hand, using ends of thumbs, index, and second fingers
	Grasps pea-sized objects with either hand using tip of index finger and thumb
Gross motor	Creeps forward using alternate arm and leg movements
Adaptive	Bites and chews hard and chewy food
Social-communication	Gains person's attention and refers to an object, person, and/or event

speech-language pathologist. The home visitor made weekly visits to the family's home over the first 6 months and was accompanied by one of the therapists once a month.

Phase 3: Providing Multiple and Varied Learning Opportunities

Providing multiple and varied learning opportunities is important for young children to practice target skills. Chapter 6 noted that an appropriate and relevant antecedent must be used to create a learning opportunity for a child to practice, perform, or attempt to produce a target skill. As an example, if targeting the skill of *crawls forward on stomach*, there are a number of antecedents that could be provided to elicit the target response, such as placing a favorite or new and interesting item on the floor a short distance from the child, having a parent/caregiver position themselves on the floor a short distance from the child and encouraging the child to move, and positioning the child a short distance from a place to view outside. Using this example, a learning opportunity occurs when any of the antecedents are used to encourage the target skill.

In ABI a learning opportunity is only created when an antecedent occurs naturally or is presented in a way that permits the child to continue an action or maintains the child's intent or interest in the activity. If the antecedent modifies or extends the child's action or attention, it should not shift his or her behavior or attention away from the activity in which he or she is interested or engaged. Using the example of *crawls forward on stomach,* a learning opportunity is not created if the child is engaged and examining an object of great interest and the caregiver tries to distract him with another unrelated object, the child is on his or her back watching something of interest and fully engaged in the observation, or the child is tired or hungry and not interested in practicing a physically tiring skill.

There are three guidelines for selecting antecedents. First, teams need to identify the potential array of existing antecedents useful in eliciting a target goal or objective. Chapter 6 included descriptions of numerous intervention strategies (e.g., interruption or time delay, visible but unreachable, physical model) that involve presenting an antecedent (e.g., object of interest) to encourage the use of a desired behavior (e.g., crawling forward on stomach to reach the object). A number of additional resources define and describe various antecedents and prompting procedures (Barnett, Bell, & Carey, 2002; Grisham-Brown, Hemmeter, & Pretti-Frontczak, 2005; Coogle, Floyd, Hanline, & Hiczewski, 2013; Meadan, Ostrosky, Milagros Santos, & Snodgrass, 2013; Noonan & McCormick, 2013; Sandall & Schwartz, 2008).

A second guideline requires that team members (in particular the caregiver) know the individual child's interests and characteristics as well as his or her target goals in order to select appropriate and salient antecedents that will create optimal learning opportunities. Meeting this guideline requires careful observation of the child across activities and throughout the day. Knowing what children like and enjoy will assist in selecting relevant antecedents that may elicit the target skill. Equally important is an understanding of what goals have been targeted. It may be useful to have a list of the targeted skills on the refrigerator or saved to a smart phone or tablet. Knowing the child's interest and the targeted goals are essential for effective intervention.

A final guideline entails that the caregivers provide multiple and varied antecedents across activities when they know the child's interests and goals. It may be an oversimplification, however, in most cases the more frequently a child is able to *meaningfully* practice a targeted goal, the more rapidly he or she will acquire the skill. Consequently, caregivers should be ever alert to use or develop opportunities to ensure the child has multiple opportunities to practice a skill such as grasping small objects. It is likely that throughout the day, with thought, the caregiver can find many opportunities to encourage the child to use his or her grasp to obtain a toy, object, or food. Of course, these opportunities should be relevant and/or meaningful to the child (e.g., the child wants a particular object or piece of food).

After selecting antecedents that will provide the child with multiple and varied learning opportunities, the team needs to be thoughtful and careful in their choice of feedback (i.e., consequences or reinforcement). Numerous types of feedback have been identified for achieving a variety of outcomes—several are logical results of using a new skill (e.g., gaining a desired object, access to a person, a visit to a favorite place, a better view or distancing oneself from an unfamiliar person, object, or animal). The appropriateness or success of the feedback selected can be determined only by its effect on the child.

To be maximally effective, feedback should be timely (i.e., immediate) and integral (i.e., directly related to or contingent on a child's behaviors/skills and associated with, connected to, or a logical outcome of the activity, action, or response). Timely feedback helps the child connect the relationship between the response and subsequent feedback. Integral feedback helps the child recognize that responses produce related and meaningful outcomes.

Chapter 6 discussed the organizational structure of the ABI approach. The chapter identified and described the intervention guides and embedding schedules as lynchpins of intervention efforts designed to address the child's targeted needs in activities throughout the day. In particular, embedding schedules designed by the child's team provide information to the caregiver about when to provide a learning opportunity to practice a behavior or skills, what to say or do to encourage it (antecedent), and how to provide feedback when necessary to the child. In home-based programs, embedding schedules are developed for a single child, using the activities and routines identified by the assessment information. The matrices of any embedding schedule are determined by what the team (most importantly, the caregiver) believes are important to include. As embedding schedules are designed, they can be developed around preferred activities. Completing this phase in the ABI approach results in an embedding schedule the family can use.

Owen's team completed an intervention guide to determine the antecedents his caregivers could use throughout the day to provide numerous opportunities to practice his targeted IFSP goals.

The home visiting professional explained her role in Owen's intervention program to his parents. She noted that it is more important for the parents, his primary caregivers, to work with him on his goals throughout the day when times and activities provide the most appropriate learning opportunities. Owen is most familiar with them and their daily routines and will be more willing to engage in familiar activities with them. She also explained that on each visit she will observe Owen as he plays and interacts with his parents to help monitor his progress, but her main focus will be to coach them to help Owen acquire his target goals.

During the first visit, Owen's parents and the home visitor discussed activities they can provide throughout the day as learning opportunities for Owen to practice his five targeted goals (see Table 11.1), and they identified appropriate antecedents that will support Owen's practice and use of them. The team then discussed the use of feedback and reinforcement Owen will receive as he begins to use the skills. The last thing they discussed was how Owen's progress will be monitored over time.

The home visiting professional returned the next day with a completed embedding schedule for the family. The schedule lists each of the activities across the day they agreed were good times for Owen to be given learning opportunities. Within the matrix were included antecedents the parents would use, the targeted behavior, and feedback (i.e., consequences and reinforcement) they would use.

Phase 4: Monitoring Children's Progress

The final phase critical to successful implementation of ABI is the need to systematically monitor child progress toward achievement of targeted goals. Monitoring progress is defined as a scientifically based practice, designed to help caregivers determine children's short-term progress and modify teaching practices to ensure they are progressing toward identified goals (DEC, 2007). As the field of EI/ECSE has shifted to more authentic practices of assessment, goal development, and intervention, collection of data to monitor child and family progress in home visit programs has not kept pace. Monitoring children's progress through data collection is the area in which home visitors report the least amount of information (Wasik & Bryant, 2001).

Other than the shift to more authentic practices, there are additional explanations for this general omission or difficulty in collecting data to monitor progress in the home setting. First, each family's circumstances are unique, and programs provide many services in many different ways, unlike classroom programs. Second, the transfer of intervention efforts from home visitor professional to primary caregiver offers many data collection challenges. Whereas the professional has acquired skills to collect data to monitor progress, the caregiver in all likelihood has not. Nonetheless, we believe through shared responsibility, progress-monitoring efforts can be undertaken to obtain ongoing information that can be used for important decision making.

Monitoring progress serves three important purposes. First, data collected through regular and continuing observations or recordings are necessary to determine the success of any intervention used (Barlow & Hersen, 1984; Grisham-Brown et al., 2005; Wasik & Bryant, 2001), as well as the fidelity to which the intervention is administered as designed (Barton & Fettig, 2013). The Decision Rules component of the ABI intervention guides (see Chapter 6) helps teams make decisions about monitoring child progress toward targeted skills. Teams determine a time frame for review of the data and make decisions about next steps, depending on evaluative feedback. Second, consistent recording of child responses to intervention across settings, objects, people, and conditions often identifies when the child is more likely or willing to practice target skills and the most salient forms of feedback. Planning learning opportunities around when the child is more open or receptive to practicing a skill may lead to its more efficient acquisition. More meaningful feedback (i.e., consequences or reinforcements) to the child may also assist in skill acquisition. The third purpose of regular and continued monitoring of progress is to help the team determine when a targeted skill is acquired and when it is time to introduce new targeted skills (Grisham-Brown et al., 2005). These three purposes of monitoring progress are critical to home-based programs in which the caregiver and child see the service coordinator or other team members only a few times a month.

Collecting Data and Monitoring Progress   Designing a data collection system for a family and child in home-based programs requires serious consideration by the team. Numerous data collection systems can be used to monitor child progress in home-based programs, yet there is no universal system that will work for every child or every goal. As the team identifies methods of data collection, there are a number of important characteristics of home-based programs that distinguish them from center-based programs and make progress-monitoring practices somewhat dissimilar.

The obvious differences of the home environment being less like a classroom and the child being younger than age 3 do not influence monitoring progress as significantly as other factors. The first important distinction in regard to monitoring progress is the focus of home visiting programs. By design, home visiting programs focus on the child *and* primary caregiver, so it is expected that the majority of interactions will be between the child and caregiver and take place throughout the day as opportunities to practice target skills occur. Therefore, the primary caregiver will likely be responsible for collecting some data that can be reported back to the home visitor and team. In order to ensure greater fidelity to the intervention plans and the ABI approach, which will provide more meaningful and accurate data, the service coordinator or other team members will be required to spend considerably more time working with, holding discussions and conferences with, and training and coaching the caregiver than they will interacting with the child. EI professionals need to be knowledgeable about Adult Learning Theory (Knowles, 1990).

A second important distinction in regard to monitoring progress in a home-based setting is the number of children on which data will be collected. In most home visits there is one child targeted for EI services and one primary caregiver. Therefore, in home visit programs, single-case designs may be the most useful system of collecting data (Neuman & McCormick, 1995). A single-case design can be used efficiently at home when the team has completed assessment and family reports, identified functional and generative target skills, and developed a variety of learning opportunities using the ABI approach. A single-case design can support collecting information across the day or over several days on the target skills (Wasik & Bryant, 2001). An example of a target skill that could be observed and recorded across the day would be locating familiar objects, people, and events during daily activities and routines. Based on caregiver knowledge and experience with the child's routines and characteristics, the team can identify daily activities and routines during which practice opportunities can occur.

One simple strategy for planning caregiver progress monitoring is to use the child's embedding schedule to also serve as a data collection form. Beside the daily activity or routine, the antecedents, the targeted skills, and examples of feedback that are listed, additional space could be provided for entering caregiver collected data.

The team will likely use a variety of methods to collect the data needed to make sound decisions. Gathering data at regular intervals on the child's performance should address the following questions:

1. Is the child making progress toward target skills?

2. Are the antecedents and/or consequences effective?

3. What accommodations, modifications, or intervention strategies are being used?

4. How often are learning opportunities provided across the day?

5. During which daily activities or routines are learning opportunities more/less likely to occur?

Another distinction between center-based and home-based programs is that the child and family are typically visited by a service coordinator anywhere from once a month to once a week. Realistically, having the home visitor as the sole individual responsible for collecting data makes little sense because intervention takes place throughout the day. Rather, data collection should be a joint effort between the home visitor and the caregiver.

Home visitor data collection can and should be done at least monthly and analyzed with the caregivers' data to help make appropriate intervention decisions. Caregivers can be provided very basic training in data collection, using straightforward and efficient gathering methods specific to their child's target skills that the service coordinator can then analyze to determine the specifics of the child's progress and use to support team decisions in monitoring progress. For example, caregivers' collection of data can be as simple as using pluses, minuses, and circles to indicate a child's progress, or a smiley face to indicate things are getting better. Some caregivers may choose to write or record a description to provide additional information. Caregivers can be encouraged to select different times of day or different activities during which to collect data using a matrix developed by the team to record results.

Gathering more global data on a child's developmental progress (e.g., reassessing using the AEPS test [Bricker, 2002] or another curriculum-based measure) helps teams make program-level decisions and increases the link between intervention efforts and accountability requirements. Although beyond the scope of this text, a number of resources exist for helping teams create data collection systems for collecting daily/weekly data, quarterly data, and annual data on child progress. For example, Alberto and Troutman (2012); McLean, Wolery, and Bailey (2004); and Sandall and Schwartz (2008) provided detailed examples of how to collect ongoing data regarding children's performance on target goals as well as strategies for collecting data on children's overall developmental progress and progress in the general curriculum. In the following section, data collection methods particularly useful within an ABI framework are discussed.

Data Collection Methods   When implementing an ABI approach, teams need to gather data related to a child's performance on target goals as well as his or her overall developmental progress. Data regarding the child's performance on target goals can be gathered using three methods: written descriptions (e.g., running records, anecdotal notes, jottings), permanent records (e.g., diagrams, photographs, video), and counts and tallies (e.g., sampling procedures, rating scales, probes). Regardless of the method, teams should ensure that data collection procedures are

- Directly linked to the criterion written for a target skill (e.g., if the criterion states that the child will manipulate three different objects with both hands performing different movements, then information regarding the number and type of objects and how a child manipulates them should be collected)

- Flexible and applicable across settings, events, and people

- Valid and reliable

- Shared by team members (e.g., direct and related services personnel, consultants, caregivers)

- Compatible with available resources (e.g., time, skills, materials)

Data regarding a child's overall developmental progress and progress monitored by a curriculum-based assessment are often gathered through quarterly administrations. These data are useful for gauging the effects of intervention on a child. Information from quarterly evaluations provides feedback about the child's developmental progress and helps clarify where intervention modifications or revisions may be necessary. In addition, administrations of curriculum-based measures at the beginning of the year and end of the year allow programs to provide accountability information.

Using the ABI Embedding Schedule developed to help provide intervention to Owen during the day and across activities, the team devised a simple data collection system for his parents to monitor Owen's progress every other day. They added space to each row in the embedding schedule in which a goal was listed so that Owen's parents could note his progress with simple signs (plus, minus, circle) or descriptions.

The home visiting professional also created a data collection form to use every other week during her home visits as she observed Owen and his parents engaging in activities. She monitored Owen's acquisition of the skills, as well as the success of the antecedent system. As a result of the parents providing intervention to Owen frequently throughout the day, Owen made significant progress in acquiring his five targeted goals, and within 2 months the team was discussing new goals for Owen to learn.

APPLICATION OF ABI IN A HOME-BASED PROGRAM

This final section of the chapter offers a second home-based program example, addressing each of the four phases of intervention.

MATEO: HOME-BASED SERVICES

Mateo is 21 months old and lives with his parents and older brother in the community where his father and mother were raised. Mateo's father works full time, and his mother stays home to care for Mateo and his brother. During the past few months Mateo's parents have noticed that he has no identifiable words and uses what they call gibberish when he wants a toy, food, or attention, for example. His parents were concerned that Mateo's language development was delayed and therefore sought a referral from their family physician to the regional EI program. Mateo's performance on an eligibility measure qualified him for EI services in his state.

Once determined eligible, Mateo began receiving weekly home visits from an EI specialist. In addition, on alternate weeks a speech-language pathologist joins the EI specialist. The team plans and executes activities that address the four phases of intervention.

Phase 1: Conducting Comprehensive and Ongoing Assessments

During the first visits, information related to Mateo's present level of performance was gathered through a comprehensive assessment conducted by his mother and father (Lisa and Arturo), the EI specialist (Jody), and the speech-language pathologist (Elizabeth). Assessment observations were based on daily interactions with Mateo and guided by the AEPS test (Bricker, 2002). Mateo was observed during several daily routines across the day, including meals, playtime, and bath time. Information was also gathered from the AEPS Family Report, which Mateo's mother completed. The following paragraphs summarize Mateo's interests and abilities related to his participation in daily activities.

Mateo wakes up from his afternoon nap, stands up in his crib, and cries until his mother comes to get him. When his mother enters the room, he holds up his arms indicating he wants to be picked up. While his diaper is changed, he uses vocalizations such as "i," "i," "i." In addition, Mateo walks up and down stairs holding onto the side rails, placing two feet on the same stair before he moves to the next. He is beginning to run, and he likes to dance to music.

While Mateo plays with his toys, he uses his index finger to turn on a music box. He can activate toys by pulling or pushing the appropriate handle. Using both hands, he can connect large blocks such as Legos or hold a container to pull out objects. Mateo can stack blocks on top of one another and place them in a row. He plays with a push toy, which he can maneuver around barriers. He also sits on the toy, pushing it around using his feet and steering around barriers. While playing, he vocalizes vowel sounds. He also vocalizes when pointing to a desired object and playing with his toys.

When Mateo needs assistance with an object, he brings it to his mother or another familiar adult. For example, he will bring a box of alphabet disks to his mother and hand them to her. She will ask him what he wants. Mateo points to the box lid to request it be opened. His mother says the word *open,* Mateo says "pu," and his mother then opens the box. Mateo removes the disks and puts them back in the box one by one. When reading books, he is able to turn individual pages in board books and correctly orient the book. When given a crayon, he inconsistently scribbles on paper using a three-finger grasp.

Mateo often plays with plastic and cloth balls with his 5-year-old brother, Emilio. Mateo throws the balls and walks around obstacles, toys, or pillows to retrieve them. He is able to throw the balls to his brother, using a one-handed grasp on small balls and a two-handed grasp on larger balls. When throwing smaller balls, he uses an overhand throw, and for the large balls, he uses an underhand throw. He is also able to kick a ball to his brother. Mateo's parents and brother report he can climb up and down inclines and play on a slide. He requires some assistance to climb the ladder.

Mateo's mother reports that he demonstrates an understanding of opposite pair words (i.e., up/down, open/closed, full/empty, big/little) by answering questions with gestures and following directions. For example, when asked, he will correctly point to a large or small ball.

When Mateo eats, he uses a bent spoon to scoop and spear food. When he wants more to eat, he says "mo." He can drink from a sippy cup independently and a cup without a lid with adult assistance. He vocalizes while eating (e.g., "i," "i," "i" and "ah," "ah," "ah"). He appears to use these expressions to communicate that he likes the food. He also makes similar vocalizations to request getting down from his high chair. When Mateo wants something to drink, he will go to the refrigerator and point.

Mateo's mother and the speech-language pathologist report that he uses other vocalizations such as "da," "eh," "hi," and "ay." Mateo waves bye-bye and says "hi" as a greeting. He will look toward his mother or father when asked, "Where's Mommy? Where's Papa?" and he will look toward his brother when asked, "Where is your brother?" He can locate items his mother requests such as a ball, book, cards, or toys.

Before bath time, Mateo removes his shoes, socks, and elastic waistband pants. He is able to remove a pullover shirt, with large head openings. In the bathtub, he vocalizes and uses some gestures. He points to the faucet to communicate he wants the water turned off or on. His mother reports that Mateo tries to imitate his brother's motor behavior.

Phase 2: Targeting Functional and Generative Goals

From the assessment information summarized in Mateo's present level of development on his IFSP, the team identifies a number of family outcomes, including using words or signs to communicate with others so that family members and friends can understand what he wants or needs. The team then writes a measurable goal and associated objectives to guide them in meeting the stated family outcomes. The team uses a revised version of the Goals and Objectives Rating Instrument (Notari-Syverson & Shuster, 1995) to ensure the goal and associated objectives are meaningful to and understood by all team members. Mateo's target goal is to say or sign 30 single words, including 5 descriptive words, 5 action words, 2 pronouns, 15 object and/or event labels, and 3 proper names, over a 2-week period. The team then takes steps to ensure his daily activities will promote acquisition and use of this target skill.

Phase 3: Providing Multiple and Varied Learning Opportunities

The three forms described in Chapter 6 (i.e., intervention guides, embedding schedules, and activity plans) are used to assist the team in creating and embedding multiple and varied learning opportunities for Mateo. His team reviews his present level of development, identifies his needs, and considers how to individualize intervention. They create an intervention guide for his IFSP outcome by selecting a target goal and associated objectives/benchmarks, outlining specific antecedents and consequences, and determining needed accommodations and modifications, and possible intervention strategies. Figure 11.1 contains an intervention guide for the target goal says or signs 30 single words, including 5 descriptive words, 5 action words, 2 pronouns, 15 object and/or event labels, and 3 proper names.

Because Mateo receives home-based services, the team discusses the family's daily routine activities, which are considered the primary context for embedding learning opportunities. Using the AEPS Family Report as a guide, the team collects information from the family regarding 1) daily routine activities, 2) the time and frequency of each routine activity, 3) the sequence of events occurring in routines, 4) a description of Mateo's current participation in routines, and 5) whether the parents believe the routine can be used to embed learning opportunities. The team identifies wake-up, breakfast, playtime, bath time, and extended family time as possible daily routines the family can use to embed learning opportunities. The EI specialist and speech-language pathologist work with Mateo's parents during their weekly visits to help them strategize and practice how to embed learning opportunities. They then develop an embedding schedule that will prompt the caregivers about which antecedents to provide and when to embed learning opportunities across the selected daily routines. Figure 11.2 contains an

ABI Intervention Guide

1. Identifying information

Child's name: _Mateo_

Team members: _Parents: Lisa and Arturo; EI specialist: Jody; speech-language pathologist: Elizabeth_

Date intervention initiated: _September 2013_   Date intervention completed: _August 2014_

2. Target goal, objectives, and program steps

Goal:

    1.0   Mateo will say or sign 30 single words, including 5 descriptive words, 5 action words, 2 pronouns, 15 object and/or event labels, and 3 proper names over a 2-week period.

Objectives:

    1.1   Mateo will say or sign five different descriptive words (e.g., big, little, hot, red) over a 2-week period.
    1.2   Mateo will say or sign five different action words (e.g., open, go, eat, sit) over a 2-week period.
    1.3   Mateo will say or sign two different pronouns (e.g., me, mine, it, my, I, you, this) over a 2-week period.
    1.4   Mateo will say or sign 15 different object and/or event labels (e.g., ball, cup, hat, bubbles) over a 2-week period.
    1.5   Mateo will say or sign three different proper names (e.g., Mom, Dad, Mateo) over a 2-week period.

Program steps:

3. Core standards

IFSP outcome: We want Mateo to use words or signs so that family members and friends can understand what he wants or needs.

Figure 11.1. Completed ABI Intervention Guide for Mateo.

ABI Intervention Guide *(continued)*

4. Antecedents, targeted and nontargeted responses, and feedback or consequences

Antecedents designed to provide learning opportunities	List of possible child responses: targeted (+) and nontargeted (-)	Feedback or consequences
1.1 Ask questions about objects, people, and/or events that require a single descriptive word/sign response (e.g., "Do you want a big block or little block?") Model single words/signs to describe objects, people, and/or events (e.g., colors, shapes, sizes, quantity). Model single words/signs to describe objects, people, and/or events (e.g., colors, shapes, sizes, quantity). Encourage Mateo to describe objects, people, and events using a single word/sign (e.g., "Mateo, say blue.").	Mateo says or signs descriptive words (e.g., big, little, hot, red). (+) Mateo vocalizes vowel sounds (-) Mateo points to objects, people, and/or events (-) Mateo does not respond to questions, models, or encouragement (-)	Provide affirmation. (+) Mateo receives the object. (+) Continue activity. (+) Imitate vocalization and model single word/sign. (-) Model single word/sign to label proper name of person he points to or looks at. (-) Wait several seconds and then ask the question again, or model the word/sign again. (-)
1.2 Provide objects/toys or people that perform an action (e.g., balls bounce/roll, lights flash, brother runs/goes, teddy bear sits). Model single action words/signs or label actions of objects, people, and/or events (e.g., open, go, sit, eat). Encourage Mateo to say or sign an action word (e.g., "Mateo, say/sign up.").	Mateo says or signs action words (e.g., open, up, go, eat, run, kick sit). (+) Mateo vocalizes vowel sounds. (-) Mateo points to or looks at objects and/or people, performing an action. (-) Mateo does not respond to models or encouragement. (-)	Provide affirmation. (+) Mateo receives the object. (+) Continue activity. (+) Imitate vocalization and model single word/sign. (-) Wait several seconds and then move the object/toy closer, refer to the person performing an action. (-) Encourage Mateo to say or sign action word. (-)
1.3 Ask questions that require saying or signing a single pronoun as a response (e.g., "Whose book is this?"). Say/sign single pronouns. Encourage Mateo to say/sign pronouns (e.g., "Mateo, say/sign me.").	Mateo says or signs pronouns (e.g., me, mine, it, my, I, you, this). (+) Mateo vocalizes words sounds. (-) Mateo does not respond to questions, models, or encouragement. (-)	Provide affirmation. (+) Continue activity. (+) Imitate vocalization and model single word/sign. (-) Wait several seconds and then ask the question again, or model the word/sign again. (-)
1.4 Ask questions that require Mateo to label objects or events (e.g., "What do you have?"). Say or sign object/event labels. Encourage Mateo to say or sign object/event labels.	Mateo says or signs object/event label. (+) Mateo vocalizes vowel sounds. (-) Mateo looks at or points to object/event. (-) Mateo does not respond to questions, models, or encouragement. (-)	Provide affirmation. (+) Mateo receives object. (+) Continue activity/event. (+) Imitate vocalization and model single word/sign. (-) Model single word/sign to label object or event he points to or looks at. (-) Wait several seconds and then ask the question again, or model the word/sign again. (-)
1.5 Ask questions about objects, people, and/or events that require saying or signing a proper name (e.g., "Who is playing with you?"). Say/sign single proper names. Encourage Mateo to say/sign proper names (e.g., Mom, Dad, Mateo, Emilio).	Mateo says or signs proper names (e.g., Emilio, Mom, Dad, Mateo).(+) Mateo vocalizes vowel sounds. (-) Mateo looks at or points to person. (-) Mateo does not respond to questions, models, or encouragement. (-)	Provide affirmation. (+) Imitate vocalization and model single word/sign. (-) Model single word/sign to label proper name of person he points to or looks at. (-) Wait several seconds and then ask the question again, or model the word/sign again. (-)

(continued)

Figure 11.1. *(continued)*

ABI Intervention Guide *(continued)*   *page 3 of 3*

5. Teaching strategies

- Ensure joint attention and then pair single words/signs with verbalizations.
- Wait at least 5 seconds for Mateo to respond before restating or prompting again.
- Use milieu language strategies including incidental teaching, mand-model, and time delay.
- Use nondirected strategies such as visible but unreachable and piece-by-piece.

---

6. Monitoring progress

Who (person responsible for collecting the data)	Where (which activities or locations)	When (how often or on which days)	How (which methods)
Parents	Home (wake up, breakfast, playtime, lunch, bath time)	Daily (3 activities a day)	Record number and type of words/signs/ Mateo uses.
Jody	Home visit during planned activity	Weekly	Record number and type of words/signs Mateo uses.
Elizabeth	Home visit during 30 minutes of speech therapy	Monthly	Collect language sample using audiotape.

---

7. Decision rules

If adequate progress does not occur in _____1 month_____ (specify time frame for when the team will review the data), consider changing:

_____ Targeted goal

_____ Antecedents or feedback/consequences

__X__ Teaching strategies

__X__ Frequency, type, and/or locations of learning opportunities provided

_____ Other (describe) _____

ABI Embedding Schedule

Focus: Individual **Setting:** Home   *page 1 of 2*

Child's name: _____ Mateo

Team members: _____ Mom, Dad, Jody, and Elizabeth

Dates schedule will be used: _____ October and November

Target skills

Family routine	Says/signs five different descriptive words (e.g., big, little, hot, red)	Says/signs five different action words (e.g., open, go, eat, sit)	Says/signs two different pronouns (e.g., me, mine, it, my, I, you, this)	Says/signs 15 different object and/or event labels (e.g., ball, cup, hat, bubbles)	Says/signs three different proper names (e.g., Mom, Dad, Mateo)
Wake-up	Ask question, "What color shoes, shirt, pants, socks?"	Label actions Mateo completes throughout the morning routine.	Sing, "Good morning to you."	Label common objects in the bedroom and bathroom.	Greet Mateo with proper name to serve as a model.
Breakfast	Describe breakfast food (e.g., hot, cold, soft, crunchy).	Label actions of placing household items on table.	Ask, "Whose seat is this?" (Say, "My seat"). Ask, "Who sits here?" (Say, "I sit" or "You sit").	Name eating materials (e.g., cup, spoon).	Greet people with proper name as they enter the room to serve as a model.

Figure 11.2.   Completed home ABI Embedding Schedule for Mateo.

(continued)

Figure 11.2. *(continued)*

ABI Embedding Schedule *(continued)* **Focus:** Individual **Setting:** Home				*page 2 of 2*
Target skills				
Family routine	Says/signs five different descriptive words (e.g., big, little, hot, red)	Says/signs five different action words (e.g., open, go, eat, sit)	Says/signs two different pronouns (e.g., me, mine, it, my, I, you, this)	Says/signs 15 different object and/or event labels (e.g., ball, cup, hat, bubbles)	Says/signs three different proper names (e.g., Mom, Dad, Mateo)
Playtime	Describe Mateo's play with objects.	Label action of child and toy (e.g., "Car go up/down.").	Use pronouns to label turn taking (e.g., my turn, your, turn).	Label toys or pictures in book.	Label pictures of family members to serve as a model.
Bath time	Describe the texture of items used during bath time (e.g., "The towel is soft.").	Label actions of water (e.g., pour in, out, on, over).		Label common toys from playtime in bath.	
Extended family get-togethers	Name family members when they get together.	Label actions with family and toys (e.g., in, out, on, over, under).	Use pronouns to label turn taking (e.g., my turn, your turn).		Greet Mateo and family with proper names to serve as a model.

embedding schedule for Mateo. The team creates an embedding schedule that allows them to incorporate the antecedents from the intervention guide into family prioritized routines. Finally, the team develops a few planned activities that the parents may be able to use. Figure 11.3 contains an activity plan for sand box play.

Phase 4: Monitoring Children's Progress

The team reviews the intervention guide to develop a data collection system to monitor Mateo's progress on target goals. A primary concern is to develop a data collection system that 1) is accessible and usable by everyone on the team, 2) keeps writing to a minimum, and 3) includes situational and performance information. To help them with the forms, the team lists possible single words/signs Mateo is likely to need and use on a daily basis. The team alphabetizes the words/signs so that anyone can easily mark when one is used. The team needs data on whether Mateo is using words or signs and how he is using them (e.g., description, action, label); consequently, the ABI embedding form also includes a means of recording this information.

The data collection system the team adopted includes the following:

- Mateo's parents will record the words and signs Mateo uses on a weekly basis (i.e., during wake-up, breakfast, playtime, bath time, and extended family time) on a form the team developed for them. The form has space to list the spoken or signed words, indicate how he is using them, and count them with hash marks. The form includes all the activities the team identified to embed opportunities so family members can collect data in any or all of them. The ABI embedding form will also help identify, through the collection of data, those activities more likely to generate practice and lead to success so family members can target high potential activities.

- The EI specialist will record the number and type of words and signs Mateo uses during her weekly home visits while his mother plays with or engages in daily routines with her son. Every 2 weeks, the EI specialist will also review all data and summarize total number and types of words and signs used.

- The speech-language pathologist will collect a language sample once a month, recording it during her visit as Mateo and his mother play or engage in daily routines.

- All team members will review the data monthly to make decisions regarding changes to the intervention strategies as the results dictate.

Once data are collected, the team plans to meet regularly to summarize their findings and make intervention decisions. Figure 11.4 contains a data collection form (the embedding schedule with added space for keeping track) Mateo's parents' use, and Figure 11.5 contains a completed data collection form used by the EI specialist.

ABI Activity Plan

1. Activity name   Sandbox play

Target child: Mateo

Target skills: Uses action words, object labels, and descriptive words

---

2. Materials

Sandbox with sand

Objects to play with in the sand (e.g., cups, spoons, cars, balls, plastic people, dinosaurs, blocks, plates)

---

3. Environmental arrangement

The sand box and objects should be accessible to Mateo.

Figure 11.3. Completed ABI Activity Plan for Mateo.

ABI Activity Plan *(continued)*

4. Sequence of steps

Beginning

Have Mateo climb into the sandbox, and ask him to name each object.

Middle

Mateo asks for objects and labels them when he buries or digs them up, using descriptor words and action words.

End

Review object label, action words, and descriptors with Mateo.

5. Embedded learning opportunities

Repeats word/sign that labels object

Describes objects he digs up or buries

(continued)

Figure 11.3. *(continued)*

ABI Activity Plan *(continued)*

6. Planned variations

1. Vary the objects that will be placed in the sand box.

2. Vary actions with toys and sand.

---

7. Other (e.g., vocabulary, peer interactions, caregiver response)

Action words (e.g., in, out, on, over, dig)

Object labels (e.g., cup, spoon, car, ball, plastic people, dinosaur, blocks, plate)

Descriptive words (e.g., large, small, color names)

Mateo's family can adapt the sandbox play by changing objects and actions.

ABI Embedding Schedule

Focus: Individual **Setting:** Home   *page 1 of 2*

Child's names: ___Mateo___

Team members: ___Mom, Dad, Jody, and Elizabeth___

Dates schedule will be used: ___October and November___

Target skills

Family routine	Says/signs five different descriptive words (e.g., big, little, hot, red)	Says/signs five different action words (e.g., open, go, eat, sit)	Says/signs two different pronouns (e.g., me, mine, it, my, I, you, this)	Says/signs 15 different object and/or event labels (e.g., ball, cup, hat, bubbles)	Says/signs three different proper names (e.g., Mom, Dad, Mateo)
Wake-up	Ask question, "What color shoes, shirt, pants, socks?"	Label actions Mateo completes throughout the morning routine.	Sing, "Good morning to you."	Label common objects in the bedroom and bathroom.	Greet Mateo with proper name to serve as a model.
Caregiver progress notes					
Breakfast	Describe breakfast food (e.g., hot, cold, soft, crunchy).	Label actions of placing household items on table.	Ask, "Whose seat is this?" (Say, "My seat"). Ask, "Who sits here?" (Say, "I sit" or "You sit").	Name eating materials (e.g., cup, spoon).	Greet people with proper name as they enter the room to serve as a model.
Caregiver progress notes					

Figure 11.4. Completed home ABI Embedding Schedule with space for caregivers to enter progress monitoring notes.

(continued)

Figure 11.4. *(continued)*

ABI Embedding Schedule *(continued)* **Focus:** Individual **Setting:** Home   *page 2 of 2*

Target skills

Family routine	Says/signs five different descriptive words (e.g., big, little, hot, red)	Says/signs five different action words (e.g., open, go, eat, sit)	Says/signs two different pronouns (e.g., me, mine, it, my, I, you, this)	Says/signs 15 different object and/or event labels (e.g., ball, cup, hat, bubbles)	Says/signs three different proper names (e.g., Mom, Dad, Mateo)
Playtime	Describe Mateo's play with objects.	Label action of child and toy (e.g., "Car go up/down.").	Use pronouns to label turn taking (e.g., my turn, your, turn).	Label toys or pictures in book.	Label pictures of family members to serve as a model.
Caregiver progress notes					
Bath time	Describe the texture of items used during bath time (e.g., "The towel is soft.").	Label actions of water (e.g., pour in, out, on, over).		Label common toys from playtime in bath.	
Caregiver progress notes					
Extended family get-togethers	Name family members when they get together.	Label actions with family and toys (e.g., in, out, on, over, under).	Use pronouns to label turn taking (e.g., my turn, your turn).		Greet Mateo and family with proper names to serve as a model.
Caregiver progress notes					

ABI Data Collection Form

page 1 of 1

Child's name: _Mateo_   Team members: ___Parents, Jody, and Elizabeth___

Collecting the week of: _November 22, 2013_

Alphabetized list	Word	Sign	Word/sign	Description	Action	Pronoun	Label	Proper name
				Summary of utterance				
Ap-ba		‖‖‖						5
Ball	‖‖‖		‖				6	
Big	‖		‖‖	3				
Bug		‖‖					2	
Cat	‖‖‖‖						4	
Cup	‖‖‖						5	
Dad	‖‖‖		‖‖					5
Down	‖‖‖				5			
Eat		‖‖‖			5			
Emilio	‖	‖‖‖						4
Go	‖‖‖		‖‖‖		6			
Green	‖	‖‖		3				
Hat	‖	‖‖					3	
He	‖					1		
Hot	‖‖		‖‖‖	7				
I	‖	‖‖‖				6		
It	‖‖‖					3		
Itsy		‖‖		2				
Me	‖‖‖ ‖‖‖‖	‖‖	‖‖‖			16		
Mine	‖	‖‖‖				4		
Mom	‖‖‖		‖‖‖					8
More	‖‖‖ ‖‖‖				10			
New				0				
No	‖‖‖		‖‖‖		10			
Owen	‖							1
Pan	‖						1	
Pat	‖‖		‖‖				4	
Red	‖	‖‖‖		4				
Run	‖‖‖				5			
Sit	‖‖‖ ‖‖	‖‖‖			10			
Stop		‖‖‖			5			
Teddy	‖‖			2				
Um-mah	‖		‖‖‖					4
Up	‖‖‖				5			
Yell				0				
You		‖‖‖				3		

Figure 11.5. ABI Data Collection Form completed by Mateo's early intervention specialist.

SUMMARY

This chapter presented information specific to EI intervention services for infants and toddlers with disabilities and their families. Federal legislation mandating services and development of the individual family service plan and types of service coordination were presented. Three theoretical models, Maslow's hierarchy of needs, family systems theory, and the ecological systems framework, and their importance to understanding and working with families of infants and toddlers with disabilities were also described. A brief history of the changing role of families in EI was presented describing the shifts from professional-centered services to family-centered services, and from therapeutic-type services to caregiver-coached interventions with their children. A number of home visiting guidelines were offered to emphasize the importance of the caregiver and child relationship. Finally, the four phases of intervention using ABI in home settings were presented and provided examples of employing ABI in the home with two different young children.

REFERENCES

Alberto, P.A., & Troutman, A.C. (2012). *Applied behavior analysis for teachers* (9th ed.). Upper Saddle River, NJ: Pearson.

Astuto, J., & Allen, L. (2009). *Home visitation and young children: An approach worth investing in? Social policy report.* Ann Arbor, MI: Society for Research in Child Development.

Bailey, D. (2003). Assessing family resources, priorities, and concerns. In M. McLean, M. Wolery, & D. Bailey (Eds.), *Assessing infants and preschoolers with special needs* (3rd ed.; pg 172–203). New York, NY: Merrill.

Baird, S., & Peterson, J. (1997). Seeking a comfortable fit between family-centered philosophy and infant-parent interaction in early intervention: Time for a paradigm shift? *Topics in Early Childhood Special Education, 11,* 19–31.

Barlow, D., & Hersen, M. (1984). Single case experimental designs: Strategies for studying behavior change. New York, NY: Pergamon.

Barnett, D.W., Bell, S.H., & Carey, K.T. (2002). *Designing preschool interventions: A practitioner's guide.* New York, NY: Guilford.

Barton, E., & Fettig, A. (2013). Parent implemented interventions for young children with disabilities: A review of fidelity features. *Journal of Early Intervention, 35*(2). doi: 10.1177/1053815113504625

Brewer, E., McPherson, M., Magrab, P., & Hutchin, V. (1989). Family-centered, community-based, coordinated care for children with special health care needs. *Pediatrics, 83,* 1055–1060.

Bricker, D. (Series Ed.). (2002). *Assessment, Evaluation, and Programming System (AEPS®) for Infants and Children* (2nd ed., Vols. 1–4). Baltimore, MD: Paul H. Brookes Publishing Co.

Bronfenbrenner, U. (1979). *The ecology of human development.* Cambridge, MA: Harvard University Press.

Bruder, M., & Dunst, C. (2008). Factors related to the scope of early intervention service coordinator practices. *Infants & Young Children, 21,* 176–185.

The California Evidence-Based Clearninghouse for Child Welfare, (n.d.). Home visiting programs for prevention of child abuse and neglect. Retrieved from http://www.cebc4cw.org/topic/home-visiting-for-prevention-of-child-abuse-and-neglect/

Campbell, P., & Sawyer, B. (2007). Supporting learning opportunities in natural settings through participation based services. *Journal of Early Intervention, 29*(4), 287–305.

Campbell, S.K., Kolobe, T.H.A., Osten, E.T., Lenke, M., & Girolami, G.L. (1995). Construct validity of the Test of Infant Motor Performance. *Physical Therapy, 75*, 585–596.

Coogle, C.G., Floyd, K., Hanline, M.F., & Hiczewski, J.K. (2013). Strategies used in natural environments to promote communication development in young children at risk for autism spectrum disorder. *Young Exceptional Children, 16*, 11–23. doi:10.1177/1096250612473126

Cook, R.E., & Sparks, S.N. (2008). *The art and practice of home visiting: Early intervention for children with special needs and their families.* Baltimore, MD: Paul H. Brookes Publishing Co.

Division for Early Childhood. (2007). *Promoting positive outcomes for children with disabilities: Recommendations for curriculum assessment, and program evaluation.* Missoula, MT: Author.

Division for Early Childhood Task Force on Recommended Practices. (2014). *DEC recommended practices: Indicators of quality in programs for infants and young children with special needs and their families.* Reston, VA: The Council for Exceptional Children.

Dunst, C. (2000). Revisiting "Rethinking early intervention." *Topics in Early Childhood Special Education, 20,* 95–104.

Dunst, C.J., Bruder, M.B., Trivette, C.M., & Hamby, D.W. (2006). Everyday activity settings, natural learning environments, and early intervention practices. *Journal of Policy and Practice in Intellectual Disabilities, 3*(1), 3–10.

Dunst, C.J., Johanson, C., Trivette, C.M., & Hamby, D. (1991). Family-oriented early intervention policies and practices: Family-centered or not? *Exceptional Children, 58*(2), 115–126.

Early Childhood Technical Assistance Center (ECTAC). (2014). *Early Childhood Technical Assistance Center (ECTAC)—Improving systems, practices, and outcomes.* Chapel Hill, NC. Retrieved from http://ectacenter.org

Education of the Handicapped Act Amendments of 1986, PL 99-457, 20 U.S.C. §§ 1400 *et seq.*

Epley, P., Summers, J., & Turnbull, A. (2011). Family outcomes of early intervention: Families' perceptions of need, services, and outcomes. *Journal of Early Intervention, 33*(3), 201–219.

Friedman, M., Woods, J., & Salisbury, C. (2012). Caregiver coaching strategies for early intervention providers: Moving towards operationalizing definitions. *Infants and Young Children, 25*(1), 62–82.

Friend, M., & Cook, L. (2013). *Interactions: Collaboration skills for school professionals* (7th ed.). Upper Saddle River, NJ: Pearson.

Grisham-Brown, J., Hemmeter, M.L., & Pretti-Frontczak, K. (2005). *Blended practices for teaching young children in inclusive settings.* Baltimore, MD: Paul H. Brookes Publishing Co.

Guralnick, M. (1997). Second generation research in the field of early intervention. In M.J. Guralnick (Ed.), *The effectiveness of early intervention* (pp. 1–14). Baltimore, MD: Paul H. Brookes Publishing Co.

Hanson, M., & Lynch, E.W. (2004). Theoretical perspectives. In M.J. Hanson & E.W. Lynch (Eds.), *Understanding families: Approaches to diversity, disability, and risk.* Baltimore, MD: Paul H. Brookes Publishing Co.

Hart, B., & Risley, T.R. (1995). *Meaningful differences in the everyday experiences of young American children.* Baltimore, MD: Paul H. Brookes Publishing Co.

Individuals with Disabilities Education Improvement Act (IDEA) of 2004, PL 108-446, 20 U.S.C. §§ 1400 *et seq.*

Johnson, K. (2009, February). *State-based home visiting: Strengthening programs through state leadership.* New York, NY: National Center for Children in Poverty, Mailman School of Public Health, Columbia University.

Jung, L. (2010). Identifying family supports and other resources. In R. McWilliam (Ed.), *Working with Families of young children with special needs.* New York, NY: Guilford Press.

Kaiser, A., Hemmeter, M., Ostrosky, M., Fischer, R., Yoder, P., & Keefer, M. (1996). The effects of teaching parents to use responsive interaction strategies. *Topics in Early Childhood Special Education, 16*(3), 375–406.

Kashinath, S., Woods, J., & Goldstein, H. (2006). Enhancing generalized teaching strategy use in daily routines by parents of children with autism. *Journal of Speech, Language and Hearing Research, 49,* 466–485.

Ketelaar, M., Vermeer, A., Helders, P., & Hart, H. (1998). Parental participation in intervention programs for children with cerebral palsy: A review of research. *Topics in Early Childhood Special Education, 18,* 108–117.

Knowles, M.S., et al. (1984) *Andragogy in Action. Applying modern principles of adult education,* San Francisco: Jossey Bass.

Knowles, M. (1990). *The adult learner: A neglected species.* Houston, TX: Gulf Publishing.

Kontos, S., & Diamond, K. (2002). Measuring the quality of early intervention services for infants and toddlers: Problems and prospects. *International Journal of Disability, Development and Education, 49*(4), 337–351.

Mahoney, G., & Perales, F. (2005). Relationship-focused early intervention with children with pervasive developmental disorders and other disabilities: A comparative study. *Developmental and Behavioral Pediatrics, 24*(2), 94–109.

Marvin, C., & Yates, T. (2007). *Promoting parent-child interactions during home visits.* Conference presentation at the Council for Exceptional Children, Division for Early Childhood (DEC) 23rd Annual International Conference on Young Children with Special Needs and their Families, Niagara Falls, Ontario, Canada.

Marvin, C., & Yates, T. (2008). DEC conference presentation, Niagara Falls, NY.

Maslow, A. (1943). A theory of human motivation. *Psychological Review, 50*(4), 370–396.

Maslow, A. (1954). *Motivation and personality.* New York, NY: Harpers.

McLean, M., Wolery, M., & Bailey, D. (2004). *Assessing infants and preschoolers with special needs* (3rd ed.). Columbus, OH: Charles E. Merrill.

McWilliam, R. (2006). What happened to service coordination? *Journal of Early Intervention, 28,* 166–168.

McWilliam, R. (2010). Support-based home visiting. In R. McWilliams (Ed.), *Working with families of young children with special needs.* New York, NY: Guilford Press.

Meadan, H., Ostrosky, M., Santos, R., & Snodgrass, M.R. (2013). How can I help? Prompting procedures to support children's learning. *Young Exceptional Children, 16*(4), 31–39.

Neuman, S., & McCormick, S. (1995). *Single-subject experimental research: Applications for literacy.* Newark, DE: International Reading Association.

Noonan, M. & McCormick, L. (2013). *Teaching young children with disabilities in natural environments.* Baltimore, MD: Paul H. Brookes.

Notari-Syverson, A., & Shuster, S. (1995). Putting real life skills into IEP/IFSPs for infants and young children. *Teaching Exceptional Children, 27*(2), 29–32.

Olson, D.H. (2000). Circumplex model of marital and family systems. *Journal of Family Therapy, 22,* 144–167.

Park, J., & Turnbull, A. (2003). Service integration in early intervention: Determining interpersonal and structural factors for success. *Infants and Young Children, 16*(1), 48–58.

Patrick, S. (2004). Barriers to family-centered services for infants and toddlers with developmental delays. *Social Work, 49*(2), 301–308.

Paulsell, D., Boller, K., Hallgren, K., & Esposito, A. (2010). *Assessing home visit quality: Dosage, content, relationship.* Washington, DC: Zero to Three.

Peterson, C., Luze, G., Eshbaugh, E., Hyun, H., & Ross, K. (2007). Enhancing parent-child interactions through home visiting: Promising practice or unfulfilled promise? *Journal of Early Intervention, 29,* 119.

Peterson, P., Carta, J.J., & Greenwood, C.R. (2005). The effects of teaching enhanced milieu language teaching skills to parents in multiple risk families. *Journal of Early Intervention, 27,* 94–109.

Roberts, R. (2005). *An outcomes-based approach to evaluating service coordination models: Final report.* Logan, UT: Early Intervention Research Institute.

Salisbury, C.L., Woods, J., & Copeland, C. (2009). Provider perspectives on adapting and using collaborative consultation in natural environments. *Topics in Early Childhood Special Education, 30*(3), 132–147.

Sandall, S.R., & Schwartz, I.S. (2008). *Building blocks for teaching preschoolers with special needs* (2nd ed.). Baltimore, MD: Paul H. Brookes Publishing Co.

Sawyer, B., & Campbell, P. (2012). Early interventionists perspectives on teaching. *Journal of Early Intervention, 34*(2), 104–124.

Shonkoff, J., & Hauser-Cram, P. (1987). Early intervention for disabled infants and their families: A quantitative analysis. *Pediatrics, 80,* 650–658.

Trivette, C., Dunst, C., & Hamby, D. (2010). Influences of family systems intervention practices on parent-child interactions and child development. *Topics in Early Childhood Special Education, 3*(1), 3–19.

Turnbull, A.P., & Turnbull, H.R. (2001). *Families, professionals, and exceptionality: Collaborating for empowerment* (4th ed.). Upper Saddle River, NJ: Merrill/Prentice Hall.

Turnbull, A., Turnbull, H., Erwin, E., Soodak, L., & Shogren, K. (2011). *Families, professionals, and exceptionality: Positive outcomes through partnerships and trust* (6th ed.). Upper Saddle River, NJ: Pearson.

U.S. Department of Education. (2014). *35th annual report to Congress on the implementation of the Individuals with Disabilities Education Act, Parts B and C, 2012.*

Warfield, M.E., Hauser-Cram, P., Krauss, M.W., Shonkoff, J.P., & Upshur, C.C. (2000). The effects of early intervention on families. *Early Education and Development, 11,* 499–517.

Wasik, B., & Bryant, D. (2001). *Home visiting: Procedures for helping families* (2nd ed.). Thousand Oaks CA: Sage Publishing.

12

Using Activity-Based
Intervention with Children Who
Have Significant Impairments

Although the framework for implementing ABI with children with significant disabilities remains the same as it would for any child, children with
multiple, significant impairments often require more intensive and structured intervention strategies and approaches than do children with less significant developmental delays. By definition, children with severe disabilities
have problems or serious delays that encompass more than one developmental area. For example, children with significant motor problems may also
have accompanying impairments in social-communication, social, and adaptive areas. Children with serious cognitive impairments may also have challenges in the fine motor, social-communication, adaptive, and social areas
of development. Likewise children with serious emotional disturbances will
have challenges in the social area and likely in other developmental areas
as well. Children with multiple impairments may also have areas in which
they do not have impairments. It is important that teams ensure continued
developmental progress in these areas and provide specialized instruction
in areas of impairment to maximize the child's functioning and minimize
secondary delays in areas in which the child is developing typically. The multiplicity of challenges experienced by children with significant disabilities is
sobering and requires thoughtful application of any intervention approach.

The purpose of this chapter is to describe how to apply the ABI approach
with children who present significant challenges and who have more serious needs in terms of habilitative interventions. The chapter begins with a
description of special considerations for using ABI with this population. It

then describes how each phase of ABI can be modified to meet the needs of children with severe disabilities, and includes an example illustrating the application of ABI for a preschool-age child with significant impairments. The chapter concludes by offering a range of suggestions for implementing ABI with children who have significant needs during child-initiated, routine, and planned activities.

SPECIAL CONSIDERATIONS

The unique needs of children with multiple impairments require consideration of several factors in providing services to them and their families. These factors include the importance of a team approach, assistive technology, positioning and handling and adaptive equipment/furniture, and family involvement.

Team Approach

By team we refer to the group of individuals who are responsible for assessing, developing goals, implementing an intervention plan, and conducting ongoing progress monitoring for a specific child. The composition of teams for children with severe disabilities is particularly important because these children often have complex medical, therapeutic, and educational needs that require a high level of knowledge about specific conditions and effective interventions. Teams working with children with severe disabilities should include three groups of people: caregivers (e.g., parents or guardians), service providers (e.g., teachers, child care workers, interventionists), and specialists (e.g., therapists, nutritionists, autism specialists). The last group should include those professionals who have the special expertise needed to address the child's multiplicity of needs (McWilliam, 2005).

Although decisions about and implementation of appropriate services and intervention strategies should be made collaboratively by these three groups, the specialists on the team (e.g., occupational therapist, physical therapist, speech-language pathologist, autism specialist, vision specialist, audiologist) have a vital role to play when devising and delivering intervention services to young children with severe disabilities. For example, when a child has a seizure disorder, the participation of a nurse or neurologist on the team may be essential. For children with feeding issues (e.g., swallowing, choking, gagging; feeding tube), a physical or occupational therapist may be critical to the team. For children with serious dietary concerns (e.g., adequate calorie intake), the participation of a nutritionist is likely necessary.

For children with significant needs, the team should always include professionals with the necessary expertise to address the special and often difficult and challenging issues presented by these children. Teams composed of several specialists require that they share their perspectives and expertise and develop collaborative efforts in which all members contribute.

Assistive Technology

Assistive technology refers to a tangible support for children to cope more effectively with environmental demands and/or to improve their ability to meet their needs. Assistive technology is important for helping children with significant disabilities participate fully in daily routines and other activities (Downing & Demchak, 2008; Kelker & Holt, 2000). An assistive technology device is defined as, "any item, piece of equipment, or product system, whether acquired commercially off the shelf, modified, or customized, that is used to increase, maintain, or improve functional capabilities of a child with a disability" (Individuals with Disabilities Education Improvement Act [IDEA] of 2004 [PL 108-446]). There are two primary types of assistive technology devices (Downing & Demchak, 2008). The first are referred to as low-tech devices and include inexpensive, relatively simple adaptations such as built-up spoon handles or picture communication systems printed on cardstock. The second are referred to as high-tech devices and include expensive and complex adaptations (e.g., a power wheelchair, a van with a motorized lift system), equipment such as computers with specialized software, and augmentative and alternative communication devices.

In most cases, assistive technology should be selected or developed to meet three important goals: 1) improvement of family interactions and satisfaction, 2) enhancement of the child's ability to participate in routines and activities outside of the home, and 3) improvement of communication with others across settings (DiCarlo, Banajee, & Stricklin, 2000). Specific examples of how assistive technology can be used during different types of activities and with young children having a variety of needs are described later in the chapter.

Positioning and Handling and Adaptive Equipment/Furniture

Positioning and handling as well as adaptive equipment/furniture are often important to consider for children who have gross or fine motor problems such as spasticity. Positioning and handling refers to a spectrum of maneuvers that specialists can perform to help ensure a child is physically situated, given his or her disability, to ensure maximum comfort, safety, and range of motion. Adaptive equipment/furniture refers to specialized equipment/furniture (e.g., standing table) or to existing equipment/furniture that has been altered to meet a child's special needs (e.g., built-up spoon handle, child chair with built-up sides).

For children who have significant motor impairments, proper positioning and the use of appropriate adaptive equipment during activities are essential to ensure the child is comfortable and able to access and fully participate in daily routines and other activities that occur throughout the child's day, whatever the setting (Dennis & Schlough, 2008). For example, an adapted chair (e.g., one with extra support or padding) might be necessary for proper positioning during meals and table activities for a child with cerebral palsy. The child might also need a wheelchair or walker to enhance mobility. It is also critical that team members who position and move children between activities and equipment work closely with specialists to understand how to position and handle them to ensure children receive the maximum benefit from adaptive equipment (Dennis & Schlough, 2008).

Family Involvement

The importance of including caregivers as legitimate members of the intervention team is a major theme in this book. We believe the more meaningfully caregivers participate the more likely children will make progress toward targeted goals and objectives. Caregiver participation is particularly important for young children with severe disabilities, as working with children who have significant disabilities often requires close communication and problem solving with families. For example, a child with a complicated medical history may have frequent hospitalizations, requiring additional collaboration when the interventionist resumes home visits for an infant or toddler, or when the preschooler returns to the classroom following an extended break. Many children with multiple impairments are unable to communicate with their families about what happens during their school day, and thus, it is particularly important that center-based staff have a regular mechanism to communicate with families about the child's school day. For example, a teacher may use a template for a daily note home that includes picture symbols for each of the day's routines (e.g., snack, free play, circle time) paired with anecdotes about what the child did during each activity. Another idea is to share pictures and anecdotal notes via a blog specifically designed for the child. (See Edelman [2014] for information about using video in early childhood settings.) Children with multiple and significant medical, educational, and therapeutic challenges require careful consideration of how to proceed with intervention efforts.

APPLICATION OF ABI FOR CHILDREN WITH SIGNIFICANT IMPAIRMENTS

This section describes how ABI can be used with children who have significant needs during each of the four phases of ABI: 1) conducting comprehensive and ongoing assessments, 2) targeting functional and generative goals, 3) providing multiple and varied learning opportunities, and 4) monitoring children's progress. To illustrate each phase, we've included an example of the application of ABI with Mollie, a 4-year-old with significant needs.

Phase 1: Conducting Comprehensive and Ongoing Assessments

Assessing children with multiple impairments can be challenging for teams, particularly if the child is not yet demonstrating particular skills on commonly used curriculum-based assessment tools that might typically be targeted for intervention given the child's age. For children with significant disabilities, it is important that the assessment tool selected is sensitive enough to provide a fine-grained analysis of the developmental sequence of skills to allow the team to document existing skills and to detect small changes in progress (Neisworth & Bagnato, 2005). For example, the AEPS (Bricker, 2002) includes programming steps that break down objectives into their component skills allowing the intervention team to assess a child's skills more accurately. Over time, having this more fine-grained analysis available also makes it more likely that the child will demonstrate progress on the assessment tool, thus providing a better description of changes in the child's development over time. It is also particularly important that a team includes individuals who have expertise in the areas being assessed. For example, when assessing a child with cerebral palsy who uses a walker or wheelchair, the assessment team should include a physical therapist who has specialized knowledge about young children's motor development.

Mollie attends Little Tikes, an inclusive community preschool program in her family's neighborhood elementary school. Mollie is 4 years old and has cerebral palsy, a seizure disorder, vision impairment, and significant delays across all areas of development. She attends Little Tikes five mornings per week. The classroom team consists of Lisa, the ECSE teacher; Jill and Andrea, the classroom assistants; and Jenny, the speech-language pathologist who spends several hours in the classroom each week. Other related service providers who are available to serve on the team as needed include physical and occupational therapists, a vision specialist, a school nurse, and an autism specialist.

Mollie's team completed the AEPS by observing her in the classroom and at home. Their goal was to observe her use of functional skills during daily routines and other activities. Because Mollie wasn't yet performing several of the skills on the AEPS, the team used the AEPS Programming Steps to allow for a more fine-grained analysis of her skills and progress. As part of their assessment, the team interviewed Mollie's family to learn about family routines and priorities. The family also completed the AEPS Family Report.

While in the classroom, Mollie was observed sitting in her wheelchair with a soft shaker toy on her tray. She batted at the toy, moving it around on the tray and bringing it to her mouth. She made some sounds (e.g., /ma/) that appeared unrelated to the activity. She was not yet observing her peers, but quieted and turned toward the ringing telephone. The classroom assistant moved Mollie from her wheelchair to an adapted chair for lunch. The assistant fed Mollie soft, mashed foods (e.g., yogurt, bananas) with a spoon. Mollie drank from a cup with handles and a lid with assistance from the adult to control the cup's tilt. Mollie coughed several times while drinking, suggesting swallowing problems. Mollie brought crackers to her mouth and gummed them with assistance from the adult to grasp the cracker.

When the meal was finished, the assistant cleaned Mollie's face and hands and carried her to the circle time area. The assistant positioned Mollie between her legs to provide the necessary support for her to maintain an upright position. During circle, Mollie sat quietly and smiled when children sang the hello song.

Phase 2: Targeting Functional and Generative Goals

For children with significant impairments, it is particularly important that the team focus on goals that promote active, meaningful participation in classroom, home, and community activities. Because the skills being taught will likely require additional time, intervention effort, and child practice for mastery, it is critical that the goals selected enhance functioning for the child and provide maximum benefit for the family. For example, being able to communicate wants and needs is an important skill for all individuals to possess. This skill, therefore, is one that teams will likely want to address for young children who have significant communication impairments. Similarly, eating, dressing, and using the toilet are important life skills that allow an individual to have dignity and independence. These skills may be of high priority, particularly as children approach kindergarten. For children with autism, foundational skills that are forerunners of later developing skills or necessary for learning other skills (e.g., imitation, initiating communication exchanges, sitting and attending during group activities) may be of the highest priority. Overall, teams need to consider the likelihood that potential IFSP outcomes or IEP goals will lead to the child's acquisition of important skills that will make a difference in the child's quality of life or will provide the foundation for later developing skills, enhancing the child's functioning at home and school and in the community.

Mollie's team selected three goals they agreed would improve her participation in classroom and family activities: 1) Mollie will maintain a supported sitting position, 2) Mollie will eat a variety of soft and crisp foods, and 3) Mollie will select an activity or object when given a choice.

Phase 3: Providing Multiple and Varied Learning Opportunities

Learning opportunities should address two important criteria: sufficient quantity and quality. Meeting these criteria is essential to ensure acquisition of targeted goals and objectives for all children; however, designing and offering learning or practice opportunities for children with significant impairments requires more effort and careful planning.

Children who have significant needs will likely require a greater number of learning trials than their peers before mastering a new skill. Thus, learning opportunities need to be carefully devised and offered to ensure an adequate number of practice opportunities for children to acquire or gain new skills. (See also Sandall & Schwartz [2008] for their discussion of child-focused instructional strategies that provide this level of support.) For example, if the child is learning to make requests, the team should provide an opportunity for the child to make requests during circle time (e.g., song choice), at outside time on adapted equipment (e.g., swing, tricycle), at meals (e.g., choice of favorite foods), during art (e.g., paint colors), and during free play (e.g., choice of games). This approach provides the child with multiple opportunities to make meaningful requests.

An important dimension of quantity is that opportunities are offered across the day (i.e., distributed) during daily routines and activities rather than only provided at one time or within one activity in a massed practice format (Wolery, 2005). For example, asking a child to request the same toy repeatedly in a brief time period likely will not be meaningful and will perhaps result in wasted intervention effort. Dispersed trials will likely produce better outcomes. Choosing functional goals that generally allow targeting throughout the day and across activities enhances dispersed practice. Distributed practice should, in turn, enhance the generalization of important skills (e.g., requesting).

The second criterion for learning opportunities addresses quality—that is, opportunities need to be of sufficient quality to ensure learning. Our definition of *quality* is that opportunities be functional for the child. The skill should be essential for participation within authentic routines, and activities and should promote interactions with others including peers. Learning opportunities should be embedded within these routines and activities. In addition, quality practice opportunities require authenticity in that what the child is doing or is asked to do makes sense to him or her. Thus, for most children, naming zoo animals in a book may be of significantly less quality than learning to name common objects in the environment.

In addition to planning and offering multiple quality practice opportunities, team members need to specify intervention methods they will use to provide the opportunity for the child to practice the skill. Furthermore, teams need to know what they will do if the child demonstrates the expected behavior, does not demonstrate the behavior, or demonstrates a different behavior. Within the ABI framework, an intervention guide, introduced in Chapter 6, is particularly important for children with significant needs because it requires the team to articulate these teaching behaviors in detail. Although a discussion of specific intervention strategies useful for children with more significant needs is beyond the scope of this book, many excellent resources are available on this topic (e.g., Collins, 2012; Downing & Demchak, 2008; Sandall & Schwartz, 2008).

The team collaborated to complete an intervention guide for each of Mollie's three IEP goals to guide their intervention efforts. Figure 12.1 provides an example of the intervention guide for Mollie's goal for selecting an activity or object when given a choice. The team also completed a group embedding schedule (Figure 12.2) to identify opportunities throughout the classroom day when they could provide opportunities for Mollie and Xang, a 3-year-old boy with autism, to practice their targeted skills. For both children, the team made sure to consider how these skills would increase opportunities for functional communication and social interactions with peers, to ensure their meaningful involvement in classroom activities.

Phase 4: Monitoring Children's Progress

Teams may have difficulty recognizing growth and change in children with more significant disabilities. Changes may be relatively small in nature and more difficult to observe than changes for children with less significant delays. For example, a child with significant motor impairments may go from maintaining a standing position for 5 minutes to maintaining a standing position for 7 minutes. Although significant to the child's progress, teams may be unlikely to notice changes without careful monitoring to document how long the child can tolerate standing before beginning to bend his knees and rest his upper body on the stander tray, indicating his inability to maintain the standing position.

The team designed a data collection form they could use to collect weekly data on Mollie's progress toward her IEP goals/objectives (Figure 12.3). This form allowed each team member to collect data on Mollie's progress. The team shared their data during weekly planning meetings and reviewed the data more critically at monthly intervals, as stated on the intervention guide, to make decisions about changes to their intervention strategies. The team used the data when informally updating Mollie's parents about her progress and for more formal reporting required by their program (e.g., quarterly progress reports toward IEP goals/objectives; Child Outcome Summary Forms [COSF], annual IEP).

PRACTICAL STRATEGIES FOR ROUTINE, CHILD-INITIATED, AND PLANNED ACTIVITIES

This section describes practical strategies for using ABI with children who have significant impairments during routine, child-initiated, and planned activities at home and in a center-based setting.

ABI Intervention Guide   *page 1 of 3*

1. Identifying information

Child's name: <u>Mollie</u>

Team members: <u>Lisa, Jill, Andrea, Jenny</u>

Date intervention initiated: <u>September 2013</u>   Date intervention completed: <u>May 2014</u>

2. Target goal, objectives, and program steps

Goal:

   1.0   During classroom activities, when given a choice of two pictures, Mollie will select an activity or object by looking, pointing, or reaching for the picture during three different activities per day, for 2 weeks.

Objectives:

   1.1   During meals, when given a choice of two food items, Mollie will select a food by looking, pointing, or reaching for the food during one meal per day for 2 weeks.

   1.2   During free play, when given a choice of two toys or objects, Mollie will select a toy or object by looking, pointing, or reaching for the toy or object three times per day for 2 weeks.

Program steps:

3. Core standards

Demonstrates progress in expressing needs, wants, and feelings appropriately.

Communicates needs and wants through a variety of verbal and symbolic forms.

Figure 12.1.   Completed ABI Intervention Guide for Mollie.

(continued)

Figure 12.1. *(continued)*

ABI Intervention Guide *(continued)*   *page 2 of 3*

4. Antecedents, targeted and nontargeted responses, and feedback or consequences

Antecedents designed to provide learning opportunities	List of possible child responses: targeted (+) and nontargeted (-)	Feedback or consequences
Objective 1.1: Hold up two preferred food items in Mollie's line of vision, and ask her which one she wants to eat. Pause to allow her to respond.	Mollie looks at, points to, or reaches for one food item. (+) Mollie doesn't respond. (-) Mollie looks away. (-) Mollie looks at, points to, or reaches for both food items. (-)	Give Mollie the food item she selects. (+) Regain Mollie's attention, hold up food items, ask question again, pause to allow her to respond. (-) Provide physical assistance to help Mollie make a choice; give her the food selected. (-)
Objective 1.2: Hold up two preferred toys/objects in Mollie's line of vision, and ask her which one she wants to play with. Pause to allow her to respond.	Mollie looks at, points to, or reaches for one toy/object. (+) Mollie doesn't respond. (-) Mollie looks away. (-) Mollie looks, points, or reaches for both toys/objects. (-)	Give Mollie the toy she selects. (+) Shake or move each toy to gain her attention, ask her again, and pause to allow her to respond. (-) Provide physical assistance to help Mollie reach toward a toy; give her the toy. (-)
Goal 1.0: Hold up two pictures of preferred toys/objects during free play, and ask Mollie which one she wants to play with. Pause to allow her to respond. Hold up two pictures of preferred foods during meals, and ask Mollie which one she wants to eat. Pause to allow her to respond.	Mollie looks at, points to, or reaches for one picture. (+) Mollie doesn't respond. (-) Mollie looks away. (-) Mollie looks at, points to, or reaches for both pictures. (-)	Give Mollie the item she selects. (+) Regain Mollie's attention, hold up pictures, ask question again, pause to allow her to respond. (-) Provide physical assistance to help Mollie make a choice; give her the item selected, and confirm the choice by pairing it with the picture and verbalizing choice (e.g., "You picked crackers"). (-)

5. Teaching strategies

- Begin by offering choices in the activities indicated above, but then expand to include choice making in other activities (e.g., choosing songs during circle time)
- Have a favorite peer assist with holding items or pictures
- Discuss favorite food items and toys with parents
- Consult with vision specialist to determine how best to present pictures and items so that Mollie can see them as well as possible.

ABI Intervention Guide *(continued)*   *page 3 of 3*

6. Monitoring progress

Who (person responsible for collecting the data)	Where (which activities or locations)	When (how often or on which days)	How (which methods)
Teacher, Lisa	Free play	Mondays, Wednesdays, and Fridays	Data collection probes
Assistant, Jill	Meals	Daily	Data collection probes

7. Decision rules

If adequate progress does not occur in _____4 weeks_____ (specify time frame for when the team will review the data), consider changing:

_____ Targeted goal

_____ Antecedents or feedback/consequences

__X__ Teaching strategies

__X__ Frequency, type, and/or locations of learning opportunities provided

_____ Other (describe) _____

_____

_____

ABI Embedding Schedule

Focus: Group   **Setting:** Classroom

Children's names: Mollie and Xang

Team members: Classroom staff and related service providers

Dates schedule will be used: First quarter (Sept. to Nov.)

Daily classroom activities and opportunities for practice

Children and target skills	Arrival	Free play	Circle activities	Breakfast/lunch/snack	Centers	Practice opportunities per day
Child's name: Mollie						
1. Mollie will maintain a supported sitting position.	Position Mollie in adapted chair near the "Who's Here Today" chart where she can greet peers (e.g., with switch device and hand-over-hand support).	Place Mollie in supported sitting with circle pillow behind her; provide toys on floor in front of her. Sit on the floor behind Mollie and provide support as needed.	Place Mollie in a crossed-leg position for first 5 minutes of circle; sit behind her and provide support as needed.		Position Mollie in adapted chair for first 5 minutes of activity, then move her to a more supported chair.	6
2. Mollie will eat a variety of soft and crisp foods.		Position Mollie in a beanbag chair in library area; provide support for safety.		Place at least two soft and/or crisp foods on a plate with suction cups and lip to help with scooping (may be selected by Mollie; see objective below); provide assistance at elbow to help her pick up foods.		Total opportunities: 4 (2 meals, 2 foods/meal)
3. Mollie will select an activity or object when given a choice.		Give Mollie a choice of two favorite activities (e.g., computer, switch toy). Have a peer give Mollie a choice of two favorite toys or materials.	Give Mollie a choice of favorite songs.	Give Mollie a choice of two favorite foods.	Give Mollie a choice of art materials.	6

Figure 12.2. Completed ABI Embedding Schedule for Mollie and Xang.

Daily classroom activities and opportunities for practice

Child's name: Xang

Goal						
1. Xang will respond to a familiar adult's social behavior.	Prompt Xang to say "bye" or wave to bus driver. Prompt Xang to say "hi" or wave to teachers and peers.	Tickle Xang or play other simple social game and pause for him to respond.				3
2. Xang will use three-word utterances.	Give Xang "I want" picture strip and choice of three activities; pause for him to make a request. Model phrases describing pictures he sees in books; ask him to repeat (e.g., "Say, I see dog").	Give Xang "I want" picture strip and choice of preferred activities; pause for him to make a request.	Give Xang "I want" picture strip and choice of three songs; pause for him to make a request. Have Xang help with weather activity and provide picture strip (e.g., "It is sunny").	Offer small amount of each food to start. Point to and model use of "I want" picture strip to request more. Offer favorite foods for snack. Model phrases (e.g., "I like cereal").	Offer choices of art materials, games; pause for Xang to make a request. Model phrases describing activities (e.g., "It is blue").	10

ABI Data Collection Form

Child's name: __Mollie__   Person collecting data: __Lisa__

Date: __March 10, 2014__

Goal/objective	Monday	Tuesday	Wednesday	Thursday	Friday
Goal 1 Mollie will maintain a supported sitting position.	+A +A + +A + -		+A +A +A - + -	+A +A + +A + -	
Goal 2 Mollie will eat a variety of soft and crisp foods.	+ + - +	+ - - -	- - + -	- + + -	- + - +
Goal 3 Mollie will select an activity or object when given a choice.	- - +A	+A +A - -			- - +A -

Key:
 + = independent
+A = demonstrated skill with assistance
 - = did not demonstrate skill

Figure 12.3.   Weekly ABI Data Collection Form used by Mollie's team.

Routine Activities

The routines in children's lives may vary from day to day as well as across time; however, most children have routines associated with meals, bathing and dressing, and transitions. Transitions are discussed for two reasons. First, because transitions occur multiple times during a day, they are a necessary part of life. Given their frequency of occurrence, transitions provide frequent opportunities for intervention that may be overlooked in the hustle and bustle of daily activities. That is, because transitions happen often and with regularity, they should be seen as potentially rich opportunities to embed targeted goals and objectives. Second, transitions can present unique challenges for children with significant impairments and the adults working with them.

Meals   Meals can present challenges and intervention opportunities for children with significant disabilities. Feeding techniques, positioning during meals, and strategies for promoting social communication are areas that should receive careful consideration. For meals at home and at school or a child care center, the child with motor impairments may benefit from adapted tableware (e.g., plate with a suction cup for stability, plate or bowl with a lip for scooping food more easily), utensils (e.g., built-up spoon handle, flat bowl on spoon), and cups (e.g., cup with a spout or lid). Successful meal-times may depend on positioning and the presence of adaptive equipment for some children so they can focus their efforts on independent eating and drinking skills. For example, a child with cerebral palsy may benefit from rolled-up towels placed on either side to help him stay upright and stable. An infant or toddler in the home setting may benefit from a high chair with a secure footrest to promote proper positioning. The types of foods offered may affect a child's ability to manage mealtime successfully. For example, a child with cerebral palsy who has difficulty swallowing may benefit from thickened liquids to reduce choking and gagging. A child with autism may benefit from the gradual introduction of textures or food temperatures the child finds aversive. (See Bruns & Thompson [2011] for information on meal times for children with autism.)

Meals provide many opportunities for children to communicate with adults (e.g., parent, teacher) and other children (e.g., friends, siblings). For children with significant impairments, meals provide a particularly good time for providing opportunities to request favorite foods or needed actions. A speech-language pathologist working with the team can help devise strat-egies for children to communicate their preferences for food items, ask for more, socialize with peers, and tell an adult they are finished. For children who are nonverbal or use only a few words, the team might try a speech-generating device or tablet computer app programmed with words or phrases commonly used during meals (e.g., *want, more, drink, all done*). Another option is to assist children with serious cognitive impairments or hearing impairments to learn signs for common food items (e.g., CRACKER, WATER) and actions (e.g., WANT, ALL DONE, MORE). A team might also use picture symbols or photos to offer food item choices to children with autism.

Meals also provide excellent opportunities for encouraging the social use of language including opportunities for children to comment on the meal itself, to talk about what has happened already that day (e.g., what children did outside on the playground), or to talk about what children will do when the meal is over. If used in classroom settings, materials should also be shared with families to allow children to have the same opportunities to communicate during mealtimes at home.

Related service provider team members should work closely with family members and center staff to ensure meal experiences that are as successful as possible for the child and respectful of the family's culture and prefer-ences for their child. For example, in some cultures, certain foods may not be eaten. In addition, the team should consider the primary caregiver's other time commitments (e.g., other children in the family) to ensure that sugges-tions offered are realistic.

In settings outside of the home, modifications to the environment (e.g., materials, adapted seating) should be carefully planned with clear roles assigned to team members. For example, it may be a paraprofessional's responsibility to set up the necessary materials prior to meals at school and to provide assistance to the child during meals. The speech-language pathologist, occupational therapist, and physical therapist may provide suggestions for feeding, positioning and handling, and promoting communication opportunities during meals. It may then be the ECSE teacher's role to provide communication opportunities, monitor weekly progress on feeding and communication goals, and provide feedback and assistance as needed to the paraprofessional during meals.

Bathing and Dressing   Bathing and dressing routines offer opportunities for practicing a variety of skills, including making choices, following directions, standing and moving around the environment, fastening and unfastening zippers and snaps on clothing, and putting on and taking off clothing items.

Communication during bathing might include offering children several bath toys to encourage them to communicate a choice. Families might offer a choice of toys using pictures prior to bath time. Dressing provides opportunities for children to choose favorite clothing items.

For a child with autism, a picture schedule of the bathing routine and dressing routine may help the child anticipate the steps in the routine. In addition, families might need to consider sensory issues such as water temperature in the bathtub and the texture of bath towels and clothing. Providing an "all done" picture and a "first/then" board with a preferred activity following bathing may help to reduce challenging behaviors during bath time.

Families may need assistance in making bathing and dressing more manageable, particularly if their child requires physical assistance to sit independently. A bath ring or adapted seating (e.g., bath chair) may help to make this routine less physically demanding for the parent and more enjoyable for the child. In addition, clothing that is easier to put on and take off may be helpful as a child with physical needs grows larger and becomes more challenging to dress and undress.

Transitions   Transitions can be challenging for children with severe disabilities such as autism. Transitions between activities can be made smoother by providing a consistent and predictable routine, using visual schedules, and alerting the child to any changes in the schedule through the use of pictures. For example, if the weather is too cold for outside play, the teacher might replace the picture of outside with a picture of the gym, and then point this out to the child when going through the schedule for the day.

For children with significant motor impairments, it is important that transitions between activities are used as opportunities for practicing mobility. For example, a child with cerebral palsy who uses a walker may need extra time to move to the next activity independently. The consistent use of a walker at transitions throughout the day provides the child with multiple opportunities to practice his or her mobility skills. For children with vision impairments, modifications may need to be made to the classroom to assist them in navigating around the environment. A vision specialist might also teach the child strategies for moving around the classroom, school, and home independently. It is important that the team works closely with the vision specialist to determine what supports are needed and to provide opportunities for the child to practice moving around independently in home and classroom environments.

For all children, transitions can provide opportunities for promoting social interactions. For example, children may be encouraged to line up with a buddy when walking outside to the playground or the bus. When lining up and walking from one school location to another, with supervision from an adult, a peer can help a child stay with the group, provide an opportunity for the child with special needs to talk with a friend, and provide support to successfully navigate through the school building (e.g., in the case of a child with a physical or vision impairment).

Child-Initiated Activities

Using child-directed or initiated activities to embed training on targeted goals and objectives is a hallmark of ABI. Because it may be more difficult for children with significant impairments to initiate a range of activities or to actively express their preferences, the team may need to invest additional time and thought into how to stimulate and how to use child-initiated actions for this population of children. For example, team members may have to consider how to assist children to ensure participation in a range of activities (e.g., through positioning to allow the child to manipulate materials, by transitioning children between activities to allow for exposure to multiple activities). In addition, the team may need to modify activities or materials to allow for active participation by the child. Team members may also need to provide an alternative communication system to allow the child to make choices, express preferences, and interact with peers. The following sections offer suggestions for modifications of three commonly occurring types of play that may permit children with severe disabilities to participate: block play, book play, and pretend play.

Block Play   Block play is a frequent activity across settings for most children, and this activity often happens on the floor. For a child with a significant motor impairment, positioning and support may be necessary precursors for child-initiated block play. The child may need to be positioned in a way that allows him or her to reach and manipulate the blocks or physical support to help the child maintain balance. Lighter-weight blocks that are soft and easier to grasp might also be provided to enable the child to stack them. To facilitate social interactions and to meaningfully involve a child with significant motor impairments, if stacking blocks is challenging, the interventionist might suggest to other children in the block area that the child with impairments play the role of knocking the blocks down.

For a child with vision impairments, the use of large blocks in bright colors might be a facilitative support that will permit the child to participate in the block play activity. Children with autism often engage in repetitive behavior such as building block towers and then knocking them down. This child-initiated activity might be used to address a communication goal of signing more by requiring the child to produce the sign to get additional blocks to build another tower. Interactions with peers can also be encouraged by creating a game of building and knocking down towers.

Book Play   Most children have access to books, and books provide many opportunities to address children's goals and objectives—even children with severe disabilities. For a child with significant motor impairments, a book with repetitive lines can be programmed into a large button device so that each time the child touches the switch, the story line is re-read. This provides a way for the child to engage in child-initiated book reading with peers if a typically developing peer reads the book with the child, turning the pages, and talking about each page, while the child with more significant impairments pushes the switch. Board books that have thick, sturdy pages that are easier to turn may help a child with motor impairments to engage in book reading activities. If children need more assistance in turning pages, pieces of cardboard tabbed out from the side of the book can be added to provide a larger area for grasping the page.

For children with vision impairments, books with large print should be included in the classroom book area. Care should also be taken to arrange the book area to accommodate children with different positioning and sensory needs. For example, there may be soft beanbags for a child with autism who likes the feeling of being surrounded by the beanbag chair. For a classroom that includes a child with significant motor impairments, there should be open space to accommodate an adapted chair on wheels that provides the child with enough support to allow his or her hands to be free to turn pages in books. For other suggested adaptations see Dennis, Lynch, and Stockall (2012).

Pretend Play   For children who are developmentally more advanced, encouraging child-initiated pretend play or games is important. For a child with autism, mini picture schedules of typical housekeeping routines (e.g., doing laundry, baking a cake) or play scenarios (e.g., going to the doctor, going to the grocery store) can be included to help the child learn the typical sequence of events in these activities. In addition, children may be taught how to engage in specific roles within the pretend play center (e.g., being the cashier at the grocery store or a waiter at a restaurant) using pictures and modeling by adults and peers. For a child with significant motor impairments, a communication device might be programmed with simple words or phrases that could be used in the center to facilitate social interactions. For example, if the play center is set up as a veterinarian's office, the device might be programmed with a picture of a cat, dog, and other animals; it might also be set up with common phrases someone would use when bringing their pet to the veterinarian's office (e.g., "My dog is sick").

Planned Activities

Planned activities require team planning and set up of materials to ensure meaningful participation by children with significant needs. For example, if a teacher is beginning a 2-week unit focused on the winter season, he may need to program communication devices for children in his classroom to reflect vocabulary that will occur within the planned activities (e.g., *snow, ice, cold, sled, mittens, melt*). He may also need to think about how to adapt unit-specific activities to allow all children to participate (e.g., by thinking about how to adapt a snowflake cutting activity for a child with a significant motor impairment and for another with a vision impairment). Many of these activities may occur only one time and will thus require special, specific adaptations, planning, and preparation to make sure all children can participate meaningfully in the activity both in terms of completing the activity and engaging with peers. Circle time and art are two planned activities common to most classrooms.

Circle Time   Several strategies can be used to help children with significant impairments actively participate in circle time. Adaptive seating might be used for a child with cerebral palsy to allow the child to focus attention on activities during circle time rather than maintaining an upright body position. A child with autism might be encouraged to bring a favorite toy to circle to help ease this transition. (For additional suggestions for adapting circle time for children with autism see Barton, Reichow, Wolery, & Chen [2011].)

For children who are nonverbal or who have limited expressive language skills, their preferred mode of communication (e.g., ASL, communication device, picture symbols) should be used throughout circle time activities to allow them to answer questions, interact with peers, and otherwise participate. For example, when talking about the weather, the interventionist might provide a board with four pictures of common types of weather (e.g., cloudy, rainy, snowy, sunny) and allow children to respond in different ways when asked about the weather. A typically developing peer might look at all four pictures and point to the correct picture and describe it (e.g., "It's raining outside"). For a child with Down syndrome, the interventionist might initially provide fewer choices, and choices that are easier to discriminate between (e.g., rainy and sunny). For a child with significant motor impairments, the teacher might use two large switches, with each switch having two pictures with voice output to allow the child to participate by talking about the weather with the class. Another option would be to provide the child with one switch with only the correct picture and a brief sentence or two describing the weather to allow the child to act as the weather reporter for the day. Children might also be paired together to act as a weather team, providing for multiple responses and opportunities for social interactions.

Art Activities   Switches can be used successfully to allow children with significant impairments to participate in art activities. For example, an interventionist might connect a large switch to a paint spinner. This activity encourages children of all abilities to participate in the activity by providing different roles that require different skills. For example, one child can put the paper in the spinner, while another child can push the switch button. A third child might squirt paint onto the paper as it spins. The activity promotes social interactions between children with and without disabilities and provides a meaningful way for a child with a significant disability to participate. Other art activities might require a range of materials adaptations to allow participation by all children. For example, a vision specialist might suggest thicker highlighted lines on paper to represent where a child with a vision impairment should cut the paper. A child might also use adapted scissors (e.g., spring loaded, mounted on a wooden stand) to promote independent cutting. It might also be helpful to tape the paper to the table to help the child steady the paper while cutting. (See Sandall & Schwartz [2008] for additional suggestions on adapting materials and activities for children with significant needs.)

SUMMARY

There are many considerations for using ABI with children who have significant impairments. This chapter has described how interventionists can implement each of the four phases of ABI with children who have significant needs and provided practical suggestions for the application of ABI during routine, child-initiated, and planned activities.

REFERENCES

Barton, E.E., Reichow, B., Wolery, M., & Chen, C. (2011). We can all participate! Adapting circle time for children with autism. *Young Exceptional Children, 14*(2), 2–21. doi:10.1177/1096250610393681

Bricker, D. (Series Ed.). (2002). *Assessment, Evaluation, and Programming System (AEPS®) for Infants and Children* (2nd ed., Vols. 1–4). Baltimore, MD: Paul H. Brookes Publishing Co.

Bruns, D.A., & Thompson, S. (2011). Time to eat: Improving mealtimes of young children with autism. *Young Exceptional Children, 14*(4), 3–18. doi:10.1177/1096250611402169

Collins, B.C. (2012). *Systematic instruction for students with moderate and severe disabilities*. Baltimore, MD: Paul H. Brookes Publishing Co.

Dennis, C.W., & Schlough, K.A. (2008). Gross motor development. In S.R. Hooper, & W. Umansky (Eds.), *Young children with special needs* (5th ed., pp. 114–166). Upper Saddle River, NJ: Pearson.

Dennis, L.R., Lynch, S.A., & Stockall, N. (2012). Planning literacy environments for diverse preschoolers. *Young Exceptional Children, 15*(3), 3–19. doi:10.1177/1096250612437745

DiCarlo, C., Banajee, M., & Stricklin, S.B. (2000). Embedding augmentative communication within early childhood classrooms. *Young Exceptional Children, 3*(3), 18–26. doi:10.1177/109625060000300303

Downing, J.E., & Demchak, M. (2008). First steps: Determining individual abilities and how best to support students. In J.E. Downing (Ed.), *Including students with severe and multiple disabilities in typical classrooms* (3rd ed., pp. 49–89). Baltimore, MD: Paul H. Brookes Publishing Co.

Edelman, L. (2014). *Using digital video in early care and education and early intervention.* Retrieved from http://inclusioninstitute.fpg.unc.edu/sites/inclusioninstitute.fpg. unc.edu/files/handouts/Edelman%20-%20Using%20Video%20in%20EI-ECE%20(5-4-14).pdf

Individuals with Disabilities Education Improvement Act (IDEA) of 2004, PL 108-446, 20 U.S.C. §§ 1400 *et seq.*

Kelker, K.A., & Holt, R. (2000). *Family guide to assistive technology.* Cambridge, MA: Brookline.

McWilliam, R.A. (2005). DEC recommended practices: Interdisciplinary models. In S. Sandall, M.L. Hemmeter, B.J. Smith, & M.E. McLean (Eds.), *DEC recommended practices: A comprehensive guide for practice application in early intervention/early childhood special education* (pp. 127–146). Longmont, CO: Sopris West.

Neisworth, J.T., & Bagnato, S.J. (2005). DEC recommended practices: Assessment. In S. Sandall, M.L. Hemmeter, B.J. Smith, & M.E. McLean (Eds.), *DEC recommended practices: A comprehensive guide for practice application in early intervention/early childhood special education* (pp. 45–69). Longmont, CO: Sopris West.

Sandall, S.R., & Schwartz, I.S. (with Chou, H.-Y., Horn, E.M., Joseph, G.E., Lieber, J., Odom S.L., & Wolery, R.). (2008). *Building blocks for teaching preschoolers with special needs* (2nd ed.). Baltimore, MD: Paul H. Brookes Publishing Co.

Wolery, M. (2005). DEC recommended practices: Child-focused practices. In S. Sandall, M.L. Hemmeter, B.J. Smith, & M.E. McLean (Eds.), *DEC recommended practices: A comprehensive guide for practice application in early intervention/early childhood special education* (pp. 71–106). Longmont, CO: Sopris West.

13

Activity-Based Intervention and the Team

As has been indicated throughout this book, acceptable developmental progress for most children who have or are at risk for disabilities requires the contribution and involvement of a range of professionals, paraprofessionals, and caregivers. Typically in EI/ECSE this range of individuals is referred to as the child's team.

This chapter addresses the team in relation to the use of ABI. The chapter begins with a brief history of the evolution of teams within special education. It then describes the three constituencies that comprise teams in EI/ECSE. And finally, it closes with a discussion of how the successful implementation of ABI requires teams to work together across the four ABI phases of assessment, goal development, intervention, and progress monitoring.

HISTORY OF TEAMS WITHIN SPECIAL EDUCATION

The practice of employing teams in special education occurred prior to the passage of the landmark Education for All Handicapped Children Act of 1975 (PL 94-142). In the 1920s, precursors to contemporary teams were initiated. Clinics that were linked to mental hospitals, social agencies, public and private schools, and institutes of higher education were established for children with disabilities (Friend & Cook, 2013). These early clinics identified specific team members (e.g., psychologist, social worker, psychiatrist) and emphasized a regimented approach to the diagnosis and treatment of children's problems. In these clinics the concept of interdisciplinary teamwork was developed. Although each team member had specific duties that contributed to the intervention effort for the child, little collaboration occurred between team members. Rather, each member was individually responsible for 1) testing, 2) working with parents, and 3) working with the child.

Fast forward to the enactment of PL 94-142 in 1975, which specifically addressed the need for special education teams. This legislation, however, did not outline the composition of the team or the procedures to be followed, leaving those decisions to individual states. States were free to interpret federal law and determine team compositions and procedures. As a result, names of these teams varied widely from state to state and included descriptions such as *child study team, school assessment team, placement team, planning team,* and *multidisciplinary team* (Friend & Cook, 1992). Equally varied was how teams functioned. Although it is widely assumed that teams were established under the law to encourage more collaboration in the provision of services, the actual intent of the law was to limit the decision-making authority of any one professional, ensure incorporation of multiple perspectives, and involve parents in the decision-making process for their children (Friend & Cook, 1992).

Initially established as multidisciplinary, numerous program and system evaluations revealed several problem areas that prevented teams from achieving their potential of providing enhanced services to children with disabilities and their families. Problems included 1) the use of unsystematic approaches to collecting and analyzing information, 2) minimal parent or general educator participation, 3) use of loosely construed or nonexistent decision-making/planning processes, 4) lack of interdisciplinary collaboration and trust, 5) territoriality, 6) ambiguous role definition and accountability, and 7) lack of experience and training for professionals to work together (Friend & Cook, 1992).

Over the years a number of solutions have been offered to address these problems associated with teaming. Subsequent legislation and amendments enacted in IDEA (1990, 1991, 1997, 2004; U.S. Department of Education, 2011) suggested ways to systematize the collection and analysis of information used to make team decisions about children's developmental and educational progress. In addition, accountability requirements developed by the federal Office of Special Education Programs resulted in significantly more systematic collection of assessment and evaluation data for young children (IDEA 2004). Texts, trainings, and consultations were developed to help teams obtain information and skills to enhance professional collaboration. Increasingly university-based personnel preparation programs have come to include training and experience in team building and functioning (Dinnebeil, Buysse, Rush, & Eggbeer, 2008).

During the nearly 100 years since early descriptions of teams working with young children with disabilities and their families appeared in the literature, the concepts associated with teams and team collaboration have evolved. An array of new language and new approaches is available to help shape our contemporary ideas of teams and their roles in EI/ECSE. To a large extent the contemporary EI/ECSE vision of teams has been affected by several philosophical changes that have pervaded the field. One of the more important philosophical changes was the shift from professional-centered approaches to the view that, in large measure, families rather than professionals should determine priorities for their children (IDEA 2004). A second change was the move away from professionals focused on their own discipline to a collaborative and integrated focus for assessment and intervention efforts (IDEA 1997). A third important change was the move to include caregivers as an integral part of the IEP/IFSP and intervention team (Education of the Handicapped Act Amendments of 1986), which is a clear recognition of the family's importance and the need to promote their strengths, capabilities, and decision-making prerogative as team members.

In addition to these important philosophical changes, other practices have had a significant impact on how EI/ECSE teams' functioning has evolved. Two important practices include inclusion and authentic practices.

Inclusion

The concept of inclusion likely began as a practice that supported implementation of the least restrictive environment (LRE) mandate first addressed in PL 94-142. The proposed practice of providing services in the LRE was in direct opposition to then-current service delivery models in which services were provided in separate facilities/programs designed especially for those with disabilities. This special education format of separate service delivery supported education in self-contained classrooms and the removal of children by assigned specialists who conducted their work in isolation from caregivers and intervention personnel. There was little interest by team members in sharing expertise or in coordinating intervention activities across disciplinary boundaries. The introduction of LRE required a significant shift in attitude and practice. Initially LRE was interpreted to mean that school-age students with mild disabilities be included in general education classes. By the mid-1980s, the interpretation of LRE expanded to include younger students and those with more moderate to severe needs.

The move to LRE was supported by the disability community, legal decisions addressing equality, and influential leadership personnel in education. These factors, along with federal legislation, resulted in a more generalized acceptance of children with disabilities into general education and child care programs. By the early 1990s, LRE was increasingly referred to as *inclusion,* which was defined as the principle and practice of considering general education as the placement of first choice for all learners (Villa & Thousand, 2003). Theoretically, this meant that supplemental supports such as equipment, assistive technology, and importantly, team expertise became integrated into center-based or classroom activities, rather than being provided in separate settings. Such change in the delivery of services required significant modification in team members' philosophical orientation and practice (Villa & Thousand, 2003). For example, new practices and approaches such as teaming, co-teaching, positive behavioral supports, and multitiered systems of support were developed. Further was the need for redefined roles and relationships among team members, requiring additional training through in-service opportunities, coursework, co-teaching, professional support groups, and other coaching and mentoring activities. The importance of team collaboration for success in this new service delivery model was apparent.

Authentic Practices

As with inclusion, the move to more authentic practices in EI/ECSE has occurred gradually over time. Chapter 2 provides a description of the development of authentic practices, now seen as recommended practice for EI/ECSE programs. As described in Chapter 2, the impetus for change from rote, adult-directed learning came from federal legislation, educational leadership, and research outcomes. As programs used more authentic practices to guide assessment, goal development, intervention, and progress monitoring, team members needed to consider children's daily routines and play in familiar environments for gathering information, delivering intervention, and monitoring progress. Consequently, routines such as mealtimes, play, or zone learning and exploring activities were seen as opportunities for children to practice targeted skills in the activities in which these skills were needed. Authentic practices supported the acquisition and use of skills in circumstances that provided a natural context for learning.

Again this conceptual as well as practical shift in how services were delivered has significantly affected the functioning of EI/ECSE teams. For the most part team members are now required to use activities of daily living to assess, intervene, and evaluate the impact of intervention. This commitment entails watching children negotiate environmental demands rather than assessing them with artificial tasks in small rooms. Recommended practice mandates that intervention no longer use multiple trial formats and other forms of rote learning, but rather that intervention is mapped onto daily activities and play. This shift requires team members to share information and to work their particular expertise into coordinated and collaborative efforts that address all of a child's goals and objectives. Related services personnel are required to share their knowledge with teachers and parents so that children benefit from ongoing interactions rather than special sessions once or several times a week (Giangreco, 2000).

THE CONTEMPORARY TEAM

The composition of contemporary EI/ECSE and early childhood education teams continues to vary across states, programs, agencies, and children. That is, one program may have a team composed of a special educator, caregiver, occupational therapist, and speech-language pathologist, whereas another agency may have a team composed of a Head Start teacher, itinerant teacher, and caregiver. Historically, the variability in team composition occurs for several reasons, including local/state requirements, availability of personnel, agency resources, location of programs, program/agency philosophy, and children's individual needs. Although we recognize the variability in team composition, teams should ideally be composed of three groups of individuals: direct services delivery personnel, related services providers, and caregivers.

Direct Services Delivery Personnel

Direct services delivery personnel are those individuals who provide daily interventions to the child or assist the family in using interventions throughout the day. Direct services delivery personnel can be divided into two subgroups: professionals and paraprofessionals.

The professional group is composed of individuals with specialized training in child development, education, or special education, and includes EI/ECSE teachers/interventionists, home visitors, and early childhood teachers. The majority of these individuals have bachelor's degrees, and many have master's degrees. Most have completed a university program of studies that results in some form of state teacher certification and attainment of professional competencies (Bruder, Mogro-Wilson, Stayton, & Dietrich, 2009). Most federally funded EI/ECSE programs require that teachers or interventionists have the state required licensure. Head Start now requires teachers to have bachelor's degrees.

The second subgroup of paraprofessionals includes child care workers, aides, and teaching assistants. Paraprofessionals are individuals who provide instructional support to special educators (including EI/ECSE program personnel) in the delivery of services to children with special needs (U.S. Department of Education, 2012). The use of paraprofessionals in special education classrooms has increased substantially since the 1980s (Giangreco, Edelman, Broer, & Doyle, 2001). In 2010, more than 45,000 paraprofessionals, 94.3% of whom were considered fully qualified for the positions (i.e., met state certification requirements in states where requirements were in place), provided services to young children with disabilities between the ages of 3 and 5 years of age (U.S. Department of Education, 2013).

Special education law (e.g., IDEA) states that paraprofessionals should play a supporting role in assisting qualified personnel (i.e., licensed teachers and related services providers) in delivering services, but they should not be responsible for planning services or making educational decisions. What paraprofessionals do on a day-to-day basis, however, can vary widely, and defining appropriate roles for paraprofessionals is an ongoing concern within the special education literature (e.g., Giangreco et al., 2001; Giangreco, Yaun, McKenzie, Cameron, & Fialka, 2005; Musick & Stott, 2000). Considerations for paraprofessionals in programs using ABI are provided in the Appendix to this chapter.

Related Services Providers

Related services providers have special disciplinary training that culminates with professional licensure and can include occupational therapists, physical therapists, physicians, nurses, communication specialists, school psychologists, social workers, mental health specialists, nutritionists, vision specialists, hearing specialists, autism specialists, mobility specialists, itinerant teachers, and family therapists. As made clear in the IDEA Amendments of 1997 (PL 105-17), teams should include the expertise and perspectives from the range of disciplines necessary to address child and family needs (Davies, 2007; Huefner, 2000; Yell, Drasgow, & Ford, 2000). Many children and families who participate in EI/ECSE and early childhood education programs have multiple challenges requiring assistance from a range of specialists (Bauer, Joseph, & Zwicker, 1998; Guralnick, 1997; Limbrick, 2005; Olson, Murphy, & Olson, 1998). Complex human needs require thoughtful solutions that can be derived only by examining the numerous facets of the problem and by developing procedures that are effective and able to be implemented. This process can best be ensured through the active cooperation and collaboration of a range of related services providers.

Caregivers

Caregivers can include parents, grandparents, other relatives, foster parents, and, in some cases, friends. The inclusion of caregivers on the team is critical to the successful application of ABI. The fundamental tenets of the approach, such as selecting meaningful goals, embedding learning opportunities in daily activities, and promoting learning through the daily transactions that occur between young children and their physical and social environment, require that caregivers be involved throughout the processes of assessment, goal development, intervention, and progress monitoring. Without the integral participation of caregivers, professionals will find it difficult to identify family values and priorities, address the needs of young children, or transform daily activities and transactions into meaningful learning opportunities (Jung, 2003).

Team Necessities

Ideally, teams should be formed with representatives from these three constituency groups; however, this is only the first step to ensure a balanced and effective team. Unfortunately, little empirical information is available concerning the functioning of teams in general, and within an activity-based approach in particular. Therefore, the majority of our knowledge about teams and the application of ABI has been derived from experience.

Having the necessary skills to fill critical roles is of fundamental importance; however, it is equally important for team members to share a similar approach toward how children learn and how to best facilitate that learning. Going through the motions of an approach in a mechanical, nonenthusiastic manner is likely to lead to little change in children. The reverse is also true; that is, nearly any approach may be effective if delivered with commitment and enthusiasm (Friend & Cook, 2003; Walther-Thomas, Korinek, & McLaughlin, 1999). To maximize children's progress, it seems best to adopt the approach with the greatest likelihood of success and then to employ this approach with genuine enthusiasm and the belief that it will be effective.

Teams wishing to adopt an activity-based approach in particular must be committed to a transactional perspective; that is, they need to recognize that learning occurs as a function of the child's interactions with, and feedback from, the environment (Sameroff & Fiese, 2000; Warren, Yoder, & Leew, 2002). Fundamental to change and growth are the daily interactions that occur between children and their social and physical environments. These exchanges or transactions should serve as the focus of team efforts. Team members should recognize that it is not the behavior of the child or adult in isolation but the cumulative effect of their exchanges that creates change (Davies, 2007).

Not only is it important to be enthusiastic about the chosen approach, but it is also important that team members bring with them an attitude that fosters collaboration with and respect for other team members. The field has acknowledged for some time that no single person, discipline, or, in many cases, agency/program can meet the needs of diverse families and their children who have or are at risk for disabilities (Dinnebeil et al., 2008; Park & Turnbull, 2003). Children may have an array of disabilities or needs that require the expertise of motor, communication, psychological, medical, or nutritional specialists. Their families may need an equally comprehensive range of services, including legal, educational, and therapeutic support, or they may need assistance with day-to-day living (e.g., food, shelter). Teams are necessary to address the many needs of children and families who are eligible for services. To maximize the services rendered to children and families, team members should convey to each other their mutual interdependence. Holding attitudes that foster respect and collaboration is an essential underpinning of effective team functioning.

In addition to displaying respect for professional expertise, similar attitudes toward caregivers should be nurtured. The inclusion of caregivers as team members should not be pro forma but instead should be a genuine extension of equal partnership rights. The information and perspectives that caregivers bring to a team are essential in creating an accurate picture of the child's strengths, interests, and emerging skills demonstrated across settings. In addition, without caregiver participation, the determination of family values and priorities is an educated guess at best.

Teams implementing an activity-based approach will need to follow a number of specific guidelines related to practices in assessment, goal development, intervention, and progress monitoring. As described in Chapter 3, ABI is a comprehensive approach that is most successful when conceptualized and implemented within a linked system. The roles of direct services delivery personnel, related services providers, and caregivers that appear necessary for the successful application of ABI within a linked system are described in the following section.

THE FOUR PHASES OF INTERVENTION: A TEAM EFFORT

The successful application of ABI requires that all team members work together across the four phases: assessment, goal development, intervention, and progress monitoring processes. Table 13.1 provides a number of guidelines or suggestions for enhancing the team's work across the four phases of intervention.

Principles to Guide Teams

Attention to developing models of team collaboration is growing by necessity, and an underlying theme of these models is that professionals and caregivers must coordinate their efforts (Bruder, 2005; Dunst & Bruder 2002; Friend & Cook, 2003). Once such models are adopted, the next stage is to prepare individuals to use them. The following seven principles should guide teams in their application of ABI.

Principle 1   Team members need to understand and be committed to the approach. Previous sections of this chapter noted the importance of appropriate attitude and enthusiasm for the approach of choice. Team members should be willing to fulfill the roles necessary for the implementation of ABI. Individuals who are skeptical about the approach (as well as team collaboration) will likely not gain the skills necessary for successful application of ABI.

Principle 2   Team members need to engage in comprehensive and ongoing observations of young children across daily activities, as noted in Chapter 9. Observing children's behavioral repertoires and determining under which conditions responses occur are fundamental to the successful use of ABI. Team members should be comfortable with the process of observing and not feel compelled to constantly respond to or direct children's actions. For example, teams should observe children during play, during interactions with friends and siblings, and during the completion of daily routines rather than pulling them aside or creating contrived testing situations. To be efficient and useful, observation needs to be focused and yield objective findings. In other words, teams should be aware of the behaviors they intend to document and encourage the child to demonstrate these behaviors during

Table 13.1   Team guidelines for four phases of intervention

Four phases of intervention	Guidelines
Assessment	Use a comprehensive curriculum-based measure that addresses all of the important areas of development and encourages participation from all team members.
	Ensure all team members participate in gathering, summarizing, and interpreting information from the assessment process.
	Select assessment procedures that identify family resources, priorities, and concerns.
Goal development	Allow and encourage all team members to participate in selecting and prioritizing target goals.
	Select priority goals that address multiple areas of development and can be addressed by all team members. For example, selecting *Manipulates objects with both hands* as a target goal can be addressed by direct services providers, consultants, and caregivers alike to promote a child's ability to play with toys and gain independence with dressing and feeding.
	Use the revised version of the Goals and Objectives Rating Instrument (Notari-Syverson & Shuster, 1995) or other measures to ensure that target goals are understandable to all team members and functional for the child.
Intervention	Use the three forms (i.e., intervention guides, embedding schedules, and activity plans) discussed in Chapter 6 as a means of organizing intervention efforts among team members.
	Include caregivers in the planning and implementation of intervention efforts (e.g., designing or selecting activities, preparing materials, providing learning opportunities), and ensure that caregivers' priorities are incorporated in the design of daily activities.
	Encourage team members to demonstrate effective meeting skills so that the limited time they do have is spent on planning individualized instruction.
	Impress on administrators the need for adequate planning time with other team members.
Evaluation	Distribute the responsibilities for data collection among team members.
	Select data collection methods and procedures that are able to be understood and used by all team members. Avoid complicated procedures that require extensive training or time.
	Use planning time to review and interpret data to make joint decisions.

authentic activities. Finally, team members should be able to discriminate between observable behavior (e.g., "Luis cried for 10 minutes following his mother's departure from the classroom") and inferences (e.g., "Because Luis was sad, he cried when his mother left the classroom"). Decisions need to be based on children's observable actions, not on adult inferences of their actions.

Principle 3   Team members need to follow or respond to children's leads (Warren, 2000; Warren et al., 2002). Team members may see their roles as organizers of children's days by planning a series of activities or sets of therapy sessions. Although such planning is required to ensure the necessary infrastructure for ABI, the structure should not be used to direct activities but to ensure that opportunities are provided for children to practice target goals and objectives and that applicable interventions are incorporated into daily activities.

Principle 4   Team members need to shape child-directed, routine, or planned activities in directions that will yield desired outcomes. Through the careful use of antecedents and consequences, team members can become adept at designing and selecting activities that retain children's interest and involvement. For example, a caregiver can place specific items within a child's reach (e.g., crayons) to encourage practicing targeted fine motor skills or use attention and comments to encourage the continuation of an activity that promotes interaction with a peer. Team members should discuss the antecedents and consequences deemed appropriate and then ensure intervention efforts are consistent. This level of collaboration and consistency often requires joint planning time and the development of intervention guides such as the ones discussed and illustrated in Chapters 6, 10, and 11.

Principle 5   Teams need to provide adequate numbers of opportunities for children to practice target goals and objectives. Our observations of center- and home-visiting programs suggest that caregivers, direct services delivery personnel, and related services personnel do not consistently recognize or make use of the many learning opportunities that could be vehicles for acquiring and practicing target goals and objectives. Often, one type of activity or the most obvious activity is selected to address a child's particular needs, and other potential opportunities are disregarded. Again, careful observation may lead to appreciating children's interests and the environmental opportunities that may capture those interests, which, in turn, may significantly increase the number of available learning opportunities that occur across a child's day. Furthermore, a team approach is necessary to ensure adequate numbers of opportunities are provided across daily activities (Jung, 2003).

Principle 6   Teams need to create a balance among the types of activities employed through systematic monitoring of child progress. Given that intervention is integrated into daily events and activities, team members need to devise and use monitoring strategies that provide accurate feedback on children's progress toward target goals and objectives (Raver, 2003). Devising nonintrusive strategies that yield reliable findings at low cost is a challenge. The appropriate use of ABI, however, is not complete without attention to evaluation of child and family outcomes. Team members should work together to devise a system for monitoring children's performance and to share in data collection responsibilities. Teams need to consider the most efficient and effective methods for monitoring children's progress (McLean, Wolery, & Bailey, 2004).

Principle 7 Teams need to collaborate to effectively implement the ABI approach. Collaboration is defined as a style of interactions between at least two equal parties, voluntarily engaged in shared decision making as they work toward a common goal (Friend & Cook, 2013). Collaborative teams in EI/ECSE require a blending of hands-on and role release skills; sharing roles; and remaining available to assist and advise through consultation, training, and feedback (King et al., 2009). Members with different disciplinary expertise need to share skills and participate in mutual training and staff development to make the collaborative model functional (Friend & Cook, 2013; Giangreco, 2000; Howard, Williams, & Lepper, 2010).

Characteristics of Collaboration

In their textbook *Interactions: Collaboration Skills for School Professionals*, Friend and Cook (2013) listed six defining characteristics of collaboration. The first is that collaboration is voluntary. Regardless of policy or program, team members must choose to collaborate. The second characteristic of collaboration is that it requires parity among participants, or equally valued team membership. Genuine collaboration cannot occur if greater decision-making power or more valued skills, knowledge, or information is believed to reside in some members of the team and not in others. The expertise of all team members needs to be recognized along with shared decision making (Giangreco, 2000).

The third characteristic of collaboration is that it is built on mutual goals. Team members do not have to share all goals in order to collaborate; however, they do need to share a sufficient number of goals to enable the team to work together. The fourth characteristic of collaboration is that it depends on shared responsibility of team members for both participation and decision making—that is, team members need to be fully engaged in team-selected activities and decision making associated with the selected activities.

The fifth characteristic focuses on sharing resources (e.g., skills, knowledge, talents) that each team member brings to the table. Each team member has resources to contribute that are valuable for reaching shared goals. Sharing knowledge and skills can result in the team better using scarce resources and enhancing the sense of ownership among team members. The sixth characteristic is individuals who collaborate need to share accountability for outcomes. That is, each team member accepts ownership of group decisions, actions, and ultimately progress demonstrated by the child.

In the team approach recommended for ABI, collaboration is the foundation that guides and directs team members' contributions. The next section addresses the four phases of intervention in the ABI framework and assumes a commitment to collaboration by team members.

Collaborative Teaming Across the Four Phases in the ABI Framework

Following is a description of how teams can collaborate across the four phases of the ABI framework: assessment, goal development, intervention, and progress monitoring.

Phase 1: Conducting Comprehensive and Ongoing Assessments   EI/ECSE assessment is a complex enterprise in most states. Collecting assessment information cannot be completed or validated unless team members understand children's and families' needs. Best practices in EI/ECSE still indicate that an interdisciplinary team assessment provides the most accurate and comprehensive pool of information for determining eligibility and designing intervention programs that match the child's needs (Division of Early Childhood [DEC], 2014).

A critical aspect of assessment is the team members' ability to observe children engaged in activities determined appropriate for the collection of assessment information. It is important for observations to take place as children engage in functional activities in their typical environments and with familiar caregivers. Using a curriculum-based measure should help provide a detailed description of the child's strengths, interests, and emerging skills and serve as a guide for identifying needs as well as a baseline to compare progress over time. Information collaboratively shared with all team members from observations is necessary for determining eligibility and for designing appropriate intervention targets.

Phase 2: Targeting Functional and Generalizable Objectives   Writing IEPs/IFSPs should be a collaborative endeavor that addresses all aspects of a child's developmental and educational needs. Team members need to ensure that all goals and objectives are functional, generalizable, and measurable. Team members have the responsibility to select goals/objectives that will improve a child's access, participation in, and benefit from a home- and/or center-based program. The targeted goals/objectives that comprise a child's intervention program should enhance the child's performance in daily activities and routines.

It is critical that the selection of goals and objectives is made collaboratively by team members ensuring that service planning, implementation, and evaluation are coordinated. Once goals/objectives are selected, subsequent intervention decisions should acknowledge a related services provider's ability to use role release and role support, and to provide in-service training for caregivers, interventionists/teachers, and paraprofessionals who can then provide interventions across all daily activities. Related services providers also need to be able to visit settings to observe, monitor, and evaluate the effects of interventions as children participate in home, center, or classroom activities with their peers.

Phase 3: Providing Multiple and Varied Learning Opportunities All interventions should enhance the child's performance and participation in familiar environments. When therapeutic interventions are used, they need to be applied across the day in various activities with different materials and with different people to be maximally effective. Team members' use of embedding schedules can provide support to caregivers and interventionists/teachers to devise appropriate ways to provide learning opportunities to practice target skills.

Improvement is directly related to practice opportunities; consequently, learners need frequent and functional opportunities to acquire necessary skills (i.e., multiple and varied learning opportunities). To enhance training opportunities, therapists can demonstrate, model, and train another adult (e.g., teacher, caregiver) to provide useful practice opportunities across the day.

Phase 4: Monitoring Children's Progress Collaborative intervention teams have the responsibility to plan and develop data collection strategies to monitor child progress. No two children are alike, so collection of data across children will vary, requiring that team members discuss options and come to an agreement on how to proceed. The developed data collection plan needs to be sustainable and doable by any team member who may be assigned the task of monitoring a child's progress on specific goals and objectives. Once a plan for data collection has been determined, responsibility for data collection needs to be assigned to specific team members. Their subsequent responsibility is to collect the assigned data as directed by the agreed upon plan.

Like intervention that is embedded into daily activities and routines, data collection should take place in the child's usual environment during daily activities and play. This often poses a challenge that the team must address. Collecting multiple trial data in isolation is far less demanding than obtaining information from children as they negotiate their daily environments. Teams need to give consideration to how to obtain valid and useful information without posing artificial constraints on children.

SUMMARY

The constitution and functioning of teams in EI/ECSE has evolved over time as philosophical orientations have changed and data have suggested better ways for teams to function. Several changes in philosophy and practice have inspired major shifts in teams. These include the recognition of caregivers as integral members of the team, the need for collaboration among different disciplines, the emphasis on inclusion, and the focus on authentic activities as the primary context for intervention. We believe that the successful application of ABI requires collaborative teams consisting of direct services delivery personnel, related services providers, and caregivers.

REFERENCES

Bauer, A., Joseph, S., & Zwicker, S. (1998). Supporting collaborative partnerships. In L.J. Johonson, M.J. LaMontagne, P.M. Elgas, & A.M. Bauer (Eds.), *Early childhood education: Blending theory, blending practice* (pp. 63–80). Baltimore, MD: Paul H. Brookes Publishing Co.

Bruder, M.B. (2005). Service coordination and integration in a developmental systems approach to early intervention. In M.J. Guralnick (Ed.), *The developmental systems approach to early intervention* (pp. 29–58). Baltimore, MD: Paul H. Brookes Publishing Co.

Bruder, M.B., Mogro-Wilson, C., Stayton, V.D., & Dietrich, S.L. (2009). The national status of in-service professional development systems for early intervention and early childhood special education practitioners. *Infants and Young Children, 22*(1), 13–20.

Davies, S. (Ed.). (2007). *Team around the child: Working together in early childhood education.* Wagga Wagga, New South Wales, Australia: Kurrajong Early Intervention Service.

Dinnebeil, L., Buysse, V., Rush, D., & Eggbeer, L. (2008). Becoming effective collaborators and change agents. In P. Winton, J. McCollum, & C. Catlett (Eds.), *Practical approaches to early childhood professional development: Evidence, strategies, and resources* (pp. 227–245). Washington, DC: ZERO TO THREE.

Division for Early Childhood. (2014). *DEC Recommended practices in early intervention/ early childhood special education 2014.* Retrieved from http://www.dec-sped.org/recommendedpractices

Dunst, C., & Bruder, M. (2002). Valued outcomes of service coordination, early intervention, and natural environments. *Exceptional Children, 68*(3), 361–375.

Education for All Handicapped Children Act of 1975, PL 94-142, 20 U.S.C. §§ 1400 *et seq.*

Education of the Handicapped Act Amendments of 1986, PL 99-457, 20 U.S.C. §§ 1400 *et seq.*

Friend M., & Cook, L. (1992). *Interactions: Collaboration skills for school professionals.* Boston, MA: Allyn & Bacon.

Friend, M., & Cook, L. (2003). *Interactions: Collaboration skills for school professionals* (4th ed.). Boston, MA: Allyn & Bacon.

Friend, M., & Cook, L. (2013). *Interactions: Collaboration skills for school professionals* (7th ed.). Boston, MA: Pearson.

Giangreco, M. (2000). Related services research for students with low-incidence disabilities: Implications for speech-language pathologists in inclusive classrooms. *Language, Speech, and Hearing Services in Schools, 31,* 230–239.

Giangreco, M.F., Edelman, C.W., Broer, S.M., & Doyle, M.B. (2001). Paraprofessional support of students with disabilities: Literature from the past decade. *Exceptional Children, 68*(1), 45–63.

Giangreco, M.F., Yuan, S., McKenzie, B., Cameron, P., & Fialka, J. (2005). "Be careful what you wish for...": Five reasons to be concerned about the assignment of individual paraprofessionals. *Teaching Exceptional Children, 37*(5), 28–34.

Guralnick, M.J. (1997). Second-generation research in the field of early intervention. In M.J. Guralnick (Ed.), *The effectiveness of early intervention* (pp. 3–20). Baltimore, MD: Paul H. Brookes Publishing Co.

Howard, V., Williams, B., & Lepper, C. (2010). *Very young children with special needs: A foundation for educators, families and service providers* (4th ed.). Boston, MA: Pearson.

Huefner, D. (2000). The risks and opportunities of the IEP requirements under IDEA '97. *Journal of Special Education, 33,* 195–204.

Individuals with Disabilities Education Act Amendments of 1991, PL 102-119, 20 U.S.C. §§ 1400 *et seq.*

Individuals with Disabilities Education Act Amendments (IDEA) of 1997, PL 105-17, 20 U.S.C. §§ 1400 *et seq.*

Individuals with Disabilities Education Act (IDEA) of 1990, PL 101-476, 20 U.S.C. §§ 1400 *et seq.*

Individuals with Disabilities Education Improvement Act (IDEA) of 2004, PL 108-446, 20 U.S.C. §§ 1400 *et seq.*

Jung, L.A. (2003). More is better: Maximizing natural learning opportunities. *Young Exceptional Children, 6*(3), 21–27.

King, G., Strachan, D., Tucker, M., Duwyn, B., Desserud, S., & Shillington, M. (2009). The application of a transdisciplinary model for early intervention services. *Infant and Young Children, 22*(3), 211–223.

Limbrick, P. (2005). Team around the child: Principles and practice. In B. Carpenter & J. Egerton (Eds.), *Early childhood intervention: International perspectives, national initiatives and regional practice.* West Midlands, England: SEN Regional Partnership.

McLean, M., Wolery, M., & Bailey, D. (2004). *Assessing infants and preschoolers with special needs* (2nd ed.). Columbus, OH: Charles E. Merrill.

Musick, J., & Stott, F. (2000). Paraprofessionals revisited and reconsidered. In J.P. Shonkoff & S.J. Meisels (Eds.), *Handbook of early childhood interventions* (2nd ed., pp. 439–453). Cambridge, United Kingdom: Cambridge University Press.

Notari-Syverson, A., & Shuster, S. (1995). Putting real life skills into IEP/IFSPs for infants and young children: Revised IEP/IFSP Goals and Objectives Rating Instrument (R-GORI) for Early Childhood. *Teaching Exceptional Children, 27(2),* 29–32.

Olson, J., Murphy, C., & Olson, P. (1998). Building effective successful teams: An interactive teaming model for inservice education. *Journal of Early Intervention, 21,* 339–349.

Park, J., & Turnbull, A. (2003). Service integration in early intervention: Determining interpersonal and structural factors for its success. *Infants and Young Children, 16,* 48–58.

Raver, S. (2003). Keeping track: Using routine-based instruction and monitoring. *Young Exceptional Children, 6,* 12–20.

Sameroff, A., & Fiese, B. (2000). Transactional regulation: The developmental ecology of early intervention. In J. Skonkoff & S. Meisels (Eds.), *Handbook of early childhood intervention* (pp. 135–159). New York, NY: Cambridge University Press.

U.S. Department of Education. (2011). *Part C of the Individuals with Disabilities Education Act: Final Regulations.* Retrieved from http://osep-part-c.tadnet.org/uploads/file_assets/attachments/12/original_Final_Regulations-_Part_C-DOC-ALL.pdf

U.S. Department of Education. (2012). *31st annual report to Congress on the implementation of the Individuals with Disabilities Education Act, 2009.* Retrieved from http://www2.ed.gov/about/reports/annual/osep/2009/parts-b-c/31st-idea-arc.pdf

U.S. Department of Education. (2013). *35th annual report to Congress on the implementation of the Individuals with Disabilities Education Act, 2010.* Retrieved from www2.ed.gov/about/reports/annualosep/2008/parts-b-c/30th-idea-arc.pdf

Villa, R., & Thousand, J. (2003). Making inclusive education work. *Educational Leadership, 61*(2), 19–23.

Walther-Thomas, C., Korinek, L., & McLaughlin, V. (1999). Collaboration to support students' success. *Focus on Exceptional Children, 30*(3), 1–18.

Warren, S. (2000). The future of early communication and language intervention. *Topics in Early Childhood Special Education, 20,* 33–37.

Warren, S., Yoder, P., & Leew, S. (2002). Promoting social-communicative development in infants and toddlers. In S.F. Warren & J. Reichle (Series Eds.) & H. Goldstein, L.A. Kaczmarek, & K.M. English (Vol. Eds.), *Communication and language intervention series: Vol 10. Promoting social communication: Children with developmental disabilities from birth to adolescence* (pp. 121–149). Baltimore, MD: Paul H. Brookes Publishing Co.

Yell, M., Drasgow, E., & Ford, L. (2000). The Individuals with Disabilities Education Act Amendments of 1997: Implications for school-based teams. In C.F. Telzrow & M. Tankersley (Eds.), *IDEA Amendments of 1997: Practice guidelines for school-based teams* (pp. 1–28). Bethesda, MD: National Association of School Psychologists.

Appendix 13

Considerations for Paraprofessionals in Programs Using Activity-Based Intervention

Paraprofessionals play a supporting role in assisting licensed teachers and related services providers in delivering services. As previously noted, defining appropriate roles for paraprofessionals is an ongoing concern within special education (e.g., Giangreco, Edelman, Broer, & Doyle, 2001; Giangreco, Yaun, McKenzie, Cameron, & Fialka, 2005; Musick & Stott, 2000). For example, experts have expressed concerns about paraprofessionals being inadequately trained to provide some services to infants and toddlers and their families with complex educational and psychological needs (Musick & Stott, 2000) and to preschoolers and school-age children with disabilities (Giangreco et al., 2001). Often those individuals with the least amount of training (i.e., paraprofessionals) are being asked to work with children who have the most significant needs, rather than the most highly skilled professionals (i.e., certified teachers and related services providers) working with these children (Giangreco et al., 2001). Under IDEA, while paraprofessionals are required to have training and supervision necessary to carry out their assigned duties, both are often lacking (Giangreco et al., 2001). Thus, how to appropriately use the skills of paraprofessionals is a challenging dilemma for new and experienced teachers alike.

Although some paraprofessionals are employed in birth to 3 services, this appendix focuses on the use of paraprofessionals in center-based programs where we believe paraprofessionals can be most appropriately utilized within an ABI framework. There are four phases within an ABI framework: 1) conducting comprehensive and ongoing assessments, 2) targeting functional and generative goals, 3) providing multiple and varied learning opportunities, and 4) monitoring children's progress. Within an ABI framework, paraprofessionals can most appropriately support interventionists in phase three, providing multiple and varied learning opportunities, and phase four, monitoring children's progress. These phases, and the use of paraprofessionals within these phases, are described in the following sections.

PROVIDING MULTIPLE AND VARIED LEARNING OPPORTUNITIES

Although the primary responsibility for providing embedded learning opportunities rests with the ECSE teacher and related staff, paraprofessionals play an important role in helping to provide additional learning opportunities for young children with special needs. Because the teacher can only be in one place at one time, having additional adults trained to provide specific opportunities for children to practice IEP goals and objectives is critical to ensuring sufficient practice opportunities.

Intervention efforts require a team approach in which all team members, including paraprofessionals, are working toward the same goal of helping children learn and develop. This can be made explicit to paraprofessionals by acknowledging the importance of their contributions to the team. The interventionist (e.g., ECSE teacher) should plan intervention (e.g., creating ABI intervention guides, ABI embedding schedules, ABI activity plans), delineate roles (i.e., who will do what and when), provide models of how to use ABI, and supervise the paraprofessional's use of ABI with individual children. It is important for the teacher to be specific about what paraprofessionals are expected to do (and not do). For example, if the team wants a child to practice transitioning independently by getting up out of his chair and walking from the snack table to the sink to wash hands, it is important for the interventionist to explain the desired opportunity, why the opportunity is provided, and what the paraprofessional should do (e.g., wait for the child to get up out of his chair and walk to sink, provide assistance with one hand only if necessary) and not do (i.e., pick up the child and move him to the sink).

Explaining rationales can go a long way in helping paraprofessionals understand a particular approach to intervention, thereby increasing the likelihood they will provide multiple embedded opportunities to support children's skill development. For this reason, it may be beneficial for the interventionist to give paraprofessionals in his or her center or classroom a brief overview of ABI, focusing on what the practice should look like in the classroom. This could be implemented as part of a professional development opportunity at the beginning of the year or more informally during a team meeting.

It is also helpful to post a copy of the embedding schedule in several places around the room (with only children's first initial to maintain confidentiality) for all team members to see and refer to. For example, interventionists might place an ABI embedding schedule with all children's goals in the free play area down near eye level in a place where paraprofessionals can easily refer to children's goals during play times. Interventionists might also post small reminders (e.g., an index card with children's goals that relate to meals) in a place where paraprofessionals might easily notice them (e.g., on the inside door of a cabinet with dishes and other things accessed prior to meals). These reminders can help everyone be aware of what skills to focus on for individual children during each routine. In addition, it is helpful to be specific about what each team member is expected to do, particularly if you have multiple paraprofessionals. For example, it may be that one paraprofessional sits at a table during mealtimes. In this case, it would be helpful to talk with that paraprofessional directly about how to work on children's goals during meals. Another paraprofessional might spend a great deal of time in the pretend play area. It would be important to discuss the ABI embedding schedule with this paraprofessional, highlighting, or maybe only including, those skills that can be easily embedded within pretend play.

Because the use of ABI in a center requires a great deal of training and practice, it is critical that interventionists model the use of ABI strategies they expect paraprofessionals to use. For example, if a child has a goal to wash hands independently, the interventionist might assist the child with the hand washing routine and ask the paraprofessional to observe in order to model the amount of support the paraprofessional will be expected to provide (e.g., hand-over-hand assistance to turn on the faucet) and prompts the paraprofessional should use (e.g., rather than getting the towel for the child, modeling how to get the child's attention, tap the paper towel container, and provide a verbal prompt, "Get a towel"). More complex skills and teaching strategies may need to be modeled more than one time.

After the interventionist models how the paraprofessional is expected to provide a learning opportunity, the interventionist should observe the paraprofessional using the strategy and provide feedback (e.g., if the paraprofessional used the wait time strategy correctly the interventionist might say, "Great job waiting for him to use his words before you gave him the crackers"; if the paraprofessional did not use the strategy correctly the interventionist might say, "Next time make sure you wait to give him time to ask for the crackers before giving him the crackers to encourage him to use his words."). The interventionist should provide the support needed for the paraprofessional to implement the strategy correctly and consistently, observing occasionally to make sure the strategy continues to be used with the child. The interventionist needs to be sure to emphasize the importance of providing the child with an opportunity to practice the skill on as many occasions as is possible.

MONITORING PROGRESS

Monitoring children's progress is another component of ABI in which para-professionals can offer assistance. Documentation of progress through data collection can become an integral component of what all individuals in the ECSE classroom do on a daily basis. Keys to making data collection success-ful for paraprofessionals are to provide data collection forms that are easy to understand, explain the forms and model their use, and post the forms in places where they can be accessed when and where children demonstrate skills on which data are being collected. For example, for a child working on the hand washing routine, the ECSE teacher could post a data collection chart on a clipboard hanging near the sink with a pencil attached. Each day before lunch, the ECSE teacher could ask the paraprofessional to record whether the child completed the routine independently (+), with verbal or physical prompts (P), or with hand-over-hand assistance (A). As with provid-ing embedded learning opportunities, including paraprofessionals in data collection requires careful planning, a clear explanation of what the parapro-fessional should do and why, and modeling and supervision of implementa-tion to make sure data collected are accurate. Involving paraprofessionals in monitoring children's progress takes more planning at the outset but is well worth the effort when summarizing a child's progress toward IEP goals and objectives.

SUMMARY

Paraprofessionals can play an important supporting role in the delivery of services to young children with special needs within an ABI framework. This requires careful planning, direct training, and ongoing supervision and mentoring of paraprofessionals by licensed ECSE teachers and related services providers. For maximum success in incorporating paraprofession-als within an ABI framework, interventionists should focus on utilizing paraprofessionals in two key areas: providing multiple and varied learning opportunities and monitoring children's progress.

REFERENCES

Giangreco, M.F., Edelman, C.W., Broer, S.M., & Doyle, M.B. (2001). Paraprofessional support of students with disabilities: Literature from the past decade. *Exceptional Children*, 68(1), 45–63.

Giangreco, M.F., Yuan, S., McKenzie, B., Cameron, P., & Fialka, J. (2005). "Be careful what you wish for...": Five reasons to be concerned about the assignment of individual paraprofessionals. *Teaching Exceptional Children*, 37(5), 28–34.

Musick, J., & Stott, F. (2000). Paraprofessionals revisited and reconsidered. In J.P. Shonkoff & S.J. Meisels (Eds.), *Handbook of early childhood interventions* (2nd ed., pp. 439–453). Cambridge, United Kingdom: Cambridge University Press.

U.S. Department of Education. (2012). *31st annual report to Congress on the implemen-tation of the Individuals with Disabilities Education Act, 2009.* Retrieved from http://www2.ed.gov/about/reports/annual/osep/2009/parts-b-c/31st-idea-arc.pdf

14

Early Intervention/ Early Childhood Special Education Intervention and Future Accommodations

Since ABI was first conceptualized and applied in EI/ECSE programs, significant change in educational and therapeutic services for young children has taken place around the world. One could argue that the field of education or services for young children with disabilities and those who are at risk

- Has made strides forward

- Has been neutralized by new challenges

- Has lost ground

Arguments can be made to support each of these positions and for the myriad of more measured or nuanced conclusions about progress in the education of young children, or lack thereof. However, we are persuaded that progress has occurred and is reflected in the quality and quantity of educational and therapeutic services available globally to young children. Nonetheless, much remains to be done.

Since their inception, the number of programs and services available to young children who have or are at risk for disabilities and their families have seen more or less steady growth in the United States. Most recently, this growth has been fueled by the national resurgence in the belief that intervening early in children's lives has both preventive and curative powers that can offset the myriad of challenges that beset many of today's young children and their families. Although those who are associated with EI/ECSE and ECE believe that intervention provided early in children's lives can be effective, we are aware that the problem is considerably more complicated than the delivery of services to young children and families.

Poor-quality programs, however early they are begun, will not produce the protective and positive outcomes politicians and voters expect from the investment of resources into early education programs. National "cure-all" expectations such as the Goals 2000: Educate America Act of 1994 (PL 103-227), the No Child Left Behind Act of 2001 (PL 107-110), and the Race to the Top Act (American Recovery and Reinvestment Act of 2009, PL 111-5, Section 14005-6, Title XIV) place considerable pressure on the field to improve the quality of programs to ensure, to the extent possible, that children enter public schools with the necessary foundation for optimal learning. Indeed, expectations have expanded from preparing young children to acquire developmental milestones to also preparing young children to have an emotionally and physically balanced life. Preparing children with disabilities and children who come from toxic environments to learn effectively and to be emotionally well adjusted is a tall order. Meeting such challenges will require that teachers, interventionists, specialists, program developers, administrators, and researchers move forward in the exploration of methods to enhance early development, adjustment, and learning.

Our hope is that growth in the numbers of programs serving young children will be paralleled by program staff's choice and use of the most effective intervention available. We believe that for most children and families, child-directed approaches such as ABI are the best choice. The success of these approaches in meeting national expectations for young children will be determined in part by our ability to describe and teach the elements and processes that compose them. That is, of course, the primary goal of this volume—to present a coherent and complete description of a comprehensive and coordinated approach to intervention for young children.

Our teachings, writings, and discussions focused on ABI have led to important insights. Three of these insights have had a significant impact on our current thinking and on how we will proceed in the future. Our first and long-held insight is that program personnel do not tend to adopt an entire model or approach unless required to do so by state or local regulations (e.g., Bricker et al., 1997). Consequently, apart from programs that mandate the adoption of an approach, individuals, when able, appear to choose parts, elements, or pieces of an approach. These pieces or parts appear to be selected because they 1) match an individual's personal belief about how to teach or intervene, 2) are compatible with an individual's present style or approach, and/or 3) can be managed or integrated into an individual's present approach. Pieces or elements of an approach that do not fit personal beliefs, are not compatible with present approaches, or simply cannot be managed because of time and resources appear to be discarded and not adopted. The outcome, then, is often anything but the straightforward application of an entire approach.

If we are correct in assuming that many teachers, interventionists, and specialists do not adopt the entirety of an intervention approach, how can we as developers present approaches composed of multiple elements so that they can be maximally useful? To date, our response to this issue has been to clearly and comprehensively describe each element of ABI. By doing so, users may be better able to "pick and choose" what parts and pieces of the approach are most compatible with their philosophy and resource base. Although we believe in a systems approach, our future challenge may be to parse ABI into more definable units that can be applied as individual users see fit.

A second insight is that teachers, interventionists, and specialists require time (e.g., months or even years) to integrate a new element into their teaching repertoires. For example, we have found that after instruction in the use of ABI, many service delivery personnel experience considerable difficulty in increasing the frequency with which they embed learning opportunities that target children's goals and objectives into child-directed, routine, and planned activities (Pretti-Frontczak & Bricker, 2001). We believe these phenomena (i.e., piecemeal application of an approach and long latencies to improve intervention techniques) are not peculiar to ABI but rather reflect programmatic and personal realities that make change slow and arduous (Rogers, 1995).

The slow adaptation to change by most service delivery personnel offers a significant challenge to developers of comprehensive intervention approaches such as ABI. It is important to analyze how to assist ABI users in the efficient adoption of approach elements into their service delivery efforts. As many have noted and most have experienced, change is difficult. This fact has significant implications for preservice and in-service training efforts. Those involved in the creation and refinement of intervention approaches need to give thought to how to improve training efforts so that students and practitioners acquire the ability to handle and welcome change that may improve their intervention efforts with young children. Training efforts must be imbued conceptually and practically with the goal of assisting the learner to adopt stances and styles that embrace and welcome change instead of dreading and fighting change.

The third insight is that most learners of new concepts and strategies benefit from being exposed to multiple examples, particularly examples that parallel their circumstances. This insight has led to the addition of more illustrations and examples of how to employ ABI than were present in previous editions of this book. We are hopeful that the expansion of examples focused on how to apply an activity-based approach will assist readers in more quickly and effectively learning and applying the elements that comprise ABI, or at least those elements that are compatible with their belief system and available resources.

However, we have come to understand that the addition of more print examples is not sufficient. Rather, intervention developers like ourselves need to consider how to incorporate a range of options for use in preservice and in-service training, such as videos, webinars, and online materials to mention but a few avenues that may offer valuable alternatives for explanation and demonstration. The move to broaden our teaching options offers its own set of challenges. For example, our experience with the development of a training video for ABI has made clear that to create effective options requires time, resources, and the inclusion of media experts. The future must include a range of alternative teaching options that can clearly demonstrate the elements of intervention approaches such as ABI.

These observations on the willingness and ability of personnel to instigate change raise two other more difficult issues: fidelity of treatment and measuring program effectiveness. Fidelity of treatment measures usually require that all elements of an approach be employed on a regular basis if a fair test of an approach is to be conducted. Most would agree that using only some of the elements or using the elements of an approach intermittently does not permit a valid examination of an approach's effectiveness or impact. Yet as noted earlier, it seems that many intervention personnel do not apply all elements of an approach but rather select those pieces that match their needs.

Consequently, an important question arises as to how many elements of an approach must be used and how frequently they must be used to constitute a legitimate application of the approach. This weighty problem has an associated dilemma in that most EI/ECSE programs have neither the expertise nor resources to adequately measure the fidelity with which an approach is being implemented over time. Thus, we are confronted with the challenge of specifying what it means to apply a comprehensive intervention approach and how to assist those in the field to determine how closely they are meeting the rigors of applying the overall approach.

The challenges surrounding fidelity of treatment raise a second issue of how to measure the impact or effectiveness of an approach if personnel employ only bits and pieces of the approach. As we noted in Chapter 8, the field of EI/ECSE needs to move to the collection of second-generation research— research that offers insights into what aspects of intervention do or do not affect outcomes. Monitoring child progress and assessing more global forms of intervention impact continues to create a multitude of challenges for service personnel as well as the research community. Bringing clarity to fidelity of treatment requirements is critical to evaluation questions. Perhaps the best we can do is to carefully define an element, then determine the use of that element (i.e., fidelity of treatment), and finally assess its effect on children. As Baer (1981) wrote so many years ago, attempting to measure the impact of comprehensive intervention approaches may be a goal that is unattainable; however, improvements are possible in current practice.

To begin we recommend the careful delineation of program features as we have attempted to do in this book. As we have noted, the adoption of an entire approach or model may not be a realistic expectation given what we know about human behavior and the lack of resources available to most service programs. We will likely accomplish more if we change our expectations to asking personnel to consider the implementation of recommended practice features or elements rather than to adopt all elements of an approach. The manner and way of implementation will need to be varied to address the realities of specific settings, children, families, and personnel delivering services. If this is a reasonable expectation, then ways to evaluate the impact of intervention approaches on children will need serious reflection and subsequent change in current paradigms. The future offers many extraordinary challenges!

This chapter underlines our expectation that ABI will be applied with thoughtful modifications. We do not expect that all consultants, caregivers, and direct services personnel will understand, interpret, or apply the elements of the approach in the same way. We expect and value variation. A major challenge is to determine how variations occur (e.g., which elements are usually applied and which are ignored), and the impact of those variations on children. Attempting to understand how approaches are individualized and the subsequent impact of this individualization is a question of great importance for the field of EI/ECSE and for all those who participate in creating and refining intervention approaches.

REFERENCES

American Recovery and Reinvestment Act of 2009, PL 111-5, Section 14005-6, Title XIV.

Baer, D. (1981). The nature of intervention research. In R. Schielfelbusch & D. Bricker (Eds.), *Early language: Acquisition and intervention.* Baltimore, MD: University Park Press.

Bricker, D., McComas, N., Pretti-Frontczak, K., Leve, C., Stieber, S., Losardo, A., & Scanlon, J. (1997). *Activity-based collaboration project: A nondirected model demonstration program for children who are at-risk disabled and their families.* Unpublished report, University of Oregon, Center on Human Development, Early Intervention Program.

Goals 2000: Educate America Act of 1994, PL 103-227, 20 U.S.C. §§ 5801 *et seq.*

No Child Left Behind Act of 2001, PL 107-110, 115 Stat. 1425, 20 U.S.C. §§ 6301 *et seq.*

Pretti-Frontczak, K., & Bricker, D. (2001). Use of embedding strategies during daily activities by early childhood education and early childhood special education teachers. *Infant-Toddler Intervention: The Transdisciplinary Journal, 11*(2), 111–128.

Rogers, E. (1995). *Diffusion of innovations* (4th ed.). New York, NY: The Free Press.

Index

Page numbers followed by *f* or *t* indicate figures or tables, respectively.